OF BEASTS AND BEAUTY

OF BEASTS AND BEAUTY

Gender, Race, and Identity in Colombia

BY MICHAEL EDWARD STANFIELD

UNIVERSITY OF TEXAS PRESS
Austin

First edition, 2013
First paperback edition, 2014

Requests for permission to reproduce material from this work should be
sent to:
    Permissions
    University of Texas Press
    P.O. Box 7819
    Austin, TX 78713-7819
    http://utpress.utexas.edu/index.php/rp-form

♾ The paper used in this book meets the minimum requirements of ANSI/
NISO Z39.48-1992 (R1997) (Permanence of Paper).

LIBRARY OF CONGRESS CATALOGING-IN-PUBLICATION DATA

Stanfield, Michael Edward, 1957-
Of beasts and beauty : gender, race, and identity in Colombia /
by Michael Edward Stanfield. —First edition.
        p.   cm.
Includes bibliographical references and index.
ISBN 978-0-292-74558-2 (cloth : alk. paper)
ISBN 978-1-4773-0222-4 (paperback)
    1. Feminine beauty (Aesthetics)—Colombia—History.   2. Beauty
contests—Colombia—History.   3. Women—Colombia—History.
4. Nationalism—Colombia—History.   5. Colombia—History—1810–
6. Colombia—Social conditions.   7. Colombia—Politics and
government.   I. Title.
HQ1220.C7873   2013
305.409861—dc23   2012044364

doi: 10.7560/745582

To Marilyn Gae and Jayne Spencer, two extraordinary women who modeled many of the powerful facets and interactive dynamics of internal and external beauty.

CONTENTS

ACKNOWLEDGMENTS

This book sprang from a creative impulse that then required the assistance and support of dedicated professionals and dear friends in both Colombia and the United States. In Bogotá, friends and colleagues Augusto Gómez and Angelina Araújo graciously shared their time, expertise, and personal insights on beauty and Colombia. Former students María José Perry, Santiago Perry, and Sonia Durán encouraged me over the years to press on with this work, regardless of difficulties in Colombia or the complexities of living in the United States. As always, my fictive Colombian family, Alberto, Leonor, Jenny, doña Carmen, Gloria, Mercedes, Wilson, and Santiago, welcomed me into their homes and shared the personal warmth that makes Colombia so inviting. At the busy and engaging Biblioteca Luís Ángel Arango (BLAA), Ángela Torres Pérez, Luz Caridad Peña Carbajal, and Alberto García F. patiently attended to my many requests; Magdalena Santamaría did the same at the Biblioteca Nacional. Mario Bohórquez Martínez and Hugo Alonso Albarracín Barriga of the Banco de la República kindly aided in the reproduction of some images from the BLAA.

In delightful Cartagena, the staff of the Archivo Histórico, Archivo General del Distrito, facilitated access to its newspaper collections. Esperanza del Valle introduced me to the headquarters and activities of the Concurso Nacional de Belleza, while Jacklin Rojas Camargo artfully assisted in the use of several images from the Colombian National Beauty Contest. In equally warm Cali, Amanda Henao J. of the Banco de la República, Cali, shared her knowledge of the collections under her care, as did the supportive staff of the Archivo Histórico, the Biblioteca Departamental, and the librarians at the Universidad del Valle.

The superb archival collections in Medellín were matched only by their dedicated and energetic staffs. Adriana Yaneth Álvarez C., Ángela María Cardona Gómez, and Carolina María Gil S. at FAES (Fundación Antioqueña para los Estudios Sociales) deserve more credit than this one line. Although FAES no longer exists as an independent organization, its collections are now found at the Biblioteca Pública Piloto (BPP) de Medellín para América

Latina, where Jackeline García Chaverra diligently assisted in the use of FAES images now housed at the BPP. Hilda María Hincapié Gil, Lucía Vásquez Molina, Jorge Humberto Yépez, and Mariela Ríos Madrid welcomed me to the Archivo Histórico de Antioquia and its superb Archivo de la Memoria Visual, a fascinating collection for this project. At the Biblioteca General at the Universidad de Antioquia, Rosa Delia Álvarez, Celina Alzate M., and Myriam Medina Muñoz made this "pobre gringo perdido en la selva colombiana" quite at home while working with that collection.

In the United States, the research and public lectures at the University of San Francisco's Davies Forum by Beverly Stoeltje, Amelia Simpson, Ellen Zetzel Lambert, Lois Banner, and Randy Thornhill all helped frame central themes found in this book. My mentors and friends Thomas M. Davies Jr., Brian Loveman, and Linda B. Hall encouraged the research and shared their views. USF's Faculty Research Fund covered most of the research costs while I worked happily in Colombia. My colleagues in the USF History and Latin American Studies departments heard about this project for far too long but remained stubbornly supportive. Patrick Steacy of USF's Center for Instruction and Technology, Santiago Perry, Marissa Litman, and Jeanine Hoy assisted in the selection and reproduction of many of the illustrations found in this book. My dear friend and colleague Cheryl Czekala, former student Liz Jones, and family members Susan Stanfield and Marilyn and Dave Searing carved up and improved draft chapters. Theresa May, editor-in-chief at the University of Texas Press, made manuscript preparation a stress-free exercise given her punctuality, professionalism, and humanity. The assistance of Kaila Wyllys with illustrations, Victoria Davis with production, and the insightful editing of Teri Sperry made publishing with UT Press a true joy. Many thanks to Jane Rausch and Frank Safford for their engaged and insightful comments on the manuscript. Peer review by my colleagues from the Latin American Historians of Northern California (LAHNOCA), organized and coordinated by Myrna Santiago and Theresa Alfaro-Velcamp, pressed me for greater comparative and interpretative analyses during a research talk at one of our initial meetings. Finally, I'd like to thank my children, Lincoln, Payton, and Sophia, for allowing their dad his "quiet time" to finish this work.

OF BEASTS AND BEAUTY

INTRODUCTION

This book chronicles the social, cultural, and political importance of feminine beauty in Colombia[1] from 1845 to 1985. Colombians have valued beauty in women throughout their history, as have peoples around the globe for thousands of years. Beauty, then, is a powerful cultural mirror through which historians can view the evolution of societies and nations. The serious analysis of beauty reveals much about our shared humanity as it unveils the power and pitfalls of a human obsession that is crucial to the image and status of nations and peoples of all colors, mixtures, ethnicities, genders, and ages.

Major and controversial questions will pepper this work. Why has beauty been of such great import to humans? What is beauty, how is it defined, valued, contested, measured, displayed, expressed, and marketed? Who is beautiful and why, and what does that tell us about gender, color, class, morality, social evolution, and political development? How and why has beauty in modern American republics reinforced notions of development, modernity, and a white pigmentocracy inherited from European colonialism over the last half millennium?

How has Colombia's tortured geography and equally tortured political history protected local and regional definitions of beauty, ones often having little to do with the North Atlantic ideal? How, when, and why has Colombian beauty merged with and emulated international beauty standards? How has beauty's meaning and expression changed in different regions over time as the mass medium of its expression has become more visual? Today, why does Colombia have more than three hundred beauty pageants each year, and what does that tell us about civil society and the state of national politics?

The masculine beast is the alter ego and engaged partner of feminine beauty in Colombia. That beast represents many of the historical and structural problems unresolved in the nation: a nonsovereign state that cannot guard the lives and property of its citizens, provide basic social services, or uphold and comply with the law; a state perceived as illegitimate and challenged by determined armed groups; periodic waves of political, economic, and social violence, insecurity, civil war, insurgency, and counterinsurgency often directed at the civilian population; elitist and exclusionary institutions, be they governmental, religious, or business organizations; social exclusion and customary racism that limit social mobility for nonwhite Colombians; extreme concentration of land and wealth and the concomitant inequality and impoverishment of at least half of the population. Colombia's national history has been defined by civil strife, a weak and ineffectual government, little meaningful reform, and murder rates routinely ten times those of another very violent nation, the United States of America. Over the last decades of the twentieth century, well over half of all kidnapping for ransom cases in the world took place in Colombia. I will argue that one major reason that Colombians value beauty so much is that the terror of the beast—violence, insecurity, racism, poverty, and the perceived illegitimacy or inadequacy of government—reinforces gender roles (women should be beautiful and men should be powerful) as it closes options for reform and liberation. Beauty, thus, represents the feminine and social constant opposite institutional, elitist, dysfunctional, and often violent male order/chaos; beauty is feminine, moral, virtuous, civil, uplifting, peaceful, and hopeful.

Pageants and festivals juxtapose beauty with the beast in spaces that are nonpartisan, civic, and celebratory, performing rituals and spectacles of great regional and national symbolism. Since the middle of the twentieth century, the Señorita Colombia national beauty pageant in coastal and tropical Cartagena has become the national obsession. Held during the week of November 11, Armistice Day, and the anniversary of Cartagena's independence from Spain, the pageant attracts representative beauty queens (*reinas*) from various departments and territories of the nation. The whole process takes months, from selecting local and departmental queens to preparing the sovereign and her entourage for the national pageant, all covered by an intense media blitz. Often, the Señorita Colombia pageant becomes the biggest media story and the most popular event in the entire nation by late October. People from all classes and sectors pick their favorites, argue and gossip over small and large details, bet their money, and anxiously await the competition to crown their new national sovereign.

Local, departmental, national, and international pageants are so important to Colombians because of the disturbing presence of the beast and because the nation has such a horrible national and international reputation. Colombians don't have many national heroes, particularly in the twentieth century; politicians usually cannot garner national respect because of partisan divisions and general cynicism; military leaders are usually superfluous given the lack of foreign wars. Colombian national soccer teams attract great attention both inside and outside the country, but even promising teams typically lose the big games, as in the 1994 and 1998 World Cup debacles, the national team thereafter failing to qualify for the World Cup in 2002, 2006, and 2010. Individual Colombian soccer and baseball players, cyclists, racecar drivers, golfers, and inline speed skaters have fared well internationally in recent decades, but their individual triumphs don't carry the national and international significance of a collective national triumph like a World Cup championship.[2] Juxtaposed with these intermittent athletic triumphs, Colombia has all the social and political problems connected with generalized poverty and violence, drug trafficking, guerrilla insurgency, paramilitary massacres, and death squad activity (the beast) with little to close the distance and fear of everyday life except family, friends, and beauty.

Colombians need beauty to literally and figuratively put a good face on the nation. They need a winner and they get one each year, sometimes each week, with the new, fresh, young, vibrant, and very feminine reinas. And once a queen, always a queen. People on the streets, on the mountain paths, and along the wide rivers remember the quintessential Colombian winner of the twentieth century, Luz Marina Zuluaga, Miss Universe 1958. She was the first Colombian to participate in Miss Universe and the only Colombian winner of that pageant to date, a fact that makes her a national icon. Since then, Colombian contestants in the Miss Universe and Miss World pageants have placed well, presenting a positive image of the nation to the global media as they promote the country's products, exports, and tourism potential. Other Latin American women, notably from Venezuela, Brazil, the Dominican Republic, Puerto Rico, Peru, Argentina, and Mexico also have excelled on the global stage. Why this is the case requires additional comparative investigation and cannot be firmly answered here, but one certainly can argue that Colombians over the last sixty years—like Venezuelans after the petroleum bust and political crises of the 1980s—have promoted their beauty queens as positive national and international symbols during times of crisis, drift, and sagging patriotism.[3] Colombians and Venezuelans, neighbors and rivals who often contest border issues and the top spots in international pageants, point with pride to their reinas and their beautiful women as proof of their nation's goodness, modernity, style, and allure when male outlets for national honor—sports, jobs, politics—lack potency.

This project evolved from a series of observations and fortuitous accidents. As a young child, I recall a moment in church when I looked over my mother's shoulder at a woman in the pew behind ours. Her beauty and angelic singing voice are as alive to me today as they were decades ago. Beauty is memorable; children, like adults, notice and remember it.[4] As I hid from my mother my various secret crushes on fellow elementary schoolmates, she shared with me her passion for motion pictures and beauty pageants. We watched movies at the local theaters, but more importantly, she would sit us kids down in front of the television for the annual Miss America pageant. Initially, I wasn't sure if Miss America viewing wasn't "girl stuff" and that maybe I should be outside playing football or watching my dad break his knuckles working on the car. But those years I did watch, I learned a few things as I rooted for Miss California, our home-state favorite. The first was that the pageant's outcome was unpredictable and dramatic and that people in the audience, as well as those participating, invested a great deal of energy into the whole enterprise. Even if Miss Texas won, with her twangy accent and big hair, at least I learned something about contests, geography, regional differences, and the larger nation.

Decades later, avoiding my dissertation, my television channel surfing settled on the Miss Universe pageant. Interrupting my couch-potato torpor, the creative light bulb sparked my brain to do a geopolitical analysis of beauty within the parameters of the pageant. Several conclusions quickly emerged. First, the African women lacked the preferred body type; they carried ample body fat in their hips and legs—a marker of beauty and fertility in agricultural societies—clearly not having had the time or inclination to work out hours a day, diet excessively, or have the fat removed surgically. The East Asian women had the right proportions, about a 3:2:3 ratio of bust, waist, and hips, but they lacked the necessary height. The North Atlantic ideal was well represented by the European, US, Canadian, and the other British Commonwealth contestants, thus displaying the wealth, development, and leisure of the modern world. But Latinas had the height, figure, face, and style to match them, and they had a sexy but familiar femininity to boot, an "exotic otherness" that was familiar and alluring while both traditional and modern.

A year later, during an editing break on my now completed dissertation, I happened upon the 1993 Miss Universe pageant held in Mexico City. Mexico was then in the process of making major changes to the Constitution of 1917 and its twentieth-century identity, gutting much of what the nation stood for after the Mexican Revolution in order to implement freer trade and NAFTA. The pageant judges, symbols of internationalism and the new order, made the error of not selecting Miss Mexico as one of the ten finalists, which threw the already boisterous and vocal audience into a rage. Mexicans could not countenance such an affront, particularly as the abrogation of Article 27, made famous by the demands and deeds of Emiliano Zapata, signaled once again that the Mexican government would champion not the interests of Mexican citizens but those of foreign investors. Their whistles and shouts forced the program into various unscheduled commercial interruptions—and still the crowd wouldn't quiet. The judges, whose backs were to the inflamed public, looked nervously over their shoulders while master of ceremonies Dick Clark visibly shook as his voice cracked. The audience then got behind Miss Puerto Rico as their replacement Latina; the top three finalists, from Venezuela, Colombia, and Puerto Rico, directed themselves to the audience by answering their final questions in Spanish. Miss Puerto Rico[5] won the crown. In essence, the crowd took control of what was presumably a corporate, international, yet "objective" event. The audience had altered the show and the outcome of the pageant, proving that it could be open to a degree of popular pressure and that the corporate pageant could be made more "democratic" and sensitive to national honor.

In 1994, I was back in Colombia doing more fieldwork for my first book[6] when a final incident galvanized my interest in researching beauty. A departmental pageant was being held in Cartagena, a pyramid pageant that would send the winner to the national Miss Colombia contest and perhaps on to Miss Universe or Miss World. The clear crowd favorite was a *morena*, of Afro-Colombian heritage, a representative local beauty with dark hair and eyes. The judges selected instead a lighter, more European-looking contestant, provoking protests from the audience. The judges, presumably, decided that a *morena* would not win the national contest, nor would she best represent the elite of the city and of the department. The audience then did something fascinating: they took their favorite into the street, crowned her their *reina*, and then paraded her around in celebration. The politics of the official pageant and the parallel ritual on the street highlighted the deep class and color issues that divide the elite and the folk of Colombia.

Fieldwork for this book started in earnest in 1997, followed two years later by another harvest of data. Newspapers, journals, and magazines abounded in libraries and archives in Bogotá, Medellín, Cali, and Cartagena, providing sources on beauty for those cities and their environs and for other countries. Travel accounts from the nineteenth century yielded insight on provincial life in Antioquia, Cauca, Santander, Cundinamarca, and along the Magdalena River as native and foreign travelers braved Colombia's difficult and sprawling geography en route to various cities. *Cromos*, the Colombian equivalent of *Life Magazine*, served as a nice longitudinal source because of its weekly publication since 1916 and because its covers are usually dominated by the images of attractive and important women. Since most humans use their eyesight so much to study and understand their world, I also focused on visual sources, like photographs, prints, and cartoons, to supplement the textual sources.[7]

Primary sources like those mentioned above serve as the major documentary base for this book because the topic is new. However, secondary sources from Colombia and elsewhere give this study greater context and comparative value. Although historians generally have avoided the topic of beauty, Colombians have published some works on it. The sixtieth anniversary of the Miss Colombia pageant in 1994 yielded one celebratory book and two muckraking ones; the former, *Las más bellas: historia del concurso nacional de belleza*, includes many full-page photographs of past beauties and provides a good overview of the evolution of the pageant along with useful procedural information. The two muckraking works, authored by Colombian journalists Eccehomo Cetina and Pedro Claver Tellez, highlight how the pageant and its contestants have been tarnished by money, fame, sex, ambition, and the rich and unscrupulous men who have been drawn to them—professional handlers and stylists, politicians, and drug traffickers.[8]

Concurrently in Colombia during the 1990s, rising interest in gender studies and women's and social history has added to the secondary base for this study. The three volumes in the *Las mujeres en la historia de Colombia* series include more than fifty articles about women's contributions to the history, politics, culture, and society of the nation since the pre-Columbian period, supplementing the fine articles found in the multivolume *Nueva historia de Colombia*.[9] Essays and monographs, like those authored by Suzy Bermúdez, Catalina Reyes Cárdenas, Patricia Londoño Vega, and Santiago Londoño Vélez, also illuminate women's roles and daily life in Colombia during the nineteenth and twentieth centuries.[10]

In the United States, historians, like their colleagues in Latin America, have tended to overlook the importance of beauty in social and everyday life. An early exception to that tendency and a work that has inspired this book is *American Beauty* by Lois W. Banner. Professor Banner argued convincingly that the "pursuit of beauty has always been a central concern of American women" and that this pursuit has bound women together more than any other fact. She focused her primary analysis on face, body, and fashion, finding three primary beauty types that have emerged and reemerged in American society. She devoted most of her attention to the period from 1800 to 1921, but then in an updated edition noted how trends she found earlier continued on through the twentieth century. Oddly, few historians have followed up on Banner's 1983 classic, especially for the period after 1921, when the Miss America pageant and motion pictures further commercialized American beauty.[11]

To fill this big historiographical hole and to further enrich this study, I've branched out in an eclectic fashion into other disciplines. Latin Americanists often use interdisciplinary and comparative approaches when confronting both the complexity of the region and the relative dearth of secondary literature. For example, linguist Amelia Simpson wrote a brilliant analysis of the blonde Brazilian television star Xuxa, emphasizing how the mega-marketing of this 1980s phenomenon reinforced female gender roles as it toyed with ambivalent and troubling notions of modernity and race.[12] Simpson's work sparked my inquiries into how color, class, marketing, and modernity reveal Colombian attitudes about themselves and their nation. From the field of English and literary criticism, Ellen Zetzel Lambert analyzed the "difficult beauty" found in the works of English female authors of the nineteenth century, a literary expression of beauty of great emotion and depth. Lambert also addressed why and how late-twentieth-century feminists had to grapple with beauty as a personal and a political issue, a goal in part shaped by the phenomenal success of another work on beauty, Naomi Wolf's *The Beauty Myth*.[13] Lambert helped me appreciate the power and subtlety of beauty, especially in its nonvisual, literary, and deep forms as expressed by nineteenth-century Colombian writers. Anthropologists, like Beverly Stoeltje, have published fine comparative studies on the power and meaning of beauty pageants, fascinating and enlightening works for me given the Colombian obsession with pageants.[14] Finally, psychologist Linda A. Jackson led me through the minefield of nature and nurture, biology and culture, and how they shape beauty and its study in her innovative book, *Physical Appearance and Gender: Sociobiological and Sociocultural Perspectives*.[15] Jackson certainly opened my own cultural windows on how and why beauty matters to human beings.

I do not claim that this research and its findings comprise anything close to a definitive or objective work. It is, instead, an introductory study meant to inspire thought and reflection. I hope that this book opens the way for other students and scholars to analyze similar cultural themes in the future. I am neither Colombian nor female, and I am writing about feminine beauty in a foreign but beloved land. I am aware of my own limitations, biases, and blinders. I do claim, however, that beauty serves as an illuminating cultural window on human beings as individuals and in society as it chronicles the development of cultures and nations over time. It tells us much about regions and their peculiar cultures, in this case in Colombia, as it tracks how the country became a more urban and modern nation. It focuses squarely on the role, image, and relative power of women, thus bringing the majority of the population and a major national theme into prime relief, a focus often overlooked in Colombian and Latin American history.

I hope that Colombians find this book and its arguments challenging and provocative, but not offensive, given that it will reframe how some citizens think about themselves and their collective past. I hope to teach non-Colombians, particularly residents of the United States, something about Colombian history and society, given the woeful ignorance demonstrated by continued and increased US funding for violence in Colombia, the further feeding of the beast. In short, I will use beauty as the hook by which I get North Americans to read about Colombia as I challenge Colombians to look at themselves and their modern situation in fresh ways. Finally, I hope that those who read this book will revise what and how they think about history and Colombia, about beauty and gender relations, about the modern and global world, and about those things humans share in common.

Nine chapters subdivide the chronology and thematic discussions that follow. Chapter 1 provides the reader with a historical and geographic introduction to Colombia as it presents major themes in the history of beauty over time. Chapter 2 begins the exploration of how beauty and ugliness were defined, expressed, and represented from 1845 to 1885. Colombia's broken and heterogeneous geography and concomitant regionalism will offer us a glimpse of elite and folk life in colonial and aristocratic cities like Bogotá, Cartagena, and Popayán in comparison with the more recently settled and less aristocratic regions of Antioquia and Santander. In its form and presentation, fashion transmits notions of beauty, modernity, and class, so we'll track what people wore and how they presented themselves in public. During this period, Liberal and Conservative Party traditionalists railed against the corset and the impact of foreign fashion during breaks from their seemingly incessant internecine battles, and often embraced the image of the rural barefoot *campesina* as an enduring symbol of a kind, domesticated, and available beauty. To understand the attitudes of the educated leaders of the day, we'll track the literary expression of beauty's internal depth when analyzing a surprising number of journals written for or by women, many of them dedicated to the "fair sex."

Chapter 3 focuses on the years from 1886 to 1914, an era of increasing exports and the related impact of imported cloth, fashions, and ideas. The sports craze of the 1890s, especially big in the United States, spilled over into Colombia as bicycling, swimming, tennis, and horse racing changed women's fashions as they did elsewhere. The sporty, athletic look made famous by the Gibson Girl in the United States pushed more elite teenagers and women in Colombia to embrace the newest international trends. Technical improvements in photography both decreased the cost and widened the circulation of two-dimensional images, many of them constructing and representing feminine beauty. Politically, these years saw a new conservative and long-lived constitution, the important presidencies of Rafael Núñez and Rafael Reyes, a bloody civil war from 1899 to 1902, and the unsettling buildup to the Great War in Europe.

Chapter 4 grapples with the era between 1914 and 1930 as the nineteenth and twentieth centuries were torn apart by dramatic events and modern trends. The Great War (World War I) not only killed millions in Europe but also changed the status and image of women in the Americas. Women were used as symbols of nationalism as they donned uniforms as evidence of their devotion to national causes. Women's hairstyles and hemlines would shorten considerably, ushering in the image of the new woman. New weekly illustrated magazines in Colombia, like *Cromos*, were full of advertisements pitching new fashion styles, cosmetics, skin creams, hair and mouth products, and sundry curatives aimed at women of various classes, thus setting and marketing the look and price of the new international feminine beauty standard. In this context of mass mobilizing for nationalism and consumption arose the prominence of the national and international beauty pageant, a trend Colombians initially joined eagerly. Foreign films from Italy, France, and the United States also heralded a break from simpler past entertainment as they brought the world and glamour of film starlets into the Colombian psyche. The growing dominance of Hollywood in film and New York in commerce eventually supplanted the traditional allure of Paris, making the United States the new fashion and beauty center for Colombians in the twentieth century. The economic bubble of the 1920s eventually gave way to the Great Depression of 1930, leaving triumphant, nonetheless, more widely diffused images and a new culture of beauty, but ones more removed from everyday Colombian life.

Chapter 5 covers the years 1930 to 1946, a period of Liberal dominance of national government and also a rare period of reform in Colombia. The first half of the twentieth century was also an era of relative peace, so the nation and its citizens did not need the saving grace of beauty as a sedative for the terror of the beast. Only two national beauty pageants were held during those years. The hope of reform also tended to open up other outlets for females in society, especially in education, sports, and the emerging job markets in the cities. In short, peace and reform made the public performance of beauty less important in Colombian civil life, leaving the magazine covers and the theatre screens to the foreign film stars.

Chapter 6 chronicles the failure of reform and renewed partisan hatreds that reawakened the slumbering beast from 1946 to 1958, a terrible era in Colombian history written in capital letters as *La Violencia*, The Violence. A Conservative return to power, the assassination of the leading Liberal reformer, and the eventual purging of Liberals from national institutions set the stage for truly awful partisan and civil war. During this period, Colombia took on the horrible reputation it would carry for the rest of the century: a place riddled with ungodly levels of violence, crime, and insecurity. Of course, feminine beauty assumed a greater role in national life in light of masculine passion and stupidity, evinced by the reemergence of the national beauty pageant in Cartagena in 1947. This period also held the one military dictatorship of the twentieth century, that of General Gustavo Rojas Pinilla. Rojas interrupted the domination of government by the two traditional parties and proved to be an adept manipulator of both power and beauty. He both enfranchised women and militarized the female image by placing many young women in uniform before the public view as mechanisms to garner support for his regime. He introduced television to Colombia and censored the press as he presided over the national beauty pageant in Cartagena, symbolically punctuating his power over the nation as the masculine general crowned the new feminine queen. Chapter 6 closes with Rojas dumped by leaders from the two traditional parties, who in fashioning the National Front tried to put Humpty Dumpty—an exclusionary democracy dominated by elites—back together again.

Chapter 7 confronts the legacy of the National Front, especially the political cynicism and ongoing violence that made beauty a civic, national, and international necessity. The year 1958 began with Luz Marina Zuluaga winning the Miss Universe pageant in Long Beach, California, bringing Colombia a unique international triumph at a pivotal time. Over the next ten years, pageants of almost every conceivable flavor flourished throughout the land at a time when elections were formal but meaningless, when unauthorized political parties could not compete with the Liberal and Conservative parties, and when civil war morphed into guerrilla insurgency. The 1960s also brought with them rock 'n' roll music and a youth and drug culture that had a dramatic, if shallow, impact on fashion and beauty. By 1968, Colombia had several guerrilla movements, an emerging marijuana sector, ongoing sharing and alternation of power by the Liberals and Conservatives, and the pageant's first "anti-*reina*," a young woman who spoke for herself instead of serving as a mouthpiece for misplaced yearnings.

Chapters 8 and 9 track the fallout from the National Front and the failure of both reformers and revolutionaries to create a more modern and just state and society. Beauty became one of the only national and cultural symbols of goodness and salvation in the country, especially in light of the persistent strength of the beast—guerrilla insurgency, paramilitary and military massacres, and the violence spawned by the drug business. Chapter 8 looks at the period between 1968 and 1979, years when more rural Colombians left the poverty and insecurity of the countryside and entered into the larger media world of the cities. Beauty continued to be an avenue of social and self-expression and offered the chance of social climbing, particularly for the young female migrants looking for mates or pink-collar jobs.

Chapter 9 pulls the various themes of the book together as it chronicles the dramatic events from 1979 to 1985. The ultimate year of this study held within it a one-week period full of natural and political catastrophes when both nature and politics seemed to damn the country and its citizens. However, neither the disaster at the Palacio de Justicia nor the devastating mudslides off the slopes of the Nevado del Ruiz interrupted the Miss Colombia pageant, occurring at the same time that year, for Colombians still hoped that beauty might deliver them and their troubled nation, albeit momentarily, from the terror of the beast.

An epilogue tracking major trends in Colombian history from 1985 to 2011 will bring my analysis of beauty and the beast into the twenty-first century. A conclusion will summarize the major themes presented in the book and will test if what I argued for 1845 to 1985 still rings true in 2011. For both personal and professional reasons, I preferred to end the narrative with the dramatic events of 1985, but I was convinced by reviewers of the manuscript to grapple with the complexities of the last quarter century. I hope that readers find the conclusion and epilogue a useful summary of recent historical currents and present circumstances.

The first chapter sets the geographic and historical stage to help readers appreciate the importance of beauty to Colombians through time, and the subsequent chapters track the chronological evolution of beauty's meaning as it mirrored the terror of the beast and the fortunes of reform. Although beauty is of universal importance to human beings throughout time and around the globe, beauty in Colombia uniquely reflected the nation's geography, its colonial inheritance, its growth into a modern, urban society, and its yearning for a positive identity. Ironically, the beast of violence reinforced traditional gender roles as it blocked avenues to reform, while beauty functioned as a positive outlet for Colombians seeking hope and relief from political and institutional failure. Tragically, violence, exclusion, and terror made beauty a powerful sedative for people in a nation dreaming of a better future.

SETTING || *Chapter 1*

Colombia is a peculiar and beautiful country. Its coasts on both the Caribbean Sea and the Pacific Ocean—an advantage unique in South America—give it favorable access to the world and its trade, but Colombian port cities are remote and hard to reach for the vast interior population. Three verdant mountain ranges highlight the nation's Andean character and provide a home for 90 percent of the population, while the vast tropical plains and forests east of them are only thinly settled. Two major rivers squeezed between the Andean ranges, the Cauca and Magdalena, along with the coastal lowlands, the llanos, and the vast Amazonian forests, underscore Colombia's tropical latitude. Its natural resources—fertile and well-watered agricultural and grazing lands, gold, emeralds, petroleum, coal—represent a bounty of potential wealth and development, but most Colombian residents are poor. Colombia, about the size of France, Spain, and Portugal combined, is more fertile, rich, and physically captivating than its Latin American neighbors, but it is the envy of few, for it is a deeply divided and troubled nation.[1]

Its geography has fostered a strong regionalism, one that bolsters provincial and traditional attitudes as it thwarts national integration and modern liberal development. A conservative Catholic Church has reinforced traditional attitudes while playing an active role in daily and institutional life. The church has actively meddled in party politics, supporting the Conservatives rather than the Liberals, both parties created and framed by the nineteenth century and slow to adapt to twentieth-century developments. The state is weak—at local, departmental, and national levels—while the economy has generally been strong. Violence haunts many regions and their citizens with threats from thieves, bandits, guerrillas, paramilitary squads, and governmental forces. Colombians cannot depend on systems (political, economic, judicial) to protect their interests or their lives. In such a tense and fluid environment, individuals rely on family and friends as their pillars of support, giving warmth to primary relationships often lacking in the efficient United States. In short, it's a beautiful and rich country, but also one that can be quite violent and full of insecurity.[2]

A recent book on the culture and customs of Colombia notes the importance of regionalism, traditionalism, and the Catholic Church in Colombian
society as it comments on the preeminent popularity of the *Concurso Nacional
de Belleza*, the Señorita Colombia beauty pageant. The authors assert that
"Feminine beauty is highly prized in Colombia, perhaps more visibly so than
in any other Western nation."[3] Although peoples across the Americas and
some Europeans might contest this statement, a closer look at how Colombian geography and history have shaped regional culture partially reveals why
beauty has been so important to Colombian identity.

Colombia's tropical and mountainous terrain divides rather than unites
the nation's population. Throughout the colonial period, the tropical lowlands
were disease-ridden and uninviting, thereby stunting settlement. The Andean
ranges were vast, steep, and jagged, thus tending to attract people to pockets
of temperate and arable land within them. Much of the middle and lower
elevations of the Andean ranges have fertile and well-watered lands that promoted the founding of self-sufficient small villages and towns. Available lands
up and down slopes enabled farmers to grow most everything their villages
needed, thereby precluding the need for long-distance trade and stunting the
development of national commerce.

Geography made trade difficult and expensive; pack mules and humans
labored over rugged paths and carried much of the goods in the Andean area,
while on the Magdalena River, the major artery linking central Colombia
with Caribbean ports, one had to contest with low and meandering water,
mosquitoes, and episodic river traffic.[4] The combination of broken and diverse
geography and human settlement in small, self-sufficient towns, particularly
in the salubrious middle elevations of the Andean region, tended to reinforce
local customs and allegiances rather than promote a more national or international orientation. However, within the four major zones of Colombia—the
Caribbean coast, the Pacific coast, the Andean region, and the eastern lowlands—popular traditions hung on through time, thereby buffering autoch-
thonous attitudes, like the definition of beauty, from being easily supplanted
by imported fashions.

The thousand-mile-long Caribbean coast, the area of Colombia most open
to international exchange, retains a number of distinct regions. The remote
and arid La Guajira peninsula has few roads and little infrastructure and is
home to scattered groups of Guajiro Indians. Further south and west is the
home of the Kogi and Sanká Indians in the highest coastal mountain range in
the world, the Sierra Nevada de Santa Marta, with peaks up to 5,800 meters
tall (more than 19,000 feet). Below their perennially snowcapped peaks,
one finds the oldest colonial city in Colombia, Santa Marta, and Aracataca,

the hometown of Colombia's most famous modern author, Gabriel García Márquez, and the huge swamp that sheltered his composite coastal town, Macondo, from time and the world in his brilliant novel, *One Hundred Years of Solitude*.[5]

At the mouth of the Magdalena River sits Barranquilla, historically an important port of entry for modern ideas and imported products for the nation and now a city of well over one million inhabitants. Although Barranquilla is bigger and busier, Cartagena stubbornly has held on to its reputation as a colonial and aristocratic city, one whose walls protected its picturesque homes and narrow streets from the surrounding waters and the pirates who appeared on them.[6]

Cartagena's quaint and dignified air is similar in ambiance and character to New Orleans, Louisiana, for both cities have become sites of revelry and tourism, in part because both were international ports of the slave trade, a trans-Atlantic pigmentartic business that transformed their respective societies by exploiting the dark many and bringing riches to a white few. Cities like Cartagena and New Orleans reshaped American societies by introducing millions of Africans to colonial America, thus creating multiethnic societies of unequal rank and order but ones where notions of beauty often collided and sometimes intermingled. Today, the Concurso Nacional de Belleza is held in lovely Cartagena, a city where thousands of Afro-Colombians participate in their own popular celebrations and the official national pageant's activities. Tellingly, however, only in 2001 did the first Afro-Colombian woman win the national title.

The Caribbean coast southwest of Cartagena has much in common with the Pacific coast: it is rural, poor, underdeveloped, and largely ignored by the Colombian government. The Chocó region bridges the two coasts near the present border with Panama. In the colonial period, African and indigenous slaves were compelled to work the region's rich gold and platinum deposits, leaving in their wake a tri-ethnic society like that of the Caribbean coast but one more African in derivation; nearly 90 percent of the Chocó's present population is of African descent, making it an important but largely ignored cradle of Afro-Colombian culture. Biodiversity in the area's rainforests is said to rival that of like forests in Amazonia, with some areas receiving 12 meters of rain annually (some 468 inches). Roads, schools, electricity, and potable water are rare, while mosquitoes, malaria, dysentery, guerrillas, exploitative foreign corporations, and smugglers are not. Further south, Buenaventura is the biggest city and most important port on the Pacific coast, and the only site along an 800-mile (1300 k) coastal stretch linked to the interior by a paved road.[7]

Over the relatively low Cordillera Occidental (Western Range) from Buenaventura, one enters Cali, which, along with Cartagena, Medellín, and Bogotá, serves as an urban hub for this study.[8] Cali sits in the wide and fertile Cauca Valley, once filled with sugar plantations worked by African slaves. Cali prospered and grew during the mid-twentieth century, making it a "ciudad alegre" and home to the most beautiful women in Colombia, according to the city's boosters. A popular saying from colonial times highlighted the relationship of local geography to beauty in the Upper Cauca Valley: "Para granizo, Guanacas; para viejas, Timaná; para muchachas bonitas, Cali, Buga, y Popayán." (For hail, Guanacas; for old women, Timaná; for pretty girls, Cali, Buga, and Popayán.)[9] Past sugar barons and present industrial and financial elites have kept the white aristocracy proud and above the poor Afro-Colombian urban dwellers and the indigenous communities in the surrounding mountains.[10] Further south, bucolic Popayán shares with Cali an aristocratic elite tradition, but one built more on colonial and indigenous foundations. Pasto is the southern urban anchor of the Colombian Andes, capital of a department with strong indigenous and royalist roots, a place therefore used as the butt of most Colombian jokes.[11]

North and east of Cali, one encounters Colombia's coffee zone, an area known for its rich soil, hardworking farmers, and natural and human disasters. The coffee zone witnessed some of the worst fighting and slaughter during La Violencia, while in 1985, the eruption of the highest volcano in the Cordillera Central, the Nevado del Ruiz (5,389 meters, 17,680 feet), brought mudslides and death to at least 23,000 people. Frequent earthquakes remind the region's inhabitants of the unpredictability of living near a hot spot of the Pacific Ring of Fire.

Medellín, north of the main coffee zone, is an important commercial and industrial hub of west-central Colombia, serving as a marketplace for coffee from the south and mineral wealth from surrounding Antioquia and the Chocó. It is also the most developed industrial and manufacturing community in the country. The city lies in a long valley surrounded by Andean ranges, its springlike climate encouraging its entrepreneurial residents to dress more casually and comfortably than the more formal and buttoned-up *bogotanos*. *Antioqueños*, or *paisas*, residents of the sprawling department around Medellín, have the reputation of being more modern, independent, industrious, and egalitarian than their main competitors for national leadership in Bogotá.[12]

More reserved and formal than their paisa rivals, residents of cold, damp, and cloudy Bogotá have long enjoyed a position of prominence, if not leadership, over much of the rest of the country. Long the political capital of the

MAP 1.1   *Colombia (Shaded Relief) 2008, United States Central Intelligence Agency, in Perry-Castañeda Map Collections, University of Texas Libraries.*

land, Bogotá is the largest and most important city in the country. It is a center of art, media, and education, a major commercial hub, and the home of the federal bureaucracy and national institutions. Although *costeños* might joke about the dreary and dark tone of the city and its residents, and paisas might challenge the presumed arrogance of capital dictates, both Colombians and foreigners must deal with Bogotá if they are to understand or thrive in Colombia.

Ethnically, many urban residents in Bogotá (and in the surrounding departments of Cundinamarca, Boyacá, and Santander) think of themselves as Spanish, thereby distancing themselves from the socially subordinated indigenous and mestizo populations in the countryside and from the majority Afro-Colombian societies of the coastal regions. However, regardless of claimed political or racial stewardship over Colombia, national elites have failed to build from Bogotá a sovereign and legitimate government. The capital has only sporadically, and weakly, exercised its central national position over the distant and diverse peoples and regions it purportedly leads.[13]

North of Bogotá in the department of Santander, travelers in the 1830s remarked on the beauty of women in the towns of Socorro and Piedecuesta. Santander was a fairly prosperous area at the time, with exports of tobacco and straw hats enhancing purchasing power for both men and women. The area's lower elevation and access to the Magdalena River and Venezuelan trade routes mixed a warmer climate than that found in chilly Bogotá or Tunja with openness to imports and foreign exchange.

In meeting señora Concepción Fernández (who had counted among her admirers Simón Bolívar) in Socorro, English painter Joseph Brown described her as a lady who "has been deservedly celebrated for eminent beauty . . ."[14] But Brown saved his highest praise for the women of the town of Piedecuesta. Brown wrote: "The women here are said to be the handsomest in all this and the neighboring provinces of Socorro and Pamplona, and this report I am ready to confirm from many pretty faces which peeped thro' the balcony rails as I rode by. The greatest curiosity is excited in these inland towns amongst all classes but more especially the females of the higher classes when any stranger makes his appearance, and so it was as I entered Piedecuesta, the windows were occupied until I was out of sight."[15] Clearly flattered by this attention, Brown seems to suggest, nonetheless, that the beauty and fame of a region's women is influenced both by climate and the progress brought by economic activity.

The vast eastern lowlands dwarf the rest of the country in size but are thinly populated. The llanos and the rain forests of Amazonia are home to a number of indigenous peoples who have been in contact with missionaries and traders over the last several centuries. Although Colombians don't think of their country as even having an indigenous population, between 1 and 2 percent of the total population is Amerindian, a larger native population in absolute and per capita measures than that of Brazil. In essence, the indigenous population and the Afro-Colombian population ring the perimeters of the nation, while the Andean region is primarily viewed as white and mestizo.[16] Today, both the llanos and the Amazonian lowlands are important regions of petroleum exploitation and of the farming of coca and its production into cocaine.

Over the course of the last century and a half, Colombia has transformed from an agricultural and rural society to a rapidly urbanizing and market-oriented one. The country held about 2.2 million people in 1851, second only to Brazil in total population in South America. In 1870, Bogotá had about forty thousand inhabitants, followed by Medellín with thirty thousand, with the next dozen largest towns having seven to thirteen thousand residents. By 1905, the total population increased to 4.1 million, with about 10 percent of that total living in departmental capitals. By the 1920s, Bogotá, Medellín, Cali, and Barranquilla were starting to consolidate their positions as leading cities in the land. By 1940, 29 percent of Colombians lived in urban areas, but it was only after 1964 that most Colombians lived in cities rather than the countryside. As of 2011, Bogotá is a city of about seven million people; Cali and Medellín have over two million each, and Barranquilla over one million, while about forty-five cities now boast more than one hundred thousand inhabitants. About 76 percent of Colombia's almost 46 million inhabitants are now classified as urban, a major recent transformation of what had been a rural and provincial nineteenth-century society.[17]

Although settlement patterns shifted fairly rapidly, both popular and elite attitudes lagged somewhat behind modern innovations. Popular culture has been nourished by the rich folklore of the countryside, brought to the city by migrants seeking perceived opportunities in urban areas as they flee the poverty and insecurity of rural life. Upper-class values continue to be markedly aristocratic, especially in colonial bureaucratic cities like Cartagena, Bogotá, and Popayán. Color, class, and familial name markers reinforce ascriptive and hierarchical barriers, as do closed political and social systems. Somewhat less aristocratic and exclusive are Barranquilla, Medellín, and Socorro, cities that grew and prospered after the colonial period had ended.[18]

Modern developments in places like Medellín illustrate not only how paisas took advantage of liberating change but also how guardians of tradition often reacted strongly against any challenge to authority. Popular lore recalls that in the 1830s, Medellín held its first masquerade ball, a hugely popular event that led to many others. However, many social events continued to be conducted as private affairs, such as dances in residences. One party hostess of the late 1830s, doña Trinidad Callejas, whose grandson Rafael Uribe Uribe became a famous Liberal leader at the turn of the century, was remembered as the most beautiful woman of her era, an illustration of how beauty punctuates social status and sticks in the collective memory of people. A big Carnival in 1881 and the emergence of youth clubs in the 1890s signaled a shift to more civic and public venues of social interaction.[19]

The twentieth century saw Medellín become a leader in industrial and business developments. Elites in the city supported public education more so than in any other part of the country, an indication that education could be the route to both social advancement and higher productivity. Changes brought by modernity in the 1920s affected women's fashions, ushering in greater freedom for women but also the beginning of a strong backlash by traditionalists. Conservatives in the community and government joined forces with local bishops and priests to regulate women's dress, reserving special concern for cloaking the female body. For example, in 1927 a local businessman placed a reproduction of the Venus de Milo in his storefront window. The statue attracted a curious crowd but also the wrath of "scandalized women" who convinced the mayor to have the nude taken down.

Over the next four decades, the Catholic Church led a campaign to regulate women's public appearance, at mass, in schools, and even on the street, to limit how much impact modern ideas and fashions could have on Medellín. Moreover, the church maintained an extensive "black list" of books and pamphlets by European authors like Voltaire, Montesquieu, Hugo, and Zola as well as banning marriage and sex manuals and the writings of Colombians like Rafael Uribe Uribe, who argued that it wasn't a sin to be a Liberal. The black list was in effect until Vatican II opened more room for modernity in the 1960s. Ironically, it was industrious and entrepreneurial Medellín which attracted the church's most reactionary and traditional sentiment to curb modern change.[20]

Coastal and colonial Cartagena, on the other hand, reveled in a sensuous celebration of female beauty, albeit ordered by rules that highlighted class and color barriers. Stories dating from the Spanish foundation of the city in 1533 remember the Colombian equivalent of La Malinche in Mexico, the Caribbean beauty Catalina, who was described as "tall, with an elegantly formed bust, large eyes surrounded by long and velvety eyelashes, an aquiline nose, a mouth of delicate contours, and arms that harmonized with the other lines of her body." She was sweet and graceful, the adored embodiment of youthful exuberance; other indigenous women admired her but envied her many fine Spanish dresses. Over the next 150 years, women like the enchanting "India Anica," whose bewitching appeal robbed a male admirer of his appetite, sleep, and soul, the Spanish girl Guillermina and her "pretty features and beautiful body," and Eva, "who although not part of the nobility was worthy of wearing a queen's crown because of her charms," highlight how the beauty of women's bodies were more visible and appreciated by male eyes on the tropical coast than they were in the colder, more concealed Andean regions.[21]

A marvelous social history of the festive dances performed in Cartagena during the early nineteenth century, penned by Conservative general Joaquín Posada Gutiérrez, illustrates the color and caste hierarchies represented in the dances themselves and hints at the African roots of what would evolve into the modern beauty pageant. Posada (1797?–1881) was a native of Cartagena and wrote in the mid-1800s, drawing from his memories of dances performed early in the century during the celebrations in honor of the patron saint of the city and during *Carnaval* (Carnival). His vivid and lively account illustrates how late colonial and early republican societies reinforced caste hierarchies in their dances, both performing a ritual of order in society as they opened room in less formal settings for cross-color mixing and adventures. Posada's account also suggests that the roots of today's pageants in Colombia and the Americas run through African as well as European culture.[22]

Regardless of venue, the dances that Posada described punctuated a society highly aware of and ordered by color, class, and caste. On the first day of the novena prior to the February 2 celebration of the Virgin of the Candelaria, a great dance hall would fill with dancers in the following order: (1) the dance for the pure white women, the so-called "blancas de castilla"; (2) that of "pardas," or free mulatas; (3) that of "negras libres," or free black females. Only those of high class and certain dress were allowed to this elite dance, a rule "understood by all." Interestingly, this order reflected the colonial ideology of blood purity or "limpieza de sangre" for whites, as it underscored the importance of being free rather than slave in a city intimately involved in the trans-Atlantic slave trade. Moreover, the order of the dance was set by the caste of the women, not the men, highlighting the role of women in setting the parameters for family and societal honor as well as for the future of their offspring in the caste system.[23]

The more popular open-air dances followed the elite lead in obeying a caste order of participation. Whites began, followed by mulattoes, free blacks, slaves or "gente pobre," and Indians. Each group, again, was led by elite members of each caste, until, eventually the young, poor, and barefoot could join in the fun. The dances included the boisterous and sensual African-derived *currulao* and its spirit-possession ritual similar to that practiced in the Candomblé religion and the even more erotic *mapalé* and its song to Eros; the more reserved indigenous *gaita*; a Spanish quadrille; and a "hispanized" waltz. The dances and music tended to reinforce stereotypical notions of culture — the African perceived as more sensual, the indigenous more restrained and defeated, the Spanish more ordered.

Non-elite whites, or "blancas de la tierra," lacking the class standing and pedigree to gain an invitation from the "blancas de castilla," avoided the popular street dances and the inevitable gossip by throwing their own house dances, to which they invited their white betters and "cuarteronas" (those of one-quarter African or indigenous blood). The cuarteronas were the cigar makers, seamstresses, and dress makers in town and were described as having "skin between mother-of-pearl and cinnamon, light eyes, and pearly teeth." Both elite and non-elite white men snuck away to dance and frolic privately with cuarteronas. Each of these dances and venues reflected hierarchies of class and color, but they also opened social space to transcend formal caste barriers.[24]

February 2 brought the climax of the previous eight days of revelry as the population dressed in its finest clothes to honor Our Lady of the Candelaria. The elite brought out their heavy velvet embroidered fabrics, the ladies donning hoop skirts, crinoline, silk stockings, and loads of gold, emerald, and pearl jewelry. The young favored the less restrictive fashions brought into vogue by the French Revolution: pants, shirts, and shoes with ties rather than buckles. Those who could not afford authentic luxury wore clothes of commoner fabrics and borrowed fake jewels and pearls and settled for silver plate.[25]

Carnival followed the February 2 celebrations closely, participation ordered again by caste and class rank. On the last Sunday of the Carnival season, competing groups of "negros bozales," or recently arrived African-born slaves, organized celebrations and parades, each with their own queen and king, princesses and princes, and royal court. The celebrations recalled the African homeland but also placed the participants and spectators in America as they rekindled monarchical African traditions while reflecting the tensions and the search for order within a colonial American slaveholding society.

The royals dressed not in African but in European garb, slave owners lending their finest clothing and jewels in which to bedeck "their" slaves in yet another round of elite competition and popular emulation. Queens wore gold jewelry and heavily encrusted crowns, worth the freedom of themselves and their families, during those short days when "the slaves were almost free." Only queens and kings could use umbrellas for shade—also a status symbol in Africa—while the princesses wore flowered garlands on their heads as they were prohibited from wearing hats. Once the competition of the different groups and their royalty had ended, the clothes and jewels were returned, and slaves had free days until mass on Ash Wednesday, after which the queens would return to "the acute moral pain and the physical penalties of slavery."[26]

This rich description points to various conclusions. First, slave owners used the Carnival season as a stage on which to compete with one another for prestige as they pitted groups of negros bozales against one another, a classic divide-and-conquer technique common in many urban areas in the Americas. Second, public celebrations in Cartagena, and by extension in Colombia, brought opportunities for both elite and popular sectors to participate in inclusive but ordered and hierarchical rituals denoting rank and power like those displayed in beauty contests. Third, the roots of modern pageants can be traced not only to European nobility and the fashion trends set by the viceregal court in the Americas, but also to Africa and the inclusion of folk traditions that crowned representatives of African American communities as sovereigns.

Perhaps part of the popularity of beauty and pageants in the Americas has to do with this blending of noble traditions from Europe and Africa in a colonial society disguised in a democratic American wrapping. Moreover, the transformation of an ordinary girl into a regal queen brings notoriety and prestige, but it won't topple institutions (slavery) or social systems (elite patriarchy) that subordinate women.

During the course of the eighteenth century, the popularity of Carnival celebrations and the African-influenced dances that came with them spread up the Magdalena River and into southern Colombia with the slaves sent to work the mines and plantations of Antioquia and the Cauca Valley. Dances like the cumbia, the currulao, and the *bullerengue* (originally a dance for young girls and a celebration of puberty) spread into the interior of the country, bringing with them a slice of the Afro-Caribbean coast and its celebration of sensuality and female beauty. Today, the currulao is associated with Cali, the bullerengue is most danced in the departments of Bolívar and Magdalena, while the cumbia has become a national and international hit. Carnival celebrations are important in the southern Nariño cities of Tumaco, on the Pacific coast, and in Pasto in the highlands. Cartagena has lost its leadership in Carnival celebrations to larger Barranquilla, but it still hosts the biggest spectacle in the nation dedicated to female beauty, the Reinado Nacional de Belleza, a platform built, in part, by its past importance as a gateway of African culture for the rest of the country.[27]

The public display of feminine beauty during dances, fiestas, or pageants can reinforce both poles around which women are constructed in Colombia and in much of the world: that of the saintly, chaste, and pure woman and that of the worldly, erotic, and objectified woman of desire and fantasy. Latin American women tend to be bifurcated by both men and women into these polar groups: that of the "good women" who reflect a Marian devotion to religion, suffering, and service to others; and the "bad women," who as sociological males are sexual, sinful, self-absorbed, and shameless. Women as sacred objects tend to be sheltered by the church and the family, especially when they are imaged as nuns, mystics, wives, and mothers, while the public women of the street, be they prostitutes, nonconformists, foreigners, or single women defined outside a familial setting, are the embodiments of corporal beauty and the objects of male sexual predation. This ambivalence in female gender construction leads to all sorts of double standards and contradictory behavior. For example, a man will venerate his mother and protect his wife and daughters while pursuing sexual fulfillment and adventure with various mistresses. Moreover, in a country like Colombia, where the "institutional commodification of feminine beauty" is underpinned by hierarchy, patriarchy, and machismo, women's legal, social, and political status is inferior to that of men. Women only gained juridical equality with men in 1974; prior to that year, women were defined juridically as minors, who were represented by their fathers or husbands. Up to 1980, a rapist who married his victim would be exonerated of the crime, and a husband could kill his wife if she was caught in preparation for or in the act of sexual intercourse with a lover.[28] Clearly, beauty for women could promote both social and personal dissonance given the contradictions and ambivalence in gender constructions in a nation where modernity and juridical equality are only partly realized.

Outside the parameters of Colombia's peculiarities, physical appearance is more important for women than for men and influences human behavior everywhere it has been studied. Why this is the case opens up the classic question of whether beauty's importance for women is more grounded in nature and biological processes or in learned behavior taught in human societies through culture and socialization. The sociobiological perspective on beauty and physical appearance uses a long lens of thousands or millions of years of human evolution. According to this approach, humans are "hard-wired" to recognize beauty in women because physical appearance is more strongly related to reproduction for women than for men; the symmetry of a face provides clues to genetic integrity, and lack of parasitic infection and a woman's hip-to-waist ratio are markers for reproductive success. Beauty, then, is a gestalt that one knows when one sees it, regardless of age, sex, or culture, one exercising a powerful force on human behavior even on individuals and societies that have lost the demographic imperative to procreate.[29]

Socioculturalists, conversely, argue that cultures and societies teach humans to value an attractive appearance more in women than in men, and therefore they research the relationship between cultural and individual values and behaviors. The quote from the late-nineteenth-century voluptuous British theater star Lillian Russell, that "men should be strong and women beautiful," would be understood as a statement about a society that valued men as bread-winners in a competitive patriarchal society while women adorned public life as part of a gendered expression of their feminine and objectified state. Like Linda Jackson, who authored an in-depth analysis of the sociobiological and sociocultural perspectives on gender and physical appearance, I will adopt elements of each approach in studying beauty's import to humans, thereby acknowledging both that we are products of nature and that we are nurtured to learn cultural and social lessons.[30]

Although physical beauty has long been interpreted as seductive and as an "expression of the perfection of human form," it has also been seen as an indicator of internal virtue; beauty then becomes a "projection of human spirituality, a source of human creativity, and a moral symbol." In the chivalric cult of the late Middle Ages, women and their beauty became symbols of the "pacific virtues of love, truth, and charity." This cult and its focus on the virtue of women and beauty, one that emerged, in part, as a protest against the brutal warfare of the earlier Middle Ages, had great resonance in nineteenth- and twentieth-century Colombia, a society also ripped apart by violence, private armies, seizures of land, and abuse of governmental authority, one hoping that female beauty could save it from the ravages of the male beast. Even when beauty was seen as a woman's duty and as a powerful tool by which women could climb social ladders and conquer powerful men, it was also seen as a moral virtue, one that brought hope to troubled societies.[31]

Beauty in the modern world is also constructed around racial typologies that themselves were conjured, in part, from the reputed beauty of eighteenth-century Circassian women who lived in the Caucasus Mountains. The Austrian biologist Johann Frederick Blumenbach devised the still familiar and unscientific racial categories Caucasoid, Mongoloid, and Negroid, by naming Caucasians for the beauty of Circassian women, said to be the fairest of all, while arguing that the other "races" devolved from the beautiful white race.[32] Such ideas of the late eighteenth and nineteenth century reinforced Europe's assumption of world leadership as it apologized for colonialism, but clearly it has no standing now given how it was constructed around the myth of Circassian female beauty, and given the archaeological findings of the twentieth century that place Africa as the cradle of evolution of a single human race. But myth mixed with pseudoscience still has a strong pull in contemporary multicultural societies, as does the enduring lesson that beauty and whiteness equal status and potential power in American societies still cognizant of colonial pigmentocracies.[33]

At the visual level, dress and fashion are a means of communicating societal and individual definitions of gender, class, ethnicity, occupation, location, power, and beauty. In general, among people who have the material means to do so, women have dressed for seduction while men have dressed for status. Male dominance over female freedom in the public sphere has traditionally meant that a woman's beauty became an important commodity for securing a future. Shifting notions of the age and shape of the most beautiful women have influenced the emphasis on the seductive quality of female fashions. In a single paragraph Rachel Kemper concludes that humans will go to great lengths to be fashionable and beautiful:

> There is probably nothing, no matter how painful or repulsive, that will cause humankind to hesitate in the pursuit of beauty; no costume, however uncomfortable or ridiculous, that will not be flaunted with pride in the name of fashion. Fashion functions and has always functioned as a means of wish fulfillment. Throughout the ages, women have wished to appear young, radiantly gorgeous, and infinitely desirable. Men have sought to look virile, distinguished, rich, and superior. In all countries, climes, and eras, both men and women have pursued the elusive goals of status and recognition, attributes which are usually the prerogative of wealth and social position. By following or, better yet, by setting the current fashion, we constantly identify ourselves with the social group, the ideal, of our choice. We are still very much convinced that clothes make the man. Intellectually, perhaps, we know better; emotionally we remain true believers. By providing us with psychological security, fashion becomes not merely a luxury but a necessity. Indeed, if fashion did not already exist, we should have to invent it.[34]

Modesty in dress reflects societal and religious standards and, ironically, aids in the seductive appeal of fashion. Humans are a curious species, often relying on vision to pursue our curiosity, measuring what we see and wondering about what is masked. Women and fashions tend to conceal or reveal the face, lips, eyes, mouth, breasts, hips, legs, waist, and buttocks depending on shifting sensibilities of morality, modesty, and personal freedom. Extremely modest sixteenth-century Spanish fashion highlighted a society of formality, order, control, and elite power. Sumptuary laws attempted to restrict the display of wealth flooding into the Americas as they also sought to limit class and caste ascension from below.

In 1571, Phillip II of Spain ordered, as part of the Laws of the Indies, that "negras and free mulatas are not to wear gold, silk, capes, or pearls," thus signaling a concern that the great wealth and relative freedom of the Americas would break down the aristocratic integrity and control mechanisms of Spanish colonial society. Sumptuary laws were dictated and reiterated—

thereby signaling their ineffectiveness—for each class and caste throughout the colonial period in Latin America, with women required to follow the dictates defined by their husband's caste. Ironically, Spain's attempts to control dress and to legislate modesty tended to stimulate attention to fashion and to the accessories that helped a person stand out from the rest.[35]

Various factors made France the fashion capital of the world during the last half of the eighteenth century, a position that Parisian designers enjoyed until after the First World War. The impact of a modern and industrial textile sector in Europe, freer trade in the Americas, and the impact of the Bourbon reforms in Spain and her colonies helped France emerge as a fashion leader. Although fashion defined the inherited and practiced parameters of a hierarchical, authoritarian, and discriminatory state and society during the latter stages of colonialism in Colombia, the French Revolution opened room for an expression of freedom and liberty that presaged the independence movement against tradition and colonialism.

After 1795, the trendy neoclassical muslin tunic weighed all of five ounces and was wrung out in water just before it was put on so as to cling to a body unencumbered by underwear. Morality and manners were much relaxed, making individuals rather than societies the arbiters of personal behavior. In the messy decade between the first stirring of independence in 1810 and Simón Bolívar's dramatic victory at Boyacá in 1819, royalists tended to mimic the established monarchical fashion while republican supporters wore the lighter and shorter fashions inspired by the French Directorate.[36]

Fashion in Europe during the first half of the nineteenth century exhibited a number of passing trends, as is often the case. The French rage for the sheer muslin chemise gave way to far heavier and layered looks during the Romantic era of the 1820s to the 1850s, leaving some room for an escapist exoticism inspired by fabrics or looks taken from Egypt, Persia, and India. English fashion, which tended to lag about five years behind French trends, took up the neoclassical Grecian look by 1800, followed the Indian inspired trend of the 1820s, and eventually draped itself in the heavy armament and fabrics of Victorian England, setting the tone for a less turbulent society than that found in France.[37]

Fashion among the elites of Colombia certainly was influenced by French and English trends, but more regional costume and an emerging "national dress" dominated during the first half of the nineteenth century. Elites knew of trends from Paris and London and made home-sewn copies of designs they found in illustrations; French and English fashions competed for the attention of Colombians set on following the latest foreign trends. Unlike today, that period saw close female friends trying to dress exactly the same in order to express their shared affection. In the 1830s, paintings in Bogotá showed evidence of the exotic Asian look popular during the Romantic era, with elite women sitting with their feet up and crossed on sofas, turbans wrapped around their heads, wearing jaguar skin pants, and smoking thin cigars while enjoying an afternoon full of conversation and gossip.[38] However, ongoing restrictions inherited from the colonial period hung on as people of various castes followed many of the strictures on dress defined by their color and class. Church power helped keep fashion modest, dark, and simple, for example, by reserving only for the archbishop the right to wear colored stockings.

Men's fashions tended to be rather dark and subdued as well, but sportswear, especially hunting and riding garb, introduced some new looks that women also noticed and some began to follow. Moreover, one finds a tendency in the 1820s and 1830s, like that found earlier in France and England, for elite women to dress down, especially when they ventured onto the street and into the public sphere.[39]

The trend toward a more uniform female fashion during the first few decades of republican Colombia was defined by internal rather than foreign influences. The prolonged and bloody wars for independence during the second decade of the nineteenth century disrupted and destroyed people, property, and commerce, leading to dislocations in the countryside, a sense of urban isolation, and a general sense of insecurity and collective impoverishment. Recurring civil wars and socioeconomic violence after 1830 fed insecurity and punctuated the lesson that in public it was best to blend in, thereby avoiding the wrath of political enemies or the attention of thieves. Those conditions, along with the search for a republican and national dress, helped make colonial peasant attire the norm even for urban elite women. The classic look of the *traje nacional* included a long wide skirt cinched at the waist by a thick belt; a blouse whose length, sleeves, and thickness were determined by location and climate; and a shawl or mantilla, again of various cuts, fabrics, and thickness given the climate, topped off with a hat similar to those worn by men. While the outfit might look the same, the quality of the fabric, the intricacy of the embroidery or the lace on the blouse and shawl, the quality and type of jewelry, and whether shoes were worn were class and caste markers. This enduring costume, one that played on nostalgic memories and one that became the basis of "typical folkloric garb" in the twentieth century, confounded foreign observers because of its longevity—seemingly another sign that Colombia was not progressing—as it sustained regional fashions that became "typical" of national dress.[40]

The costume of the mestiza *ñapangas*, who worked in the homes of the elite of Popayán and Pasto, however, illustrates how fashions that later would be called "typical" evolved in a particular socioethnic context, in this case as a uniform for domestic servants, one blending more Spanish than indigenous styles as markers of employment and caste. The beauty of the ñapangas became legendary in southern Colombia, with their uncovered head and bare feet noticeable on the streets as they went about their lady's chores, a beauty also close at hand in domestic settings. It was said that wealthy families in Popayán maintained two armies: one male and ready for war; one female, ready for strolls and parties. The barefoot ñapangas, in their hoop skirts, cotton blouses, and light shawls, were proud symbols of household status, of rural to urban migration, and of a "whitening" process where women of African or indigenous roots ascended in class and caste through occupation and social location.[41]

Beauty is always relational, comparative, and dynamic; the flipside of beauty is ugliness, and for mid-nineteenth-century elite observers, the beauty found in towns and cities was often juxtaposed with the destitution, marginality, and ugliness of the rural poor. In contrast to the fine dress of urban slaves who worked in elite homes in Cartagena, the slaves who toiled on the plantations and in the mines were almost nude for lack of clothing—nudity, among rural slaves or Amazonian Indians, indicating a lack of status and marginality from Western progress and civilization. In contrast to the beautiful women of Piedecuesta, the surrounding peasantry was described as "swarthy and not healthy owing probably to the atmosphere of malaria from this redundant vegetation." The English painter Joseph Brown depicted rural working women with either dark complexions or harsh facial features, portraits that revealed low social status, the harshness of rural work and life, and the social and aesthetic distance between rural ugliness and urban beauty. Although the beauty of mestiza peasant women was often idealized, as when they revealed their toasted breasts while bending to gather water at the town fountain, in many cases beauty was a marker of urban status and progress, while the ugly, dirty, and marginal were reminders of the poverty and struggle that most Colombians endured.[42]

Beauty also masked the beast of civil war and political violence. Eight major civil wars rocked the country between 1831 and 1902, the last one, the War of a Thousand Days (1899–1902), by far the bloodiest. Fourteen local civil wars broke out over the same period, disrupting production and commerce, squandering public resources, and often leaving more debt in their wake. Insecurity from the threat or reality of violence was a sensation that many Colombians in the nineteenth century experienced. And although the frequency of civil war declined in the twentieth century, violence continued to plague the nation because, "unlike many other Latin American nations, Colombia never overcame the nineteenth-century political divisions between Conservatives (clericals) and Liberals (anticlericals), never resolved the nineteenth-century issues of centralism versus federalism, never established a national government that truly forged and administered a nation, and never replaced personalism, factionalism, and the quest for partisan hegemony with a modern political agenda."[43] Beauty, then, became an alternative and positive expression of civic and Colombian pride, one often embraced as an alternative to entrenched racial and caste inequalities, to the ugliness of being poor or rural, and to the cyclical beast of male violence.[44]

Colombia's heterogeneous geography and society found ugliness amongst the rural, poor, diseased, and nonwhite population and beauty among the moral, prosperous, urban, and educated minority; beauty marked both ecological and economic health and sociocultural status. Beauty also became a handy trope to bridge the inheritance of American colonial pigmentocracy—white is best, black is bad—to modern pseudoscientific racial categories that maintained racial inequality into the twenty-first century. The adoption of the traje nacional revealed both an attempt to create a national fashion identity and a defensive stance in the midst of societal insecurity and partisan violence. Interestingly, the mania for pageants in Cartagena, Colombia, and the rest of the Americas may rest in both European and African noble traditions performed in the colonial era and re-created in modern American societies disguised as democracies. Both the beast of violence and the definition of beauty served to maintain socioeconomic inequalities as beauty emerged as the alter ego of the beast, each needing the other to maintain traditions and institutions.

"LA MUJER REINA PERO NO GOBIERNA," 1845–1885

The four decades following 1845 witnessed the formation of Colombia's two dominant political parties, the Liberals and the Conservatives, an opening to the international economy, and a greater familiarity with foreign fashion. The slowly growing population was still strongly rural and self-sufficient, but urban elites increasingly imaged the nation's future around white and Hispanic ideals. These were decades of great political conflict and civil war, of rebellions, coups, and failed revolutions. The period began with the political presence of Conservative-turned-Liberal Tomás Cipriano de Mosquera and ended with the Liberal-turned-Conservative Rafael Núñez, both leaders switching parties with changing partisan fortunes, both searching for a wider political base from which to govern. It was a time of deep factions within parties and strident political combat over the role and perquisites of the Catholic Church in government and society. Slavery was abolished, indigenous and church lands privatized, federalism and freedom—of trade, expression, religion, the press—flourished, as socialist idealism filled the heads of intellectuals and some urban artisans. It was a time when change confronted continuity, when republicanism and liberalism challenged colonialism and tradition, confrontations and challenges often left incomplete and passed on as a problematic inheritance to twentieth-century Colombians.[1]

The Conservative and Liberal parties emerged ideologically from the challenges presented by eighteenth-century Enlightenment Europe and out of Colombia's independence wars with Spain and subsequent civil wars over power. Conservatives generally stressed the need for order and morality in society and government and, therefore, the need for strong church-state ties. Liberals, more the heirs of Enlightenment ideas, stressed liberty and freedom of individuals in modern society and government and, therefore, the need for the separation of church and state. Conservatives tended to favor strong central government, while Liberals preferred that governmental power be limited and dispersed to independent states. Both parties favored international trade as an avenue for Colombia's future progress and civilization, making economic policy differences difficult to distinguish. Conservatives tended to be slightly more socially elite, but both parties were, and still are, run by economic and social elites. Artisans might be ideologically liberal but belong to the Conservative party for religious or commercial reasons; rich merchants might be Liberal because of economic self-interest but still believe that their social inferiors should not vote. Indians tended more toward the Conservative camp because of the Liberal assault on *resguardos* (communal lands) while Afro-Colombians, particularly in Cauca, identified with the party of abolition, the Liberals. Nonetheless, poor rural voters often adhered to the party of their *patrón*, typically a big landowner. Regardless of the difficulty of teasing out ideological, class, color, occupational, or personal reasons for partisan membership and fervor, one can point to a key issue that fused religion and politics into one explosive cocktail: the role and prerogatives of the Catholic Church, which Conservatives wanted continued or expanded by close church-state ties, and which Liberals wanted curtailed as evidence that Colombia was a modern state.[2]

Radical Liberals, the faction most confrontational on the church question, laid the groundwork for many important freedoms but also for huge future headaches. Radical refusal to negotiate with other factions of the Liberal party or with Conservative party or church leaders led to various armed confrontations and the weakening of the Liberal party in general. Liberal economic principles opened room for agricultural and forest product exports and for more and varied imports, but this opening to foreign trade hurt the economic, social, and political interests of an important urban constituency, the artisans. Strongly federalist governments and constitutions weakened intrusions of government into private and public life, but a flourishing arms trade and a weak state combined to fan high levels of political and social violence; armed urban artisans were overrepresented in the myriad violent conflicts of the era, a reality that began to worry Liberal elites. Although urban Liberals might have some grasp of ideological issues, rural Colombians often found that the Liberals, who first favored a wider electorate, sought to restrict male suffrage once in power for fear of voter manipulation by priests or hacienda owners, while out-of-power Conservatives favored universal male suffrage. Rural folk often chose a partisan side influenced by family, marriage, friendship, and godparents, or out of local rivalries that predated the republic. Even though much of Colombia was only lightly or hardly settled, campesinos often needed patróns and their parties if they were to successfully defend their land claims from rivals or expand into frontier zones. In short, Radicals pressed the Liberal agenda, but they created problems within their own party and sparked confrontations with Conservatives; they weakened the

Colombian state and left room for violence to flourish, and their political and ideological inconsistency helped complicate and politicize rural life.[3]

Partisan conflict, greater participation in elections and politics, and constitutional flux all characterized mid- to late-nineteenth-century Colombia, making political violence normative. Colombia had four constitutions during its first quarter century of independence (1821, 1830, 1832, 1843) and four more between 1853 and 1886 (1853, 1858, 1863, 1886). Constitutional flux revealed the inability of Colombia's scattered elites to frame a national legal order acceptable beyond regional or partisan loyalties. Liberals asserted their partisan agenda starting in 1853, with Radicals imprinting their ideology in the constitution of 1863, following the bloody Federal War of 1859 to 1862. Rebellions and civil wars rained down on the people and regions of the nation throughout the nineteenth century. Four national civil wars erupted just between 1876 and 1899 (1876–77, 1885–86, 1895, 1899–1902). Tossing elections on top of violent partisan warfare only made matters worse as fraud, intimidation, insults, and coercion became part of the theater of suffrage; partisans screamed "Viva" for themselves and "Muerte" to their opponents during electoral rituals that often presaged yet another civil war.[4]

Economically, Colombia muddled through the last half of the nineteenth century, experiencing some episodes of economic growth between busts in export markets for agricultural or forest products. One persistent problem hinged on a large public debt inherited from the wars of independence; from 1845 to 1905 a series of interest and debt renegotiations failed to bring fiscal order as payments lapsed and debts went into delinquency. An indebted national government, already weakened by internal political strife, could not attract global capital as a necessary ingredient for economic development. Nonetheless, various exports brought a degree of economic prosperity and stimulated international trade.[5]

The opening to freer trade during the first Mosquera administration (1845–1849) signaled elite agreement that only the international economy would introduce progress and civilization to Colombia. A rich country with numerous natural resources and fine agricultural and grazing land, Colombia managed to enjoy various "boomlets" for its gold, cotton, coffee, tobacco, quina, rubber, and straw hats during the last half of the nineteenth century. Increased foreign trade inflated the pitiful incomes of elites, who prior to 1845 lived more off their social prestige than their annual income, allowing them to import Parisian fashions, exotic carpets, and heavy pianos. Slowly, coffee emerged as the engine of Colombian exports, with cultivation starting in the eastern mountains and then moving west, a pattern mimicked by Colombian migrants during that century. In the 1870s, coffee brought in about 20 percent of export earnings, increasing to 50 percent by 1898.[6]

Mosquera also tackled Colombia's daunting geography when attempting to develop an infrastructure for trade. However, promotion of trade and infrastructure could carry ominous consequences for Colombian sovereignty; the strategic Isthmus of Panamá effectively became a U.S. protectorate with the Bidlack-Mallarino Treaty of 1846. Designed as a defensive and entangling alliance between the Colombian and U.S. governments to block French and British designs on Panama, this treaty opened the Isthmus to at least ten armed U.S. interventions in Panama from 1852 to 1903,[7] most without consultation or agreement with the Colombian government, effectively gutting Colombian sovereignty over its Isthmian territory. Framed in the context of Manifest Destiny, the U.S. expansionist war with Mexico (1846–1848), and the incorporation of the Southwest into U.S. territory, this first U.S. protectorate with Colombia over Panama not only signaled a sea change in U.S. foreign policy—an entangling alliance—but also served as a model for twentieth-century U.S. protectorates in various Central American countries, the Dominican Republic, Haiti, and Cuba.[8]

Closer to the mountains and valleys of the Colombian heartland, the first Mosquera administration also established a steamship line on the vital Magdalena River and began a road building program (one ignored by later administrations). The Magdalena shipping service gave Colombian exporters a vehicle to reach international markets, but the river was not navigable all year. Poor or nonexistent roads kept transport costs very high, stunting market development as cargo weighed down on the backs of humans or mules. Many Colombians who participated in the import/export trade had better information and knowledge of international realities than they did of their own country; many regions remained hidden in an isolating but beautiful natural environment. By 1875, three telegraph lines linked Bogotá to Medellín, Barranquilla, and Buenaventura, making it only a matter of minutes to share news around the nation—yet as late as 1920 it might take two to four weeks for a load of coffee to be shipped from Bogotá to any of those cities at the other end of the telegraph line.[9]

Socially and demographically, the Colombian population grew slowly until 1870 and then expanded noticeably, tending to self-identify more as white and mestizo and less as Indian and black. Tables 2.1 and 2.2 highlight these demographic and social trends.

Colombian males self-identified as "whiter" and less indigenous in 1912 than estimated in 1852, with white percentages doubling and indigenous numbers dropping by more than one-half. Mestizos were the largest group

TABLE 2.1 COLOMBIAN SOCIAL CLASSIFICATION,
1825–1912

Year	Social Classification	Percent of population
1825	Mestizos, mulatos, negros	43
	Indians	35
	Whites	22
1852	Mestizos	47
	Negros, mulatos	17
	Indians	14
	Whites	17
1912	Mestizos	49
	Negros, mulatos	10
	Indians	6
	Whites	34

Sources: Ocampo López, Historia básica, p. 227; Palacios, Entre la legitimidad, p. 17.

TABLE 2.2 COLOMBIAN POPULATION, 1825–1912

Year	Total Population
1825	1,327,000
1851	2,243,054
1871	2,951,111
1912	5,072,604

Sources: Ocampo López, Historia básica, p. 227; Bushnell, Making of Modern Colombia, p. 286.

in all three census years, with a tendency in 1852 and 1912 to distinguish Indo-mestizos and Euro-mestizos from Afro-mestizos. This trend tended to diminish the black percentage of the population between 1852 and 1912 as Colombians—both ideologically and socially—began to think of their nation as less black and more white, more European and less indigenous. Regardless of these attitudes, which still hold true today, departments like Cauca in 1912 revealed a decidedly less mixed, less white, and more indigenous identity: 32 percent of those males participating in the census self-identified as indigenous; 25 percent white; 19 percent black; 19 percent mixed; and 5 percent not specified.[10] Again, Colombia's regionalism influenced how its pockets of population thought about social, ethnic, and "racial" categories, and, hence, how beauty was imaged.

On a national scope, Colombia became less indigenous when privatization of resguardo lands brought more "Indians" into a market economy and into the cultural and economic sphere of *mestizaje*. All groups tended to practice "caste mobility" during the nineteenth century, with each caste moving up a notch or two: indigenous to mestizo; negro and mulato to mestizo; mestizo to white. This general trend toward "progress" and "civilization," as measured by urban western European standards, also continued a colonial pattern of "whitening" via class or occupational mobility, a process hastened by racial ideology, location, occupation, and the declining recognition of nonwhite blood in the family tree.[11]

Liberalism brought a mixed bag of results for women. Liberalism's rhetoric of "liberty," "equality," and "individualism" opened some room for public discourse on the role of women in a modern society. The fluorescence of the popular press, particularly under Radical influence from 1863 to 1885, resulted in numerous publications written by or for women. The separation of church and state after 1853 resulted in a narrow window when civil marriage and divorce were legalized (1853 to 1856). Women in the Provincia de Vélez, in present-day Santander department, actually gained the right to vote in municipal elections in 1853; Colombian women had to wait more than a century, until 1957, before female suffrage became legal nationwide.[12]

However, liberalism's reign ended in 1885, leading to Conservative dominance of the Colombian government until 1930. Moreover, the social and economic impact of liberalism took root later in Colombia than it did in other Latin American nations, like Mexico, Argentina, and Chile, in part because of Colombia's political violence and lack of institutional reform and its poor infrastructure over such a mountainous and tropical terrain. Traditional attitudes about marriage, patriarchy, and how women "ought to be"—religious, private, self-sacrificing, and invisible—persisted well into the twentieth century, thus blunting the impact of liberalism in opening up more opportunities for women in the public sphere.[13]

Greater import/export trade did, however, modify the textile market and therefore encouraged changes in fashion. President Mosquera's freer trade policies set duties on the weight of textiles rather than on their place of origin or market value. Thereafter, imported fabrics, like silk, had a lower duty placed on them than heavier Colombian woolens. Some evidence suggests that this measure hurt the domestic textile sector and altered, slowly, Colombian popular dress. For example, in 1888 a woman's peasant outfit was valued at $78.60 pesos, about half of that sum being taxed ($39.58 pesos). It took a female firewood and coal seller two years to earn the $78.60 to purchase the outfit, a washerwoman ten months, an agricultural worker in coffee country fifteen months. However, many Colombians operated outside the consumer market for textiles, spinning their own yarn and weaving their own cloth, with techniques and designs inherited from pre-Columbian and Spanish colonial traditions. The homespun tradition held on in many areas of Colombia because of local traditions and because of low wages and high textile costs and duties. Observers often decried the persistence of traditional attire in women's fashions as an example of Colombia's lack of progress and modernity, with black the color de rigueur and with mantillas covering shoulders, heads, and faces, a look familiar to residents of the Cordillera Oriental centuries earlier.[14]

A closer look at various regions around Colombia allows us a glimpse of how the opening to the international economy affected fashion and the definition of feminine beauty. Bogotá, although remote and difficult to reach for foreign and domestic travelers, tended to attract much commentary as the nation's capital and largest city, with about fifty thousand inhabitants in the 1850s. Its cold, grey, and damp climate often struck commentators as dark and somewhat grim, an image that carried over into their descriptions of the city and its residents. Poverty, beggars, and prostitution gave many neighborhoods an insalubrious reputation, as did the garbage, rummaging animals, and lack of sewers. Newspaper articles complained about the scarcity of jobs for women, which sustained a poverty that forced many women to beg or prostitute themselves. They also complained that neither Liberals nor Conservatives seemed interested in their well-being and that the municipality charged high taxes but ignored essential public services. Moreover, they lamented that most women in Bogotá wore such dark colors—mostly black—and that the somber air and lugubrious shade implied a life passed in mourning.[15]

However, when the sun broke through to reveal the deep blue sky, allowing young women to stroll through Bogotá's narrow cobblestone streets unencumbered by heavy, dark shawls, when guitars came out to enliven the outdoor meetings of friends, Bogotá took on a lighter mood as the beauty of the capital's women became a point of focus and commentary. Fridays and Saturdays were market days in the central square of Bogotá, which filled with rural peddlers and urban shoppers. The scene appeared biblical to some, with barefoot rural women in long skirts, embroidered blouses, long flowing shawls, and perhaps a straw hat filling their ceramic jars with water at the square's fountain, while others sat on the ground surrounded by their wares. Produce, color,

FIGURE 2.1 *Bogotanos at Choachi, from Issac E. Holton,* New Granada: Twenty Months in the Andes *(New York: Harper and Brothers, 1857).*

and aroma were all around as Bogotá's women scrutinized and bargained for fruits and flowers. One Brazilian observer, Miguel María Lisboa, noted in 1853 that most residents were Caucasian, with perhaps a slight admixture of noble Muisca blood, which, along with the damp and cool climate, gave Bogotá's women a beautiful color, making them the most beautiful women in all of South America. On Sundays, Lisboa saw elite women dressed "à la francesa" enjoying Bogotá's north side in the company of many gentlemen. He mentioned that most of the time, however, elite women dressed "à la colombiana," donning their French attire only on special occasions.[16]

Isaac Farwell Holton, a Yankee botanist and chemist from Middlebury College in Vermont, found similar variety in women's fashion during his travels in Colombia in the 1850s. Holton's wonderful descriptions of people, their attire, and behavior make his book *New Granada: Twenty Months in the Andes*, one of the best travel books about mid-nineteenth-century Colombia. In and around Bogotá, Holton observed elite women dressed in imported European costumes, topped off with bonnets and shaded with parasols, while their gentlemen escorts wore frock coats, britches, ties, and topcoats, their elite status anchored by a walking cane. But elites mixed in public settings with working Colombians, whose attire marked their common status: simple sandals or bare feet, rough-cut local cloth, and straw hats rather than top hats or bonnets.[17]

Venturing out of Bogotá, Holton found more representative fashions and venues where beauty was displayed and measured. In Fusagasugá, southwest of Bogotá in warmer *tierra caliente*, Holton witnessed the famous *bambuco*, a dance that in late-twentieth-century pageants would become a marker for authentic Colombian beauty and grace. To perform the dance, a young woman removed her shawl and hat, revealing hair in long braids. She wore a long, full skirt and a scooped embroidered blouse that left the shoulders, neck, upper chest, and back bare. This formal but common dance kept the woman's eyes focused down toward the floor as she resisted the temptation to betray a smile. Holton described the dance this way: "One couple needs the whole floor in the bambuco. It is decided that *he* is to dance it. Then they wonder who *she* will be. He bows to *her*. She borrows a pocket-handkerchief (mine, perhaps), and steps out. She moves to the music, but *ad libitum* as to the direction, and he follows her motions as faithfully as a mirror. If she moves east, he dances west; when she goes north, he goes south; when she turns a little, he turns as much, and in the contrary directions. Thus they advance, recede, turn side to side, or even entirely round; so they dance without ever touching each other, till she becomes tired, drops a curtsy, and sits down." The restraint of the dance and the young woman's guarded demeanor was not shared by her mother, whom Holton describes as a "coarse Bogotana, with a cigar in her mouth and a turban on her head . . ."[18] The turban was in fashion when the mother was a younger woman, while cigar smoking, although unusual to the Yankee Holton, was quite common for Colombian women in the middle of the nineteenth century.

THE BAMBUCO.

FIGURE 2.2   *The Bambuco, from Issac E. Holton*, New Granada.

Beauty for Holton was measured primarily by intelligence, demeanor, and character and secondarily by external physical appearance. He encountered Señorita Manuela Pinzón, a pretty young woman who took pride in her fashionable riding dress, one that gracefully blended European and Colombian elements. But it was Manuela's "cheerful and lively turn of mind," her conversational skills, and her familiarity with the novels of Alexandre Dumas and Eugène Sue, that added to her beauty in Holton's eyes. Holton found many Colombian women who, not lacking physical attractiveness, lived in a prison of isolation, one that limited women's opportunities to study, learn, and experience the world. He wished that "it were more common for old women to be pretty here, but that can not be without education." Like many Colombian writers of the nineteenth century, Holton found beauty not just in an external projection, but in an internal "difficult" beauty revealed by an educated mind, a kind heart, and a solid character.[19]

Travelers Rosa Carnegie-Williams and Miguel Cané found other varieties of feminine beauty in Bogotá during their respective stays in the capital in the early 1880s. As in the United States in the nineteenth and twentieth centuries, various notions of beauty existed simultaneously at any given time. But unlike the United States, where historian Lois Banner found the sickly "steel engraving" genteel lady, the voluptuous immigrant, and the natural athletic look marking the transitions of an agricultural to an industrial economy in which immigrants reshaped nineteenth-century society, Colombia received few immigrants and did not industrialize during that period.[20] Instead, different models of beauty, like those observed by Carnegie-Williams and Cané, revolved around the ethnic identity and fashion of Spanish, Indian, and black women, a continuity of colonial caste categories. Cané, an Argentine writer and diplomat, and Carnegie-Williams, a British lady who penned one of the few travel accounts written by a woman in nineteenth-century Colombia, both noted the multitude of Indian women who came into Bogotá for market. Both noted their bare feet and typical common dress, commenting more on their mere presence than on their beauty. Carnegie-Williams reported her surprise on seeing a black woman in Bogotá, well dressed and in shoes, for typically "servants don't wear shoes in the street or in the house" and because most of the city's inhabitants were "good looking" (bien parecidos). Her comments revealed a general attitude that beauty and class were reserved for the Spanish or white ideal.[21]

Carnegie-Williams often commented on the "Spanishness" of Colombian women, a notion still embraced in a country proud of the white side of its mestizaje with Indians and blacks. She was struck by the dark-eyed Spanish beauties who peered out through the bars of the windows that kept them imprisoned and mysterious, and of the "dark specimen of Andalucian beauty" that she encountered in her social calls. The "Spanish look" reconnected Colombia to its European and colonial roots, a connection that would become a staple of Colombian beauty on through the twentieth century. She also reported on how dashing "bogotana beauties" looked in their riding wear, the precursor of more liberating sportswear that would become more common in subsequent decades.[22]

While sportswear very slowly opened up the possibility of greater freedom of movement and expression for women—along with the tyranny of fitness and discipline to look good in the more revealing fashions—Carnegie-Williams also noted the conservative influence of the Catholic Church in maintaining propriety in women's appearance, especially during mass. Part of the uniform of women in Bogotá in the 1880s was the black mantilla, of cashmere and lace for the elite, of common wool for the rest, which was the essential passport for admittance to mass. Rosa noted that women were not allowed in church if wearing a hat or bonnet, a rule that, along with the tax on cloth, pushed the cost of common mantillas to five times their true value. The Catholic Church, more so than in the United States, managed to restrict modern and revealing fashions in Colombia well into the twentieth century.[23]

The Argentine Cané commented on the grace, style, and allure of Latin American women in general, noting especially their singing, dancing, and musical skills and the appeal of their "enchanting speaking voices." He suggested that "our American women" drove foreigners crazy because they brought together appealing aspects of European women: the distinguished and elegant French air, the sculpted Greek body, Spanish grace, an Italian soul, English facial symmetry. The women of Bogotá he found collectively beautiful for the "soft fire in their eyes, the elegant undulation of their head . . ." and for their primordial and continuous grace. He found their speaking voices irresistible because of their musical cadence. He described *bogotanas* as small in stature but very well proportioned, and very attractive because of their purity of color. Cané's comments compare Bogotá to a European point of reference—in contrast to the more indigenous north of his native Argentina—thereby reinforcing the natural allure of bogotanas as well as Colombia's image as both a white and Andean society.[24]

North of Bogotá in the department of Santander, thriving cottage industries and export markets opened up economic opportunities for women, making these women noteworthy and desirable. A Radical Liberal stronghold with easier access to the Magdalena River and Venezuelan trade routes, Santander's more temperate and tropical climate nurtured tobacco plants and chinchona trees, whose bark yielded quinine. Tobacco and quina exports supplied the currency to buy imports, especially textiles, in the 1850s, with rubber and coffee bringing in more earnings by the 1870s. By the latter decade, elite women in Bucaramanga were following French fashion trends, while their spouses and brothers mimicked English ones.[25]

Although textile imports hurt segments of the national cloth sector, another artisan group in Santander, one dominated by females, enjoyed decades of prosperity. Some three thousand straw hat makers in and around Bucaramanga produced eighty-three thousand hats annually, bringing home about two hundred pesos each annually for their labor. A basic lifestyle cost about one-half of that (ninety-two pesos annually) in the 1850s, so thousands of women in Santander earned a sizable disposable income. They spent money in the local markets and purchased fine fabrics for their typical garb: a skirt, embroidered blouse, and light shawl, topped off, of course, by a straw hat. The women in towns like Girón, ten kilometers from Bucaramanga, smoked more cigars than most men, a marker of their status and income. Be they white, mulata, or mestiza, the women of Santander stood out because of the quality of their dress and because of their pride and happiness in their independence. The women of nearby Piedecuesta, south of Bucaramanga, enjoyed fame for their beauty, a beauty enhanced by a warm climate, less confining and brighter fashions, and the allure of women who had money, pride, and public prominence.[26]

West of Santander stretched another diverse and entrepreneurial region that emerged to rival Bogotá and Cundinamarca for national prominence, Antioquia. Of the 734 municipalities in Colombia in 1870, only 21 counted more than ten thousand inhabitants, with only Medellín, the capital of Antioquia department, and Bogotá counting more than twenty thousand inhabitants. *Antioqueños* or paisas, the proud residents of the department, often compared themselves favorably to bogotanos whom they judged to be overly formal, parasitic, and haughty. Paisas prided themselves on their industrious work ethic, their greater investment in primary education, their commercial and entrepreneurial skills, and, of course, their attractive and hardworking women.[27]

Ethnically, Antioquia was an example of Colombian mestizaje, with Afro-Colombians who worked the western mines, surviving indigenous groups, and descendants of Spanish conquistadors and more recent immigrants mixing to produce a variety of hues between color lines. Like Bogotá and Santander, Medellín tended to "whiten" as the city grew and prospered. One explanation for Antioqueño business success, a notion still widely held in Colombia, was that Jews dominated the commercial sector in Medellín. Manuel Uribe Ángel, a Colombian who traveled through the region in 1862, challenged this stereotype, counting just four Jewish families in town, along with numerous Basques, Galicians, Asturians, and Aragonese from northern Spain. Like Cané, Uribe Ángel found the soothing accent of antioqueñas more refined than in other areas of the country, as he remarked on how both women and men dressed more decently than other Colombians. He found it worrisome that elite antioqueño children were sent off to Europe for their education, for the young ones forgot their family and culture while the older ones indulged in the libertine corruption of cities like Paris.[28]

However, Uribe Ángel did revel in the allure of the biblical authenticity of rural antioqueña women. He commented on the pretty girls he saw working in the countryside, their alabaster white skin, red cheeks, bare feet, modest typical dress, and hair braided in twin pigtails, as they shepherded flocks, collected firewood, cooked meals, cared for children, and comforted the aged with "the tenderness and exquisite love of biblical care." For Uribe Ángel, like other Colombians appreciative of the peasant ideal, all this placed Antioquia in the context of the sacred texts, as it reminded him of "the sacred traditions of the desert, of Lebanon, of the land of Canaan, of the shores of Genezareth and of all the sacred regions spoken of in the scriptures."[29] This biblical and sacred image of feminine beauty, at once timeless, traditional, and holy, was one that antioqueños continued to hold dear, even as Medellín became the most modern and industrial city in the country.

The German traveler Friedrich von Schenck found much to like during his travels to Antioquia in 1880. He found antioqueños to be healthy, tall, athletic, strong, hardworking, and serious—similar, perhaps, to an ideal image of a northern German. He found them particularly attractive compared with the "lazy mulatos and the worn-out inhabitants of the low country" toward the coasts, a reminder that notions of beauty and attractiveness also reveal notions of those deemed to be ugly and repugnant. The antioqueñas of the mountains wore short skirts—probably to keep their hems out of the mud— and hats similar to those worn by men, had twin braids of long hair hanging down their backs, and were barefoot, as were most of the department's inhabitants. They worked hard in the countryside, a virtuous habit, but Schenck was troubled that females worked as beasts of burden, carrying heavy loads on their backs over mountain passes, loads harnessed by a strap stretched across their foreheads. This arduous work, decried by Alexander von Humboldt eighty years earlier, conflicted with the European notions of beauty, race, and femininity as it revealed that life in the Colombian countryside was hard, indeed.[30]

Schenck found antioqueños more measured than other Colombians. They had fewer secular and religious holidays, saving more time for productive work. They strictly regulated prostitution to outlying and infamous neighborhoods—unlike Bogotá, where prostitution flourished seemingly everywhere—while they deported and incarcerated recalcitrant prostitutes in the unhealthy forests of Patiburú. The large number of rich families in Medellín did not display or flaunt their wealth in public, a wealth earned primarily from gold mines and commerce, and secondarily from agriculture and ranching. While elites in Medellín, Antioquia, and Manizales might wear European garb at home—men in top hats and jackets, women in Parisian fashions and wearing powders to lighten their complexion—they donned the "typical national dress" (el traje típico nacional) when out in the countryside or on trips, perhaps wearing shoes, unlike most of the department's inhabitants.[31] Whereas states like Antioquia and Santander were known for their commerce and relative prosperity, they were also known to be places where many people carried weapons and used them; homicide rates in these "white" and prosperous places were higher than in more indigenous and Afro-Colombian zones.[32] Elite discretion in not advertising wealth and in donning the national dress when venturing out into the countryside explains both why elites opted to blend in while in public and why "typical national dress" held on so long in many areas of Colombia where violence prevailed through the twentieth and into the twenty-first century.

Schenck overlooked the other side of Medellín in the 1880s, a city where three thousand of the city's thirty-seven thousand inhabitants lacked homes, regular food, and gainful employment. The urban underclass of Medellín worried the city's elites—another hint about why they dressed down in public—and it explains why the region that became the most economically modern of Colombia remained socially conservative. Paisa elites voted Conservative not only to counter Liberal strength in regions like Santander and Bogotá; they also supported the party that promised greater social control of the masses.[33]

Schenck found the geopolitical and socioethnographic location of ugliness among the black and indigenous dwellers of the Cauca and Magdalena river valleys. Along the Magdalena, he described the black and mulatto population as physically undesirable, especially because of the common skin diseases endemic among those populations. Ringworm, spread by fungus; scabies and mange, spread by parasitic mites; and leprosy, spread by a bacterium, scarred the skin of some Afro-Colombians Schenck observed. He described them as uncivilized, semisavage, hardly Catholic, and generally lost in unhealthy forests. Similarly, in the Magdalena river valley, he found the female indigenous of El Peñón to be "very ugly" as measured by their physical appearance and by the region's poor economy and sad and neglected ambiance.[34] Schenck's comments highlight two basic lessons: First, the racialism and social Darwinism of the late nineteenth and twentieth centuries were grafted onto earlier colonial pigmentocracies and sustained ideas of the beauty and development of whites while casting blacks and natives into the pool of the undesirable. Secondly, however, his comments also remind us that notions of beauty are often defined as nutritional and health markers—tall, athletic, strong, good skin, shiny hair, clear eyes—whereas ugliness, at times, reveals severe environmental stress and poor diet, parasitic infections, or chromosomal damage. Beauty and ugliness imaged in racial or ethnic terms not only reveals prejudice and racist ideas but also a modern political economy still shaped by colonial inequalities.[35]

South of Antioquia, in what is now the coffee country of the department of Caldas, both Schenck and other writers found evidence of the influence of paisas in regional culture. In Manizales, a town founded by paisa colonists in 1848, Schenck found that both Liberals and Conservatives jointly participated in town fiestas in 1880, having completed a four-year hiatus because of civil war. The fiestas lasted three days and included horse races, bullfights, masquerade balls, and, unfortunately, a few knife fights. The days' events followed a strict order, with the first day organized and paid for by local merchants, the second by the makers and distributors of aguardiente (a cane liquor spirit), and the third by public employees and artisans. This ordering of festival days had its roots in colonial customs and continued into the twentieth century with the ubiquitous beauty contest.[36]

Antioqueños also had an influence in the social life of little towns like Salamina (Caldas), located between Medellín and Manizales. Popular theater companies, organized in town or based in Medellín, performed plays featuring Mexican and Brazilian actresses. Little Salamina had access not only to local and regional theater but also to international actors with their distinctive styles, cultures, and fashions; foreign actresses had more social room to be daring, seductive, and "exotic." Salamina's females also practiced a popular pastime in which thirty to forty married and unmarried women would take to the streets on moonlit nights to sing and dance. This display of female celebration and solidarity must have been an attractive sight, indeed.[37]

Notions of beauty in Cartagena mirrored some of those found elsewhere in Colombia, but with a decidedly Caribbean and coastal twist. Like the lowlands of the Magdalena and Cauca river valleys, Cartagena's population suffered many tropical diseases, epidemics, and the effects of urban poverty, scourges that left their marks on body, face, and society. Cholera devastated the city in 1850, followed closely thereafter by a yellow fever outbreak; lepers were housed at the hospital on the island of Tierra Bomba. The lack of an adequate urban water supply meant that many residents drew their drinking water from wells and cisterns; during the dry season water levels dropped, leaving the water brackish and foul tasting.[38]

Class and neighborhood helped distinguish the range of attractiveness and beauty in and around the city. José María Samper described the señoras (ladies) of town in 1858 as "generally very beautiful, spiritual, extroverted and happy, uniting an elegance or gentility in form with a grace in their speaking voice, in their look and smile, all truly enchanting." The poor women of the working class, however, he described as "painfully ugly: skinny, long, sullen, pale as ghosts, lugubrious like the shifting shadows in the midst of tombs." Samper, an important author and politician of nineteenth-century Colombia and the husband of Soledad Acosta de Samper, ignored the ways in which poor diet, nonpotable water, disease, and poverty made working-class women ugly, instead employing a metaphor to describe Cartagena as an immense ruin and tomb, one that could only be saved by its integration with the development and civilization of the larger world.[39]

Cartagenans themselves were quite willing to express varied and sometimes contradictory attitudes about women, beauty, and morality. While sensuous poems extolled the beauty of women's bodies—poems that would have raised scandal in the more reserved Andean regions—other articles in local newspapers in the 1870s repeated attitudes that placed women's origins in both heaven and hell. Some said that women were heaven's emancipation; others that they were a miscarriage from the abyss. The Eve/Virgin Mary dichotomy, of woman as bad/good, whore/saint, lost/saved, reminded readers that "one woman lost the world, another saved it."[40]

On women's education, a particularly sensitive subject in the nineteenth century, a sentence below the masthead of the newspaper *El Amigo de las Damas* (The Ladies' Friend) suggested that women should cultivate and exercise their intellectual and moral faculties by reading good books, ones that reinforced their destiny forged by God, that of being daughters, wives, and mothers. Education, then, was an instrument not of liberation and modernity but of intellectual and moral training on the ways in which women could excel within the place delimited by traditional gender roles. In this guise, education was a conservative exercise.[41]

Education, though, could also add to a woman's beauty and charm, as the careful schooling of Margarita and Rosalia illustrate. Margarita was a young woman of twenty, of medium height and nice figure. It wasn't, however, her corporal beauty that made her seductive, but her swan-like and soft movements that gave her an enchanting grace. Likewise, Rosalia, who at thirty was no longer considered young, had a face unmarked by her years, while her sweet and tranquil eyes revealed that "a pretty woman is always young" and that "beauty has no age." But both women were more beautiful and attractive because of the careful moral and ethical education that they had received.[42]

Another article in *La Floresta*, a "literary newspaper dedicated to the fair sex of the state," played on the generation gap between a nephew and his uncle and on Liberal/Conservative debates on the roles of women and the Church in Colombian society. The nephew explained to his uncle that he sought a woman of strong spirit, a vigorous athlete, one who would be active and quick to defend right and to create a better future. He didn't want a quiet, passive, devoted wife, especially if devotion to the Church interfered with their marriage. The nephew's desire for an engaged, modern, and secular mate—instead of an old-fashioned and religious type—struck the uncle as an example of youthful enthusiasm and naïveté, as the uncle chided his nephew for repeating ideas that had been around a long time.[43]

The contradictions and complexities of Cartagena—an aristocratic and conservative city that reveled in coastal and Caribbean freedom—were exposed during Carnival and costume balls. Locals began to think about Carnival at the beginning of December and started preparing their costumes by New Year's Day; old clothes were preferred as Carnival celebrations included the precision throwing of water, eggs, ash, paint, and stinkier substances at any and all persons found on the streets. Those who could afford it hired bands and hosted street dances; hunts were organized, bulls were run through the streets, and a large *cumbiamba* (cumbia concert and dance) filled the main square nightly. Women dressed like men and vice versa, switching the usual gender performances; women bought men at dances, a switch from the usual business of prostitution and power. Yet, men still gave women sweets, aguardiente, and decorations for their dresses. The elites of town—the *gente decente*—stayed off the streets until late afternoon, when they emerged to dance bambucos or *guarachas cubanas*. They left their doors open, dissolving the usual limits of private space, giving refuge to those trying to escape bombardment from the myriad street projectiles. Carnival in Cartagena—and in Barranquilla in the twentieth century—celebrated absolute, but fleeting, liberty as it challenged the usual tyranny and repression of everyday life.[44]

Along with the "innocent fun and the joy of life" brought by Carnival, costume balls also brought opportunities for Cartagena's residents to throw off the usual constraints of daily life. The university hosted such balls for years, but one author wanted them moved to the nicer, more central Casa Municipal. He also proposed that masked revelers be required to wear name cards, both ideas suggesting that past balls had become too rowdy and out-of-hand. It also seems that older elite men wanted access to the fun, as the writer suggested "that one needn't worry if some half-old guys showed up

FIGURE 2.3   *Camisón, from Issac E. Holton,* New Granada.

for the ball, the young girls are sure to win."[45] Like earlier dances in honor of the Virgin of the Candelaria, Carnival and costume balls in late-nineteenth-century Cartagena were a theater for the expression of freedom, liberty, beauty, and fantasy.

Along the Magdalena River and in southern Colombia, reality rather than fantasy, work more than celebrations, and racial and political tension more than orchestrated harmony dominated most of the calendar year. During the 1850s around Mompós, in the hot and humid lower Magdalena River Valley, the Yankee professor Isaac Holton was surprised, and maybe a little scandalized, by how little clothing working women wore. Some women wore a *camisón*, a loose, sleeveless shift with narrow straps at the shoulders, cut to the knee, and gathered at the waist. Many cut their hair short—cooler in the hot climate—and went barefoot. This rather modern look, one popular in late-twentieth-century cities, struck Holton as a bit scanty. In another town, he commented on how all the women wore blue skirts, be it for the availability of indigo or that the town was solidly Conservative.[46]

In and around Cali, in the Cauca Valley, Frederick von Schenck commented negatively on the Afro-Colombian population, stating that their bad habits and poor appearance made them all the more ugly. He found the women uglier than the men, noting their unfeminine habit of riding horses like men. He worried about the violent proclivities of the Afro-Colombian community, recalling that black and mulatto Liberal troops had wreaked much destruction upon the lives and properties of Conservative elites during the 1876–1877 civil war in the Cauca Valley. In the context of this intense partisan and racial strife, the valley was also shaken by a series of strong earthquakes throughout the 1870s, further unnerving regional society. Nonetheless, Cali's emerging reputation for beautiful women found an early reference when in 1875, Romelia Rojas, the "prettiest girl in Cali," "who could have won any beauty contest anywhere at any time," married a lucky suitor. Political and social violence, natural disasters, and beautiful women shaped the memories of those troubled times in the 1870s, as they would in much of Colombia throughout the twentieth century.[47]

Cali maintained its rivalry with Popayán for leadership in the Cauca Valley, with Cali emerging as the bigger commercial city to challenge the aristocratic and political elite of Popayán. Popayán and its environs were more indigenous and less Afro-Colombian than Cali, with poor rural women wearing a camisón similar to that seen by Holton in the lower Magdalena. The ñapangas of Popayán maintained their reputation as beautiful symbols of racial mixture, while in El Bordo, on the road between Popayán and Pasto, barefoot beauties, wearing low-cut, scoop-necked dresses, danced a bambuco in a salon with Afro-Colombian partners.[48] In Pasto, the poverty of the mostly indigenous population distanced the town's female residents from the beauty ideal. They wore layers of cloth imported from Ecuador, adding to the sense that Pasto and *pastusos* were almost foreigners to other Colombians. However, even if their physical appearance was defined as "disagreeable and repugnant," the townspeople were complimented on their hospitality and morality.[49]

For residents in the tropical lowlands of southern Colombia, the lack of clothing used by rural women raised questions about nature and civilization. Were bare-chested Afro-Colombian female gold washers in steamy Barbacoas free in a natural wonderland, or were they trapped in nature and therefore uncivilized? Were the shapely and mostly unclothed indigenous women of the Putumayo and Caquetá beautiful and alluring in their innocence, or were they dangerous and savage cannibals? These ambivalent and contradictory questions about civilization and nature are particularly common when asked of nonwhite women, their beauty, and their bodies.[50]

For women in Europe and the United States, fashion was an important venue to display modernity, class, and beauty. Fashion trends during the 1840s to 1880s usually included some variation on the hoopskirt, crinoline, or bustle; tight corseting was de rigueur. Dresses tended to be heavy, some consuming up to fourteen yards of material. Actresses often set fashion trends, with some of their more revealing, sensuous, and racy dress in vogue decades later. By the 1850s, photography provided the vehicle for middle- and upper-class women to show off their fashions, beauty, and figures—with finished photos already being altered and retouched to create the image of, for example, a smaller waist. The sewing machine simplified dressmaking, and by the end of the century less excessive undergarments led to a lighter and more form-fitting silhouette.[51]

Competing beauty ideals in the United States in the nineteenth and twentieth centuries revealed that beauty's definition is always plural and contested. The severe, slight, and rail-thin "steel engraving lady" of the 1830s (later reprised in the 1920s with the flappers and in the 1990s with the "heroin chic" look), a more voluptuous and mature look in the 1860s (and 1930s and 1940s), and the "natural beauty" of the 1890s (and several periods throughout the next century) marked transitions in a society that became more industrial, urban, and modern. The immigrant working class competed with the elite "fashionables" in setting beauty trends, revealing a certain amount of democratic contestation of beauty.[52]

Colombian definitions of beauty were also plural and competitive but not the same as those found in the United States or Europe. Colombia modernized far later than either the United States or Western Europe, stunting the explosive growth of urban areas, the market economy, and homogenizing images and standards of beauty. Colombia received few immigrants—compared with Brazil, Argentina, and the United States—so "imported" notions of beauty had less room to dominate and overwhelm regional standards of beauty. Instead, Colombia followed the logic of a multiethnic and regional reality, one formed in the colonial era and maintained in the nineteenth century, where rural ideals competed with urban ones, where caste, color, and nationality informed a plural but still hierarchical sense of beauty alternatives.

Modernity and its fashions were, however, influencing how some literate urban dwellers thought about beauty and the nation's future. A wonderful source for marking this transition is found in the surprisingly large number of periodicals written by or for women, many of them focused on fashion and literature, and "dedicated to the fair sex." Many of these weekly or biweekly magazines were published in the 1860s and 1870s, during the decades when Radical Liberals opened up more room for a freer press. Each publication had its own voice and tone on women, fashion, and beauty. Some, for example, were edited by men who celebrated women's beauty; others that were edited by women insisted that females play a more active role in building a modern nation.

Published in Bogotá in 1858 and 1859, the *Biblioteca de Señoritas* was a weekly literary journal, edited by men, that alternated between a "revista parisiense" focused on French fashions, the theatre, opera, and high society, and an edition on interim weeks that ran local stories, poems, and Bogotá social news. Although published in the capital, the *Biblioteca de Señoritas* seemed to have national distribution, as most of the larger cities and towns had agents to market it. Some articles focused on the essence, beauty, and character of women, using the depth of the written word and of analysis to move beyond facile and superficial understandings. In an article that asked, "What Is Woman?" (Qué es la mujer?), female beauty, purity, and innocence were all accepted as given attributes while female nature was described as illusive. Girls were compared to angels from heaven while young women left the realm of angels to become goddesses, nomenclature that took female nature into the supernatural realm. As "Other," women were as mysterious as God and the first mystery of creation.[53]

On a more tangible and social level, another tale followed the bored wanderings of an urban dandy who was trying to kill a Sunday in Bogotá—a most difficult task, he lamented—when he happened across a young woman and her sister bathing in and relaxing along a river. He retired and left them to their privacy, but then the woman sent her sister to tell him they were done and that he could now bathe if he so chose. Their subsequent interaction and dialogue revealed the woman to be beautiful both for her appearance—tall, slender, healthy, strong, with an interesting and intelligent face—as well as for her directness, thoughtfulness, and spirited character.[54] While the author apologized to his readers for not adequately relaying more of the attitude and accent of this beautiful and unexpected woman, another article criticized the ignorance of men for making women frivolous; women only focused on fashion and small talk because men kept women educationally and socially distant from matters of substance.[55]

Fashion did, however, appear often in the pages of the *Biblioteca de Señoritas*, but in an analytical and critical light. The women of Paris were criticized for being fashion mad because it led to debt, disgrace, and the dissolution of families. For the women of Bogotá, the female mission was to *conserve* the honor of the family and the fortune of her husband, to *educate* the heart and spirit of her husband, children, and servants, and to make a world full of challenges more *pleasant*. Señoritas were urged to pay special attention to please (*agradar*) by "cultivating our heart, our spirit, our person under all conditions by making them as beautiful, as agreeable, and as seductive as possible."[56] That way, women could use their "palpable and effective" influence on men and society without it even being felt. The women of Bogotá could, then, seek

elegance in their dress and take pride in pleasing the eyes of those who con-
templated them because it was natural for women to want this and because it
was part of their mission to make the world a better place.

Ideas about fashion, like passing fashion trends in the mid-nineteenth
century, often conflicted with one another. Advice columns reminded women
of which shades looked right depending on a woman's skin and hair color, to
wear light fabrics if heavy and heavy ones if slender, and to remember that
taste, tact, and grace were the true flowers of civilization. Women were told
that they no longer had to live with the fashion tyranny alive in their grand-
mothers' day and that they didn't want to dress like their mothers. They lived
now in a time of liberty, which, ironically, made each woman's beauty her own
responsibility, freedom bringing obligations.[57]

One piece of underwear, the crinoline, raised howls of protest in the pages
of the *Biblioteca de Señoritas*. Heavy petticoats or hoop skirts made of whale-
bone or steel were ridiculed as grotesque and unwieldy exaggerations. Nonetheless, the crinoline was taking over everywhere you looked: on the streets, in
church, in the theaters, and in the salons. The nineteenth wasn't the century
of steam power, or the railroad, or the telegraph; it was the century of the
crinoline. It was attacked by nationalists as a foreign import that was robbing
the new nation of its own nature. It was decried by artisans and by those worried that imports and the culture of luxury were gutting the national economy
and leading it to ruin. No matter. The crinoline was winning each battle,
and rapidly the war, as it took over Bogotá's fashionable north side. At least
one could see national fabrics and ruanas in the west side markets, the ruana
emerging as, and remaining, a symbol of Colombian fashion and tradition.[58]

One defender of the crinoline noted that attacks on fashion were often in
inverse proportion to the decency of the look; the more decent, the harsher
the attack. The crinoline, he reasoned, gave women twenty times their natural
volume and did so in a decent way. He was more worried about the low-cut
trend then in vogue — of wearing an undershirt without a bodice. But his
main point was the importance of good hygiene, a practice, he said, often
overlooked by the elegant women of Bogotá. A woman might look good from
a distance, but come near and her natural and pungent odor and stained teeth
would not allow one to confuse her with an angel.[59] Satire and fashion are
old friends.

The pursuit of beauty through fashion was expensive, however, as husbands complained that it now took four times as much imported fabric to
clothe their wives in the latest style. Moreover, gala dances, like those in the
Colombian senate and congress in 1858, could involve nearly ten thousand
pesos spent on new gowns just for one dance. In such a poor city as Bogotá,

one in need of bridges, theaters, and other urban services, such events and spending seemed excessive. However, an article in the *Biblioteca de Señoritas* noted that the splendid gathering of all types of beauties gave the evening a magical air of illusion. Yet, once the ten-hour dance ended, the city returned to its deserted and pale self. Another dance at the residence of the Peruvian minister in Bogotá was noteworthy in that all the gentlemen dressed in white ties, a first for the city, and because among the elegant beauties were a few who could drive to distraction even the most dispassionate.[60] The dances and their requisite fashions were for some, then, a social opportunity to shine and an interruption in the monotony of an otherwise dreary existence.

A six-year hiatus passed before *El Iris* took up the task of serving as the capital's "literary journal dedicated to the fair sex" as was its precursor, the *Biblioteca de Señoritas*. The male editors thanked "the beautiful daughters of Granada" for their support of this nonpolitical, nonpartisan literary magazine. They named it "Iris" as a symbol of peace, women being the symbol of concord, generosity, healing, comfort, and love. Symbolically, women were equated with creativity, life, artistry, and beauty, nonpartisan and nonpolitical creatures who lived in the midst of an untamed and violent nation. Women were asked to contribute pieces to *El Iris*, but for the most part women and their beauty were used, as they still are in Colombia, as a font of peace and hope in the midst of chaos and violence.[61]

The literary side of *El Iris* included love poetry written by men for women, oftentimes couched in terms of a father writing about his daughter in order to avoid overt sexual overtones. Women were often compared to flowers—pure, aromatic, delicate—as "girls and flowers are always sisters." As a symbol of nature and beauty, women as flowers also served as society's base, and "if their hearts were cultivated they would bear fruit in proportion to the seed planted within." A woman's education should then focus on moral, spiritual, and practical instruction; the editors suggested that females avoid studying for professions that were "outside their orbit of attributions."[62]

El Iris covered French fashion trends, paying special attention to the gowns worn by the nobility at large and sumptuous dances hosted by the emperor and empress. Colombia's elite would then know which fabrics, dress styles, jewelry, gloves, hats, and hairstyles were then in vogue among the elite of Paris. But *El Iris* also complimented Bogotanas for their fashion flair, one pulled together without a great deal of money or affect. For their style, one article suggested, "We've heard that Bogotanas have no other rivals besides North American women . . . and if coquetry hasn't bastardized the grace of our beauties then decorum and grace and innocence reign in social gatherings."[63]

There was some worry, however, that the rising popularity of theater actresses, especially the sensuous, voluptuous, and blonde actresses then the rage in the North Atlantic, would tempt some elite women "to convert themselves a little into actresses."[64] The search for male attention and the sex appeal of modern actresses would then lead to a social deterioration of women and the elite. *El Iris* articles often placed a crown on the heads of women to mark them as sovereigns and elites. Whereas modernity warmed to a more corporal, sensuous, and democratic beauty, tradition found in the crown a symbol of heritage, permanence, and detachment from the modern. However, the crown could be one of thorns because of the duties and pains that came with being female. Moreover, with or without a crown, women might reign, but they did not govern ("la mujer reina pero no gobierna"), a reminder of separate gender roles and of the limitations placed on women's social and political power.[65]

Political struggles between the active and often dictatorial Tomás Cipriano de Mosquera and Radical Liberals from the Cordillera Oriental dominated national and state politics in the mid-1860s. A Conservative revolution in Antioquia in 1864 ousted the Mosquerista governor imposed on the state, a move that Mosquera's opponents supported as a tactic to limit the general's power.[66] In this volatile and politicized setting, *La Aurora: periódico dedicado al bello sexo*, began its publication run in Medellín in 1868. Similar to *Biblioteca de Señoritas* and *El Iris*, *La Aurora* explored topics on beauty, women, morality, "progress," and literature in a gendered and nonpartisan voice but with a decidedly Antioqueño twist. Its imagery was more Christian and biblical, an indication of Conservative Party politics and their expression during Liberal dominance of national government. It was more satirical, less literary, shorter and cruder in format, markers of paisa pride in simplicity and informality. True beauty, of course, was to be found in Antioquia, a beauty that was traditional, moral, genuine, and familiar, springing from the state's abundant nature and solid faith.[67]

God and nature had granted Antioquia the spectacular beauty of the women who graced it. Their beauty was biblical and timeless because Providence had graced no other country with "beings more angelic, more noble, more saintly than are our beautiful antioqueñas."[68] *La Aurora* was claiming that its "country" had the most beautiful women in Colombia, a status claim fitting of an enterprising booster but also of a region trying to get out from under Bogotá's heel. This very political message was, however, veiled in a nonpartisan cloak when *La Aurora*'s editors claimed, "Our magazine will be clean, pure, noble, like the soul of the virtuous antioqueñas to whom it is dedicated."[69] Beauty is often used to smooth jagged edges left by male contests over status and power.

Although Antioquia's beauties could rival and beat any of those in Europe, the problem of keeping up with Parisian fashion offered fruit ripe with satire. Fashion was decried in a satirical piece in the pages of *La Aurora* as "the abyss for the vortex of luxury," but that didn't concern Medellín's women, who didn't want to look passé. As Paris moved away from the bustle and crinoline in 1868 and toward a longer and more angular look, antioqueñas were faced with giving up clothing items they now loved. An imagined convention was called of the "poor American Indians" ("pobres indias americanas") who were confused and didn't know what to do. A speaker suggested that the bustle be ditched and that the crinoline be trimmed so that Antioquia's women would remain in fashion and not be left behind. The meeting ended with the stirring cry, "Down with the bustle and crinoline! Viva the long narrow dress! Long live the European ladies!" ("¡abajo la cola i la crinolina! ¡viva el traje alto i angosto! ¡VIVAN LAS EUROPEAS!") The police pledged to put down the bustle; readers were told not to go to the theater or on a midnight stroll unless they followed the imitative commands of European fashion. At a staging of *Uncle Tom's Cabin*, it wasn't the actors or script that stirred the crowd's energies but the fashions of some European ladies in the box seats.[70] The editors and writers of *La Aurora* spoke with pride about their region's beauty while they poked fun at the dictates of imported and external fashion.

East in Bogotá, beauty's demands and its limitations and strictures were themes often addressed in the pages of *El Hogar*, a literary journal "dedicated to the fair sex" published between 1868 and 1870. José Joaquín Borda, its editor, often explored the question of why physical beauty wasn't sufficient in a woman. Without virtue, intelligence, grace, deference, and soul, beauty was only a temporary and fragile mirage. Beauty needed substance to be true; only with virtue and intelligence guiding beauty could one find the "model woman." For Borda, women carried great social and spiritual responsibilities, ones that vanity, coquetry, and reckless love would undermine and lead to female declension. Only with the balancing of good character, mental acuity, and service to God and humanity could a woman be truly beautiful.[71]

Vanity's trappings and their connections to gender roles and to modernity and progress were themes that Borda touched on insightfully in January 1869. He suggested that vanity became more common among peoples and nations undergoing economic and social development. People began to scrutinize themselves and one another as exemplars of status, taste, and progress, creating both greater demands and opportunities for individual prominence. He suggested that elite women were made vain because of their limited opportunities in the male-dominated world of economic, social, and political power. Left to the domestic sphere and to the relatively easily earned attributes of beauty, virtue, and a careful education, women entered into the foggy realm of vanity and pride as both a protest against and a pursuit of the glories reserved for men.[72]

Fashion's dictates and the obsession with appearance could lead women away from true beauty. An article on fashion began with a critique of the frivolous pursuit of the latest look but ended with an in-depth description of those latest French fashions. *El Hogar*, like many such publications of the time, tried to reach a balance between character and appearance, vanity and beauty, morality and materialism, tradition and modernity, nationalism and internationalism—an elusive and difficult equilibrium still de rigueur in present-day pageants around the world.[73]

Two types of women received criticism: the gender-bending virile woman and the unfaithful wife and mother. Women who dressed, worked, smoked, rode, or shot like men, and women who were vulgar, assertive or who supplanted or challenged men and their authority were reminded that "women should have the waist of Venus and not the staff of Mars" and that they should please men with their sweetness, tenderness, and modesty. While this admonition suggests that some women were clearly gender-bending and challenging the precepts of patriarchy, the opprobrium reserved for the poor wife who sold her virtue for gold, leaving her husband in a murderous rage and her daughter in dishonor, reminded *El Hogar*'s readers of severe patriarchal claims over women and their sexuality and behavior in daily life.[74]

The balancing of contrasts left room for a romantic poem to the beauty and nobility of a black woman ("A una negra"). Because of the beauty of contrasts, her eyes, lips, and teeth complemented her skin color; her body's curves and sway moved the air as she walked down the street, leaving men faint but grateful to God for the variety and allure of female beauty. The beauty of *la negra* was noble yet accessible; she was a sovereign of noble Ethiopian lineage, robbed of her crown by a cruel slave trader, but she was there in the street, a queen for the common man. Like other varieties of beauty in the pages of *El Hogar*, the poem to la negra found variety and contrasts in the beauty of women.[75]

Questions about color, attraction, love, and a suitable mate were all raised in a potboiler of a story strung through several editions of *El Verjel Colombiano*. *El Verjel* (Vergel? Garden or Orchard) was published in 1875 and 1876 and was Bogotá's successor to *El Hogar* as the "literary journal dedicated to the fair sex." The story told of a young man's awakening interest in and attraction to a neighborhood *morena* (an Afro-Colombian) whom he found re-freshingly candid, innocent, multifaceted, and talented, but ugly. He enjoyed the morena's company and speculated that she might make a good wife; she was tender, sensible, docile, virtuous, sufficiently educated, well-connected socially, adept at domestic chores, and of high moral conduct. Moreover, he reasoned that her lack of beauty might ensure a tranquil marriage, minimizing jealousies or the unwanted attention of other men. He was set to make the rational choice when he spied "divinity in human form . . . ," a young gentle beauty with snow-white skin at the peak of her enchanting charm. In seeing her he fell desperately in love and then understood romantic love; realizing that his infatuation with the morena had passed, he decided not to marry her.[76]

Subsequent stories in *El Verjel Colombiano* played on this tension between form and substance, attraction and love, the spiritual and the physical. In the article "La coqueta," the male author described the attributes of a natural and enchanting coquette—one who was young, educated, beautiful, tal-ented, heartfelt—and contrasted her with the more calculating and common flirt.[77] In this case, a naturally beautiful and attractive young woman was ac-ceptable, whereas the conscious pursuit of attention and conquest was not. Poems sought ideal beauty in a woman, suggesting that beauty was an in-tense yearning and desire found beyond but close to one's self.[78] Beauty was found in theaters, not necessarily in the faces and bodies of foreign actresses, but in the acting, music, and song that inspired reviewers and audiences.[79] Beauty was found in good wives who gave their husbands hope and inspira-tion, when during civil wars even old friends of the same party warred against one another. In this case, marrying beauty would keep family and society intact as it helped men through destructive and ugly political and military battles.[80] Finally, an article on beauty ("La belleza") distinguished between the heavenly and divine beauty of the soul and the external, corporal, and earthly beauty of the body. To be a good woman, one always had to maintain the focus on the interior beauty of the soul and its character, rather than being seduced by the form of corporal symmetry.[81] In each of these articles, beauty was described and analyzed in a complex and interactive manner; it was nu-anced, multifaceted, difficult, natural, physical, and spiritual.

Soledad Acosta de Samper (1833–1913) ably explored the demands and contradictions of being female and beautiful. A prolific writer and histo-rian, Acosta de Samper gained both national and international recognition from her many publications. In 1878 she founded and edited *La Mujer*, which claimed to be the first periodical written by and for women in all of Latin America.[82] Acosta had collaborated in the publication of *Biblioteca de Seño-*

ritas twenty years earlier but pledged in *La Mujer* that women would not be "compared to fragrant and beautiful flowers, created and born only to adorn the garden of existence." Instead, the focus would be on how women in their particular domains helped men through "the rough road of life and helped them carry the great and heavy cross of suffering." The focus, then, was not on gender emancipation or liberation but on the duties and responsibilities incumbent on every human being.[83]

La Mujer was a well-written and serious publication, one highlighting women's history, European politics, science, literature, and poetry. Peppered throughout its pages were advice columns keeping women focused on dedicated and conscientious work, on educating their children, and on excelling in everything they did. Fashion did creep into its pages, however, usually covering the latest trends in Paris or, in another instance, of the jewelry-mad women of San Francisco, California, where diamonds, sapphires, opals, and pearls were all the rage. However, Soledad had a dim view of extravagant and profligate consumption, reminding her readers that most French women didn't exaggerate their looks but showed grace with simple style.[84]

Soledad was an Anglophile—her mother English, her father Colombian—so it wasn't unusual that the fame and beauty of Lillian Langtry merited comment in the second issue of *La Mujer*. Langtry, a courtesan and former mistress of the Prince of Wales who counted among her admirers Oscar Wilde, became a "professional beauty" in England in the 1870s and then, short of money, took her notorious and aristocratic show to the stages of the United States in the early 1880s. Acosta de Samper commented on Langtry's pervasive popularity at social events, remarking on her perfect grace, elegant body, and singular features, but noted that her most powerful quality was in uniting snow-white skin, jet-black hair, and blue eyes the color of a tropical sky.[85]

Acosta de Samper lambasted fleeting French fashions, which she often found to be outrageous, savage, and in bad taste. She noted the social damage done to family, society, and self when image and fashion became a paramount concern for women. Applauding Queen Victoria for banning certain exaggerated French flourishes from the British court, Soledad expressed a wish for a similar ban in Colombia. She noted that two Englishwomen had died as a result of extremely tight corsets and reprinted some advice from the Princess of Wales about avoiding overly tightened corsets and high heels.[86]

Duty to others and duty to God weren't possible when women became slaves to fashion. Soledad counseled her Colombian readers on how to dress economically and in good taste, thereby not allowing fashion to become an obsession that would hurt the family and the marriage. She clearly believed that women needed to perform their familial and social duties and that they should maintain their separate sphere and not meddle in the affairs of men. She differentiated between the positive aspects of modesty and pride but critiqued vanity, writing, "You can't have modesty without pride, nor pride without apparent modesty. On the other hand, vanity, which we sometimes confuse with pride, doesn't have within it an atom of modesty or of pride. Vanity, when it becomes the owner of the heart, doesn't permit any other rival sentiment and reigns despotically."[87]

The themes of duty, honor, and urbanity continued in a series of advice columns to young women. Acosta de Samper quoted from books of etiquette penned by Madame Celnart and Manuel Antonio Carreño. She had a no-nonsense attitude about life and female comportment, saying a good heart joined urbanity in happy synthesis with morality, grace, elegance, and self-respect. She warned the señoritas that life was full of sacrifices and challenges, that dances were a form of social combat, and that marriage had many illusions but was usually full of incessant battles. Framing her presentation around the pillars of religion, family, society, and urbanity, she delineated etiquette guidelines while at church, the home, social and illness calls, dances, the street, and funerals. She argued that a good woman, one who was kind and gracious, was much more worthy of love than a beautiful woman, but that if these two qualities came together, then a good and beautiful woman's influence would be all-powerful.[88]

By the mid-1880s, Acosta de Samper was editing *La Familia*, a publication open to articles by women and men, and one more openly political. This period marked the demise of liberal reforms and of Radical Liberal influence. Erstwhile Liberal and soon-to-be Conservative Rafael Núñez heralded this change in partisan and political tides and the movement toward bipartisan government during various presidential terms in the 1880s. Articles focused on how mothers ought to set examples for their children and for society on the benefits of order, industry, prudence, economy, and authority. Women who supported liberal educational reforms were warned that education should not be separated from religion and morality—a Conservative stance—and that women should not stray into partisan or sectarian politics, but keep their focus on the family. But family life was no bowl of cherries; wives were counseled to keep their distance and preserve their respect and dignity when dealing with their husbands, guarding against too much intimacy. Mothers were told to demand too much respect rather than grant too much familiarity to children and servants, a message focusing on order in domestic life while the civil war of 1884–1885 punctuated political disorder at the same time.[89]

Soledad's conservative streak was widening as the Conservative Party prepared for control of the presidency under Núñez in 1886, power that it would not relinquish until 1930.

Both tradition and geography laid heavily on Colombia as it became a republic. Caste distinctions between Spanish, indigenous, and black still demarcated power and beauty. The Catholic Church doggedly protected paternalistic order as it pressed for feminine restraint. The geography and climate of Colombia allowed for more corporal freedom on the hot and humid coast and tighter control in the highlands. Radical Liberal freedom opened expression for female reality and social purpose, but in a literary and controlled medium. The beauty found in women's journals stressed the traditional importance of morality and virtue to mark a woman's interior beauty and character while other articles focused on modern Parisian fashions. Nonetheless, these four decades allowed a deep inquiry into the literary and moral definitions of beauty, one still focused on the feminine purpose of making this shared world a better place. Yet women reigned but did not govern, a structural and institutional reality that limited beauty's promise.

Colombian political leaders failed to bring either the liberty fervently pursued by Radical Liberals or the order cherished by Conservatives in the transition from the nineteenth to the twentieth century. The Radical Liberals lost control of the presidency to Independent Liberal Rafael Núñez, who forged working relationships with Conservatives after 1880. The beast of partisan war erupted in 1885, giving Núñez the political space to frame a new nationalist and centralist constitution in 1886, one that would survive until 1991. But Núñez's Regeneration of the nation failed to end the cycle of political violence as Liberal exclusion from national government led to new revolts in 1895 and to a full-scale civil war from 1899 to 1902. Notions of beauty and the nation were pulled back to conservative Hispanist traditions but also toward modern innovations during these same years.[1]

Núñez focused on practical and pragmatic policies in his Regeneration and in the Constitution of 1886 framed by his Conservative partner Miguel Antonio Caro. Federalism was abandoned, replaced by a centralized national authority. Presidents enjoyed more formal power, and their term increased to six years. States became departments, the president naming the governors who selected all mayors. This institutional authoritarianism also mirrored the restoration of powers to the Catholic Church in social, legal, and educational matters and shut Liberals out of patronage and power positions, fertilizing partisan divisions and the future possibility of sectarian violence.[2]

The alliance between church and state made Catholicism a cornerstone of social order and Colombian nationality. The Church regained full control over marriage, with patriarchs ruling over wives and children as legal minors. Oversight over curriculum, school texts, and teacher appointments in public schools promised the order and morality of a church institution becoming more reactionary to modern trends. An influx of energetic and crusading foreign clergy, many of them displaced by nationalist and anticlerical movements in late-nineteenth-century Europe, bolstered the religious and social reaction to secularism and modernism. The institutional and social power of a resurgent but backward-facing Colombian Catholic Church would survive well into the twentieth century.[3]

About four million people lived in the country in 1886, most still in small towns and rural areas. Bogotá had about one hundred thousand inhabitants, the rich enjoying a hint of modern conveniences like telegraph, telephone, and electrical services. But the capital resembled a sprawling rural town, with open sewers and with pigs, horses, chickens, and cows commingled in many urban plots, regardless of the human residents' class. Half of all newborns were birthed to unwed mothers, with many children left without a father or a chance at an education. Class tensions intensified in the colonial core of the city, especially among artisans, who faced a wave of imported commercial goods stocked in downtown stores in 1887–1888 and increasing urban rents that displaced many to the city's peripheral neighborhoods.[4]

Modern conveniences opened greater social distance for elites to mark their privileged urban status. The capital's small elite and middle class referred to themselves as "la gente buena" (the good people), dismissing the majority rural and urban working class as "indios" (Indians), a social binary maintained into the 1920s.[5] While most city residents drew their water from open ditches or from Bogotá's public fountains, downtown elites and bureaucrats enjoyed piped-in water from a new aqueduct system by the 1890s.[6] Electric light created a brighter, more modern alternative to the formerly dim urban landscape of the colonial era for elites and public workers. The novelty of electric light brought an aura of elegance and romance to the streets and walls of Bogotá's colonial La Candelaria neighborhood. Most residents embraced the splendid lighting that they now unequally enjoyed, but traditionalists warned "God Help Us" for the sin that was sure to increase during nocturnal parties and dances.[7]

Dances provided the opportunity for young dandies and ladies to shine in their European fashions, latest hairstyles, and elegant shoes and accessories. In a room decorated with fragrant flowers and filled with a flowing waltz, a coquettish look could trigger a budding romance and a future call. European fashions trickled into the capital through merchants' shops and European magazines. Elites might change clothes several times a day and bathe with imported soaps, further distinguishing their separate status from the barefooted masses ("descalzos") by wearing shoes.[8]

In contrast to the proliferation of women's magazines during Liberal governments in the two decades after the 1850s, Conservative rule tended to blunt such publications in the 1890s. However, Ismael José Romero and Fernando A. Romero began editing *La Mujer* in Bogotá in 1895. Written for and about women and gender but mainly by male authors, articles in the second iteration of *La Mujer* promised to be short, simple, and innocent for its young readers, avoiding scandalous French customs and literature and possible censorship from the Colombian government. Many articles touted the strength and virtue of Colombian women, with themes of morality, talent, and beauty appearing often.[9]

Although some might opine that women were weak, worthless, a defect from male nature, *La Mujer* noted that women made up half of humanity and were strong and resilient and able to put up with more than a man could take. Classical and religious lessons pointed to the fact that a woman's beauty made her not male, and that God had placed women on Earth because the distance between males and angels was just too great.[10] A man was only one-half a woman, with women always leading men to the march for social justice. Although a woman's beauty placed her on a pedestal of perfection and adoration, that beauty had power. If man could only win a woman's heart with love, a woman could enslave a man with her beauty. If beauty was irresistible, a domination of the senses, then beauty was power and power was force. But the principal beauty had to be moral and internal; it was found in the heart, not in the face and form. That internal beauty of a generous heart of delicate and virtuous sentiments, coupled with physical beauty and a seductive voice, made men vassals to an obviously superior woman.[11]

Beauty was the work of God, and ugliness a sign of human depravity. Both beauty and ugliness were heritable across generations. Perhaps after three generations, the vice and bad passions of a grandparent could be diluted by good moral conduct. Beauty certainly had its advantages; a person born with good looks and pleasant proportions had it easier than an ugly person who had to struggle to stay on the road toward goodness. But women born beautiful could mask an ugly character, one revealed only with careful scrutiny of their actions. The signs of true and sublime beauty always included virtue.[12]

La Mujer included humorous popular jokes like this one: "Rubias y Morenas: Con la sal que derrama una morena, se mantiene una rubia semana y media." (The salt that a brunette spills can maintain a blonde for a week and a half.)[13] Notwithstanding these early brunette jokes, *La Mujer* also defended feminist struggles for more inclusive opportunities in the job market in the United States. Colombian women, as well as men, had the right and duty to work, especially the 50 percent of women who never married and needed to support themselves. Women should perform all jobs and delicate professions that men did badly: sewing, embroidery, painting, bookkeeping, typing, telegraphy, and nursing for female patients. Women typically invisible in the press, such as artisans' wives, were extolled for their diligent work at home and market, usually caring for a group of children as they worked.[14]

In "The Three Ages of Women," readers were warned of the dual dangers of contact with men and of aging. At fifteen, a woman was compared to a fragrant flower, a radiant blue sky at the dawning of beauty and love; she was irresistible, charming, pure, innocent, and a sovereign over men. At twenty, the world and its traps had caught up to her; although she was interested in marriage, age and contact with men had wilted her flower. The age of thirty frightened her and she hid her age. At thirty, she was either married or socially obsolete, facing the twin female agonies of aging and death.[15]

The social necessity but problem of marriage concerned the editors. Although many young women married in Medellín, few married in Bogotá. The capital was filled with blonde and brunette beauties, and although marriages often were not eternally happy, writers still could not comprehend why weddings were so rare. The blame was fixed on economic, cultural, and educational grounds. Economically, the lack of an industrial and vibrant commercial base made dowries modest at best. Big weddings and a fascination with foreign imports made marriages both remote and expensive. Only the rich could afford the luxury of a wedding, complete with silk, velvet, diamonds, grand banquets, and fine French wines. And while the youth of Medellín received a practical education, one focused on hard work and upward mobility, girls and boys in Bogotá both suffered through a theoretical and impractical curriculum, one ill-suited for real life. In short, the ideal of marriage buckled under the combined weight of poor local economies and imported foreign fashions.[16]

Tight-laced corsets and the pseudoscience of the fashion industry also attracted the ire of *La Mujer*. Corsets worn day and night, and often laced so tightly as to compress the waist to eighteen inches, damaged internal organs, led to eating and digestive disorders, caused nosebleeds, and killed some three hundred women annually. The corset wasn't the culprit; it was the mania of fashion, the abuse of the corset, and the exaggerated alteration of the human torso that gained the blame. Moreover, vendors in beauty shops in France and Germany who promised, for a small price, an end to ugliness, using ointments to smooth a face scarred by smallpox, a touch to the end of the nose to create a Grecian profile, or facial mud treatments to guarantee rosy cheeks and perfect eyes, were dismissed as charlatans.[17]

According to *La Mujer* director Fernando A. Romero, bogotanas needed no cosmetic manipulation of their natural and cultural beauty. Although their admirable bodies were still cloaked by the mantilla negra, their rosy cheeks, sweet smiles, and pure accent mixed with their grace, virtue, and honor to create irresistible and extraordinary beauties. They were defined as Spanish, not mestiza, indígena, or negra, and were refined, educated, and tasteful.

They dressed well and richly, not because they had to, but because it was un-necessary. Their cultural superiority allowed them to speak a few indigenous words, if only to be understood by "them."[18]

Although Bogotá's population embraced its Spanish colonial image, hundreds of bogotanas signed a letter in 1896 addressed to the Reina Regente de España calling for an end to Spanish violence in Cuba. Cuba's struggle for independence met increasingly harsh Spanish repression, reminiscent of Colombia's independence process, recurring actions that Bogotá's female signatories termed an affront to religion, morality, and women. This petition to the Queen suggested that the beast of machine guns, concentration camps, and firing squads threatened Spanish Catholic beauty.[19]

The ultraconservatism of the "Spanish Race" held back modern social progress for women in Medellín, according to Leocadio Lotero in an article forwarded from a Medellín magazine to La Mujer. Lotero noted that women voted in some areas of the United States and that even the imperious and proud English allowed women voters for some town council elections. But in Antioquia, the grinding daily regime of agricultural life or the hawking of foreign imports by urban merchants kept progress contained, leaving women to the roles of servants, beasts of burden, or toys, not allowing them to fulfill their full human potential. Progress would come once Medellín's young men colonized new lands, planting coffee or cacao, or mining the red earth for gold. Once wealth was produced from Antioquia's soil, more jobs and social status would trickle down to women in the city.[20]

The "Eastern" physiognomy of Antioquia's women placed them in a separate "race" from other late-nineteenth-century Colombians. Described as tall and thin, with small mouths, long fine noses, dark eyes, and a dreamy and deep look that mirrored the sadness and sweetness of the surrounding mountains, these women, purportedly, loved work and the home. They matured early, marrying just after puberty, receiving more education and birthing more children than women in Bogotá. Although Antioqueños took pride in their progress, intelligence, and industriousness, nothing was better than their women.[21]

According to two antioqueñas, the women of the Chocó, the gold mine of Colombia, were dark, spiritual, intelligent, and hard working. As befit a rural society, they dressed simply and honestly, unburdening their fathers and husbands from the social cancer of fashion. They danced gracefully and with a smile, giving them an enchanting and sweet air. Although they lacked education, they still filled the role of queen and lady with their pious nobility and irresistible style.[22]

Away from the newspapers and foreign fashions, women in rural provinces attracted comment about their character but not their appearance. The women of Santander and Tolima garnered praise for their industriousness, steadiness, loyalty, responsibility, and charity of purpose. As Santander's fame for beautiful women harkened back to mid-century, when it was a prosperous region of coffee, tobacco, and thriving artisan industry, Tolima was emerging as a new agricultural frontier. In both places, women gained respect for their simplicity, religiosity, nobility, and ability to cope with the daily challenges of survival in the Colombian countryside.[23]

On the north Caribbean coast, the women of Bolívar were described as the least beautiful of all Colombia. The department held verdant and fertile lands, while its tropical sun, warm sea, and refreshing mountains opened Colombia to foreign trade and progress through the ports of proud Cartagena and upstart Barranquilla. Although poor health, tropical diseases, or dark skin presumably dropped them from consideration for beauty, they were seductive for their enchanting grace, simple elegance, and modest self-abnegation. Like other provincial women, they were described in the pages of *La Mujer* as industrious and virtuous, with a hint of sexual prowess in the phrase, "seductresses in the home, and with you at the sick bed, sublime!"[24]

Rather than a regional description of Colombian beauty, Soledad Acosta de Samper offered a broader context of women's place in her 1895 book, *La mujer en la sociedad moderna*. Written for a Colombian, European, and American audience, Acosta de Samper noted the outstanding achievements of female reformers, writers, orators, politicians, painters, poets, doctors, and scientists in modern societies. She argued that a self-respecting and independent woman could maintain her virtue, particularly if she was judicious about marriage. Women, she argued, didn't need to marry losers; if they chose to marry, it should be to honorable men. Women could build a more just and honorable society and a better future for themselves by rejecting impiety, corruption, and immorality, by judging men who acted poorly.[25] On the issue of beauty, Acosta de Samper focused on Latin American women of the "Spanish Race," noting their physical beauty but also their vivacious spirit and good hearts. But it was the accomplishments of fellow female writers in Bogotá, Antioquia, Cartagena, and Santa Marta that gained more of her interest.[26]

North of Colombian shores, the 1890s marked a shift in U.S. beauty images toward a modern, athletic look. The Civil War buxom beauty and the allure of foreign stage stars still held sway, but feminist critiques of fashion opened space for a healthy athleticism of freer garb and more meaningful lives in which women wore skirts and blouses for sports, donning suits for the street. Corset-free, the tan, healthy, and athletic California girl showed more waist and less bust and hips. But it was from New York and the lithographs of the "Gibson Girl," a drafted icon of the mass media that imaged the "ideal woman": a tall, beautiful, athletic, and modern woman but one of traditional virtue.[27]

The bicycle craze of the 1890s had a tremendous impact on the athletic, modern, feminist woman. The safety bicycle, with its pneumatic tires around wheels of equal size, increased comfort for the rider while adding to the thrill and freedom of human-powered locomotion. Regardless of high prices and poor or nonexistent brakes, elite women, rebellious actresses, college girls, and exercise advocates took to the bicycle with relish. Women rode step-through bicycles either in dresses, which could get caught in the pedals, chains, or wheels, or in modified bloomers and a shirtwaist blouse. Girls on bikes challenged the isolation of women from public space and the restrictions of confining and heavy fashions.[28]

By 1898, the bicycle made its splash on fashion and gender relations amongst the high society of Bogotá; primarily from the city's distinguished elite, female cyclists numbered in the hundreds. Magazine articles embraced the liberation and salubrious effect of the bicycle on women's health: "if there are people in this world who owe a special debt of gratitude for this great advance in civilization, it is without doubt the beautiful women of cultured Bogotá whose ancient traditions and customs had condemned them to a cloistered life, mother of anemia and neurosis . . ."[29]

Bicycle riding liberated women from stifling dress and social restriction as it gave them more freedom astride a modern and snappy conveyance. It filled their lungs with the clean air of the countryside as it developed their muscles and added color to anemic cheeks. The bicycle challenged key aspects of elite society as it changed the language of the young sporting crowd. The English words "sport," "lunch," "sportsman," "starter," and "handicap" all became part of the hip, sporting vocabulary. Over the next ten years, clothing for hunting, mountaineering, golf, tennis, rowing, swimming, and motoring appeared in Bogotá's illustrated periodicals, adding fashion choices for the sporting crowd.[30]

However, modern changes often rile social conservatives, as evidenced by a small demonstration in 1899 against women riding at the velodrome. The 350-meter banked bicycle track, built inside the 1,200-meter horse track, attracted both wealthy and more modest spectators. An article in *El Sport*, a magazine published in Bogotá, dismissed the protestors as "Hottentots," people lost in the past who refused to see how the bicycle improved the health of young men and women alike. Noting that female cyclists sprang from the distinguished lines of the Holguín, Nieto, Caro, Manrique, Pombo, Mallarino, Samper, Camacho, Mancini, Núñez, Escobar, Restrepo, Sordo, Valenzuela,

Sayer, Dupuy, Cortés, and Borda clans, the magazine suggested that elite inclusion in modern transformations would not lead to social decomposition.[31]

Colombian decomposition came not from modern technology and mores but from political exclusion, partisan divisions, and economic distress. The War of a Thousand Days (1899–1902) revived the beast of nineteenth-century Colombian civil war, dragging the country and its people back toward insecurity, chaos, hatred, envy, and death. Six months of conventional battles in Santander gave way to two years of unconventional warfare in the Magdalena Valley and in the new coffee frontiers west and south of Bogotá. Casualty estimates, numbering as high as 100,000 dead, equaled the percentage of population killed in the U.S. Civil War of 1861–65. The United States played a key role in brokering the peace between Liberals and Conservatives in November 1902, but also in backing Panamanian secession from Colombia in 1903. U.S. sovereignty over the Canal Zone limited Panamanian independence and left Colombia out of the commercial bonanza reaped from canal traffic. U.S.-Colombian diplomatic relations and Colombian distrust of the "Giant to the North" remained acute over the next two decades.[32]

Soledad Acosta de Samper, now in her sixties, responded to the fallout of civil war and the loss of Panama by editing *Lecturas para el Hogar: revista literaria, histórica e instructiva*, a new journal working to her strengths as a writer, historian, and educator, but one now focused on the home and on education. With external society in disarray and with schools closed during the war years, Acosta de Samper returned her focus to the domestic, female space. From 1905 to 1906, the pages of *Lecturas para el Hogar* offered mothers advice on how to find good schools for their children or on how to educate them at home. Fashion no longer garnered any ink as it had done twenty-five years earlier in her first journal, *La Mujer*. Apparently, the importance of education and the role of women in shaping future societies trumped cloth and cut for both Acosta and her readers.[33]

In 1912, a year before her death, Acosta de Samper reinterpreted the Virgin Mary for the twentieth century in an article in *El Hogar Católico*. Ever the educator, Acosta summarized the plight of women in antiquity as that of slaves, beings kept for their labor and beauty and then cast off cavalierly by husbands when they so chose. It was Mary, Mother of God, of human and divine virtue, who brought dignity to women in this world; the image of Mary rehabilitated women. Acosta feared that the twentieth century would rob women of their dignity and return them to male mistreatment and pagan tyranny. If women forgot their dignity and composure, then men would sever the female connection to Mary and forget how to treat virtuous women.

Soledad's widening religious streak might have reflected her life's course but could also be seen in a social context of insecurity and unpredictable change.[34]

In the same edition of *El Hogar Católico*, the editors translated Cardinal Cavalari's lambasting of what he deemed to be indecent modern fashions. The Cardinal of Venice cited St. Peter's admonishment for women not to over-dress and adorn themselves, but to look inward to an interior life of virtue and merit. Cavalari found immodest dress repugnant and refused to admit godmothers into church (his house) for confirmation if they dressed immodestly, for he deemed them to be living in a state of habitual sin. The cardinal's barring of the doors presaged future confrontations over female fashion and traditional propriety in Colombian churches.[35]

While traditional religion closed the doors to public beauty, political reorganization used public beauty as a tool to punctuate order, progress, and power. Elected president in 1904, General Rafael Reyes organized a bipartisan cabinet and implemented power-sharing agreements between Liberals and Conservatives down to the local level. With mottos like "Less politics, more administration," he restored fiscal order, sought foreign investment, professionalized the armed forces, and supported railroad construction and shipping improvements. By early 1905, he ruled without Congress, establishing a mild dictatorship. In effect, Reyes established the political ground rules for peaceful bipartisan administration for most of the twentieth century.[36]

Reyes adeptly used public relations and spectacle to punctuate the order he directed. A new illustrated magazine, *Bogotá Ilustrado*, became a vehicle for Reyes to demonstrate his political and social primacy. In the competitions his government supported, like the Juegos Florales (Flower Games) and the Concurso Hípico (Riding Display), Reyes, his wife, Sofía, and then his daughter Nina entered in succession with ritual pomp, reflecting political and social power. Reyes participated in these ceremonies as a demonstration of national reconstruction, orderly events where political power, public beauty, and social order flowed through the Reyes clan.[37]

Reyes's degree of political control directly mirrored his ability to determine who won these social contests of beauty and power. As an incoming president in 1904, Reyes could not yet impose his political will, and his daughter lost the queen selection to the Liberal candidate's daughter, an outcome attracting much public attention in Bogotá.[38] At the height of his political clout from 1906 to 1908, one of Reyes's daughters, either Nina or Amalia, garnered the honor of Reina de la Fiesta (Queen of the Party) in the Juegos Florales competitions. But in early 1909, Reyes's fall from the presidency was telegraphed at the outcome of the Juegos Florales competition. Now in his final months as president, he had alienated political elites and university students with his hold on the presidency and angered nationalists with his negotiations with the United States over compensation for the loss of Panama. In the midst of a nasty epidemic that took notable elites to their graves, the Reina de la Fiesta selected was not Nina Reyes but Cecilia Holguín; Cecilia's father, Jorge Holguín, succeeded Rafael Reyes as interim president in mid-1909. Although Reyes had inaugurated the Juegos Florales in Bogotá, the fall of his clan's queen highlighted his political demise with the assumption of his successor's daughter as party queen.[39]

In Medellín, Reyes's policies and social rituals took root under the direction of the Sociedad de Mejoras Públicas (Society for Public Improvements) in 1912. In a solemn act, the society inaugurated an annual Juegos Florales, one in which the winner of the poetry contest chose the queen for the year. The photograph on the first cover of the society's new publication presented Señorita Marcela de Márquez Madriñan as the queen of the Juegos Florales. She was pictured with a direct gaze, her hair up, shoulders bare, a fine shawl covering her bodice, and a rose off her left arm. Her feminine beauty complemented the poet's literary skills, but her beauty also represented progress to city leaders bent on achieving it. This early publication became *Progreso* by the late 1930s, but Medellín's industrial development was symbolically birthed by a queen's cultured and modern beauty.[40]

While downtown residents of Medellín and Bogotá enjoyed the modern marvel of electricity in the early part of the twentieth century, traveler Felix Serret found the infrastructure of Cauca's capital, Cali, woefully underdeveloped. No bicycles, automobiles, or trucks circulated on the poorly paved and rough roads of the city; irregular mail service and a nonexistent fire department reminded Serret of conditions found in France centuries before. High prices and low salaries impoverished much of the city's population, leaving them barefoot even for First Communion. For those of means, courtship and engagement rituals remained prolonged, formal, and tense, mainly focused on a suitor winning the favor of his chosen's parents. Elites privately hid the shame of unwed pregnancies, while working-class women who wed were assumed to be sexually experienced. Class, caste, courtship, and city conditions harked back to the past in Cali.[41]

But movies offered city residents a glimpse of a wider modern world. The first film was shown in Cali in 1897, followed ten years later by the first film shot in Cauca. From 1914 to 1928, fifteen films were produced in Colombia, five of them in Cauca. While the Di Domenic family screened European films in Bogotá and Medellín, Cali's thirty thousand residents lived within traditional limitations but could catch the glimmer of modern image-making through film.[42]

In 1904 near Cali in Buga, a small weekly tabloid, *Zig-Zag*, sponsored a photographic beauty contest among eleven of the city's unmarried elite young women. The editors suggested that victory and glory in this competition didn't require rifles and cannons, because beauty represented a product of nature, providing objective proof of the beauty of heaven and the power of God. And when that beauty was found in a young, innocent girl, one not yet worn by pride and pretense, then victory would signify a true and ideal achievement. The winner, Carmen Becerra Escobar, had the best photo and most refined look, representing an ideal pacific beauty removed from the fields of violent conflict.[43]

One thousand kilometers north, in colonial and coastal Cartagena, tradition and modernity fused in asymmetrical style. Compared to Rio de Janeiro, San Francisco, and Sydney in its geographic beauty, the city dripped with inherited colonial grandeur. Merchants, hotels, and restaurants all banked on booming business before and during the city's "Batalla de Flores" celebrations culminating on November 11. Merchants advertised hats, fabric, and lace for costumes and outfits a month before the onset of street parades, which featured would-be queens astride ornate, flower-clad wagons.[44]

Advertised fashions in Cartagena's *El Porvenir* newspaper looked back to a corset drawn so tightly that it compressed the model's waist almost to the circumference of her neck, and forward to the modern wonder of a three-hundred-page Spanish-language Montgomery Ward catalogue. Wards shipped its catalog for free, so one could shop from the comfort of a hammock while perusing the world's largest store and its high-quality, low-priced goods, with delivery and satisfaction guaranteed. Beauty's image was increasingly visual, framed by fashion and beauty photographs and by the moving pictures of film. These new technologies and aggressive marketing made U.S. fashions, like the interchangeable blouse and shirt, more common in cities like Cartagena.[45]

Another article in *El Porvenir* (The Future) struck a decidedly romantic and modernist tone in its interpretation of the city's youth suffering through the malaise of the prewar world. With religion, society, politics, and morality all in question in artistic and literary circles, the author lamented that youth had forgotten how to have fun, to laugh, and to play. Fashion dictated that one be serious, pessimistic, and disengaged from life. Pessimism pervaded among young women, who saw life as cruel, marriage as disappointment, men as worth little, favors badly rewarded, friendships ending in betrayal.

Although one could interpret this article as a typical indictment of youth by their elders, it also foreshadows the angst and anomie of fin de siècle Europe, a society soon to be ripped apart by the madness of World War I. That war and its aftermath would have strong reverberations in Colombia, ones that redefined modernity, identity, and beauty in much of the world.[46]

Pulled back toward notions of Catholic order, Hispanist traditions, and the "Spanish Race," Colombia at the century's turn also encountered the modernity of advancing technology. While bicycles, electricity, and motion pictures initially found root in urban spaces, over time and with a little ingenuity, they also touched the countryside and the majority population. A resurgent Catholic order, bolstered by Conservative administrations, brokered Colombia's encounter with modernity, giving it a bipolar, back-to-the-future quality. Fallout from the War of a Thousand Days prompted photographic beauty contests to reimage positive aspects of the nation and the modernizing and bipartisan administration of Rafael Reyes to use public beauty and social control as levers of political power. From 1914 to 1918, the industrial and modern World War I shredded much of the traditional order of the past while ripping the twentieth century from the nineteenth; beauty tilted toward modern definitions in the next fifteen years marked by the Great War.

Historical context orients our sense of the past even given the complications of overlapping but often contradictory layers of regional, national, and international events. Internationally, 1914 marked the arrival of twentieth-century material modernity but also the horror of industrial and pathological World War I. The 1920s heralded a spectacular decade of industrial productivity and exuberant speculative greed, culminating with a burst bubble called the Great Depression. Nationally, Colombian elites managed to fashion an era of bipartisan peace and economic growth fueled by coffee exports to the United States. The Colombian population increased by half from 1912 to 1929, a product of regional peace and some urban public health improvements. Culturally, elites looked to France and Spain as the exemplars of culture and beauty until the 1920s, when thereafter the economic and cultural pull of Hollywood and American enterprise shifted constructions of beauty and modernity toward the United States.[1]

The image of the modern woman underwent significant changes during these fifteen years. In 1914 Paris, the athletic Eastern exoticism of the Ballet Russe marked a radical change in female appearance. During the war years (1914–1918), hemlines moved up to the calf, rising to the knee by the mid-1920s; higher hems and exposed arms made shaving more prevalent. Females in factory jobs or in uniform signaled both socioeconomic opportunities and national duty. The war made the modern woman more masculine, as a demonstration of both patriotism and freedom. Body image was juvenile and flattened, more linear and shapeless, and hair was cut short. The flappers of the late 1920s—hipless, waistless, boneless—symbolized the new look for young, free, sensuous party girls.[2] In Colombia, modern forms of communication like the photograph, phonograph, radio, telephone and telegraph, and motion pictures opened urban elite and middle-class consumers to the new fashions. By the 1920s, the impact of WWI, silent movies, and North American factory production oozed into Colombian cities, bringing with it the archetypical fashion standards of the decade.[3]

The illustrated weekly magazine *Cromos* began publication in January 1916, serving as a vehicle to present the modern, the beautiful, and various facets of Colombian identity. With an Art Deco title at top, slick color cover, short uplifting articles, and numerous illustrations, *Cromos* presented itself as the photo album of the nation. Still popular and in circulation today, *Cromos* became the Colombian equivalent of *Life* or *People* magazine in the United States, an entertaining, illustrated national publication marketed in a large, diverse nation.

Cover illustrations during its first year of publication looked back to mid-nineteenth-century fashions and forward to the new look inspired by French fashions and the World War. Retrospectively, viewers saw romanticized paintings from the Colombia of their grandparents and in subsequent editions studied images of a distant, modern present heralding a new future. Inside the cover, photographs of notable daughters of elite families from Bogotá, Medellín, Cali, Cartagena, and Barranquilla and from smaller provincial towns like Pamplona, Titiribí, and Manizales presented the viewer with "bellezas nacionales" (national beauties), an elite but modern definition of Colombian beauty. Internationally, women in Red Cross or military uniform and mobilized to support the Allies gave *Cromos* a decidedly pro-French fashion nationalism. In the juxtaposition of beauty and the beast, war and ugly destruction opposed female beauty and French fashions.[4]

During the final year of the World War, the covers of *Cromos* transitioned from illustrations or watercolors to photographs, bringing a sharper realism to the presentation of Colombian beauty. The photo album inside the magazine featured young women from more provincial towns like Ocaña, Cúcuta, and Sincelejo, expanding notions of the nation and, presumably, the magazine's appeal and circulation. Hair was either worn up, mimicking the trends in Europe, or, more provocatively, left long and full to fall around the face onto the body.[5]

Cromos helped build the image of modern and Colombian beauty during the tail end of WWI, reaffirming elite station and loyalty to French cultural and national icons. It also stimulated spin-off publications like *Tolima, Revista Ilustrada*, which in one of its few editions used a photograph of the pretty smiling face and well-proportioned body of Señorita Merceditas Vela on its cover. *Tolima* editors, like those at *Cromos*, realized that female beauty sells copy and advertising. Moreover, Merceditas, like other provincial beauties, democratized modern beauty in Colombia. In large established cities the queens selected were elite women of high social rank, whereas for young provincial women like Merceditas, their beautiful image, not their class, was immediately salient.[6]

FIGURE 4.1   *La Farsa de Colombina,* Cromos *cover, Aug. 26, 1916, courtesy* Revista Cromos.

In rural areas removed from national images and international homogenizing trends, an older and non-European culture of beauty survived. In 1916
the Augustinian monk Bernardo Merizalde del Carmen reported on the appearance of indigenous and black women of coastal Nariño. The indigenous
women along the Rio Tapía dressed as did their ancestors ("los antiguos sal-
vajes") in a wrapped skirt worn to the knee, tied at the waist, sometimes
covering their breasts with a cotton blouse. They painted designs on their

SEÑORITA SOFIA ANGULO PALÀU

FIGURE 4.2   *La Cruz Roja,* Cromos *cover, Sept. 21, 1918, courtesy* Revista Cromos.

faces, arms, legs, and breasts, and wore heavy necklaces around their necks. The black women around Tuquerres and Barbacoas wore similar skirts, sometimes covering the bust in the presence of strangers. Boys and girls were nude until the age of ten or twelve. The women wore heavy necklaces made from Argentine coins, raw gold, and old, valuable jewels. They preferred bright colors in their dress, tying their hair with showy ribbons.[7] As in many rural areas in the country, these southern women of Nariño maintained continuities with the past, disconnected as they were from urban and European trends.

International currents brought the deadly Spanish Flu to Colombian cities in 1918 and 1919, leaving an estimated 1,900 dead in Bogotá alone. The poor died in the capital's streets, while others took to the sick bed. Unlike a normal flu, this one killed young, otherwise healthy adults at a high rate, including some of the city's young beauties. In Cartagena, the traditional November independence celebrations were postponed until late December because of the flu pandemic. By the following year, Cartagena returned to normal, with five days of heavy drinking and public dances to celebrate independence, despite the scrubbing of many proposed activities because of poor planning; the swimming, running, and cycling races were canceled because the judges failed to show up. To protect social order, the city's elites held private events to avoid the public chaos of the street festivities.[8]

Over the next five years, class conflicts defined the November festivities in Cartagena. The city's population more than doubled in a decade, allowing the popular masses to swell in number and influence in street celebrations. Masked celebrants, firecrackers, and heavy public drinking served to challenge elite control and definitions of patriotism. Elites claimed that public disorder threatened the city and the nation if the masses could not be taught to respect tradition. In some years, the elites retreated to private clubs, electing queens while protected from public view. But in 1923, Alicia I, Queen of the Students, promulgated a new constitution, formed a cabinet, and decreed a dry law in her domains. Stricter rules for that year's November celebrations followed, prohibiting firecrackers at public ceremonies where women were present, prohibiting costumes during daylight hours, and allowing the flag only to be flown at public buildings. In this case, the queen became the instrument of elite tradition and the preserver of patriotic order.[9]

In both Cartagena and Bogotá, postwar movies and advertisements signaled a youthful and modern trend. New magazines targeted young moviegoers, highlighting films, actors, and film screenings in the city and out in the provinces. Young people began to practice kissing like movie stars while emulating their favorites' moves and look. A Bayer aspirin ad in *El Porvenir* noted that "since the creation of time, pain has been the patrimony of women," given menstrual cycles and their "peculiar physical and nervous systems." The ad promised that Bayer aspirin with caffeine would cure these tortures that many women endured, suggesting that both pain and beauty were peculiar to women.[10]

Colombians seeking progress in the early 1920s found models in various countries. Modern international culture continued to flow from both Europe and the United States. Sports, cars, and airplanes replaced the war as modern exemplars in the early postwar years. Automobiles and airplanes promised speed, comfort, and mobility, while sports like boxing, soccer, tennis, and horse racing served as competitive but social pastimes. The United States emerged as the modern economic model. Spain, England, and France remained beacons of culture, while revolutionary Mexico rose as the intellectual leader of Latin America. Thanks to German immigrants and airplanes, Colombia boasted the first airmail service in the world, along with a new commercial airline in 1919. But it was from the United States that elite material culture felt its strongest pull. From automobiles and the need for better roads, to U.S.-style country clubs (including fashion shows and classes in etiquette and international cuisine for women and children), to night clubs where one danced the fox-trot, ragtime, and jazz, to imported household appliances, modern material culture often came with a North American stamp by the 1920s.[11]

Beauty culture also mixed European and North American influences. France still served as a fashion hub, and French beauty products promised youth, health, and a firmer, larger bust. American cosmetic and beauty products flooded into the country, and the movies provided an oversized and powerful visual reimaging of modern beauty. But Colombians saw on the covers of *Cromos* from 1919–1921 not French or American models but traditional and attractive examples of Spanish beauty, of Andalucian beauties wearing mantillas. Spanish beauty, graced by a lace scarf worn over the head and shoulders, represented Colombia's European and national roots, a beauty familiar and constant in an era of modern and technological change flowing from North America.[12]

While the covers of *Cromos* from 1921 to 1924 looked back to barefoot, rural women in garden or natural settings, diverse advertisements dominated about one-half of the pages inside the magazine, promoting imported modern beauty for sale. Weight-loss elixirs, wrinkle-removing cream, and hair tonic to restore vitality and cover gray packaged the young lean beauty of the 1920s. For those wary of or unfamiliar with the new products, Pepsodent offered free tubes of toothpaste, claiming that the product would remove film from teeth and brighten smiles. Articles about American movies and their stars revealed Colombian elite resistance to the new genre coming from a northern nation with little high culture. Stars like Mary Pickford, who as both leading actress and United Artists entrepreneur, representing Saxon beauty, were juxtaposed against French artists who claimed the cultural superiority of Latin beauty. In short, the 1920s proved to be an active and highly contested era of modern commercial beauty.[13]

But what was beauty and femininity in a modern contested milieu, and how was feminism understood in a Colombian environment? Male authors

VENDEDORAS DE FLORES
(Cleo de Roberto Pizano).

Cromos

Valor, quince centavos.
N.° 368 - Agosto 25 - 1923.

FIGURE 4.3   *Vendedoras de Flores,* Cromos *cover, Agosto 25, 1923, courtesy* Revista Cromos.

in 1923 argued that beauty was a gift from God, not a commercial product. Beauty was conditioned by harmony, equilibrium, and health; healthy skin needed only good nutrition and a little soap and water, not noxious creams. Because the face was the mirror to the soul, bad passions (envy, vanity, arrogance, ignorance) marred the face, robbing its natural beauty. Beauty inspired art, poetry, transcendence; it freed men from the spines in the road during their lives. Feminists, imaged in a North American guise, were counseled not to give away beauty in the rush to dress and act like men. To maintain their feminine attraction, women should remain delicate, tender, and sweet in their actions and expressions; if they acted male (assertive, rude, brusque, violent) they lost their enchanting power over men. Enchanting women were morally superior to men but shouldn't argue over politics, science, or art.[14] Similar arguments published in Cartagena in 1925 lectured women on the definition and politics of feminism, using logic, math, and grammar to assert male superiority over women.[15] In essence, these arguments maintained a separate but unequal sphere for women, beauty, and feminism, one complementary to men but subordinated to established male order.

Although conservatives desired the maintenance of an orderly, hierarchical past, economic innovations and international influences pushed toward modernization. Colombian coffee exports boomed in the early twentieth century; the country exported one million sixty-kilo bags in 1913, two million in 1921, and three million in 1930. By 1924, 80 percent of Colombia's export earnings came from coffee, a value six times higher than in 1898.[16] In 1921, Colombia ratified a treaty whereby the U.S. government agreed to pay Colombia twenty-five million dollars for its role in the loss of Panama in 1903. The indemnity increased the amount of gold in national banks by tenfold. Loans from Wall Street bankers increased liquidity, allowing the government to spend on infrastructure and public works projects. Imports tripled from 1923 to 1928, with unfinished textiles, toiletries, and musical instruments flooding in. By the mid-1920s, the Colombian peso was on par with the U.S. dollar; Colombia was the number-one gold producer in Latin America, number one in emerald production, number two in coffee production, and third in population in South America.[17]

A vibrant economy reinforced the growth of urbanization and modernization. A faster urban rhythm and the industrial engines and recorded music mixed with church bells and mule carts in developing cities. The moneyed class began seeking the quiet and health of suburban developments, leaving the din of the city behind. Big cities installed water purification plants; when Bogotá began adding chlorine to city water, typhoid mortality dropped from 250 to 50 per 100,000 inhabitants. Salaried work expanded, opening opportunities for social climbing to educated, well-dressed youth.[18]

But modernity and opportunity touched Colombia only in pockets, not broadly across the whole country, a pattern common in much of Latin America. While the coffee economy stimulated greater public works projects and more salaried jobs in Antioquia, Caldas, and Tolima, Cundinamarca and Santander experienced less dynamism. Although coffee emerged as the export motor of the national economy, most coffee growers lived in small, crowded single rooms without running water or latrines, ate poorly, and suffered from anemia and malaria. Landowners used debt peonage to hold indebted workers under their control. Political bosses and priests continued to exercise local power in much of the countryside, reinforcing traditional deference to superior power. If modernity is measured by individualism, merit, and expanding freedoms, then much of rural Colombia lived a social life more traditional than modern.[19]

The dialectic of tradition and modernity was most apparent in Antioquia and Medellín in the early twentieth century. Long a center of gold production, it added coffee as a revenue source and then became the center of Colombia's industrial enterprise. Textile mills, flour mills, and cigarette and cigar factories created great demand for young, single female workers, who worked for one-third to one-half the wages of male workers. Especially in textile factories in and around Medellín in the 1920s, women comprised 75 percent of the work force. Many young women migrated from rural areas to seek work in textile factories, a pattern similar to that of New England a century earlier, or to patterns of migration and employment inspired by Mexican maquilas in the late twentieth century. Medellín's population doubled from 1918 to 1938, from 80,000 to 168,000 inhabitants; 56 percent of the city's population was female, placing women on a very visible cutting edge of modern, industrial production.[20]

To manage this new gendered modernity, factory owners blended Catholic faith, hierarchy, discipline, and the patriarchal family as mechanisms for orderly and productive labor relations. In Medellín in 1912, Jesuits and elite women formed the Patronato de Obreras (Foundation for Female Workers), creating centers to reinforce traditional moral teachings and to warn young women of the evils of the secular world. Christian paternalism excluded married women from the workforce and was vigilant in seeking to protect single, young women from moral failure, thereby defending the model of the paternalistic family. Some factories mandated that women work barefoot, to decrease envy between the shod and the barefoot. A 1920 strike in Bello, an important textile center just north of Medellín, suggested that female workers weren't content with the traditional order; they struck for higher wages and the right to wear *alpargatas* (espadrilles of rope sole and a fibrous or cloth upper) on their feet at work and insisted that managers who sexually abused workers be fired. The Patronato responded with more attention to dorm rooms, home economics and sewing classes, and other activities to

FIGURE 4.4 *María Gómez (Medellín) 1913, Benjamín de la Calle, courtesy Biblioteca Pública Piloto de Medellín/ Archivo Fotográfico.*

FIGURE 4.5 *Matilde de Santa Teresa (Medellín) 1913, Benjamín de la Calle, courtesy Biblioteca Pública Piloto de Medellín/Archivo Fotográfico.*

FIGURE 4.6 *Enrica Espinelli (Italia) (Medellín) 1916, Benjamín de la Calle, courtesy Biblioteca Pública Piloto de Medellín/Archivo Fotográfico.*

FIGURE 4.7 *María Loaiza (Itagüí) (Medellín) 1918, Benjamín de la Calle, courtesy Biblioteca Pública Piloto de Medellín/Archivo Fotográfico.*

oversee and direct workers' free time. Ironically, or predictably, these centers of industry experienced stubborn resistance to modern freedom, reinforcing nineteenth-century morality and religion.[21]

Catholic bishops became stout defenders of order and morality, not only warning of the evils of liberalism, materialism, and communism, but also dictating dress codes for women. In 1927, the Bishop of Santa Rosa de Osos, about seventy kilometers north of Medellín, issued a pastoral letter warning of a hellish end for those women who dressed provocatively or immodestly. Modesty and shame, hallmarks of controlled women, were lost when women elegantly revealed more of their bodies. The bishop was particularly worried by women who dressed like men and who rode astride a horse, sins against custom, nature, and God. In 1930 the Vatican issued a worldwide directive to all bishops on modest female fashions, barring fashionable girls and women from Holy Communion and immodestly dressed godmothers from confirmation and baptism.[22] Dress codes remained vigilant for the next four decades, directed by religious leaders uneasy with modern challenges to orderly tradition, and by economic elites interested in imposing their social power over female employees.

Medellín's boosters presented a gendered vision of the city's progress. From their perspective, the male sector focused on transportation (ground travel to Bogotá took 50 hours; to Cali 67 hours; and to Pasto a whopping 233 hours), infrastructure, technology, urban development, business, civics, history, and social problems, while the female sphere focused on literature with photos of the new female authors. Allegorically, young women represented charity and humility for the city's independence celebrations in 1926.[23]

One of the city's new female authors emerged as a leading political organizer in the 1920s. María de Los Angeles Cano Márquez was born in Medellín in 1887, a member of an educated and politically active middle-class Radical Liberal family. In the open intellectual climate of her home, María read Enlightenment philosophy and humanistic literature from Balzac and Hugo. Industrial development in her hometown fixed her focus on social injustice, human suffering, and the abandonment of children and led her to collaborate with workers and explore socialist critiques of industrial capitalism. On May Day 1925, María Cano was selected "La Flor del Trabajo de Medellín" (The Labor Flower of Medellín), an honorific post usually centered on charity for workers and their families. But in María's hands, the post became a political platform from which to organize labor to challenge the structural conditions that kept workers poor.[24]

Although later championed as an early feminist, María Cano was more focused on class issues and socialist goals than on gender issues. However, as

"La Flor del Trabajo de Colombia" (The Labor Flower of Colombia), María undertook seven tours of the country from 1925 to 1927, through industrial and labor hot spots like the petroleum sector in Barrancabermeja, and the banana plantations of the Caribbean coast. Union activism led to strikes against the Tropical Oil Company in Barrancabermeja in 1927, and against the United Fruit Company in the banana sector the following year, both enclaves controlled by U.S. companies and attacked by María Cano as agents of Yankee imperialism. She successfully worked to free jailed union leaders, became a national labor leader and founder of the Partido Socialista Revolucionaria (PSR) in 1926, and was jailed a number of times for her political work. She retired from activism in the early 1930s following a bitter ideological split in Socialist ranks with the emergence of a Communist orientation.[25]

María Cano, the educated, active paisa, lived as a modern woman regardless of traditional restraints. In 1930 she wrote, "Between us, there is a norm that women lack their own criterion, and that they only act as a reflection of a priest, a father, or a friend. I think I've sufficiently shaped my own criterion to orient myself."[26] As an educated and self-aware person, she became a political agent for change and social justice. As the "Flower of Labor," she initially played an accepted social welfare role but then expanded that role to exercise greater political freedom to act outside traditional gender constraints, serving as a leader and resource for those seeking modern social, political, and economic change. Extolled later by women's groups in Medellín, María Cano reflected on her political work in 1960, saying, "Certain rights and liberties for women that we now recognize did not exist then. But then and now, the essential was and continues to be to mobilize the people; to awaken them from their stagnation; to line them up and put in their hands the flags of concrete tasks. And that women take their places!"[27] María died in 1967 at age 80, a modern active woman born into a country experiencing uneven modernization and dogged conservative retrenchment.

While Medellín's movie theaters in the late 1920s were dominated by U.S. releases from Paramount, MGM, and Warner Brothers, in Cali the highbrow crowd still wanted to see French films, leaving the Eddy Polo cowboy flicks to their social subordinates. Downtown, new water and sewer lines attracted nice shops around the plaza. The elite dressed finely to attend the opera, still sending their servants out to make necessary purchases. The first suburbs grew out from the city center, as did the first factories. At the movies, blonde, blue-eyed Pearl White dazzled viewers with her "fascinating beauty that left viewers breathless."[28] Caleños took pride in the fact that Spanish director Máximo Calvo shot his romantic film "María," based on the popular 1867 novel by Jorge Isaacs, at the Hacienda El Paraíso. Cali, like Medellín, was awakening to industrialization and modernization while preserving its class and color distinctions.

As a colonial and aristocratic city, Cartagena tended to look back to the past, ceding the modern future to Barranquilla, where shipping and port improvements made it the hub of North Coast modernity; from 1905 to 1938, Barranquilla grew faster than any other city in Colombia.[29] At a more deliberate pace, rituals in Cartagena in the 1920s surrounding the anniversary of October 12 and the November 11 independence celebrations framed how elites grounded the present in the past. October 12 is a powerful but contested day of memory in the Americas; seen as either Columbus Day, Día de la Raza, or later as Indigenous Peoples' Day, the day marks origins, cultures, race, and memory. October 12 sparks debates especially in diverse societies where memory is racially selective. In a 1924 newspaper article entitled "Making humanity better and more beautiful," the author suggested that eugenics, the study of human improvement through genetic control, would make humans more beautiful and moral by restricting marriage to the healthy, by tracing genealogical trees to clarify pedigree, and by performing obligatory autopsies to confirm cause of death so surviving family members might be saved from life-threatening conditions. The first two measures, especially in a city controlled by a small white elite and with a large black population, signaled elite fear of contact or mixing with darker social subordinates. The tradition of protecting white privilege, a hallmark of colonial social power relations throughout the Americas, found in eugenics a twentieth-century justification for the exclusion of nonwhites.[30]

Another article five years later, in 1929, framed October 12 as "El Día de la Raza" but with a decidedly pro-Spanish and non-Mexican twist. Arguing that races only grow and thrive with expansion, the author suggested that Latin Americans use the anniversary to celebrate Spanish heritage, not mestizo creation as in Mexico, thereby building the regional grandeur of Ibero-Americanism across national boundaries. This union of Latinos would then form a strong racial block of intelligence and spirit, presumably against the growing power of Anglo America.[31] The focus on Spain and Europe as the seed of civilization and identity reflected a traditional prowhite bias comfortable for Cartagena's newspaper readers. In this guise, the equation of "Spanish heritage plus race equals regional progress" necessarily reinforced traditional exclusionary social power.

The "Queen of the Students" symbolically reigned over the October 12 celebrations. Queens were expected to possess talent and grace and to lead fellow students by example into a better future with their wisdom, spirit, and intelligence. Queens encouraged honor, beauty, poetry, art, love, action, and a generous heart, and warned their subjects not to be sad, heavy, melancholic, weak, distrustful, or inactive. As an animating force and spiritual leader of the students, the queen demonstrated that with strength and tenacity, one could reach the peak of success. The Student Queen of Ibagué, Tolima, ordered independence celebrations in 1925 to benefit the lepers isolated near the Magdalena River at Agua de Dios, thus fulfilling her social welfare duties.[32] The ubiquitous queens of the 1920s, be they of students, labor, or sports, all served as examples of the socially desirable, momentary sovereigns reigning to animate subjects toward a better but ordered future.

Similar to the masquerade balls, dances, and parades of the October 12 festivities, the November 11 celebrations encouraged a carnivalesque, Mediterranean bacchanal. While writers continued to complain about the chaos, poor organization, and lack of patriotic zeal among the masses, the celebrations didn't center on the defiance of Spanish colonialism and the birth of Colombian national independence, instead focusing on the enchanted, magical, and transformative qualities of a four-day party. In 1927, Rudolph Valentino's film *The Sheik* inspired most of the costumes, with turbans, veils, and flashing eyes giving the night an intoxicating, crazy, and bewitching air. One man discovered on the morning of the 12th that the woman with whom he had spent his night, and on whom he had spent his money and whiskey, was indeed a man dressed as a woman.[33] Gender-bending, cause for concern among women for the Bishop of Santa Rosa de los Osos in Antioquia, was in Cartagena an amusing illustration of the freedom possible for men during specific moments in the city's annual calendar.

Beauty contests began in Colombia following World War I, stimulated by both local and international influences. In 1919, the Pictorial Review of New York sponsored a photographic competition of Colombian beauty, with *Cromos* covering the contest in Bogotá and *La Época* in Cartagena. Readers voted for the most beautiful candidate, who could be single or married, over a three-month period, a democratic exercise also good for circulation. In 1922, the magazine *La Bodegón* of Cartagena ran a similar photographic contest—without the later trappings of parades and swimsuits—the winner garnering 382,742 votes, requiring multiple and enthusiastic voting. These photographic beauty contests, popular in the United States since 1905, framed beauty in a visual, mass-circulated medium, a harbinger of twentieth-century developments.[34]

Initially promoted by hotel owners to boost the tourist trade, in 1921 the Miss America contest began in Atlantic City, New Jersey. Winner Margaret Gorman had been selected by readers in a newspaper beauty contest prior to the pageant. She bested the other seven girls from cities nearby Atlantic

City, most from fifteen to seventeen years of age. Nationwide newspaper coverage of the event made it a major event in the United States, increasing the number of contestants to seventy-five from across the nation by 1927. The Miss America contest enshrined the revealed body and exposed skin of the bathing beauty as the icon of modern beauty, commodifying women's bodies as the measure of gender, race, class, morality, and development for the viewing nation.[35]

Colombia did not immediately emulate pageants like the Miss America contest, underscoring the importance of culture and society in shaping historical evolution. In the United States, some women had gained the vote, mobilized to win the war in Europe, and thrown off some of the Victorian limitations on fashion and behavior. Feminists backed away from the stance of female moral superiority, while the business of beauty promised that all women could be, and should be, beautiful. Modernity was both liberating and limiting for U.S. women during much of the rest of the century.[36]

In Colombia, pockets of industry and modernity were reshaping fashion and gender relations, but change was widely dispersed and checked by powerful secular and religious institutions. Colombian women only enjoyed effective suffrage in the mid-1970s, while traditional perceptions of female moral superiority blunted the drive toward equality with men. Instead, where race and class divisions defined social life, Cartagena's decision to include a beauty queen in the 1920 independence celebrations was inspired by elite desires to select a queen from their ranks to preside over the popular mass audience, punctuation on the privilege of traditional social power.[37]

From postwar Paris, Colombia's verdant nature and mild, rich coffee dressed the stage of the Moulin Rouge in an exotic interpretation of Latin beauty on a coffee plantation. Some models wore oversized Zapatista hats, others wide hoopskirts, still others chic modern hats and cloaks hemmed at the thigh and leaving the legs bare, with the words "Suave de Colombia" (Soft Colombia) sewn on the back of the cloak. Paris's love for the natural, primitive, and savage, often coded racially black, opened its entertainment scene to American jazz and to the spectacular and alluring stage shows of Josephine Baker in the mid-1920s. Baker, the St. Louis–born Parisian expatriate, became a multifaceted rage in Europe by 1927: a celebrity stage and film star, journalist, and fashion icon. Being the only black woman to appear in *Cromos* during its first eleven years of publication, Baker was described as black, mulata (her father was Spanish), a more or less pure, more or less hybrid incarnation of a new race, of the new concept of beauty. Her beauty, talent, and fame presaged nobility and the transcendence of race. She received daily marriage proposals from counts, barons, dukes, and princes, not to mention mil-

FIGURE 4.8 *Grupo de Mujeres (Medellín) S.F. (~1930), Francisco Mejía,
courtesy Biblioteca Pública Piloto de Medellín/Archivo Fotográfico.*

lionaire industrialists and champion athletes. She made three million francs a year but spent six million, a super consumer of the modern age. As described in *Cromos*, she was the darling of Europe, the heavenly star of Paris, a symbol of modern internationalism and free sensuality.[38] As the woman of the day, Josephine Baker in a Colombian context was free, independent, desirable, and modern, while remaining a traditional symbol of the sexually available bronze beauty inherited from the ñapangas of the Cauca Valley or the morenas of the Caribbean coast.

By the late 1920s, New York pushed ahead of Paris in *Cromos* as the advertised leader of modern elegant fashion. French hats still held their own, but Hollywood actresses modeling American dress designs doubled the panache of New York fashions. By 1929, models and actresses from the United States supplanted French fashion dominance, reorienting the construction and geography of modern beauty toward the United States. Newspapers in Cartagena carried more national and international news from wire services, with U.S. movie and baseball stars gaining greater copy. Sweet, feminine voices over the radio hinted that the voices might flow from the beautiful body of a Californian actress. Studio photographers in Medellín posed young women who came to their studio to accentuate the look of 1920s modernity.

The mobilizations and catastrophes of the Great War shifted much of the world from traditional order toward modern change. By the 1920s, urban beauty in Colombia shifted toward international modernity, with more revealing fashions and mass-produced images from photographs, advertising, and motion pictures. Traditionalists railed against the perceived immorality of the freer behavior and modern fashions aided by a stubbornly conservative Catholic Church that imposed dress codes to preserve female modesty. However, many Colombians outside the modernizing cities dressed much as they had in the past. Queens, be they the politically assertive Queen of Labor María Cano or the energizing but socially conservative Queen of Students, could represent either modern freedom or traditional order. From mass media, advertising, and the booming United States consumer society came the modern beauty pageant, a model that took root in Colombia in succeeding decades. But the 1920s modern boom met its bust in the Great Depression after 1929, an international capitalist failure that stimulated political and social reforms in Colombia as it moved into the 1930s.[39]

The year 1930 marked an economic and political turning point for Colombia as it did for much of the world. The financial and industrial meltdown of the Great Depression lowered prices for Colombian exports, decreased government revenues, and dried up foreign loans. In the context of this economic shock, the half-century Conservative hold on the presidency ended as the governing party split, opening the presidential playing field to sixteen years of Liberal Party leadership. Colombian nationalism intensified, thanks to a border war with Peru, and in general, Colombians looked inward both as a response to international fracture and as an effort to shift the nation toward a more modern socioeconomic trajectory.[1] Colombian beauty similarly swung back to a national orientation, blunting for most of the 1930s the wave of internationally defined modernity that had dominated the previous decade.

The Conservative Party split in 1930 demonstrated the remarkable power wielded by the Catholic Church at the party's top levels. In previous Conservative Party disputes, the competing factions allowed the archbishop to arbitrate and settle disputes. But in 1930, Archbishop Perdomo, new to the post, vacillated between the two contenders until ordered by the Vatican to back the candidate supported by the existing government and the Conservative Party machinery. But eight bishops refused to toe the line, as divisions rippled down through the lower clergy and into their congregations. With the church and the party divided, Liberal candidate Enrique Olaya won the election of 1930, heralding the beginning of the "Liberal Republic" (1930-1946). Although some provincial parish priests still refused to give Communion to known Liberal voters, Liberals had mellowed from their past confrontational stance with the church. Some political violence erupted in the transition of government, as some Conservative officeholders only grudgingly relinquished their posts to entering Liberals.[2]

Although overshadowed by his successor, President Enrique Olaya Herrera (1930-1934) achieved some notable reforms. Olaya's administration implemented an eight-hour workday (still with a six-day workweek), granted labor's right to union organization, guaranteed married wives equitable property rights with husbands, and allowed female secondary schools to grant the degree required for future university admission. The latter two reforms raised howls of protest from conservatives bent on protecting the traditional patriarchal family. Increases in income taxes, banking and currency regulation, and nationalization of the public foreign debt all set the tone for forming a more centralized and activist state, a direction followed by the next three administrations.[3]

A successful border war with Peru in 1932–1933 over control of the Amazon port of Leticia stoked patriotic and nationalist sentiment. For once, Colombians weren't engaged in civil war but in defending their territory from an aggressive foreign neighbor. The activism and nationalism stimulated by the war reached individuals, municipalities, and social clubs around the nation, as patriots sent money and even family jewelry to the national government to pay for the war effort. Increased military spending during the war and tariff policies that encouraged import substitution industrialization—a trade and development policy to reduce dependency on foreign countries by producing industrial goods locally—helped Colombia recover from the initial economic shock of the Great Depression earlier than many countries.[4]

Although the war received some coverage, the big news in *Cromos* in 1932 was the organization of the first Miss Colombia contest. Repeated two years later and then in hiatus until 1947, the 1932 contest resulted from an invitation sent to the Colombian press to select a Colombian representative for the Miss Universe pageant in Spa, Belgium. Out of the ruins left by the Great War and the restructuring of Europe, the promoter behind Miss Universe, Maurice de Waleffe, started the Miss France contest in 1921 and Miss Europe in 1929. Roberto Pinto Valderrama, residing in Paris and a member of the Special Coffee Mission in Europe, forwarded de Waleffe's invitation to Colombia. The Colombian press was instructed to pick a woman eighteen to twenty-five years old, of good family and ancestry, and "a representative type of the highest society of the country," to be among the thirty international representatives invited first to Paris and then to Spa for the contest. The journalists accepted the offer and called on their colleagues and outstanding society leaders in department capitals to participate in a national effort to identify "honorable, handsome, and beautiful" candidates whose "dignity and noble demeanor" could win the contest.[5]

Photographs, interviews, and profiles of Colombian beauties dominated the pages of *Cromos* from April until the end of the year. The Hollywood studios' promotions of their films and stars faded from focus, as the Colombian press pursued a national search for the woman who would represent the nation to the larger world. By May, candidates and delegations from various

departments arrived in Bogotá, with dances, parties, and receptions organized around the city to honor and highlight various candidates. President
Olaya was photographed greeting Miss Valle, but it was Aura Gutiérrez Villa,
Miss Antioquia, who won the first title of Miss Colombia. Aura returned to
Medellín to a parade of four hundred cars that led her to the Club Unión for
a congratulatory reception. In Spa, she placed fifth among the six finalists, the
others all from European nations.[6]

The timing of the first Miss Colombia contest in 1932 merits comment.
Like the 1919 photographic competition, the organization of Miss Colombia
in 1932 sprang from international sources. The Miss Universe pageant, held
from 1926 to 1930 in Galveston, Texas, moved to Europe with the collapse of
the U.S. economy, and it was Colombian coffee promotions in Europe that
helped engender the invitation to Spa. Nationally, Liberal reforms pushed to
promote a more modern and national state as pageant candidates from various
departments vied to embody both modern beauty and traditional nobility.
Antioquia, the epicenter of encounters between modernity and tradition, and
the gold mining and industrial motor of 1930s Colombia, saw its candidate
place first.

Colombian beauty was emerging from under Hollywood's direct shadow
but still enjoyed some of the shade. While Colombian identity was reasserted
in the 1930s, modernity implied an ongoing dialogue with international
trends. A Spanish-language film release from MGM, *Sevilla, de mis amores*,
starring and directed by Ramón Novarro, wove the technological sophistication of American cinema with the new sound technology that allowed
Colombian viewers to have a more culturally familiar experience, even if the
film originated in Culver City, California. That film and the Colombian embrace of Spanish beauty made mantillas and sevillaña attire a popular party
look throughout the 1930s. The eight-hour workday allowed more leisure
time, so there was the option, given disposable income, to partake of films,
sports, and music. By the 1930s, the way of life and beauty defined in U.S.
films became the model for the aspiring middle class. In Bogotá, Sunday became the day of rest, relaxation, and recreation even as church bells tolled
from the tower, a tradition still enjoyed today. More bogotanos made the
annual five-hour trek to Útica during December vacations to enjoy its warmer
climate. More social freedom and contact with imported material culture,
whether in sports clothes, matinees, or foreign automobiles, opened hope for
some urban women that they might soon gain greater personal freedom and
social ascension.[7]

The pace and intensity of Liberal reforms increased with the administration of Alfonso López Pumarejo (1934–1938) and his "Revolución en

Marcha," which placed social and labor issues center stage. Like Franklin Delano Roosevelt, López was a patrician with a heart, who worried about the political and social cost of ignoring the mass of illiterate, hungry, barefoot, and marginalized Colombians. Reforms during his administration included the nation's first agrarian reform law in 1936, one that included a redefinition of property rights to include property's social function to the larger society, allowing for the expropriation of private property for the social good. López asserted the state's authority in education over that of the Catholic Church, making schooling obligatory and asserting the right of all children, including those children born to unwed mothers, to an education. The elimination of literacy requirements opened political participation to all adult males, but both the Liberal and Conservative parties shied away from enfranchising women. Higher taxes on unproductive large estates and on foreign firms like United Fruit reinforced national sovereignty and shifted some income toward rural and social development.[8] Like his contemporaries Getúlio Vargas in Brazil and Lázaro Cárdenas in Mexico, López Pumarejo became a champion of the working class, an ally of labor, and a leader of a socially active and modernizing state.

Mirroring the politics of the "Revolución en Marcha," modern beauty in mid-1930s focused on athletic women participating in competitive sports. Basketball appeared most commonly, with young team members photographed in matching uniforms. Queens of sports replaced the stylized photographs of pageant candidates run prior to the 1932 Miss Colombia contests, with Hollywood starlets also fading from view. Mass culture and mass politics both echoed the goals of mobilization, organization, competition, and public participation. Cartagena hosted the 1934 Miss Colombia contest, but the event received little attention from the Bogotá press. Cartagena was marking its four hundredth anniversary and wanted to boost tourism, while Bogotá focused more on modern reforms.[9] The Miss Colombia contest ceased until 1947 as the Great Depression and rising tensions in Europe ended the international pull from the Miss Universe pageant. Moreover, Colombians had reason to believe that the social and political reforms being pursued might yield a more inclusive and just nation, making the selection of a symbolic sovereign unnecessary.

Cromos readers in 1935 got a dose of social realism in a photojournalism series run that year. Editions often juxtaposed photos of young unmarried elite women with stark photos of rural poverty and urban marginalization. Photographs of young children in tattered clothes, the barefoot unemployed resting on the cathedral stairs, gaunt women begging on the street—images that most bogotanos took for granted—gained higher relief when arranged on a single page and in the context of the Revolución en Marcha. The beauty of elite refinement and the crude reality of poverty lived in the same society but in different social worlds. That chasm was the one that worried López. Rural scenes on the *sabana* (savanna) around Bogotá or of market day in Boyacá presented a picture of solid and hardworking people, most wearing ruanas, Colombian ponchos viewed as a social marker of the rural poor.[10]

The marketing of fashionable ruanas for urban women represented an interesting geographic and social transformation of Colombian national fashion. These ruanas, sporting bright colors and fine fabric, included stylish collars, buttons at the top front, and matching caps. The ruana had left its rural and rough roots to become a sophisticated and original piece of modern, urban fashion. It was versatile, practical, and elegant, designed and made in Colombia, and striking distinctly nationalist chords; this was no foreign copy, but a truly original Colombian addition to fashion.[11] Although originally marketed to elite women, the ruana represented the social leveling implicit in the Revolución en Marcha, as it boosted Colombian national pride. In the democratic and nationalist climate of the mid-1930s, the chic feminine ruana symbolized a nation's encounter with itself.

Twentieth-century urban culture evolved with coffee culture, industrialization, infrastructure modernization, and mass media. Bogotá had an estimated population of 235,000 in 1930, Barranquilla at 140,000, Cali at 125,000, and Medellín at 119,000 inhabitants. Nineteen other secondary cities counted over 30,000 people, and thirty-three had over 10,000.[12] Colombia was becoming a nation of cities, most in Andean regions with access to the Magdalena or Cauca rivers. Piped water to upper- and middle-class neighborhoods of Bogotá allowed bathing at home, making trips to the bathhouses unnecessary for those residents who enjoyed water service. Urban sophistication also led to a crackdown on *chicherías* in Bogotá starting in the 1920s. *Chicha*, a homemade corn beer, and the three hundred chicherías in the city, drew the ire of temperance advocates and the Catholic Church, both interested in halting or limiting the hours and locations of chicha sales and consumption. In the first four months of 1929, thirsty working-class consumers polished off seven million liters of chicha, compared with only 496 bottles of brandy. The chichería, a rural cultural space in the midst of modernizing cities, appeared to be a threat to both social and moral order, and lacked the refinement of bottled and taxed brews and spirits. By the 1940s, chicha was seen as a "social disease."[13]

Gender roles also displayed the tension between tradition and modernity. The iconic image of the Virgin Mary still defined the traditional feminine values of celibacy, modesty, and self-sacrifice. The founding of twenty-six new female religious orders between 1929 and 1948, almost doubling the total of all female religious orders in Colombia, signaled a growing attraction to schools or convents led by nuns; male religious orders only increased by four during the same period.[14] Opposite to the uniforms, habits, and order of convents and Catholic schools for girls, the negative image of the "mala mujer" found more space on the streets and in public life. The "bad woman" was symbolically defined by Eve, whose independence, curiosity, and search for knowledge introduced to the world sin, pain, sex, and death. With modern progress tending more in Eve's direction, the cloak of the Virgin Mary promised protection and purity from the sexual activity and the male gendered behavior of Eve. But in urban areas, prostitution, venereal disease, modern female fashions, and erotic images of women all were common. Municipal tolerance and regulation of prostitution in cities like Medellín in the 1920s begot the creation of clinics for venereal disease, centers for the control and regulation of public women, and prophylactic institutes. By the 1930s, gender-bending elites signaled public knowledge of homosexuality and a third sex, expanding the dualism of sex to wider expressions of sexuality and gender.[15] In short, church-based gender roles collided with the freedom and sexual expression opened by the individualism, liberation, and volition of modern society.

Joining cinema from early in the century, radio broadcasts brought Colombia greater communication with itself and facilitated interactions with a wider world. Elite radio owners initially listened in to radio shows from the United States, Mexico, Cuba, and Buenos Aires. But the number of transmitters in Colombia increased rapidly in the 1930s, growing from seventeen in 1934 to seventy by 1941. More radio broadcasts, serviced by towers on mountain ridges, could knit together inhabitants in formerly isolated mountain valleys into a larger regional and national culture. Although the number of radio sets remained small in the 1930s, exploding with transistor radios in the 1960s, the building of national mass media had begun. Radio theater and coverage of sports and politics took off in the 1930s. The 1935 "breaking news" radio coverage from Medellín of the plane crash and death of Argentine tango superstar Carlos Gardel initiated radio journalism in Colombia, demonstrating the on-the-spot power of modern media.[16]

Interviewed on the radio from the Hotel Americano in Cartagena, doña Amirita I addressed her subjects about the duties and protocol of being their queen. From the San Diego district of Cartagena, Amirita Mouthón bested five other contestants from competing neighborhoods to be named queen of the 1937 independence celebrations. She received the most votes, and her committee raised double the money to support the festivities as did the second-place finisher. Amirita played the role of the benevolent sovereign, denying that feminine pride or social concerns fueled her drive for the crown, stating instead that the crown "symbolizes the glories of the past and the noble yearning for the material and moral aggrandizement of my home region."[17] While both embodying and personally transcending her role as queen, Amirita did what local sovereigns often do: won an election to gain a coveted post, raised energy and money in the community for the common good, and effectively connected pride in the past to a positive vision for the future.

As Europe once again erupted into world war, Cartagena's press and the November festivities focused outward. By 1939, the war in Europe, American football, and Hollywood stars regained newspaper columns. The most popular and original parade float that year came from Lucky Strike, the U.S. cigarette brand. Dances in movie houses and theaters remained popular, with females paying one-half the admission fare of males. By 1943, higher municipal and national taxes on dances threatened to halt this popular diversion, but some enterprising theater owners simply dropped admission rates, both to attract a larger audience and to pay lower taxes.

In the North Coast region, Barranquilla was clearly outshining Cartagena, attracting more industry, business, migrants, and better-developed social events. In November 1941, Barranquilla hosted the national Olympic Games, complete with an elite court and enchanting lady of high society, Atlántico department queen Jacqueline Smith, to open the games.[18] Beauty, sports, class, and national measures were no longer focused on traditional leader Cartagena, now outgrown by its upstart modernizing neighbor, Barranquilla. Cartagena only managed to shift beauty and class leadership back home after 1947, when it reinstated the Miss Colombia pageant.

Selecting queens to represent and promote modern sports remained popular in Cartagena and in Cali. The election of the "Queen of Basketball" in Cartagena in 1941 raised both popular participation and media coverage for the election and for the sport. In Cali, the Jantzen apparel company sponsored the Jantzen Basketball Team, supplying shorts, tank tops, and warm-ups for the team from a local retail distributor. The first women's basketball and soccer teams emerged in the late 1930s and early 1940s, with queens of those sports chosen from amongst teammates. Improved sports facilities and the organization of sports federations created the structure for larger sports audiences and greater mass appeal. But the queen was a necessary element in the spectacle to feminize a largely male-gendered competition.[19]

Dichotomous images of beauty and the organization of pageants in Medellín signaled that city's development as an emerging national leader. Photographs of prominent young women published in *Progreso* juxtaposed the wholesome innocence of single girls with more sensuous poses of young married women. This juxtaposition of "the girl next door" with the siren both reinforced the appeal of sex and reinforced the traditional notion that only married women should revel in their sexuality. Pageants to select queens of Antioqueño sports, civics, university students, and "La Raza" reinforced the belief that something naturally special set paisas apart from other Colombians. A call from the national Society of Public Improvements (Sociedades de Mejoras Públicas) to elect a national Queen of Public Spiritedness (Reina Nacional de Civismo) reveals some of the mechanics and problems encountered in such a venture. Twelve articles established the rules of the game for reinado elections, selections, expenses, and profit sharing. The election of queens was by vote, but each society and voter had to pay to play: the funds to pay for the roundtrip journey to the pageant, with the excess profits distributed among the various societies in each department. Aspiring queens and their supporters were reminded not to hound merchants, industrialists, or professionals for votes, allowing room for those elites to make their own decisions. Some candidates refused to participate; others waffled, while lack of coordination between social clubs and sports leagues yielded only two potential princesses, so the local society invited other potential candidates to participate. Perhaps the process was too cumbersome, maybe the title "Reina Nacional de Civismo" failed to strike an emotional chord, and probably young candidates had better things to do.[20]

For Medellín's boosters and business elites, air travel represented the technology that would knit the country together. Medellín's centrality relative to Cali, Bogotá, and Barranquilla facilitated rapid transportation of people and goods, reinforcing Medellín's reputation for being the commercial and industrial hub of Colombia. One could fly to Bogotá or Cali in less than ninety minutes, or take ground transportation and spend a day and a half in transit. Via road or river, it took four days to reach Cartagena, but just two hours by air, costing only one-third more than ground travel. Some places could only be reached by air, like Turbo, Medellín's port outlet on the Caribbean adjacent to Panama. Airplanes promised the machinery necessary to lift elites over Colombia's diverse and difficult geography, enhancing their power and privilege but also introducing the larger nation into their consciousness.[21]

Educational advancement also promised greater polish, technical training, and critical inquiry. Women were now admitted to some universities, but their numbers and those of total university students remained small until the 1960s. In 1937, about 60 percent of all Colombians remained illiterate, with higher rates in rural areas. Only Antioquia, Caldas, and Valle del Cauca could boast illiteracy rates lower than 50 percent for both men and women. In Boyacá and Cauca, illiteracy levels for women topped 70 percent. Given the norm of illiteracy in much of the county, to be educated, literate, and technically trained became a crucial social marker of mobility. Pedagogy included lessons on appearance and social grace, refining the performance of modern sophistication with emphases on materialism and decorum. For women in the late 1930s and early 1940s, business school offered the most obvious technical and social skills for future employment, so females dominated the student body in both public and private business schools.[22] Presumably, lessons on appearance and comportment were also vital components in the education of these young women.

The pace of reform slowed during the administration of Eduardo Santos (1938-1942), although economic policy was more robust than under López. Keynesian deficit spending and public investment in foundational industries both helped the economy survive a stubborn depression and laid the groundwork for later industrial development. War was again raising its ugly head in 1937-1938, with the Japanese invasion of China, the Italian invasion of Ethiopia, and the Spanish Civil War all serving as rehearsals for the Second World War. The tracking of international events reopened Colombia to international beauty images and products, with Hollywood beauties and a plethora of beauty products dominating more of the pages and columns of *Cromos*. An update of the magazine's layout in 1939 signaled that *Cromos* was now pitching to younger consumers, especially females, as tips and secrets on how best to use beauty products to enhance one's looks dominated more of the magazine.[23]

The impending war in Europe set the social calendar in Bogotá in November 1938. A costume ball at the Club Alemán competed with the costume ball at the French Legation while the Italian Legation and community commissioned a bust of Marconi for the city. As during the Great War a generation before, Colombian elites demonstrated their cultural and national affinities for competing European powers at social ceremonies. Perhaps dressing up like a Bavarian milk maid or an Alsatian woman was just good fun, but the carefully crafted costumes also revealed a desire to take a side in the distant drama unfolding in Europe.[24]

While Europeans began to line up in uniform for war, Colombians lined up in uniform for sports. Men's and women's basketball teams from Bogotá and Medellín competed for top honors in the country, while the men's subchampion in soccer from Atlántico signaled Barranquilla's rising national stature. While the fallout from WWI and the Great Depression led Europe toward catastrophe, marketing promised the extinction of ugliness to female readers of *Cromos*. If, as the magazine article implied, beauty is about how you present yourself and since beauty is relative and changeable, with fashion, makeup, and well-managed proportions, anyone could be pretty. The ugly woman became one who did nothing to be pretty. But beauty was not enough, according to a 1940 Colgate toothpaste ad run in *Cromos*. You might be the prettiest girl at the dance, but if you had bad breath, boys would flee. After a trip to the dentist and a tube of Colgate, that concerned girl becomes the prettiest and most popular at the party.[25] Within a year, *Cromos* readers saw the announced extinction of ugliness and the lesson that being beautiful was not enough, messages that made beauty available to anyone but also insufficient without merchandising.

Full-blown world war in the early 1940s produced a clearly defined gender order: war, death, and destruction, male; sex, beauty, and glamour, female. Advertisers focused on pitching beauty products to women, when males were absent or when big-ticket items, like automobiles, weren't being manufactured. Juxtaposed with the photographs of armies, weapons, planes, and ships, *Cromos* ran lots of photos of Hollywood glamour girls and of beauty queens from Texas, Florida, and California. Many of the photos were alluring, even erotic, often featuring a slim, busty young woman stretched out on her back, awaiting the embrace and imagination of the viewer. Sex symbols like Jane Russell pushed the censorship limits in films like Howard Hughes's *The Outlaw*. Blondes reemerged as a fascination, with the verbiage of sex appeal adding "oomph" and "pin-up" to the established "it" and "glamour" as signifiers of market worth and mass sex appeal. With Europe closed or uninviting because of the war, Colombians increasingly headed to the United States for business, travel, or university education. When Colombian beauty appeared, it was in the context of a social event in Medellín or Cali, or in the selection of the Carnival queen in Barranquilla. Once again, as the world's leading powers clashed in war, Colombian beauty reopened to international influences.[26]

Comparisons and characteristics of blondes, brunettes, and redheads both taught and revised stereotypes about female appearance and nature. Although diversity of female hair, eye, and skin color was not new to Colombia, the blonde/brunette/redhead triangle bounced modern diversity off northern European parameters. Opinion polls of Colombian youth in May 1941, patterned after similar polls given to German, English, and North American youth, sought to track what seemed to be a generational shift in western civilization. Although the sample was tiny and unscientific, Colombian males tended to be more critical of the past generation and more cynical about politics and international affairs, while females were more deferential to their elders while still wanting to be free and independent. To the question, "Should America participate in the war?" respondents interpreted "America" to mean Colombia, Latin America, or the Americas, not as the United States of America.[27]

After the United States entered the Second World War in late 1941, Colombian beauty felt the reverberations. Max Factor Hollywood promoted products that purportedly delivered beauty from another world. This new world, courtesy of the laboratories of Max Factor Hollywood, "the Mecca of world cinema," offered ingenious chemistry, surprising and experimental cosmetology, and new styles of makeup, promising the user the enchanting and fascinating beauty of movie stars. Users were asked to economize use of these indispensable products until victory in the war delivered joy and peace. The tag line at the bottom of the print ad branded Max Factor as the "cosmetics of the stars," one where "estamos unidas . . . todas las Américas" (we are united, all the Americas), a nice play on Estados Unidos (United States), the wartime leader of pan-Americanism and the home of otherworldly Max Factor. By 1943, Colombia entered into belligerency status with Germany after U-boats sank a Colombian schooner. Subsequent shortages of women's stockings became an issue in elite women's fashions. With silk stockings disappearing and nylon stockings scarce because of wartime demand, women could revert to coarse and bulky wool stockings or use makeup to simulate nylons. In climates like those of Bogotá, to leave legs bare in the cold air risked continuous viral colds. It seemed that women's stockings had become such requisite fashion apparel that women in Bogotá could not support a strike against the high price and scarcity of stockings.[28] Although this wartime "non-story" lacked substance, it did suggest that Colombia was part of the war environment even if it was not an active participant.

The pull of Hollywood and the U.S. war effort offered clear advantages and cautionary lessons. Hollywood's branch of the Office of Inter-American Affairs opened jobs at NBC and CBS for Colombian radio personality "Aramis" (Carlos Gutiérrez Riaño) to work with Veronica Lake, Linda Darnell, and Bing Crosby. The six-month job stretched into two years of work, with "Aramis" photographed surrounded by the day's stars, and shown directing the radio show "Juventud de las Américas" (Youth of the Americas). In this case, supporting the United States opened hemispheric doors of access. But the peculiar and tormented history of race relations in the United States opened a stark contrast with much of Latin America. An article in *Cromos* suggested that Spanish American emancipation during its independence wars erased the "Negro Problem," whereas emancipation long after the establishment of the republic firmly planted it within U.S. society. Although the complex histories of slavery and race were simplified in this contrast, in this case Spanish America was the leader, the United States the follower. *Cromos* noted that wartime U.S. society experienced greater racial tension—white prisoners at San Quentin refused to take meals with black inmates—but that propaganda photographs often included blacks mixed with whites to accustom whites to working with blacks. Interestingly, *Cromos* ran a photograph of Lena Horne, identified as *blanca*, next to Hazel Scott, identified as *negra*, to illustrate this pattern, even though Horne was imaged as a black woman in the United States. While intermixing had reduced the size of the black population in Spanish America, the U.S. black population had remained constant at 10 percent of the total population since the Civil War, an illustration of different cultural definitions of race and the wide abyss between white and black society in the United States. In terms of race relations, Colombia appeared more progressive than the United States, where even the illusion of makeup could not easily blur the color line.[29]

In both the United States and Colombia, one way to address the shortages of silk underwear and stockings, hair spray, and makeup was to incorporate feminine beauty into the war effort. In November 1941, Miss National Defense, a bathing beauty selected at Venice Beach, California, toured all U.S. military bases on the eve of Pearl Harbor. By October and November 1943 in Cartagena, beauty contests proliferated, with notable additions of queens of local navy bases and of the national Colombian navy. This was traditional queen season in Cartagena, but the inauguration of the Reina de la Armada Nacional pageant resulted from that queen being pulled out of the Reina de Todos los Barrios contest because of some unspoken conflict over money and distribution of proceeds. The first queen of the exclusive Reina de la Armada Nacional pageant attracted three times the votes and money than did the winner of the more inclusive and popular Reina de Todos los Barrios contest, suggesting the attractive power for civilian and military elites of segregating themselves from the popular as they endowed beauty with national and martial symbolism.[30]

A series of Gem razor blade ads run in Cartagena's press in November 1944 brought the sexual politics from a U.S. setting to beauty queen–mad Cartagena. The illustrated ad showed a young, curvaceous woman in the arms of an older man, perhaps her boss, date, or local cop. She was attracted to him because his smooth face showed no sign of five o'clock shadow and the rough bristles that would grate against her soft face. So the message of the ad was clear: to catch the babe, older men had to smooth and groom their appearance. If women's fashions had shifted toward a more masculine norm a generation earlier, the Gem blade ad suggested a feminizing of male facial texture to win female favor.[31]

On a more political note, Colombian women used the liberal space opened after 1930 and the emerging global goals coming out of WWII to push for greater equality. In 1930, Georgina Fletcher organized a congress in Bogotá to discuss divorce and prenuptial agreements. By 1936, the first women were admitted to Colombian universities. In 1944, Lucila Rubio de Laverde became the first woman to address Congress as the spokesperson for the Unión Femenina de Colombia. Rubio de Laverde subsequently used the Charter of the United Nations, whose preamble includes equal rights for men and women, as the basis to push for full legal and political rights for women in Colombia, including the right to vote. She published a book to share her vision, one that included her insights on how Colombia had changed in the previous decades. Rather than getting a basic education and marrying early, women now had the choice to study longer, marry later, bear fewer children, and work outside the home. For Rubio de Laverde, the Hollywood girls helped Colombian women become more assertive, even if both had to watch their weight and shave their legs. When she took her children to see the animated movie "Snow White," her son cried after Snow White was poisoned, illustrating the power of modern media but also the room left for capable mothers to teach their children about the beauty and love flowing from the supreme creator.[32] Once again, the modern and the traditional danced through the transition to a postwar world.

By 1946, the tide of Liberal reforms had long since ebbed. Price inflation and stagnant wages raised economic difficulties in cities. The Liberal party split, as had the Conservatives in 1930, opening the door to the opposition. The Liberal party machinery backed the moderate Gabriel Turbay while Jorge Eliécer Gaitán led the more activist wing of the party. Gaitán, the non-elite from a lower-middle-class economic background, had transformed urban politics in Colombia by closing the gap between politicians and common people, attacking oligarchs in both parties who played politics for their own ends as they blocked effective reforms. With the Liberals divided, the Conservative candidate won the 1946 election, ending Liberal governance.[33]

The Señorita Colombia pageant in Cartagena reemerged in 1947 as the focus on societal reform and the Second World War faded from view. Contestants from competing departments now dominated the cover of *Cromos*, displacing the Hollywood stars at least momentarily. *Cromos* gave the event lavish coverage, starting in September with the selections of departmental queens, through November with the selection of the national sovereign. Urban newspapers like *El Relator* of Cali and *El Tiempo* of Bogotá sent reporters to Cartagena to cover the contest, with stories mainly tracking the local favorite and her entourage. Hometown favorite Piedad Gómez won the title of Miss Colombia, even after refusing to appear in a bathing suit upon request of her archbishop. Shapely Miss Tolima, who pushed for the bathing suit contest, became the crowd favorite, and when she was not selected as the winner, the crowd outside protested. The judges restored order by quickly naming her Queen of the Sea (Reina del Mar), arranging for her return to Cartagena some months later to preside over a baseball tournament. Most candidates adopted the New Look of Christian Dior and the wavy hair of Katharine Hepburn. Six thousand people greeted the queens as they arrived at the airport, fifteen hundred attended the pageant, and three thousand tourists overwhelmed the city's hotel capacity.[34] The modern mass diversion from Colombian reality, the one that would dominate the rest of the twentieth century, had begun.

Nonetheless, political mobilizations continued through 1947 and 1948. Gaitán, now the clear leader of the Liberal Party, chaired a convention to discuss equal political status for women, including the first steps toward female suffrage. The Conservatives countered by following Pope Pius XII's lead of enfranchising women to block the advance of communism (in Italy) and to gain female favor for the Conservatives in Colombia so they would vote against Liberal reforms. Beyond political mobilizations, political violence erupted in 1947 as it had in 1930 with the transfer of government from one party to the other. Gaitán led a large silent protest march against political violence and as a show of political strength in February 1948 in the Plaza de Bolívar, Bogotá's main plaza. Gaitán seemed to be the sure Liberal party candidate for president in 1950.[35]

Through the first four months of 1948, Colombian candidates for the 1947 Miss Colombia pageant dominated the cover of *Cromos*. Bogotá was described as a city of peace, Medellín as a city in love with itself. But then on April 9, 1948, Gaitán was assassinated in downtown Bogotá by an unknown gunman. The dreams of a new leader connected to the real struggles of urban Colombia died with Gaitán. Mobs suspected that Conservatives were behind the killing and sought vengeance, rioting in downtown neighborhoods. The office of *Cromos* was burned and no editions of the magazine circulated for one month. When *Cromos* reemerged in May and June, readers saw photo spreads of destroyed downtown neighborhoods, social shots of Colombian beauties (often unsmiling and tense) in indoor locations, and Hollywood stars back on the cover. The violence sparked by "el nueve de abril" (April 9) made the streets and the public sphere, which had shaped Gaitán into a popular icon, dangerous terrain to tread.[36]

Once the Cali daily *El Relator* restarted printing its newspaper on April 12, reports tracked and interpreted the violent fallout of Gaitán's assassination west and south of the capital. The paper blamed the violence of April 9 on

FIGURE 5.1 *Tense Reinas, post-Bogotazo,* Cromos *cover, Junio 26, 1948, courtesy* Revista Cromos.

a communist uprising and noted that Colombia had broken diplomatic re-lations with Russia [sic]. By the twelfth, calm had been restored in Bogotá, but Gaitán's assassination wasn't even mentioned in the page one story. A page seven follow-up noted a "commotion" in Manizales following the news of Gaitán's killing. Over the next two days, the paper reported that Cartago was under military occupation, Buenaventura sacked, and Puerto Tejada torn apart. In Puerto Tejada, prominent Conservatives had been murdered and decapitated, Liberals playing soccer with the severed heads in the main plaza. Popayán experienced violence, forty were dead in Ibagué, and troops patrolled areas of Caldas, Antioquia, and Cauca searching for troublemakers.[37]

Liberal, modernizing reforms turned Colombian beauty inward in the 1930s, as athletic and uniformed beauty displaced international celebrities from popular magazines. From a Europe rebuilding out of World War I and in the midst of the Great Depression came the initial spark to host the Miss Colombia pageant in 1932, held again in 1934 mainly to honor Cartagena, but thereafter the pageant slumbered until 1947. Interestingly, wars in Europe set the stage for national and international pageants, but Colombians didn't need them when effective national reforms made symbolic sovereigns unnecessary. Once reforms ebbed as political violence flowed, pageants regained importance in Colombia. The killing of Gaitán and el nueve de abril riots, like those across U.S. cities twenty years later following the assassination of Martin Luther King Jr. in April 1968, were about more than an isolated killing in one location, but about popular rage erupting after the taking of a leader who promised to change the rules of the game to make politics and society more inclusive, representative, and just. The assassination of Gaitán ended the elite bipartisan governance that dominated most of the first half of the twentieth century, and formally opened the next era in Colombian history: that of La Violencia, the capital "V" Violence that would dominate the next decade. That breakdown of elite politics and popular and partisan civil war placed beauty and pageants center stage as the symbolic, nonpartisan, civic, and peaceful ritual of positive Colombian national identity. Beauty and the beast joined in a passionate tango, each partner with proscribed steps, with neither able to part from the other for the rest of the twentieth century.

Chapter 6

EXCLUSIVE BEASTS, 1948–1958

Between 550 and 2,600 Colombians died countrywide in the violence sparked by Gaitán's murder.[1] The day after his death, Liberals agreed to reenter a coalition government with Conservatives, a position they maintained for the next year until Congress was closed in 1949. As Conservatives asserted their power, Liberals were purged from institutions like the judiciary and the police, politicizing both those institutions along partisan lines and leaving Liberals distrustful of Conservative law and order. Violence and disrespect for the law dominated this first stage of La Violencia, from 1946 to 1953, with partisanship fueling the dynamics of the violence and killing. Colombia had the highest homicide levels in Latin America from 1950 to 1980, before those levels tripled in the 1980s and early 1990s.[2] Modern Colombia's deserved reputation for violence stems from the fracturing of the state after 1948 in the midst of socioeconomic modernization; government came apart just when it needed to become more robust and inclusive.

President Ospina could count on Conservative support in the waning years of his government and enjoyed support from the army and the Truman administration in Washington, DC, which imaged partisan violence through a Cold War lens. But as political order fractured, party elites had little direction or control over local guerrilla leaders. The distance between the political class and the people, which Gaitán sought to bridge, widened with the violence. The local dynamics of violence ruled many areas as people fought for land, especially in coffee country, over political scraps in poor areas, or became opportunistic or survival bandits as normal life broke down. Liberals who converted to Protestant faiths faced a double threat of attack on both partisan and religious grounds. Ironically, as the country stumbled through a state of siege, the economy grew by about 5 percent annually from 1949 to 1958, a period of notable economic growth including import substitution industrialization. The violence and the poverty of the countryside pushed migrants to the growing and more productive cities. The urban population of Colombia increased from 39 percent in 1951 to 52 percent in 1964, years when violence and lack of opportunity defined rural life as cities promised a better future.[3]

The uncontested election of ultraconservative Laureano Gómez for the 1950–1954 presidential term marked a formal end of bipartisan elite governance, as fashioned by Núñez and Reyes in decades past, and the beginning of a particularly ugly phase of violence. Liberals claimed that they could not run candidates nor participate in elections given partisan attacks and perceived the Gómez government as illegitimate. Gómez, a personal friend of the Liberal reformer López Pumarejo, was the pessimistic shadow side of Gaitán; whereas Gaitán optimistically trusted the power of the people, Gómez argued that only a rigidly hierarchical society and government could direct the racial and geographic confusion of Colombia. A Hispanist, corporatist, and Falangist Catholic, Gómez governed as the Roman Catholic Church under Pius XII followed a strongly anticommunist line, one allowing clerics and Conservatives to paint Liberal opposition as pro-communist. Liberals organized guerrilla bands and attacked the government and its supporters while progovernment vigilantes acted as occupying armies in contested terrain. Most of the violence was rural and raged in pockets of the Llanos, the eastern fringe of the Cordillera Oriental, south of Bogotá in the Sumapaz, in various locations in Antioquia, and in coffee zones in Tolima and Caldas. Conversely, the northern Caribbean coast and deep south Nariño escaped most of the tumult. Some one hundred to two hundred thousand people died in this intensely charged period of the early 1950s.[4]

Gómez pushed an industrial program that mixed paternalistic state oversight of business and labor, government subsidies for investors, and repression of independent unions. Workers were to enter into solidarity with their employers and industrial owners were encouraged to share profits with workers. Yet given recent history and a Cold War setting, business leaders imaged political mobilization, like that practiced by Gaitán, as a threat to social and economic order. Loans from the World Bank and the U.S. Export-Import Bank for infrastructure improvements joined electoral demobilization, control of unions and repression, and state agency in industrial development as aspects of the ultraconservative elite order of Gómez.[5]

Violence and political breakdown opened room for both social engineering and promotion of alternative mass spectacles that were nonpartisan. The long history of the chicherías in Bogotá neared its end in early 1949, when a new law stipulated that beer had to be bottled and contain less than 4 percent alcohol. Chicha could not be served where food was, and only people over twenty-one years of age could legally enter chicherías. Chicha consumption was crippled within six months as it was labeled a "social disease." The working class customers of chicherías, the prototypical plebe of Gaitán, lost both their leader and their homemade and cheap corn beer. Cabrito beer filled the cheap beer niche, advertised as a low-priced but healthy and nutritious beer, complete with a drawing of a campesino wooing a campesina, both in ruanas, hats, and alpargatas, symbols of their rural highland roots. She was demure and pretty in her pollera skirt, he was confident with a liter of Cabrito in his right hand as his left touched her ruana-covered arm. The simple but powerful visual message that beer brings confidence, appeal, and romance was clearly accessible to viewers with little or no education.[6]

Mass spectator sports emerged in the early years of La Violencia, stimulated both by the worldwide sports craze of the post-WWII period, and by Colombia's unique predicament. Professional soccer emerged in 1948, with Colombian teams fielding famous Argentine players thanks to a national strike in Perón's Argentina. The first bicycle race around Colombia, the "Vuelta a Colombia" began in 1951; soccer and bicycle racing remained very popular in Colombia for the rest of the century. Mass spectator sports helped calm political passions in the context of La Violencia, as did reinados, beauty pageants.[7]

Beauty contests became quite popular at the departmental, national, and international levels from 1949-1951. Beauty queens pictured with soccer players or with men in uniform linked gendered images in a single frame. Commercially, beauty was paired with coffee, cotton, beer, tobacco, and airlines, while other queens represented traditional values like kindness and charity. In these years, Colombian beauties dominated the cover of *Cromos*, only occasionally displaced by American beauties, like Marilyn Monroe, when she hit it big in 1951 in the midst of the Korean War. Oddly, the reality of La Violencia was absent from the magazine's pages, a reflection of both official and self-censorship and of the urban and modern orientation of the magazine; the violence was rural and backward, while beauty, commerce, and institutions were purportedly urban and modern.[8]

Beauty queens filled the national void of Colombian identity as the beast of violence haunted the late 1940s and early 1950s. Beauty feminized and complemented mass spectator sports, especially soccer, with beauty queens photographed surrounded by admiring players. Queens presented bouquets to team captains as symbols of beauty and civility. At times, women selected as "Queens of Sports" suited up and played soccer, appropriating team names like Boca Junior and Deportivo Cali, gender bending the normal competition, complete with female referees and male team mothers. Beauty queens attracted more spectators to the stands as they symbolically presented female power in a largely male arena.[9]

The larger international world of beauty also reached into Colombia for talent and markets. The Colombian tour of Miss New Orleans in 1949 attracted much media and public interest as she showed off her figure and swimming skills in Bogotá and posed with soccer teams on the pitch in Cali. She was in Colombia to encourage Colombian participation in a beauty contest in New Orleans. Additionally, Mexican studios recruited Colombian beauties for screen tests in Mexico. For some young women, leaving Colombia for calmer settings made both personal and economic sense. Elite young women increasingly opted to study in the United States during La Violencia, a trend that held firm for most of the rest of the century.[10]

The annual Miss America pageant also garnered attention in the pages of *Cromos*. The USA emerged from World War II as the military, financial, economic, diplomatic, and cultural power of the world. The Miss America pageant presented modern developed beauty to the nation and to the larger world. One had to be white to participate in Miss America, as one had to be white to participate in Miss Colombia, a rule that taught lessons of national, racial, and gender identity. When Miss Jeannine Holland, Cotton Queen of the USA, visited Medellín in 1951, she bridged cultural and national divides between the two countries. She modeled elegant modern dresses designed in Medellín and then donned the traditional "traje colombiano" with hand-painted scoop blouse, long embroidered skirt, straw hat, and alpargatas, thereby embodying modern beauty within traditional design. Her visit brought American beauty to the city, while Medellín's entrepreneurs showed off their products as Miss Holland, presumably, encouraged future commercial relations as well.[11]

In the midst of La Violencia, the 1949 Señorita Colombia contest attracted fewer participants and spectators but greater controversy. Whereas fifteen candidates participated in the 1947 pageant, only seven did so in 1949. The relatively peaceful North Coast departments were overrepresented while war-torn areas to the south, like Meta, Huila, and Tolima, did not send candidates. Although the pageant was heralded as an event of national cohesion and a sedative for political tensions, the pageant didn't and couldn't deliver a salutary healing of the nation. The stunning beauty and hometown crowd favorite, Ada Porto Vélez, was barred from competing for the crown, under threat that the National Beauty Contest might dissolve if another Cartagenan kept the national crown. The national emergency and regional rivalries framed the outcome of the 1949 pageant, not the merits of the candidates. The Colombian judges deadlocked in a tie between two candidates, one broken by the Chilean ambassador, who selected Myriam Sojo Zambrano, from Barranquilla, representing Atlántico department. At age ten, Myriam won a Shirley Temple look-alike contest, and a few months before her Miss Colombia triumph was named Miss Sarrapia Soap (Señorita Jabón Sarrapia). Following the pageant, the other candidates received queenly titles of Congeniality, Sports, and the Sea, and graced the cover of *Cromos* in subsequent months. Myriam received a round-trip ticket to New York courtesy of Grace Lines, cash from Coltejer, the biggest textile firm in Medellín, was named Queen of the Carnival in Havana, and Queen of Central America and the Caribbean in 1950. She then married, moved to the outskirts of Medellín, and subsequently dedicated the next phase of her life to her home and her seven children.[12]

When Myriam was crowned Queen of Central America and the Caribbean in Cali, she was accompanied by a young soldier in formal dress uniform, illustrating two trends: one toward regional beauty contests in Latin America, and inside Colombia, the militarization of the state. Along with the Cali contest, a pageant in Lima in 1949 fielded eight candidates from around Latin America, with the Peruvian representative of the *limeña* aristocracy declared the winner. As in sports, home-field advantage can determine the outcome of a pageant as it often does with a game. The trend of picturing beauty queens with men in uniform foreshadowed the formal seizure of power by the Colombian military as it signaled the weakness of civilian democracy. The selection of the Queen of the Colombian Air Force (Reina de la FAC) in May 1949 garnered extensive media attention and made the cover of *Cromos*. As in the era of Reyes at the beginning of the century, the Reina de la FAC on the cover of *Cromos* revealed contemporary trends as it foreshadowed future developments.[13]

While crowns, titles, uniforms, and insignia all signaled hierarchical rank and authority, another interesting trend in these early years of the 1950s was what could be termed the "feminization" of the Liberal Party. In the context of partisan violence and the purging of national institutions of Liberal leadership, *Cromos* ran photographs of elite Liberal matrons at garden parties. Well dressed and nonthreatening, these women in furs, pearls, and stylish hats represented their clan and party proudly at a time of national political crisis. Whereas a group of Liberal men might be seen as a military or political threat, photographs of matrons both softened and legitimized a proud and established political party.[14]

The breakdown of the Colombian political system raised questions of race. Critics suggested that the country lacked experience, maturity, and a true culture, one in which sixty percent of the population was illiterate. Racially, it was a nation of mestizos, millions of whom were damaged by disease, malnutrition, and alcohol. Socially, there were two worlds: the minority cultured and the majority savage. Five stark words summed up this racial pessimism: "somos un país de cafres" ("we are a country of niggers.")[15] Given this racial

FIGURE 6.1   *Reina de la FAC,* Cromos *cover, May 28, 1949, courtesy* Revista Cromos.

pessimism, beauty in 1951 re-embraced the noble Spanish motif, one incarnating whiter cultural and spiritual virtues. Preparing for the 1951 national beauty contest, the queen of Santander won praise for her refined Spanish air, one typical of Santander's women, punctuated by their delicate and exquisite manners.[16] The winner that year, Leonor Navia Orejuela, was the fairest of the ten candidates, had green eyes, curly brown hair, and was the first national queen from Cali. The judges were all North Americans, including Clay Shaw, a New Orleans merchant and part-time U.S. intelligence source, later indicted for conspiracy to assassinate John F. Kennedy Jr.[17]

Cali began to develop its reputation as the home of Colombia's most beautiful women following Leonor's win. Migrants displaced by rural violence and attracted by the city's new jobs stimulated urban growth of seven percent per year from 1951 to 1964. Cali's rate of increase was second only to São Paulo, Brazil, for urban growth in all of Latin America. The city's land-owning elites diversified into industrial operations while the city developed cultural and intellectual centers. This was Cali's moment to stand out from the rest of the nation and it did so in part by boasting of its beautiful women; the city's hot climate and social composition paralleled that of Cartagena, giving Cali's bathing beauties a tropical and alluring image distinct from the covered layers of Bogotá. Pageants and queens drew huge crowds, attracted powerful and important business and governmental leaders, and provided the opportunity to drink, dance, and party. Cali reveled in its newfound fame.[18]

Medellín's boosters maintained traditional explanations for unique Antioquian beauty, pulling from biblical, mineral, and racial motifs while adding a modern pitch to market the city's textiles to a wider market. A retelling of a biblical story likened Antioquia's women to Rebekah; tall, generous, and laborious, she represented the best race in the midst of a larger desert. Antioquia still claimed to have the best-developed ethnic group in the nation, symbolized by the excellence of its women. Its women were also likened to the mineral wealth of the department, whose beauty and richness could change the daydreams of the world. While calling for national peace, the boosters' pitch for the city's textiles expanded to national scope by including photographs and articles of attractive women from all around Colombia. As violence intensified in 1949 and 1950 and as the national market became more insecure, *Gloria*, the slick magazine of Fabricato, ran articles on Ecuador, suggesting a move toward international marketing.[19]

The battle between tradition and modernity found ample ground in Antioquia. On one side, priests in Antioquia and eastern Caldas attacked daughters and their mothers from the pulpit (pulpitazos) for gendered or behavioral infractions. Home dances, walks or swims with the opposite sex, riding horses or bicycles, or wearing pants could earn a girl and her mother a public denunciation in mass, requiring both to return ribbons or medallions that identified them as Daughters of Mary or Catholic Mothers. Prohibitions in Medellín against women wearing tight sweaters—too sexy and revealing of feminine curves—demonstrated this tension and gave newspaper cartoonists amusing material. Yet, for elites in the Club Union, tennis fashions hastened an androgynous look, with women dressed in shorts and shirts much like men. As with the bicycle craze a half-century earlier, tennis fashions gave elite women greater freedom of movement both physically and socially.[20]

In the context of La Violencia, elite beauty moved indoors with clubs and hotels hosting pageants, fashion shows, and upscale cocktail parties. The student pageants and those for departmental queens attracted local photographers and radio broadcasters, offering wealthy, older men the opportunity to socialize with younger, attractive women, a classic gendered encounter. Fashion shows fulfilled a number of social tasks; part get-together and gossip session for some, for others it was an intense opportunity to judge the presented fashions worn by models, questioning whether that "look" would work for the viewer. Cocktail parties, with the ubiquitous cigarettes, provided the social space to see and be seen in an elite setting, with photographers close at hand to chronicle the scene. The city's emerging middle class held its social events in restaurants rather than in private clubs.[21]

Cartagena's elites continued their controlled contact with most of the city's inhabitants in the annual Reina Popular de las Fiestas (Popular Festival Queen) in November. The 1955 queen, Albertina Porto, a striking Ava Gardner look-alike from the Papayal neighborhood, was crowned poolside amidst allegations of voting irregularities. The national beauty pageant followed, receiving increasing national attention, so restrictions on popular culture increased; street games, fireworks, and gambling were all restricted, and those poor deemed to be vagrants and crooks were rounded up by police preemptively before the festivities began.[22]

The Cold War goal of confronting communist aggression brought Colombia and the United States together during the Korean War. Laureano Gómez was the only Latin American president to pledge significant troops and naval assistance for the war on the other side of the world whilst Colombia exploded in civil war at home. The one–thousand-man Colombian Battalion fought bravely, took significant casualties, and earned high praise from United Nations officers. Its officers, Gustavo Rojas Pinilla, Alberto Ruíz Novoa, and Álvaro Valencia Tovar, all formed close working relationships with United States military officers, and went on to become major players in Colombian politics and the military for the next twenty years. Colombian assistance in Korea earned the nation greater U.S. military assistance as it bolstered the power of the Colombian armed forces and shaped a pattern of militarized United States assistance to Colombia for the next sixty years, as U.S. officials frequently perceived Colombia to be facing serious disorder and imminent collapse.[23]

While the Korean War and La Violencia dragged on inconclusively,

FIGURE 6.3   *Hotel Nutibara, Fondo Carlos Rodríguez, courtesy Archivo de Memoria Visual de Antioquia. A:H:A.*

FIGURE 6.2   *Hotel Nutibara, Reinado estudiantes, Fondo Carlos Rodríguez, courtesy Archivo de Memoria Visual de Antioquia. A:H:A.*

FIGURE 6.4   *Hotel Nutibara, Coctel Roberto Soto (1958), Fondo Carlos Rodríguez, courtesy Archivo de Memoria Visual de Antioquia. A:H:A.*

FIGURE 6.5   *Hotel Nutibara, Fondo Carlos Rodríguez, courtesy Archivo de Memoria Visual de Antioquia. A:H:A.*

Gómez vacated the presidency due to illness from 1951 until June 1953. Upon his return to office, Gómez faced not only staunch Liberal attacks but also disapproval from the Ospinista wing of the Conservative party. He also lost support from the Catholic Church, which along with Ospinistas faulted Gómez for his ideological rigidity and for the ongoing political violence. Suspecting an emerging plot from Ospinistas and military officers, Gómez removed General Gustavo Rojas Pinilla as commander of the armed forces, but by that evening Rojas removed Gómez as president of Colombia in a rare military coup. Both Liberals and Ospinistas cheered the removal of Gómez and awaited the next chapter under the general.[24]

Although Rojas Pinilla lacked a coherent political platform upon his seizure of power, he did have ambitions and a clear sense of ceremony. The selection of departmental queens set the stage for the 1953 national beauty pageant in which the general and his family played prominent roles. Although the pageant only attracted eight candidates—some representing two to four departments—heavy press coverage and a national radio broadcast provided an inviting venue for Rojas to reign over the national spectacle. Seated in lavish dress uniform in the front row with his wife, Carola, Rojas introduced national political power and the power of the military to the pageant. He accompanied the winner, Luz Marina Cruz, to her throne, crowned her personally, and then escorted her out of the Teatro Cartagena on foot to a reception in the Club Cartagena. The scepter, crown, and sash of Luz Marina were matched by the scepter, crown, and sash of the president's wife, Carola. His daughter, María Eugenia, appeared at various functions with the candidates, looking a little tense and out of place. The theme and protocol of the 1953 pageant mirrored that of the coronation of Queen Elizabeth of England; in Cartagena, both Luz Marina and Rojas received national coronations.[25] Like Rafael Reyes a half-century earlier, Rojas Pinilla connected his presidency to the social and political power wielded by public beauty to build consensus and legitimacy for his government during troubled times.

Luz Marina, a native of Cali, reinforced that city's reputation for beautiful women, yet she represented not only Valle but also Antioquia, Cauca, and Nariño. Political and business leaders in both Medellín and Cali counted Luz as their winner, having bettered the runner-up from Bogotá. She was typical in that she had finished high school in the United States prior to her coronation as queen of Colombia. She refused to appear in a voluntary swimsuit competition, as did about one-half of the contestants, bowing to the orders of their bishops. Upon her triumphal return to Cali, 150,000 people greeted the new sovereign, a crowd larger than any politician could dream of attracting.[26]

To build political legitimacy for his presidency, Rojas Pinilla had a friendly Assembly give him a four-year term in office in 1954. The Assembly also approved female suffrage, a symbolic reform because Rojas never called direct elections during his presidency. Moreover, succeeding National Front elections through the mid-1970s allowed little free electoral contestation, thus blunting the democratic impact of female suffrage. However, Rojas did achieve many firsts for women and government; he appointed the first female governor, the first female cabinet officer, and he integrated women into the police force. Young women in uniform served to soften the image of the armed forces, as it mobilized female support for Rojas. It also offered cartoonists amusing material, featuring grown men dressed as lost boys who approached shapely female officers seeking aid, the female officers not knowing what to do with so many lost boys. As Rojas courted female support for his government and with Bogotá's nightlife returning to the streets, it seemed that the new government had restored order to the nation's capital. Some Liberal guerrillas in the llanos agreed to amnesty terms with Rojas, something they could never do with Gómez.[27]

Rojas crafted a fusion of measures from both the Liberal and Conservative parties during his administration. He dedicated the nation to the ideals of Jesus Christ and continued repression of Colombian Protestants, bolstering support from both the Catholic Church and Conservatives. However, he borrowed plays from Liberal reformers of the 1930s and from Gaitán's populist appeals of the 1940s. With coffee prices high, Rojas expanded spending for public housing, health, education, and infrastructure, from railroads, highways, and airports. He formed his own labor federation to compete with federations directed by the Catholic Church and the Liberal party in order to build political support for his government. Influenced by the successful program of Juan Perón in Argentina, he tried to fashion a new political coalition of the people, the government, and the armed forces, going beyond the established party elites to address the country's problems. He also placed his daughter, María Eugenia, in charge of SENDAS, a national relief agency akin to the Eva Perón Foundation in Argentina, María Eugenia becoming an effective advocate of her father's government. By 1954, he was distancing himself from the Ospinista wing of the Conservative party and from the "oligarchy," reviving the pitch of the magnetic Gaitán.[28]

While presenting himself as an alternative to dysfunctional partisan politics, Rojas could not tame the beast of La Violencia. Some groups had morphed into criminal organizations, whose ends were economic, not political. Local areas came under the control of mafia groups who employed paid assassins to steal, extort, and kill in service to their employers. In the rugged Sumapaz region south of Bogotá, Rojas waged total war on guerrillas who refused his amnesty offers. Those leaders had established independent peasant republics in 1930 and subsequently allied with the now illegal Communist Party to defend peasant property from elite and state control. Military aid from the United States provided the hardware for an air assault on the people below, with the inevitable—and politically destructive—civilian casualties. Some of the survivors of this repression in 1954–1955 formed what became the largest and toughest guerrilla movement in the late twentieth century, the FARC (Fuerzas Armadas Revolucionarias Colombianas). In essence, La Violencia in the mid-1950s transitioned away from its initial partisan definition toward the economic and ideological logics that defined the beast of Colombian violence for the rest of the century.[29]

While the beast howled and morphed into new forms, the covers of *Cromos* in 1954 balanced glamour shots of Hollywood actresses during the first six months of the year, followed by a focus on Colombian attractions—beauty queens, Rojas Pinilla, Bolívar, rural landscapes, and attractive socialites—for the remainder of the year. Photographs of voluptuous stars like Marilyn Monroe, Ava Gardner, Elaine Stewart, and Jane Russell oozed sex appeal, while the refined beauty of Donna Reed and Audrey Hepburn made striking covers. The post–World War II reemergence of the Miss Universe pageant also pushed pageants towards an overt display of sexy female bodies as the marker of modern beauty. The post-WWII Miss Universe and Miss USA pageants began when the 1951 Miss America winner angered the major sponsor of the pageant by refusing to display herself in a Catalina swimsuit. Catalina withdrew its sponsorship from Miss America and partnered with Universal, a for-profit entertainment corporation, to create Miss USA and Miss Universe, where all contestants had to appear in Catalina swimsuits and where physical beauty, not educational achievement, talent, or civic service as in Miss America, was the key requirement. Although Colombia did not yet participate in Miss Universe, the international bathing beauties, suggestively eating hotdogs with their smooth legs placed forward, edged Colombian beauty pageants toward the Miss Universe model.[30]

Judging from the pages of *Cromos*, the focus for much of 1955 centered on the upcoming national pageant. The Cartagena city council established an organizing committee for the pageant and work started in earnest in February. The editors of *Cromos* started running articles about their role in the selection of Señorita Cundinamarca in May, six months before the pageant began in Cartagena. The pageants, both departmental and national, were praised for their economic multiplier effect and promotion of tourism, and as an expression of the level of civilization of the people organizing them. The event was big business with millions of pesos spent on clothing, transportation, food, drink, and accommodations. The favorites for the crown traveled with an entourage of forty to sixty people all needing accommodations close to their candidate; Señorita Antioquia momentarily quit the competition when her legation's request for rooms for forty was answered by the local organizing committee that it only had rooms for three. The Valle queen was expected to travel with a large party, and the eventual winner arrived with sixty. The preparation of a candidate's trousseau became news, the favorites shopping in Miami prior to their fashionable entrance in Cartagena. Television covered the 1955 Miss Colombia and Miss Universe pageants for the first time, with Miss Colombia contestants all posing in swimsuits on the beach for photographers. Señorita Santander, Esperanza Gallón, won that year's competition and was crowned by Minister of War General Gabriel París. Esperanza promised to work with SENDAS and won praise for her pearly white skin, large

FIGURE 6.6   *Esperanza Gallón and Brigadier General Gabriel París, in* Las más bellas, *p. 49, courtesy Concurso Nacional de Belleza (Cartagena, Colombia).*

dark eyes, and native intelligence. The newspapers in Cali produced documents proving that she was baptized in Cartago, making her at least partially vallecaucana.[31]

While Rojas promoted television mass media and mass politics in the mid-1950s, he could not stem elite opposition to his government. By 1956, leaders of the Conservative and Liberal parties formed a National Front to dump Rojas from power and to share power equally after his ouster, an initiative supported by a Catholic Church miffed by Rojas's challenge to its labor confederation. In the midst of declining coffee prices and economic recession, two events that year cemented opposition to Rojas. In January, former President Lleras Camargo, the National Front leader of the Liberal party, arrived at the bullfight ring in Bogotá to a ten-minute standing ovation from the crowd. A few minutes later, Rojas's daughter, María Eugenia, arrived with military escort and was booed out of the arena. At the ring the following Sunday, armed plainclothesmen shouted "vivas" for Rojas and those remaining silent were beaten; eight died and about one hundred were wounded. In August, seven army trucks loaded with dynamite exploded in Cali; thousands died or were hospitalized with forty blocks of the city damaged or destroyed. Rojas lashed out and blamed the National Front for the act, a statement he soon retracted. By May 1957, a reunited Conservative party led by Gómez and Ospina, and the Liberals led by Lleras Camargo, found support from business leaders to nudge Rojas from power. Unable to maintain support from high-ranking officers in the armed forces, Rojas left the country and went into temporary exile.[32]

Both the transition to the National Front system and significant trends in Colombian beauty filled much of the rest of 1957. A December plebiscite on the National Front included female voters for the first time in modern Colombian history, with women urged to fulfill their patriotic duty to bring peace to the nation. Trends in beauty feathered together both modern directions and traditional continuities, both seeking to mold an understanding of women's place in a space of social and political transition. By July, the media build-up to the 1957 national beauty pageant in Cartagena intensified when a seventeen-year-old Peruvian woman, Gladys Zender, won the Miss Universe crown. Zender subsequently toured Colombia, promoting the Miss Universe pageant and acting as a talent scout for the 1958 contest. Thereafter, media and business interest in both national and international pageants intensified.[33]

Zender's victory marked one track toward modern international beauty, one that had a strong ripple effect throughout Latin America. Although Colombia did not compete in 1957, three of the five finalists were from Latin America. Thereafter, Latin American contestants have won the Miss Universe crown twice as often as contestants from Europe or Asia, and three times as often as candidates from the United States. Wearing the requisite Catalina swimsuit and high heels, modern international bathing beauties embodied the revealed female body for all to ponder. Colombian newspaper columns advised women to wear the new nylon bras and lighter but still tight girdles and corsets, adopting the 3:2:3 bust to waist to hips ratio expected of modern beauty, while also mixing in folk recipes to whiten the skin or fade freckles. In reaction to the revealed female body in Miss Universe, the 1957

Señorita Colombia pageant warned all participants, under penalty of disquali-
fication, to wear discreet outfits, never swimsuits, at all times when participating in the national pageant.[34]

In preview of the coming plebiscite, *Cromos*, partnering with Avianca
and Televisora Nacional, promoted a series of twelve television programs in
which the Señorita Colombia candidates would be presented to the viewing
public. The series ran from September 26 to November 5, inaugurating the
television blitz that would define the pageant thereafter. Moreover, *Cromos*
placed coupons in its September and October editions, asking the public to
write the names of their favorites and to predict the winner. This precursor to
the popular vote in December to decide the fate of the National Front encouraged mass participation, rewarded multiple votes, and promised cash, trips,
and free *Cromos* subscriptions to those voters who returned the most coupons
with the name of the winning queen. *Cromos* articles mirrored those presented
on the television programs, weaving together a tight multimedia campaign by
which voters became familiar with the departmental queens on a first-name
basis; Doris, Luz, Mercedes, Nazly.[35]

While tens of thousands of coupons flowed in to *Cromos*, sent primarily
by women, the representation of beauty took on new forms. The Organizing
Committee of the National Beauty Contest thanked the director of *Cromos*
for his support in promoting the 1957 pageant, one promising to bring the
"Spiritual Pacification" of Colombia.[36] The national beauty contest and the
search for peace became linked, a linkage maintained for much of the rest of
the twentieth century. Nazly of Chocó became the first Afro-Colombian to
participate in the national pageant, thirteen years before the same barrier was
broken in the Miss America pageant in 1970. Nazly, backed by well-dressed
black professionals, was praised by her singular beauty which presented a "fortunate synthesis of American beauty and symbolized the positive virtues of
the Chocoan people."[37] Nazly subtly reintroduced the African component of
Colombian identity, broadening it beyond its Hispanic preference.

To link Colombia to the larger world, the United Nations initiated the first
Interamerican Folklore Festival in Manizales, one where music and dance that
had survived through "anonymous tradition" would be presented and judged
for its authenticity. Of course, beauty queens attended the departmental competitions for the national and international contest, linking modern beauty
with traditional culture presented in music accompanied by "authentic"
dancers wearing "typical" costumes.[38] As beauty became more corporal, competitive, and international, folklore became more insistent that women perform the timeless, the traditional, the local, the authentic.

As the national pageant neared, it became clear that the representatives

Una escena chocanísima: la estupenda belleza morena de Nacly Lozano Eljure, Señorita Chocó, rodeada de tres figuras representativas del gran departamento olvidado: Velaia An... re, a la izquierda; Adán Arriaga Andrade, al centro, y Diego Luis Córdoba, en el homenaje de la Chocó Pacífico a Nacly. (Fotografía de SADY).

FIGURE 6.7   *"Una escena chocanísima,"* Cromos, *Nov. 4, 1957, courtesy* Revista Cromos.

from some of the most war-torn areas of La Violencia, Antioquia, Caldas, and Tolima, were emerging as the favorites in Cartagena. Born poor and criticized as merely a "reina popular," Luz Marina Zuluaga Zuluaga, representing both Caldas and Nariño, not only won endorsements from Bavaria, the biggest beer company in Colombia, but also a rare endorsement from Max Factor cosmetics. Also rare, Luz Marina was photographed at Liberal party headquarters, where she urged women to vote for the upcoming plebiscite. Luz Marina's candidacy effectively joined the national to the international, and national politics to the national pageant. Newspapers in Cali ran photographs of Luz Marina trying on shoes and shopping in Cali, giving her that magic Valle del Cauca touch. In the coupon voting tallied by *Cromos*, Doris Gil of Antioquia won with 10,041 votes, followed closely by Luz Marina of Caldas with 10,036 votes, with the statuesque Mabel Villaveces from Tolima taking third with 9,940. Letters to the editor of *Cromos* on pageant day, November 11, were full of letters comparing two favorite candidates, but only one letter addressed the decadelong violence in the country, the most savage violence seen in Latin America. The author, a campesino from Caicedonia and an assiduous reader of *Cromos* and *El Espectador*, asked when politicians would be concerned with common people's problems, when the guilty would be judged, and when Colombians would be evolved enough to respect the rights of others. Although his voice and concerns were recorded in *Cromos*, that publication, the national and international beauty pageants, and the upcoming National Front scheme promised that the saving grace of beauty would only temporarily mollify the persistent terror of the beast.[39]

With KLM, Grace Line, Fabricato, Postobón, and Palmolive offering prizes, Doris Gil of Antioquia edged out Luz Marina Zuluaga for the 1957 Señorita Colombia crown. Doris was crowned by Miss Universe, Gladys Zender, who was convinced that Doris would be her successor as Miss Universe. General Gabriel París returned to accompany the new queen to the reception at the Club Cartagena, as he had done two years before. Doris was eighteen, had a boyfriend five years her senior, spoke French, and improved her English at a convent boarding school in the United States. The judges, two North American men, and a Venezuelan who served as a judge for the Miss Universe pageant, seconded the popular election of Doris run by *Cromos*. She married her boyfriend the following year, and therefore could not represent Colombia at the 1958 Miss Universe pageant, replaced by Luz Marina Zuluaga for that contest in Long Beach, California.[40]

Coverage of the pageant continued over the next month in the pages of *Cromos*. The magazine published the names and addresses of the winners of the coupon contest, the top nine all being female. It ran photographs of some of the candidates in swimwear, which was good for circulation and no longer a violation as the pageant had concluded. And finally, *Cromos* connected the 1957 pageant and its coupon contest to the upcoming plebiscite on the National Front. The photograph showed the resolute and well-dressed queens around a table in the process of signing a petition calling all Colombian women to the plebiscite. This invitation came from Doris of Colombia and from the other departmental queens, urging all Colombians, especially women voting for the first time, to participate in the process of restoring democratic institutions and peace to a country ripped apart by hatred and fratricidal bloodshed. Once again, beauty fronted the campaign to defeat the beast.[41]

The plebiscite reaffirmed the Conservative stance that Colombia was a Roman Catholic nation, and that government would protect and respect the Church as a guardian of social order. However, Article 1 stipulated that women would have the same political rights as men, and Article 12 stated that national government would spend ten percent of its budget on public education, measures that cheered reformers. Politically, the National Front established a sixteen-year period when the presidency would alternate between the Liberal and Conservative parties, and when all public positions in government would be equally shared by the two traditional parties. Although this agreement ended partisan discord between the Liberals and Conservatives, its elitist and exclusionary characteristics were clear in that no other parties were

FIGURE 6.8   *Doris Gil and Luz Marina Zuluaga (Nov. 1957),*
Fondo Carlos Rodríguez, courtesy Archivo de Memoria Visual
de Antioquia. A:H:A.

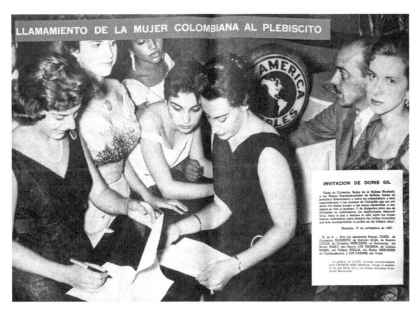

FIGURE 6.9   *Llamamiento de la mujer colombiana al plebiscito,* Cromos *(Dec. 2, 1957),*
courtesy Revista Cromos.

allowed to participate in government and in making popular elections meaningless as party elites decided their partisan outcome ahead of time. The exclusive measures helped spawn leftist guerrilla insurgency in the 1960s and its
elitist quality never addressed the overall patterns of inequality in Colombia,
realities that followed Colombia through the rest of the century. Nonetheless,
the plebiscite saw 1.8 million female voters, 42 percent of the total vote, with
95 percent of total voters accepting the plebiscite and the National Front fix.[42]

As Colombia transitioned from the partisan stage of La Violencia and the
Rojas Pinilla dictatorship to the elite-directed National Front, the late 1950s
marked another transition from the stylized elegance of the fifties to the more
turbulent and sexually expressive 1960s. *Cromos* followed the emergence of
Fidel Castro, the surprise of Sputnik, the raw energy of Elvis Presley, and
the captivating and bountiful beauty of Sophia Loren, Jane Mansfield, and
Brigitte Bardot. The popularity of television hurt the film industry in Hollywood, reopening space for Italian and French films and fashions to compete
with the Americans. The reemergence of Latin Europe as a leader in modern
beauty and fashion, a position dominated by Hollywood since the 1920s, created space for Latin American beauty to take the international center stage.[43]

Colombian beauty did exceptionally well in the United States in 1958.
In May, Pan-American Week in Washington, D.C., brought a large group
dressed as "paisas" (Antioquians) to the capitol steps, with their Antioquian
queen, the Colombian queen, Doris Gil, selected as Coffee Queen. In June, the
fifth place finisher in the 1957 national pageant, Mercedes Baquero Román,
was crowned Queen of the Americas in Miami, ahead of competitors from
El Salvador, Cuba, Paraguay, Guatemala, Peru, Jamaica, Mexico, Ecuador,
and Brazil. Mercedes reportedly had lunch with President Eisenhower following her coronation. And in late July in Long Beach, 1957 runner-up,
Luz Marina Zuluaga, was crowned Miss Universe, 1958, the one and only
time Colombia has taken that crown home.[44]

Luz Marina already had a number of regal titles. She was Queen of her
hometown Manizales, of the Club Campestre, the Journalists' Circle, the
departments of Caldas and Nariño, the Intendancy of Amazonas, and the
Folkloric queen. Following the national pageant, she traveled in Europe with
a number of national and international beauty queens, brought some of them
home with her for a Colombian tour, and traveled to Long Beach, California,
without great expectations. She had lost weight since the Señorita Colombia
pageant, and was listed with the preferred 3:2:3 bust to waist to hips ratios.
Apparently, her figure caught the judges' eyes during the swimsuit competition. Serving on the judge's panel, Peruvian Alberto Vargas had become
famous in the 1920s as an illustrator of the Ziegfeld Follies, for sensuous

Hollywood movie posters in the 1930s, and for the *Esquire* magazine "Varga Girls" pinups of the 1940s. Conscious of her role in representing Colombia, Luz Marina hoped not to embarrass herself and her country by getting cut in the first round and was relieved to make the top fifteen, surprised to make the top five, and shocked to be named Miss Universe. As *Cromos* summarized following her victory, "the name of Colombia will now be identified with a sweet and poetic figure of a woman."[45]

Luz Marina coverage dominated the pages of *Cromos* for the next two months. Reached at the Beverly Hills Hotel by long-distance telephone, she said that she was "thinking about Colombia, about Caldas, and about the Colombian women who are struggling for a better country." She vowed to let everyone around the world know that Colombia produced the best coffee and that the folklore festival in Manizales was an international attraction. Reportedly, she received a telegram from the Military Junta in Bogotá requesting that she not return to Colombia until after August 7 when Dr. Alberto Lleras Camargo assumed the presidency. She sent her greetings to Colombians back home, amusingly adding "Un saludo de Frente Nacional" (regards from the National Front).[46]

Luz Marina's victory was a godsend for the National Front. How could one not be excited by this great success on the international stage? Once news reached towns and cities, people poured into the streets in celebration, not in retaliation as on April 9, but cheering a collective and national victory. People filled the main streets in Bogotá, church bells ringing, car horns honking, factory whistles blaring, musical groups playing, people dancing, shouting "viva Colombia" and singing the national anthem. Revelers partied in Manizales for three days, and when Luz Marina returned to the Bogotá airport she was greeted by a crowd of 100,000, one fellow departmental queen stating that "Luz Marina es nuestra bandera de paz" ("Luz Marina is our banner of peace"). Partisan pundits argued that the spectacular beauty of Colombian women born after 1930 was a result of Liberal reforms of that decade. When President Lleras Camargo received Luz at the presidential palace, he was praised for his great statesmanship and serene and visionary thinking, while she was extolled for perfectly incarnating the intelligence and integrity of Colombian women.[47] In the end, Luz Marina represented all.

She arrived home with $11,000 in cash, $6000 in contracts, a V-8 Chevy convertible, furs, stockings, clothes, gloves, jewelry, luggage, beauty products, toiletries, and the Miss Universe trophy. She returned home rich, her beauty as celebrity the vehicle of a radical personal and social ascension that removed her from Colombian reality. She lost sleep, her privacy, her boyfriend to a good friend, control of her calendar, and promptly got sick. Colombian cus-

FIGURE 6.10   *Luz Marina Zuluaga, Miss Universo (1958), in* Las más bellas,
p. 61, courtesy Concurso Nacional de Belleza (Cartagena, Colombia).

toms boasted that they quickly imported the U.S. convertible into the country, whereas it took the rigidly bureaucratic Peruvians nine months to process and clear their Queen's car the previous year. The good people of Caldas gifted Luz Marina and the family with a mansion valued at 250,000 pesos, full of so many items that it took Luz Marina and her mother considerable energy just to unpack them all. She was a celebrity, as was her laborious Mama Universo, and ninety-three-year-old Abuelo Universo. They all now connoted a larger yet constrained universe. When Luz Marina toured Medellín in the company of Doris Gil, they both wore prominent and large jewelry encrusted with Colombia's famous emeralds. According to *Cromos*, the two most beautiful women of Colombia—Doris, the Queen of Colombia, who had just had her wisdom teeth pulled, and Luz Marina, Queen of the Universe, with a throat infection and high fever—proved that the country was not just rich in precious stones.[48]

Colombia needed beauty in the decade following Gaitán's murder as violence raged, the economy grew, and administrations went from Laureano Gómez to Rojas Pinilla, and then to the National Front. Beauty softened and civilized the competitive masculine worlds of mass sports, the military, and vicious partisan and socioeconomic violence. The chaos of La Violencia led to an affirmation of Colombia as a Spanish nation, as French and Italian films reasserted a Mediterranean beauty type favorable to Colombia in international pageants. General Rojas Pinilla manipulated the power of beauty and pageantry, as had Rafael Reyes a half-century earlier, to build support and legitimacy for his administration. It was clear in 1958, as it was before and after that year, that Colombia was a country rich in resources and beautiful in its cultural and physical geography. But even as Luz Marina was crowned Miss Universe, it was also clear on the ground in Florida, Valle del Cauca, that the nation's beauty could not domesticate the beast of ongoing violence. In Florida, eighteen people lay dead on the ground, shot, slashed with machetes, some decapitated, proving that the "pájaros" (paid assassins) still massacred Colombians in significant numbers. The pájaros, dressed in uniforms and armed with shotguns, rifles, machetes, and pistols, slaughtered with impunity and terrorized at will—precursors of the paramilitaries of the next generation.[49] They came from the other, larger Colombia, the one that worried López Pumarejo and energized Gaitán, the one that supplied the foot soldiers of La Violencia, the one completely alien to the elites of the National Front and to the beauty queens now on the global stage.

Chapter 7

FROM MISS UNIVERSE TO
THE ANTI-REINA, 1958–1968

The decade between Luz Marina's victory and the year that rocked much of the world contained a number of important transitions. The end of the Rojas Pinilla dictatorship and the implementation of the National Front system signaled a return to civilian government but also the continuation of an exclusionary democratic system. The partisan quality of La Violencia faded, but predatory economic violence remained, joined in the mid-1960s by revolutionary guerrilla bands. The marketing of Colombian beauty as the pacific and positive face of the nation intensified with the proliferation of regional pageants and festivals meant to be nonpartisan, participatory, and inclusive. In essence, the elite-directed National Front promoted the celebration of the best of feminine beauty and the best of traditional culture as a pitch for popular support for what was truly an exercise in embracing Colombia's elitist and nonmodern core.

The constitutionally delineated rules for equal sharing of all elective and appointive positions and the alteration of the presidency between the Liberals and Conservatives rebuilt a stable Colombian state through its formal duration until 1974. Thereafter, another amendment stipulating "equitable" power sharing between the two traditional parties continued coalition rule until 1986. More assertive National Front governments used state patronage as a source of employment and monies in order to become the new patron for clients who formerly had relied on local power brokers. National Front governments reasserted state presence in some pockets of Colombian territory traumatized by violence and then either demobilized or confronted armed bands and local political bosses. This focus on national systems over local networks reinforced the sense of a functional national state, but divisive geography, lack of resources, elitism, and resistance made the goal of national sovereignty incomplete. Moreover, exclusion of third parties blunted political participation and encouraged new forms of violence, and although the National Front signaled a victory for elite Colombia, its programs and organization never strengthened popular sovereignty by bridging the chasm between the rich few and the majority poor.[1]

Colombia's population increased by 64 percent between 1951 and 1964, fueled by a higher than average birth rate compared with that of the rest of Latin America. However, infant mortality was 60 percent higher than the average for the region, suggesting poor or nonexistent public health programs in many areas. The urban populations of Bogotá, Medellín, Cali, and Barranquilla all boomed over this time, a trend consistent with the rest of the century. A crisis in the coffee sector from 1957 to 1970 fed rural-to-urban migration. Illiteracy rates in urban areas decreased from 21 percent in 1951 to 14 percent in 1964 but remained significantly higher in rural areas (50 percent in 1951, 41 percent in 1964). Income and land tenure patterns remained among the most concentrated in the world. In the early 1960s, Colombia's primary school enrollment ratios were lower than those in Ecuador and Peru, and the working poor could not send their children to secondary schools. Colombia's elite enjoyed technical training but maintained aristocratic values, whereas lower-level technicians and manual workers lacked social status.[2] Colombia was still a country where a select few were born into privilege — symbolically, the queens of the land.

Colombia went queen and pageant crazy during this decade, riding the success of Luz Marina on the global stage and in the process of reinventing its image out of the ruins of La Violencia. Women were now citizens of the nation, but the National Front made elections merely formal exercises to approve premeditated elite decisions. Pageants placed young women and their bodies before mass audiences, a consumer site where individuals met societal assessments about modernity, tradition, identity, nationality, gender, sex, fashion, race, class, morality, and propriety. As pageants and beauty mean more than one thing for more than one audience, these measures emerged as vehicles to track Colombia's social transitions for the rest of the century. Although popular in appeal, they were elite directed, much like the National Front. At the international level, pageants like Miss Universe and Miss World (a London-based competitor of the former) opened the world stage for Colombia to compete among the "civilized" nations of the world, where contestants promoted the beauty, potential, and the allure of themselves and their countries.[3]

Luz Marina's victory at Miss Universe brought some of the world's media attention to Colombia and its beautiful women, increasing the potential for international tourism. Started in 1957, *Colombia Turística*, the official national tourism magazine distributed nationally and internationally, used photographs of Colombian models and beauty queens as propaganda to promote business and the nation. Obviously, Colombian promoters had to contend with the violent and chaotic image of the nation framed by La Violencia, but they had Luz Marina. She led a Colombian delegation to an international tourism convention in New York City and became the focal point of the event. Success at this eight-day convention was considered vital for future tourism development, and Luz Marina carried the water. As an ambassador for Colombia, as the embodiment of spectacular but respectable sexuality and of a domesticated nation, Luz Marina was the nation before the world.[4]

Colombia's unplanned success on the global stage led to reinterpretations of beauty's relationship to nature, landscape, race, and blood. The regal city of Manizales, hometown of Luz Marina, became the symbolic queen with its happy symphony of curves, clean streets, and modern structure. Bordered on the east by the snow-capped peaks of the Nevado del Ruiz, whose glistening white snows met the deep blue western horizon in the endless and edenic valley of Risaralda, the landscape around Manizales offered beauty, purity, life, and fertility. The fusion of nature and race found in Luz Marina brought pride and happiness to Colombians as she conquered the heart of the universe with just one calm smile, one caressing look. She embodied Colombian race: that air, that gesture, that carriage, the oval face, expressive eyes and lips, the shape of the nose said "I am Colombian" to all Colombians, who knew one of their own immediately. The diversity but also the commonality of Colombian blood found prideful union in Luz Marina. In contrast to Gladys Zender, who was not representative of most of Peru, Luz Marina and Mercedes and their last names, Zuluaga and Baquero, truly represented a larger nation and a unique race. As paisa, Luz Marina was superior and white, and in the combined victories of queen and nation she and Colombia transcended self, "because now she is not her but her race."[5]

If beauty was the nation, then traditional culture was its muse, with stages built in former conflict zones to reproduce Colombian identity. One of Luz Marina's official Miss Universe duties involved a tour of South America to attract participants to Manizales for the first International Folklore Festival. Her victory and the transition to the National Front coincided with the inauguration of a number of regional and national festivals, ones often including music, dance, food, parades, and, of course, beauty. Particularly in areas of Huila, Tolima, Caldas, Valle del Cauca, and the Magdalena Valley deeply scarred by La Violencia, these festivals became vehicles to rebuild civil society, revive the economy, and integrate regions into the larger nation and world. Beauty queens from local, regional, national, and international sites both attracted large audiences and feminized the image of a rebuilding nation. This powerful cocktail of beauty, folklore, culture, La Violencia, and the National Front bridged divides between the elite and the folk, the local and the na-

TABLE 7.1. FOLKLORE, PAGEANTS, AND THE NATIONAL FRONT, 1959–1961

1959	Primera festival folclórico internacional, Manizales, Caldas
1959	Primera festival folclórico, Ibagué, Tolima
1959	Primer festival turístico, Girardot, Cundinamarca
1959	Fiesta nacional de petróleo, Barrancabermeja, Santander
1959	Reinado de la caña de azúcar, Cali, Valle del Cauca
1959	Primera fiesta del mar, Santa Marta, Magdalena
1960	Primera festival de cine, Cartagena, Bolívar
1960	Reinado nacional del café, Calarca, Caldas (Quindío)
1960	Reinado del bambuco, Neiva, Huila
1960	Primera festival de arte, Cali, Valle del Cauca
1961	Festival de la frontera, Cúcuta, Norte de Santander
1961	Primera festival de los cereales, Tunja, Boyacá

Sources: Melo Lancheros, *Valores femeninos de Colombia*, pp. 765–766; "Ferias y fiestas en Colombia," http://www.turiscolombia.com/ferias_festivales_fiestas_colombia.html; *Cromos*, Oct. 26, 1959.

tional, the past and the future, the traditional and the modern, the masculine and the feminine, the beast and beauty.[6]

The resurrection of bambuco as the national dance and music of Colombia involved another search for the roots of identity. Emerging in the late colonial period in the Cauca Valley and intertwined with battles during the independence wars of the early nineteenth century, bambuco in the middle twentieth century pointed Colombia back to its traditional and complicated past. With unclear origins (some pointing to the aristocracy of Popayán, others to the slaves of the Chocó, still others to an indigenous people of the Pacific Coast), bambuco's diverse creation myths recalled the heterogeneity of a rural and nostalgic society. When imaged as Spanish and racially white, bambuco became the refined and restrained art of the highland elite; as African and black, it recalled the pain of slavery; as indigenous and brown, it was taciturn and melancholic but deeply rooted. From 1960 onward at the Reinado del Bambuco in Neiva, Huila, contestants had to impress the judges and the public with their traditional costumes and by how well they danced the bambuco, a stylized eight-part dance that many of them struggled to learn but that became a litmus test for Colombian authenticity.[7]

While bambuco looked backward to the rural Andean interior, tropical music from the North Coast increasingly became the sound heard in urbanizing centers around the country. Geographically linked to the Caribbean coast and racially black, tropical music was danceable, lively, happy, and sexier than the music and dance of the colder, more restrained interior. During the trauma of La Violencia, the North Coast was much less affected by political violence, making the coast, its people, and its culture seem to be life affirming in contrast to the death-delivering interior. If the music and dance were sexy, they could be seen as both stereotypically traditional—blacks are more sexual and the coast less controlled by the Catholic Church—or modern, as the coast has long been Colombia's window to the world in the context of a liberating sexual revolution. Entrepreneurs in Medellín marketed tropical music around the country in the 1950s and 1960s, shrinking the size of the bands and simplifying rhythms with electronic instruments while reaching a large audience both inside and outside Colombia. Tropical music, be it cumbia, salsa, or vallenato, homogenized the heterogeneity of Colombia's geography and society as it became the modern mediator between the local, national, and international markets. By the 1960s, tropical music supplanted bambuco's popularity in the country.[8]

Beauty in Colombia in 1959 likewise engaged in dialogues between local, national, and international realms. As the National Front built its foundation of stable national government in Bogotá, a *Cromos* article proudly announced that "Bogotá dictates fashion for Colombian women" (Bogotá dicta la moda para las colombianas), suggesting a linkage between political and fashion leadership. Ironically, all of the fashions presented to the nation juxtaposed the modern look in front of colonial architecture but came from French designers like Christian Dior and Yves Saint-Laurent. Departmental contestants for the national beauty pageant that year included the blonde Yolanda from Norte de Santander, who had traveled through most of Europe and the United States, and Rocío of Antioquia, described as either *trigueña* or morena (a woman who would be termed black in the United States) and the only candidate who had a job. Photos of the contestants often mixed the modernity of swimsuits and sports cars with more traditional shots of well-dressed young women cooking, reading, playing the piano, or tending flowers. *Cromos* continued its popular election of the winner, asking readers to pick their favorites. The crowd of forty thousand who poured into the streets of Cartagena to greet the queens reportedly had much more liberty than under the reign of Rojas Pinilla. The judges that year included Inger Stevens, Miss World 1957, who was just starting her film career in the United States.[9]

The judges asked the contestants to parade out of view of the public in swimsuits not once but twice because they could not reach a decision. The winner was Stella Márquez Zawadzky from Nariño, a department that had

FIGURE 7.2   *Stella Márquez as indigenous princess (1959), in* Las más bellas, *p. 70, courtesy Concurso Nacional de Belleza (Cartagena, Colombia).*

FIGURE 7.1   *Stella Márquez in modern American dress (1959), in* Las más bellas, *p. 70, courtesy Concurso Nacional de Belleza (Cartagena, Colombia).*

not sent its own candidate in a dozen years. Stella had returned to Colombia only two weeks before her victory and only had a visa to stay in the country for two months. She had left Colombia with her family four years before for the United States, where she finished high school, started university, and took some modeling classes. While living in the United States, she won beauty pageants in New York and Hollywood, in the latter representing Honduras because that Central American nation lacked a candidate. She won praise as the best representation of typical Colombian beauty: dark eyes and hair, light brown skin, a big wide smile with sparkling teeth, perfect proportions, and a sweet and simple personality. Her age (eighteen or twenty) and place of birth (Tumaco, Cali, Pasto) were contested. Her "typical dress" was of a Sibundoy Indian from a valley between Andean and Amazonian societies: hair down, white blouse falling off the shoulder, long wide skirt, big jewelry, with a ruana over her arm. On her allegorical float, she road atop a white flower in "Indian dress," symbolically a white woman becoming indigenous. By representing

Nariño, even if she were born in Cali and lived most recently in the United States, Stella tried to bring the nation's attention to an underappreciated and forgotten department of Colombia. Highland Nariño is culturally more like Ecuador than Colombia in being Andean and indigenous, and residents of Pasto, the departmental capital, are the butt of many Colombian jokes that poke fun at the simplicity of pastusos. Stella, by dressing indigenous, not only made herself culturally and nationally authentic but also became an advocate for a department often ignored by Colombians because it was indigenous.[10]

Stella's "typical Latin beauty" worked whether she was in New York, Hollywood, or Cartagena. Upon her arrival in Bogotá, her luggage included seventeen suitcases, five cardboard boxes, various small bags, a monkey, a parrot, an ocelot, and, in her hand, a coconut spiked with aguardiente. Stella's baggage demonstrated that winning in Cartagena both required extensive resources and rewarded the same. Upon her triumphant return to Nariño, ships' whistles blared in Tumaco and a big crowd greeted their sovereign in Pasto, most people claiming to have won at least one bet on their new queen. By representing that department and winning the national pageant, Stella helped make Nariño more recognizably Colombian. Max Factor paid Stella's expenses to Long Beach for the Miss International Beauty Contest, which she won, and to Miss Universe (which by then had moved to Miami), where she was a finalist. Although she planned to serve as a diplomat, Stella went on to amass seventeen national and international crowns, the most for any Colombian beauty queen, and subsequently married a millionaire from the Philippines and moved into a palace there.[11]

Around Stella at the national pageant one found dreams, hard work, and a carnival. Elites in Cartagena dressed as "negritas e indios" (blacks and Indians) at a reception in the Club Cartagena, thereby demonstrating their elite white status as they appropriated the color and culture of the subaltern. The candidate from Tolima, a recent arrival from Great Britain, dreamed of becoming a journalist and of bringing real peace to her troubled department. Rocío Correa of Antioquia revealed the stamina required of contestants: over the eight days of the pageant, she only slept twenty hours, spending most of her time working the contest by dancing, parading, dressing, bathing, promoting the pageant, conversing with judges, and giving interviews to journalists. She lost three kilos (6.6 pounds) over the eight days as she ate very little, and returned home to Medellín very fatigued, met by another large crowd and still more questions, her arms feeling like lead after waving from a float for four hours.[12]

At the local level in Cartagena, the election of queens from the neighborhood to the national level maintained social hierarchies as it promoted popular participation. In 1959, Señorita Bolívar, Xenia Méndez, played the role of both charitable patroness and ruling sovereign of the city. As patroness, she presented checks for one thousand pesos to two charitable organizations, and as sovereign she crowned the candidate from the Getsemaní neighborhood as reina popular. These neighborhood popular queens had to work as hard as their departmental peers; dances, parties, receptions, social visits, and invitations from Coca Cola bottlers all took considerable energy, with contestants expected to exhibit grace at all times. Neighborhood queens had to demonstrate stamina and patience as they were under continual social pressure and always on the hot seat. Generally, they were light-skinned mestizas or morenas, usually a head shorter than the departmental queen, while the queens of the Club Naval were white. By 1963, after the implementation of the U.S.-funded Alliance for Progress, a dynamic Peace Corps volunteer, Ivonne Rivenbark, announced to the local press the coronation of the queen from the Blas de Lezo neighborhood who had won the support of her barrio, its committee, and the Peace Corps.[13]

Cali's rapid urbanization and its fame for beautiful women made the city as queen crazy as Cartagena by the late 1950s. Selections of neighborhood queens, many of them titled Reina de Civismo (The Queen of Public Spirit), dominated the local news in early November 1959, leading to the eventual selection of the Reina de los Barrios de Cali. In the following days, the city's new sovereign, Rosalba Arango, was photographed in new dresses gifted to her by a local fashion shop, presenting flowers to team captains prior to their soccer match, and enjoying the first touch of the ball (el saque de honor). Cali's explosive sprawl, the creation of new neighborhoods by recent migrants, and its more intense contact with La Violencia made neighborhood queens important symbols of a dynamic city, one focused more on the future than was Cartagena.[14]

Cali's success as a queen maker in the Reinado Nacional de Belleza in Cartagena during the 1950s made the city a site of pilgrimage for contestants seeking the next crown. Stella Márquez stopped in Cali on her way to Cartagena in early November and was greeted by the Reinas de Café, Folclore, and Algodón (The Queens of Coffee, Folklore, and Cotton). Cali's importance as an agricultural center in the wide and fertile Cauca Valley made product promotion by queens more common there than in Cartagena. The year ended with the Reinado Mundial de la Caña de Azúcar (The World Sugarcane Pageant), with the Colombian Air Force (Fuerza Aérea Colombiana) responsible for transporting the international contestants to the city. Cali was all dressed up for the affair, with thousands of visitors and tourists overfilling the city's hotels to partake in the festivities. National queen Stella Márquez and Cali queen Rosalba Arango opened events, with the governor hyperbolically affirming, "This is peace!" (¡Esto es la paz!).[15]

The governor's pronouncement, the role of the Colombian Air Force, and the symbolism of the queen of sugarcane all merit comment. First, an urban festival complete with parades, music, dancing, feasting, drinking, pageants, and general merrymaking is peace only in a narrow space. It is a moment of civic participation and social peace wrapped in a secular ritual. It does not mean the absence of violence and discord at the regional or national level. Whether peace was declared at the fiesta in Cali in 1959 or at a soccer match in Medellín in the early 1990s, neither ended the violence fueled by structural inequality and political exclusion. Second, the Colombian Air Force transporting the precious cargo of international beauties continued the man in uniform/woman in gown dualism, with each wearing costumes of gendered power. It also points to a connection to La Violencia and to Rojas Pinilla, where the Colombian state became militarized as a response to social and political decomposition. Finally, sugarcane as sweet, succulent, and swaying with the wind suggested the charms of young women's bodies as it transformed sugarcane's past connection to slavery in the Valle del Cauca. However, sugarcane, whether planted, harvested, and refined by slaves in the colonial period or symbolized by international beauty queens in the mid-twentieth century, relied on inequality and the exploitation of human bodies.

By 1967, when Cali bid to host the Sixth Pan American Games, promoters plugged the city's sports facilities, hotels and businesses, culture and history, and beautiful women. Promotional materials included two full pages of caleña beauties, twenty-six young women identified only by their first names. Like Brazilian soccer stars, they were famous, but as young women without titles or surnames, they were also accessible and unattached to familial or marital claims. They were the available human capital marketed as value added to the larger world. Cali won the bid and hosted the games in 1971, the only Colombian city to do so to date. The highlight of the opening ceremonies included twelve thousand girls dancing in native costume.[16]

Development, be it nuclear and catastrophic or urban and modern, framed both Colombian and international contexts. In *El Tiempo*, Bogotá's biggest daily newspaper, a series of cartoons compared the power of nuclear weapons to female beauty. Whether men were distracted by an attractive woman and consequently walked into an exposed manhole labeled "atomic" or a man propositioned a curvaceous woman on the street, labeling her body a super weapon against his poor megaton, female beauty became the modern equivalent of total power.

On the flip side of this international angst about global annihilation, all

FIGURE 7.3   *Los monos de Barti; Cali, solo para mayores de 21 años (Dec. 20, 1965), courtesy* Revista Cromos.

the more real after the Cuban Missile Crisis of October 1962, a new journal for Colombian linguists, poets, and writers brought urban intellectuals into mediated contact with rural poverty. Although most of the articles in *Noticias Culturales* focused on ethnolinguistics, the accompanying photographs of dirt streets, barefoot locals in simple dirty clothes, and the working folk of Putumayo, Caquetá, Bolívar, Córdoba, the Chocó revealed that the progress and development of the National Front had not arrived and would not arrive to rural areas. This was traditional Colombian culture, and it wasn't beautiful; it was dirty.[17]

Culturally, the 1960s started out as a continuation of the stylized 1950s and ended up its own unique decade. Initially formal and regal, the 1960s became sportier, with shorts, slacks, blouses, skirts, and bikinis transmitting a fashion of outdoor athleticism. South American countries triumphed repeatedly at the Miss Universe pageant between 1957 and 1963, with Peru, Colombia, Brazil, and Argentina all winning the crown. The international "sex bombs" of the era, the blondes Marilyn Monroe and Kim Novak as well as the Latins Sophia Loren, Brigitte Bardot, and Natalie Wood maintained the northern and southern European poles of white beauty. Sex became a topic of conversation, culture, and concern, as reliable birth control and the resulting sexual freedom challenged conservative gender stereotypes. JFK's charisma and Jackie's fashions made them the most popular icons among Colombian high school students.[18]

By 1962, Colombia had at least one hundred queens crowned each year. The Reinado del Folclore in Ibagué, Tolima, received a great deal of press attention; one article in *Cromos* literally referred to it as "UN SEDANTE PARA LA VIOLENCIA" (A SEDATIVE FOR THE VIOLENCE). A new women's magazine, *Mujer*, "focusing on women's issues while not neglecting beauty, fashion, the kitchen, themes that women in all times consider important," addressed why pageants garnered so much attention by Colombians. Alluding to the grace, beauty, and social talent required of pageant participants in describing the thousands of women who had to stand in line, state their true age, and accept crude photographs on their national identification cards as a prerequisite for full citizenship, the article likened pageants to participation in modern Colombian society. Behind many fragile thrones rested real economic power: coffee in Manizales, sugarcane in Cali, steel in Sogamoso, petroleum in Barrancabermeja, cereals in Tunja, cotton in Buga, onions in Ocaña. The elements from classical Greek mythology gave Tuluá and Villavicencio the Queen of Fire, Salamina the Queen of Air, and Santa Marta the Queen of the Sea. Beneficent queens represented Charity, or became the fairy godmothers of potable water systems, or in one Tolima town, the Queen of the Cemetery (to push through a small land reform to gain turf to bury the dead). While the Queen of Queens competition to select the Colombian contestant for the Miss Universe pageant still seemed to be in the hands of the Max Factor Company, some young women made being a queen their profession, while a few women moved up the ranks in government administration in Bogotá.[19]

With pageants becoming more popular and more lucrative, their out-

UN SEDANTE PARA LA VIOLENCIA

Noblemente, la candidata del Meta aceptó el fallo del Jurado y desautorizó toda campaña contra la Reina Nacional Elsa Bateman

Aquí están las tres finalistas: Elsa Bateman (Magdalena), Aura Galindo (Meta) y Marcelena Martínez (Antioquia).

"Aunque estoy profundamente agradecida con el pueblo tolimense que quería que se me eligiera reina nacional del folclor, debo reconocer también que el jurado que acogió el nombre de la señorita Elsa Bateman, representante del Magdalena, estuvo acertado en su fallo. En esta clase de certámenes debe existir también gallardía y nobleza. Estoy satisfecha con la corona de virreina nacional del folclor. Me complace, además, infinitamente el triunfo obtenido por mis paisanos del conjunto "Cantares y copleros del Llano", al ganar el primer gran premio de la Cass Daro".

Con aquellas palabras nos recibió Aura Galindo, del Meta, al día siguiente del acto de coronación de la señorita Elsa Bateman y cuando aún en las calles se discutía acaloradamente el fallo del jurado, que estuvo integrado por los señores Manolo García, Bebe Martelo, Julio Corredor y la señora Beatriz de Gálvez. Y en esa forma, ella misma ponía fin a la polémica. Y hablaba así precisamente en momentos en que numerosos partidarios suyos recorrían las calles de Ibagué a los gritos de "Viva la señorita Meta" e invitaban a coronarla en uno de los cafés de la ciudad o en una caseta —aún no tenían decidido el sitio—, como según decían, "por decisión soberana del pueblo". En realidad, no solo en la noche del 26 de junio último, cuando se efectuó la coronación en el Teatro Tolima, sino durante varios días siguientes, numerosas personas no se resignaban a aceptar el fallo del jurado. Se obstinaban en que la reina fuera la señorita Aura Galindo, pues durante todos los desfiles había entusiasmado al pueblo en su traje llanero, con pistola al cinto y cartuchera cruzada al pecho, a la bandolera y acompañando con maracas a un conjunto musical representativo de su joven departamento. Después se supo que fue precisamente ese hecho uno de los motivos que tuvo el jurado para no elegirla reina nacional del folclor. Consideró impropio que en los desfiles siempre hubiera estado vestida de hombre llanero y que debió haberse presentado con el traje típico correspondiente a las mujeres de su región, tal como lo hicieron las demás candidatas, aunque en esa forma hubiera despertado entusiasmo popular.

Y a pesar, pues, de que continuaban las aclamaciones populares para la señorita Galindo, ella misma insistía en no aceptar una coronación en un café y pedía respeto para la señori-

CROMOS, JULIO 9, 1962

FIGURE 7.4   *Un sedante para la violencia, Cromos, July 9, 1962, courtesy* Revista Cromos.

come became more contested. The 1961–1962 queen seasons became particularly controversial. In 1961 at the Señorita Colombia national pageant in Cartagena, the clear popular favorites were from Caldas, Cundinamarca, and Santander, but the finalists came from Bolívar, Caldas, and Antioquia. The judges, non-Spanish speakers using a new point system, angered not only the crowd but also most of the other contestants after naming Cartagena's own, Sonia Heidman, queen. Like Jackie Kennedy, Sonia was taller and thinner than most of the women around her and was graceful as controversy whirled around her. Runner-up Luisa Marina of Caldas complained about the judges' decision and likened the bathing suit competition to a dog show or cattle fair. She set the record straight by denying pageant propaganda that said that she had university training, stating plainly that she spent her time idly not studying. Only one other candidate attended a reception for Sonia the next day, while ten others were notably absent in protest. After an eleven-year hiatus, Cartagena kept the crown at home but paid a steep price in negative national publicity.[20] Likewise, the point totals by the judges at the Reinado Mundial de la Caña de Azúcar in Cali placed Bolivia first and Colombia second, but the announced winner was Miss USA, Caroline Lee. No one seemed to know who switched the judges' decision, but it was clear that Colombian sugar producers were trying to get a larger quota of the U.S. sugar market; that "coincidence" was not lost on the readers of *Mujer*. Finally, at the Reinado del Folclore in Ibague, the pistol-packing blonde, blue-eyed firecracker from Meta, Aura Galindo, won the crowd but lost the judges because she only appeared in a cowboy outfit. The crowd again attacked the judges' decision and planned to exercise popular sovereignty by crowning Aura in a parallel but popular pageant. From the tough land of the grassland cowboys of Meta, Aura Galindo commanded the crowd to accept the judges' finding, halting plans for a parallel ceremony. In all three cases, popular emotions contested sovereignty when confronted with shady and exclusive elite procedures during the same year that Conservatives took the presidency from Liberals per the design of the National Front.[21]

The business of being beautiful, glamorous, a model, and a queen proliferated in the early 1960s. An English-language advertisement run by the Colombian Tourism Agency (Empresa Colombiana de Turismo) in the *New Yorker*, the *New York Times Sunday Magazine*, *Sports Illustrated*, *Esquire*, *Holiday*, and the *Saturday Review* built off Clairol's catchy and titillating pitch, "Does she . . . or doesn't she?" asking, "Is she or isn't she a Colombiana?" The model, from Chicago and not colombiana, wearing a classic sheath and dark mantilla over her hair, looked both elegant and traditional. According to the ad, Colombia was an unspoiled tourist opportunity, complete with French restaurants, jungle safaris, bullfights, and exquisite and affordable emeralds. One could enjoy a Caribbean beach and be skiing the Andes the very same day. Golfers could drive a golf ball seventy-five yards further than they had in their lives in the thin mountain air of Bogotá. The country was full of attractions and cheap—a two-mile cab ride cost 15 cents! All of these delights were fronted by a provocative question of an attractive young woman who might be an exotic Colombian beauty.[22]

At the top of the pageant pyramid, the Colombian representative during her speech at the 1962 Miss Universe contest invited everyone to visit Colombia soon so that they could enjoy the ancient and the modern attractions of her country. She assured the listeners that all would be greeted very warmly and made to feel at home. The Max Factor Company still covered many of her expenses and managed the queen's affairs. The journalists of Bogotá claimed that the new Miss Universe would visit their city first, having posted the $2,000 weekly fee. At the Jesuit university in Bogotá, the new Universidad Javeriana queen planned to improve sports programs for women, extend cafeteria service, improve the library and language labs, and promote a new music hall. Closer to the ground in Vélez, Santander—famous for its beautiful women a century earlier—the town queen shared a more traditional view of the role of women, asserting that "good homes bring good children, and good children become good citizens" (buenos hogares dan buenos hijos, y los buenos hijos son buenos ciudadanos).[23]

Modeling became another associated trade for Colombian queens. Publicity agencies, stores, and clothing lines from Jantzen, McGregor, and Peter Pan all needed models. Queens made some side money as models, practicing their walk, movement, and gestures. A new school of "glamour," run by a Spanish woman teaching the French method, became the first modeling school in Bogotá, teaching young women how to sit, stand, walk, speak, and smoke with grace, including instruction for younger girls on how to greet people and to eat with proper manners.[24]

The beginnings of a small countercultural movement also emerged in the early 1960s. Those of the "new wave" (la nueva ola) were teenagers or college students who let their hair go wild and dressed in faded blue jeans, oversized jackets, and, in the case of girls, black stockings or with legs bare. Influenced by the fashions of Marlon Brando and James Dean and by the Beatniks of San Francisco and Paris, those of the new wave reportedly experimented with drugs and pursued sexual awareness and freedom. A more intellectual challenge came from the *nadaistas*, influenced by dada and existentialism, but also by the violence of Colombian society. The nadaistas became active and aggressive in their antitraditionalism, inveighing against establishment writers and especially against the Catholic Church and religious symbolism. Like the Beats, they lived on the margins of bourgeois society, sleeping where they wanted, exchanging favors to get along.[25]

The Miss Colombia national pageant became an annual event in 1962, with Mexican actor Cantinflas joining four North Americans on the judges' panel. Recent plastic surgery made it impossible for Cantinflas to smile; he reportedly looked younger and less ugly but was only able to gesture with his eyes. Miss Bolívar also raised eyebrows by putting on six kilos following injections of the anabolic steroid Primobolan, later used by Arnold Schwarzenegger and Alex Rodríguez, to burn fat and build muscle. Like sex, plastic surgery and steroid use were now out of the closet. Five-foot-seven-inch winner Marta Restrepo lost five kilos during the pageant (from 132 pounds to 121), danced the twist, didn't work or study, and spoke to the four American judges in English; she planned to study other foreign languages in preparation for international travel. Hailing from high-society Barranquilla, she received two thousand dollars from her sponsoring department to buy her trousseau in Miami. Cantinflas, who nightly gambled in the casino until 4:00 a.m., rewarded the winners and himself by inviting the top three finishers to a film festival in Mexico.[26]

In the wake of the Cuban Missile Crisis and the ugly violence in Oxford, Mississippi, over desegregation of the University of Mississippi, Miss Chocó, Carmen Arango, knew that she would not win the 1962 Miss Colombia pageant because her race did not represent most Colombians. With the same preferred measurements as the winner (90/60/90 cm or 35.5/23.5/35.5 inches), and as a woman of African ancestry, she was in Cartagena representing her department to the larger nation so Colombians would at least remember that Chocó and its people were part of the country. Although Colombia, Brazil, and most other Latin American countries did not institutionalize segregation through law and democracy as was done in the United States, social discrimination still maintained the colonial hierarchies of pigmentocracy. *Cromos* suggested that Colombia might emulate Brazil in selecting the most beautiful mulata queen each year, stimulating lackluster interest in pageants among the black population. However, pageant promoters proudly asserted, without providing any evidence, that only in Colombia and England could people of color and whites sit at the same table and share a meal.[27]

Education and information about sex and the tensions it raised among parents, schools, and adolescents in a Catholic society framed a provocative 1962 article in *Cromos*. Asking why, if sex is so basic in human existence, Colombians knew so little about it, the article pointed to taboos taught by the Catholic Church and to parents who did not want their children learning about sex in schools but then failed to teach them anything about it at home either. The generational silence about sex seemed legitimate to parents but left adolescents in the dark. The article concluded that parents should take the lead in teaching their children information about anatomy, sexuality, and sexual reproduction and in educating youth so that they could understand their sex drive and voluntarily control it. Sex as a topic of conversation was in the larger modern culture, but both religious and secular schools avoided contact with that fact.[28]

By early 1964, *Mujer* ran articles diametrically opposed to one another about sexuality. The first piece reprinted sections of *The Housewife's Handbook on Selective Promiscuity*, in which a woman from Arizona openly discussed her three marriages and divorces, described her sexual affairs with seventeen men, and chronicled about a hundred sexual experiences. She argued that sexual expression was normal and healthy, and that women had a right to enjoy orgasms. Although the U.S. courts ruled the advertisements for the book obscene, she argued that the ignorance of sex and of the body were the true obscenities. Conversely, Angel Valtierra, S.J., published an article in a Universidad Javeriana journal arguing that the celebration of erotic pleasure in Western civilization signaled a future social catastrophe and a Cold War strategic risk. In contrast to the decadence of the West, he found a moral dignity and great reserve concerning sex in the Communist Bloc and in the Third World, suggesting that if the idol of sexuality were not contained, then Colombians would be discredited before God, communism, and the Third World.[29]

Cromos reprinted an article that year by Rosemary Ruether that placed the discussion of birth control within a Catholic framework. As a Catholic mother, she argued that birth control was necessary because the Church-approved "rhythm method" was ineffective and caused strains between couples and within the family. It placed wives in the role of policing the conjugal bed, and it forced husbands to choose between the salvation of their souls and that of their families.[30]

Marriage became another bipolar issue in the early 1960s. While *Cromos* gave lavish attention to the fairytale weddings of famous beauty queens that fulfilled the Cinderella story, another sober article criticized the laws and state of marriage in Colombia. Since the civil code defined marital dominion as a husband's rights over the person and goods of his wife, husbands routinely mistreated, beat, and even killed their wives as proof of that rule. Some elite and middle-class wives only expected their husbands to pay their bills, ignoring domestic or child-rearing duties. Many Colombians refused to marry, worried about entrapment until death in a bad marriage, choosing instead to form serial unions with various partners over time. Fifteen Latin American countries had legalized divorce, but Colombia had not, instead enforcing disastrous and dysfunctional marriages, which divorce could at least address.[31]

Media interest in the Miss Universe pageant remained high in Colombia, with some articles hinting at the grimy side of the business. Max Factor and Catalina sponsorship of the Reina de Reinas pageant at the Hotel Tequendama in Bogotá underlined corporate control of the Miss Universe business over the increasingly uniform-looking contestants. At the 1963 Miss Universe contest in Miami, judge Peter Sellers invited seven North American and European contestants to accompany him to Hollywood, where a pleased Sellers was photographed for an MGM promotion, surrounded by the seven beauties while lounging and reading a script. *Cromos* reported that the seven would be in Sellers' next film. It was clear that the thirty-eight-year-old notorious playboy was enjoying his role as a judge of fetching eighteen-year-olds in international beauty pageants. Sellers followed his 1963 Miss Universe duties with service at the 1964 Miss World pageant, where other beauties reportedly spent time around Sellers' pool. The tight connection between beauty, sex appeal, power, and fame invited liaisons between Sellers and his bevy of beauties, or earlier and more singularly in 1950, between that of judge Carlo Ponti with fifteen-year-old Miss Rome runner-up Sophia Loren.[32]

The leering middle-aged male judges of the 1963 Señorita Colombia contest certainly enjoyed their work when the shapely blonde, blue-eyed, eighteen-year-old Leonor Duplant passed closely by their patio tables wearing a swimsuit and heels. She was the shortest of the contestants but was young, fresh, and happy; dubbed a Colombian Brigitte Bardot, "she distilled femininity through all her pores."[33] One of eleven children, she was from Cúcuta, a city on the border with Venezuela, and served as the private secretary of the governor of Norte de Santander. Many of the contestants that year knew that they would not win the crown but went to Cartagena to make their hometown folks proud, get some goodies, and have a good time. Honored and fortunate to receive the crown, Leonor pledged to help the poor and needy but then revealed the angst found in many people her age and a discomfort at being on such public display, saying, "pero en mi todo es feo" (but in me everything is ugly).[34]

When asked if pageants might take people's energies away from more useful or constructive tasks, judge Mark Sulkes, president of Diner's Club, said that people needed "their little gods to adore." He suggested that ancient pagan devotion to fertility lay deep in the modern psyche. Little goddesses, many crowned during November reina season at pageants for young girls,

El jurado no puede ocultar su
admiración ante la aparición de la
belleza cucuteña. Ella es Leonor Duplant.
Tiene 18 años, mide 1.61, pesa 53 kilos
y sus medidas son: 89-58-91.
Dicen que se parece a Brigitte Bardot;
a pesar de ser una de las más bajitas,
se ha destacado en Cartagena.

FIGURE 7.5 *El jurado no puede ocultar su admiración,* Cromos *(Nov. 18, 1963),*
courtesy Revista Cromos.

came in the form of goddesses to the sea who needed to look great in a swimsuit and swim well to win. The first national queen of deaf-mutes was crowned
in 1964 and photographed with scepter and tiara for *El Tiempo*, placing her
peer group before the national stage.[35]

Politically, the National Front mechanics passed the presidency from Liberal Lleras Camargo (1958–1962) to Conservative León Valencia (1962–1966),
back to Liberal Lleras Restrepo (1966–1970). Most presidents came from
elite families of former presidents, casting elections back toward past memories rather than forward to future dreams. The majority Liberal Party experienced widening splits within its ranks between moderate and Marxist-
affiliated factions, while Conservatives still split between Gómez and Ospina
factions. Although formally excluded from the National Front, the third-

party ANAPO (Alianza Nacional Popular) led by now returned Gustavo Rojas Pinilla, played an active role in electoral politics throughout the 1960s. The populist, anti–National Front, anti-elitist pitch of ANAPO and Rojas Pinilla echoed some of the rhetoric of Gaitán and found strong resonance among young and working-class urban voters, allowing ANAPO to increase its electoral support in presidential elections from 2 percent in 1962 to 28 percent in 1966 to 39 percent in 1970, when ANAPO almost won the election outright.[36]

Other challengers adopted revolutionary and violent tactics to confront the National Front. Both the FARC (Fuerzas Armadas Revolucionarias de Colombia) and the ELN (Ejército de Liberación Nacional) emerged about 1964, the FARC from survivors of peasant republics from previous decades and from revolutionary factions of the Colombian Communist Party, the ELN from urban militants who built rural nuclei of insurrection inspired by the successful Cuban revolution of 1959. The EPL (Ejército Popular de Liberación) mixed both Cubanist and Maoist elements and began military operations in 1967, totaling three insurrectionist movements in the 1960s. All remained small during that initial decade, making political and military mistakes and meeting significant repression from a national army bolstered by U.S. counterinsurgency assistance and training and from paramilitary units employed by elite interests. The biggest group, the FARC, represented continuity in Colombian history, from the reform era of the 1930s, to the violence of the 1940s and 1950s, to the exclusion and elitism of the 1960s, a reminder that Colombia's biggest challenges are found at home even if the ELN and the EPL later gained inspiration from Cuba.[37]

Father Camilo Torres Restrepo became the highest-profile revolutionary convert to the guerrilla cause, although a unique example. The thirty-six-year-old priest, educated in Louvain, Belgium, and from an elite Colombian family, organized an urban reformist movement but then radicalized and joined the ELN. His political activism led to his forced abandonment of the priesthood in 1965. In an interview with *Cromos*, Torres argued that revolution was the only possible option to end the poverty, misery, and inequality in Colombia. He hoped that 85 percent of Colombians would support the revolutionary cause, leaving open the possibility of peaceful change through elections if supported by the armed forces. However, if the National Front elites would not release their hold on official power, he vowed that violence would become the mechanism of structural change. He died in combat as an ELN guerrilla in 1966, killed by Colombian troops led by Korean War veteran Colonel Álvaro Valencia Tovar, one year before Ernesto "Che" Guevara joined the ranks of revolutionary martyrs in Bolivia. Unlike those in Brazil, Peru, and Chile, the Colombian Catholic hierarchy did not embrace the theology of liberation breathed into the church following the Second Vatican Council (1962–1965), instead emulating the Argentine church, which stood with traditional elites. Nonetheless, the Colombian church did embrace the National Front, thereby disconnecting from its traditional enmity for the Liberal Party and quietly accepting government reforms in education and even in birth control policies.[38]

While the sociologist Torres didn't know how to fire a gun when he announced his violent intentions, fellow Catholic Efraín González carried with him a crucifix and images of the Virgin and of the sacred heart of Jesus as he slaughtered scores of Liberals as part of his partisan holy war. The pious and prayerful González started out as a sergeant in the Rural Police of Boyacá in 1956 but then formed his own gang by 1959, robbing and killing at will. He received political and economic support from Conservatives and from the Church, and he wanted to serve as a priest through the early 1960s, but then he was killed in Bogotá following a five-hour shootout with police in 1965. The morning after his death, people flocked to the spot where he fell; ice cream and cheese vendors set up shop, and troubadours and guitarists composed songs to honor his bravery, asking, "Why did you kill him, criminals?" Like other leaders of armed bands formed during La Violencia, González fell to official violence but was lionized as a popular hero.[39]

Socioeconomically, Colombia changed during the 1960s. By 1964 more Colombians lived in urban areas, some pushed out by rural violence, and others pulled by jobs, schools, and perceived opportunities in cities. A coffee depression between 1957 and 1966 pushed down real wages, leading to a wave of labor actions, especially among middle-class workers. Union membership almost tripled, but fragmented and competitive labor confederations kept the labor movement weak. More women became literate, attended university, and entered the job market. Urban dwellers had more contact with mass media, both the self-censored national outlets and more provocative international music, film, and television. The opening of family planning clinics in urban areas after 1965 made contraceptives more widely available, eventually trickling into rural areas. Colombia's population growth rate fell from 3.2 percent in 1960 to 2 percent twenty years later. The disconnection between sex and procreation clearly marked a decline in the social power of the Catholic Church, as it introduced new values and social conduct across gender.[40]

Culturally, the mid- to late 1960s held within it a fascinating encounter between inherited conservative values and provocative challenges to the established order via rock 'n' roll music and youth counterculture. A 1964 survey of high school students found JFK twelve times more popular than Fidel Castro, with Charlton Heston the most popular artist, three times more popular than

Cantinflas, even though some Colombian youth complained that "life is a thing that's imposed on us without our consent."[41] Señorita Colombia 1964, Marta Cecilia Calero, a blonde, green-eyed, sixteen-year-old who lied about her age, declared after her victory that "politics should be the exclusive activity of men. We women should stand out in the home." She married less than a year later. All of the 1964 candidates spoke against divorce and civil marriage, while in the background one heard the competing rhythms of bossa nova, bolero, and the Beatles.[42]

Marta Cecilia represented the tradition of beauty useful to social and economic elites. She appeared on the first cover of the magazine *Antioquia Turística*, where she was lauded as "the august consecration of beauty and the incarnation of the moral attributes of the Colombian woman."[43] The two hundred thousand people who greeted her in Cali and at her Cinderella wedding reinforced the equation that through a young woman's beauty one gained economic success and social security. Pageants won praise for stimulating tourism, and queens for generating charity that purportedly would end the plight of street children. *Mujer* ran articles in 1965 on feminine beauty and coquettishness meeting on the street with male flirtatious compliments (piropos) and on intimate but acceptable relationships between the new secretaries and the new bosses—both young, capable, and attractive—reflections of changing times guided by traditional gender relations. Another article in *Mujer* claimed that ugly women need not exist any longer, as plastic surgery could perfect any face or figure.[44]

The Beatles' splashy success in the United States trickled into the pages of *Cromos* in late 1964. As the idols of youth the world over, John, Paul, George, and Ringo dressed up for success, with carefully coifed hair over their ears, their music as well as their comportment bridging the gap of class, culture, artist, and audience. They acted like free clowns to bring a little joy to a world threatened by wars and atomic weapons. They were a younger, softer form of masculinity, appealing to younger males and females alike.[45]

As the Beatles were born into World War II, the Colombian band members who covered their songs were born into La Violencia. Covering songs in English from the Beatles, the Rolling Stones, Ray Charles, and Ricky Nelson, groups like Los Speakers and Los Flippers introduced the sounds and styles shaping youth culture in Britain and the United States. Band members of Los Speakers donned suits and wore their hair a little longer than the norm, as did the Beatles, displaying a discernible level of independence from parental control. Individual performers like Oscar Golden(berg), Harold, and Eliana wrote songs in Spanish, mixing influences from Bob Dylan and Colombia's nadaistas, bringing poetry to music with a social message. Colombian adherents of "yeah-yeah" and "go-go" gathered on the north side of Bogotá to dance and drink in discotheques, whereas middle- and working-class fans seemed to start the social phenomenon on the south side, where creative and free fashions led to social leveling. Dancing was structured but liberating, allowing one to release spirit and energy, which was said to be good for a healthy body. Go-go fashions in 1966 might still involve a suit and perhaps a slightly fuller mop of hair for males, and short skirts, boots, and sweaters for females.[46] Not since the introduction of the modern bicycle in the 1890s had the youth of Bogotá so reveled in the liberation offered by rock 'n' roll music and the fashions of the 1960s.

Go-go involved more than music and fashion. It offered society a fresh, new life, one transforming human behavior as it destroyed and then re-created new myths, values, customs, feelings, and gender relations. Youth, in huge postwar numbers, shaped reality to their liking, challenging tradition and the establishment in improvised dancing that yearned for equality between the sexes. The spirit of youthful rebellion against the hypocrisy of past generations had even triumphed in that bastion of tradition, England. The long flowing hair, the long undulating legs, and the crystalline eyes of go-go beauty brought the hope and excitement of rejuvenated youth to a weary and apathetic world.[47]

Although go-go promised a radical reshaping of reality, it started small in Bogotá and then branched out to Medellín and Cali, its growth limited by linguistic and cultural incomprehension. Students and young intellectuals found more resonance in its ideas and styles, yet political restraints and censorship limited free expression. Oscar Golden, wearing a suit and well-trimmed beard, spoke like Gaitán when he criticized the ruling class as he pressed for greater freedom to record protest songs. Although it was not formally prohibited, Golden claimed that record companies would not release protest music for fear of government sanctions. A concert featuring Golden, Los Speakers, and go-go dancers was canceled in Manizales in 1966, as the mayor's office cited concerns about morality and public order related to a concert in Medellín by the same performers fifteen days earlier. Described as the idol of Colombian youth in 1967 and a supporter of nadaísta poetry and songs, Golden sold records in various countries in Latin America, even as he and other artists faced de facto censorship at home.[48]

"Ye-Ye" and "Go-Go" fashion shows in 1966 and 1967 signaled elite acknowledgement of the new trends. Shows in Cúcuta benefited a local institute for needy children as they presented the bright colors, geometric designs, and short skirts emblematic of London designers; although the new fashions started on the streets, English designers quickly pounced on them and made them a mass commodity. On its 59th anniversary, Coltejer sponsored a go-go fashion show in Medellín's Club Unión, highlighting both Colombian fabrics and designs. Outside of Bogotá in Guatavita, the vision of fashion 2000 included a model in fishnets, miniskirt, stylized ruana, and space-age hat. The show also included Colombia's first black model, sixteen-year-old Anisia Perea. All the shows recognized the vitality of the new fashions, as elites consumed them as they maintained their social privilege. It was clear, in the era of Twiggy, that the new fashions looked good on the young and lean, that despite reported "radical changes" young women still liked a good crooner, and that young women in Greenwich Village preferred men who needed protection, a reflection of their maternal nature. Clearly, all the talk of a new and fresh reality couldn't topple existing power structures, be they in New York, London, or Colombia.[49]

"La nueva ola," the new wave, hit the 1965 Señorita Colombia pageant. Contestants wore much heavier makeup, à la Twiggy and Mary Quant, some sporting a "flip" hairstyle. Harold and his group performed a few of the new-wave songs. By the next year, one heard the music of the Beatles and the Colombian group Los Flippers in the background, as miniskirts, hot pants, bikinis, and long hair appeared among the contestants. Internationally, the new cinematic beauties Julie Christie and Raquel Welch earned comment and emulation. By 1967, the pop culture mania for the campy television series *Batman*, the liberating spirit of hippies, and the power of LSD became amusing themes at costume parties prior to the coronation.[50]

The hippie culture of the San Francisco Summer of Love and the stylized eroticism of the new cinema's film *Blow-up* bounced into the pages of *Cromos* in 1967. Sporting buttons reading "el nadaismo es la verdad" and "pray for sex" on his Mexican vest, Colombian reporter and poet Dukardo Hinestrosa found the young people flocking to the Haight Ashbury in San Francisco to be united by pacifism, antimaterialism, drug use, and sexual freedom. The fog of marijuana smoke and the ubiquitous hits of acid did not obscure the fact that "hippie-land" lacked an original intellectual or artistic vitality, yet it did signal youthful rebellion against a rich and powerful nation entering a crisis. Michelangelo Antonioni's first English language film, *Blow-up*, used the cultural freedom of mid-1960s London to weave a tale of a photographer's accidental brush with murder as sexual freedom and drug use punctuated the story, its eroticism pushing the limits of censorship.[51]

The eroticism of *Blow-up* and the sexual freedom in the Haight Ashbury were made possible, in part, by technology and the birth control pill. The social and cultural impact of the birth control pill raised radical questions of gender in Colombia. If the pill challenged gendered ideas on sexuality, changed behavior, and reconstructed the meaning of sex and marriage, the outcome might be greater equality between the sexes. Even the much more innocuous baby bottle, filled with infant formula, disconnected babies from their mothers' breasts, opening the possibility that men, not just women, could raise infants. With a record number of babies being born in Colombia in 1967, the demographic wave would overwhelm the existing political economy of Colombia, making birth control policies essential for stable government in the future. While the pill and IUD were effective, in poor or rural areas the hope was that the cheaper and more available condom and sponge might offer effective measures of family planning.[52]

Although the concept of female inferiority found in the 1546 Council of Trent doctrine of Original Sin still held sway with the Concordat between the Vatican and the government of Colombia, French Protestant feminist Evelyne Sullerot presented a sophisticated and fashionable image of the modern woman. Sullerot, praised in the pages of *Cromos* for her enchanting style, critiqued traditional gender constructions, Freudian theory, and the socioeconomic need to objectify women to sell commercial products. For Sullerot, the mania for "cover girls," beauty pageants, and erotic images of women in the 1960s represented a reactionary and retrograde response to real changes in modern women's lives. It was clear to Colombian women's rights activist Ana de Karpf that continuing sexual repression of women in the midst of an erotic wave of mass media would objectify women and lead to new myths to maintain female subordination. For other Colombian women of great accomplishments—politicians, lawyers, doctors, writers, journalists, the types of women who heartened Soledad Acosta de Samper three generations before—the modern educated professional woman was elite and not representative of most women in Colombia.[53] In short, although rock 'n' roll, go-go, drug use, sexual liberation, birth control, and changing gender roles signaled significant changes, in institutionally conservative Colombia those changes touched only a minority of the nation's population.

In 1968, *Cromos* ran a Julie Christie look-alike contest, sponsored by MGM and the Venezuelan airline VIASA. The fifty-nine contestants, about half blonde and about half from Bogotá, sought to emulate the stylish but natural beauty of the British actress on the heels of rare victories by blondes at the 1962–1965 Señorita Colombia pageant. With beauty marketing moving toward a natural but developed beauty, *Cromos* ran a long article on the cosmetics and beauty business. Ironically, the business of looking natural included some of the seven billion dollars spent on beauty products in the United States in 1967. According to the business executives and psychologists cited, consumers bought hope, youth, class, well-being, confidence, and magic. As cosmetics made people feel better—and didn't kill them, as did na-palm—executives saw no harm in the industry, concluding that "where there is vanity, there will be cosmetics."[54]

The rising cost of beauty pageants troubled a reporter covering the 1967 Señorita Colombia national pageant. The traditional street events for Carta-gena's November independence day festivities involved the people, the people of color. Pageant events increasingly were closed to the public, with ticket prices beyond reach for the city's black population. The pageant no longer belonged to the local society but to an exclusive national elite. That exclusion from opportunity also pushed the Colombian singer Leonor González out of her native country, first to the Soviet Union and then to Spain, where she recorded with R.C.A. Victor, the fourth Latin American to do so, the first being Carlos Gardel. González mastered the music and culture of the Pacific Coast and of the environs of Cali, mainly recording boleros, pasillos, and bambucos. She left for greater opportunity and to record music for the people, a goal blocked by Colombian recording and media executives. Her songs were included in the 1965 film *Tierra amarga*, a film shot in Quibdó by Cuban di-rector Roberto Ochoa and banned in Colombia. She criticized the imposition of U.S. power throughout the world, blamed politicians for the neglected and backward state of Colombia, wouldn't comment publically on Tirofijo—a top commander of the FARC—saying there were certain things that you shouldn't and couldn't say, and encouraged women to make their own liberty, mindful that men would only change slowly. Known as "La negra grande," González left the restrictions and prohibitions of her home country, as had Josephine Baker four decades before, emblematic of the political and social exclusion found in both Colombia and the United States.[55]

By 1968, Leonor was giving concerts at Radio City Music Hall in Man-hattan, performing protest songs for the first time, one a lament for the re-cently assassinated Martin Luther King Jr. *Cromos* praised her for her drive, her ability to speak to many audiences, and the energy she gave to various com-mitments. The magazine predicted that as a singer with a strong voice that would last, like that of Ella Fitzgerald, Leonor would be part of the music world for some time; indeed, Leonor became one of the biggest Colombian singers of the twentieth century. She transcended the destination of her early hit, "A la mina" ("To the mine"), later singing to peoples around the world who had struggled for centuries to break their bondage.[56]

Marta Traba likewise drew the attention of *Cromos* as an iconoclastic rebel, admirer of the Cuban Revolution, trained historian, and art critic who pro-moted the new wave of Colombian artists. An Argentine by birth, she left her home country and became a professor of art history at Bogotá's Universidad Nacional and the Universidad de los Andes. A disciplined worker, she founded the Museo de Arte Moderno in Bogotá, along the way publishing several books on the history of Colombian and Latin American art. She suggested that intellectuals could become dangerous, not just inconvenient, in a conservative state when they defined their politics and relentlessly pursued public critiques of the inequities found all around them. She was stylish and hip in her fashions, blending strong visual and intellectual messages. As a Marxist and from a socialist perspective, she paid political and professional costs for her support of Cuba, losing university positions. She was critical of "The Boom" in Latin American literature and the anointing of Cortázar, Vargas Llosa, Fuentes, Cabrera Infante, and García Márquez as the chosen ones, because other Latin American writers like Rulfo, Arguedas, Onetti, and Sábato likewise deserved critical attention and often outwrote their more famous colleagues. She was expelled from Colombia in 1968 after she criticized the government for the military occupation of the Universidad Nacional.[57]

Barranquilla-born, Cali-educated writer Fanny Buitrago dressed in paisley and surrounded herself in her apartment with the chaos of half-finished manuscripts, overflowing ashtrays, matchboxes, and party invitations. Described by *Cromos* as not white, not black, not yellow, not mulata, not mestiza, but with a piece of all those in her, this maverick's enchantment depended on not being definable. Called the best female writer of her day, Fanny mixed intense days of writing with three days of partying. She described herself as not so intelligent but a good writer, clumsy and needy, unable to cash a check or multiply numbers, vain, intuitive, weighing forty kilos nude, and ugly but lucky. Often linked to the nadaistas, a connection she at times denied, Fanny was a complicated and talented writer, another free voice of 1968.[58]

One week after the article on Fanny Buitrago, *Cromos* ran a titillating article on the "Guerra de los bustos" (the war of the busts), featuring the prominent cleavage of European and North American film stars including Sophia Loren, Jane Mansfield, Raquel Welch, Brigitte Bardot, Jean Seberg, Anita Ekberg, and others. Dominated by alluring photographs, this six-page photographic spread struck a much more visibly accessible cord of female substance; it was physical and soft, maternal and sexy. If Colombian women like Leonor, Marta, and Fanny pushed for greater expression in a still confined Colombia, the voluptuous film stars and the exuberant beauties who suddenly seemed to be overwhelming Wall Street pointed modern commercial beauty back to the traditional goal of female sex appeal used to attract male attention.[59]

In 1968, Avianca stewardesses sported new wardrobes, complete with skirts cut above the knee and stylish red ruanas, to make the airline and its female representatives distinctive around the world. In 1968, *Cromos* ran an article by nadaista founder Gonzalo Arango on the popular underside of the November festivities in Cartagena. Whenever possible he stayed away from the official pageant events, those absurd "comedies to sell cosmetics, whiskey, and to break the tedious boredom of high society."[60] Instead, he found, paraphrasing Camus about Paris, "that Cartagena during the pageant is a dirty city where the people have black skin." He hung out with the drunks and the transvestites, the ones of "popular madness preparing religiously for Carnival and its cult of dance and liberty." With the majority of the men dressed as women, who "coquettishly took morbid satisfaction at their sexual metamorphosis, their ambiguity of being confused with the feminine eternal, giving them secret excitement, a certain nostalgia, and devotion to the cult of the prohibited."[61] In 1968, women's liberation activists protested at the Miss America pageant in Atlantic City, likening the pageant to a meat market or cattle fair, one where women were objectified, commodified, and made obsolete, a site where woman became synonymous with the worst of racism, sexism, militarism, and capitalism.[62]

In 1968, María Victoria Uribe Alarcón, Bogotá's representative to the 1968 Señorita Colombia contest, sported a short, stylish haircut à la Mia Farrow in *Rosemary's Baby*. María Victoria's expressive eyes and big smile welcomed others even as her hairstyle—cut to highlight the face, ears exposed—and her hippie fashions, including the button on her wide-brimmed hat advertising "I'm a Virgin," hit so many modern cords that they confused some Colombians. Invited by Mayor Virgilio Barco to represent Bogotá with her intelligence and to speak her mind, she initially refused, saying she was a hippie and a pot smoker, but then spoke out on abortion, euthanasia, and free love, breaking many unwritten rules as she upset the pageant from the inside. She was both representation and self-represented, object and subject, feminine and smart. Referred to as the "modern queen," the "liberated queen," or the "anti-queen," María Victoria added a new look but also greater substance to the role of beauty queen. She was free-spirited, independent, intelligent, unafraid, and confident. Asked about the meaning of beauty, she said, "Something beautiful is something that is. I'd say that the beautiful is the everyday, that beauty is the real. Today, the beautiful woman is the one who lives her life, the one that doesn't worry about physical beauty or being well dressed. The beautiful woman today is the nonconformist with statutes, with dictated norms and that stuff."[63] Her openness and candor won over the other contestants who elected her most congenial (*mejor compañera*). Asked how modern women should be, she said, "I think they should be vital." Asked how she meant "vital," she said, "Well, active, obviously." María Victoria didn't win

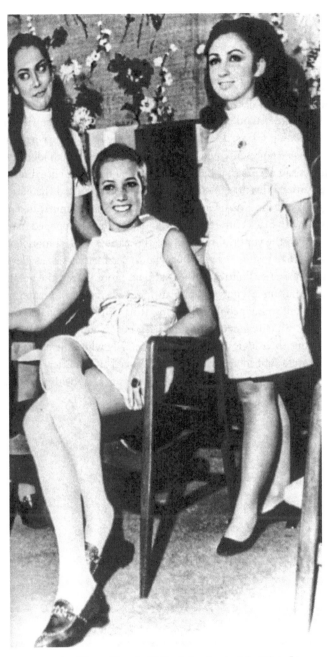

FIGURE 7.6   *María Victoria Uribe, la "anti-reina" (1968), in* Las
más bellas, *p. 119, courtesy Concurso Nacional de Belleza (Cartagena,
Colombia).*

the crown but did go on to study archaeology, anthropology, and history, and she still works at Colombian universities to understand the dynamics of violence in her country and around the world.[64] Both literally and figuratively, she appropriated beauty to sabotage the formal stage of the pageant and then went on to probe the meaning and aesthetics of the beast of violence.

Much changed in the decade between 1958 and 1968, from Luz Marina, who still couldn't understand all the fuss about her, to María Victoria, who purposefully kicked up a fuss. The proliferation of regional beauty pageants and folkloric festivals represented efforts to reproduce Colombian identity in civic and nonpartisan events that had popular appeal but were elite directed, much like the National Front. Fallout from La Violencia shifted the nation's positive image toward the North Coast, popularizing tropical music in a mediated encounter with black culture. Culture and attitudes also opened to rock 'n' roll music and to the youthful rebellion of the sixties, while a more lethal path led to Colombian insurgents rebelling against a state they saw as illegitimate and antidemocratic. Politically, the National Front played the game of continuity and exclusion, even as Colombian voters abstained in greater percentages, with many young people still seeing Rojas Pinilla as a viable alternative to the stale old elite game. As in the past, beauty and beast inhabited distinct realms, but their logics intertwined, especially when the elitism and exclusion of the state rubbed against currents of social and political inclusion and as Colombia moved into the international dynamics of the drug trade.

The cultural threads of 1960s freedom and expression dropped into the early 1970s with hippies, marijuana, and nonconformity adding to the tumult of rapidly expanding large cities. By the early 1970s, Colombians became more cynical about the National Front and about the Concurso Nacional de Belleza in Cartagena, both seen as elite fixes rooted in the past. By mid-decade, the challenge of revolution—be it political or cultural—had subsided, but so too had the delivery of meaningful and positive reforms. By the late 1970s, the drug trade brought a new inflow of dollars, spiraling homicide rates, and a new florescence of the violent beast in both rural and urban areas.

Politically, the active and reformist energies of the Lleras Restrepo administration (1966–1970) pressed for land reform, export promotion, and currency stabilization, the latter two leading to a larger and more diversified economy, the thwarting of land reform, continued rural marginalization, and increasing cynicism about the state. State promotion of Import Substitution Industrialization (ISI) protected some industries, like the new Renault automobile plant, making the boxy, utilitarian, high-clearance "4" model the ubiquitous "carro colombiano" for the next three decades. Export promotion of cut flowers from the sabana around Bogotá and of bananas near the border with Panama created new sources of wealth but also social problems and violence in the banana zone. As a showcase of the U.S.-sponsored Alliance for Progress and to promote land reform, Lleras Restrepo backed the creation of the Asociación Nacional de Usuarios Campesinos (ANUC) to support rural development and land reform, an initiative effectively blocked by large landowners and the politicians they controlled. Land concentration, inequality, and absolute poverty in rural areas increased in the 1960s through the 1980s.[1]

National Front requirements that at least 10 percent of the national budget be spent on education led to an increase of children seven to thirteen years old attending school and a decrease in illiteracy. Alliance for Progress monies helped push that budget percentage to 14 percent in 1964, increasing to 20 percent in 1978 when the federal government assumed school funding responsibilities from departments. Secondary school attendance increased even faster in the 1960s and 1970s, but still less than half of Colombian teenagers matriculated. In rural areas, by the late 1980s, a startlingly low 7 percent had access to postprimary education, while university attendance in urban areas increased from 1 percent in 1950 to 10 percent in 1985. In short, the government focused more on export agriculture and urban industrial development, leaving the countryside in a marginal and unattended position ripe for non-state actors like guerrillas, trafficking organizations, and paramilitaries.[2]

More Colombians saw and were influenced by television by the mid-1970s, often watching a set at a neighbor's home, out front in furniture stores, or in restaurants and bars. Commercial programming in 1971 from the United States included *The Brady Bunch, Gilligan's Island, Lassie, The Wonderful World of Disney, The Virginian, Mannix, Ironside, The Mod Squad*, and *Get Smart*. Many of those shows presented a world of affluence and wealth unavailable to most Colombian viewers. The Spanish-language telenovelas (*Simplemente María*, for example), dubbed films, news programs, and broadcast of sporting events brought viewers closer to the society and geography they knew, but still pushed attitudes and fashions far beyond the local or regional level. Colombians saw the broadcast of humans arriving on the moon, of events from the other side of the world, images framing long-term visual memories. By the 1970s, the government cut its sponsorship of creative programming made in Colombia, so good programs were less available, yet television remained the medium that allowed one to forget the daily grind.[3]

The man who introduced television to Colombia in 1954 on the one-year anniversary of his seizure of power, Gustavo Rojas Pinilla, made news and brought drama to National Front politics during his 1970 run for the presidency. The seventy-year-old former general, boosted by his energetic daughter, María Eugenia, ran as a Conservative since it was that party's turn to control the presidency. He kept alive Gaitán's railing against the oligarchy, handing out food and money at mass rallies, promising to increase the value of the Colombian peso from six cents to fifty cents the day after the election. He garnered strong support from the urban working and lower middle class, gaining strong majorities in urban areas of recent migrants. Popular support for the National Front slipped precipitously from the totals for the 1957 referendum—the one pushed by that year's spectacular beauty queens—of 95 percent supporting the National Front and 73 percent participating in the election. In 1970, only 40 percent supported the official National Front candidate, Misael Pastrana, and just 19 percent bothered to vote at all. Rojas Pinilla easily won the major national cities, and the primary and secondary regional cities, and radio broadcasts announced him the victor. Then official broadcasts ceased until the next morning, when Pastrana was announced the

STATIC GOVERNMENT, SOCIAL EVOLUTION ‖ 159

winner; Pastrana won in country towns and rural communities, places where loyalties to the traditional parties remained strong, and places slower to report vote totals. Nonetheless, even to non-ANAPO supporters and to foreign election observers, it appeared that the election had been stolen. Pastrana totaled 40.6 percent of the vote, Rojas Pinilla 39 percent, the rest going to two other dissident Conservative candidates. Much like the disputed 1960 or 2000 presidential elections in the United States, or the 1988 presidential election in Mexico, effective partisan machinery determined that elections are won by those who count the ballots, not by those who mark them. Pastrana entered office with minority support, as did Salvador Allende in Chile the same year, the National Front's coalition losing more credibility, with deep resentment about the outcome of the 1970 election leading to the creation of a new insurgent group, the M-19.[4]

Youthful rebellion against the status quo establishment flourished throughout the world's urban areas in the late 1960s. The confrontations in Berlin, Paris, Mexico City, and Berkeley seemed to inform the growing protests in Bogotá, Medellín, Quito, and Caracas. A conference in Mexico City in 1969, a year after the massive repression in Tlatelolco plaza, found that at least fifty countries on five continents were experiencing youthful rebellion; the conference focused on the causal factors feeding this activity. Although social factors differed from place to place, the student movement fed the new social movement that distrusted the previous generation and authority. Mass media, accelerating scientific and technological breakthroughs, and socio-economic ferment all strongly challenged traditional social structures of power. Culturally, taboos about sex were disappearing as drugs, hippie culture, and rock 'n'roll opened new avenues of consciousness and generational communication. The global confrontation of the Cold War fed a global anguish about a future of uncertain destruction. The anxiety of youth mixed with a critique of their elders passively delivering a world on the edge of destruction, further disconnected youth from parents, allowing youth to identify with the oppressed, the working class, underdeveloped third-world countries, and with indigenous cultures. Conferees concluded that young people longed for the authentic, saw through the fake, and yearned for a new critical university, rejecting the mechanistic, bureaucratic, industrial university.[5]

The rector's firing of a professor sparked a student strike at the Universidad Nacional in Bogotá in November 1969, the students demanding his immediate reinstatement and petitioning that students be consulted on future personnel issues. December exams were canceled because of the strike, and by February 1970, the semester was suspended. The students responded with large protest marches, a mass meeting in Bogota's central square, the Plaza de Bolívar, receiving support and solidarity from other universities in the capital and in Cali. The protestors employed the tactic of the sit-in while in the Plaza de Bolívar, waving white handkerchiefs, symbols of resolute but peaceful protest. Women appeared prominently in the photographs of the protestors, evidence that a more gender-inclusive Colombia was now in occupation of the ceremonial heart of the nation.[6]

In 1969, hippie culture took root in a park at Carrera 7a and Calle 60 in Bogotá, the small group cleaning and decorating the park to make a suitable meeting spot. Interviewed by Fanny Buitrago, group members said that they were looking for their true selves as thinking beings, developing both their bodies and their spirits. They focused more on a spiritual reencounter with God, first being aware of self with others, then with self and the infinite. Their dress was a disguise, but one liberated from the normal disguises of suit and tie, the uniform de rigor for the upwardly mobile on Bogotá's main avenues. In a society plagued with violence, sterile politics, and mechanized routine, the group of hippies in the Parque 60 offered an alternative truth.[7]

A larger gathering of the hippie tribe occurred June 18–20, 1971, at the Parque del Ancón, on the southwestern edge of metropolitan Medellín. With three days of rock bands, the estimated 50,000 to 300,000 attendees sprawled out along the river and up the hillsides, some paying about fourteen pesos admission, re-creating a "Colombian Woodstock." The paisa promoters reportedly made a tidy sum of money from the gate, while a Medellín organization monopolized the sale of marijuana at the venue, intimidating concertgoers trying to make small sales to cover their admission costs. Mescaline, LSD, and mushrooms were also available, with some reporters disappointed at the lack of nudity and erotic orgies. Much of the audience came from Bogotá, Medellín, and Cali, those interviewed reveling in their communion with nature while speaking favorably for peace, love, and liberty, and against violence.[8] A year later, a more dedicated back-to-nature hippie commune sprang up on the Rio de Miel, a tributary of the Magdalena River near La Dorada. Rather than a permanent community, people seemed to flow in and out of this "hippie paradise"; Colombian students and professors, English, Canadian, American, and Argentine travelers, all enjoying the warm weather and refreshing water, gathering psilocybin mushrooms in the morning, tripping through the day.[9]

The Ancón concert became a mass event, in part, because of the growing popularity of rock music and the proliferation of drug use among Colombian youth. From 1967 to 1971, the estimated number of marijuana users increased by 100 percent, as the production and distribution of drugs for both internal and external markets expanded. By 1973, one estimate suggested that

62 percent of urban students 13 to 22 used or were addicted to street drugs. About five thousand dealers, many of them mixed among the street vendors found in all large cities, serviced customers across class lines: working-class users buying marijuana and barbiturates; the biggest users, the middle class, tending toward marijuana and mescaline; elites, marijuana and heroin. Cheap and plentiful marijuana—about twenty-five cents for three grams—could be found in urban centers and around secondary schools and universities. High-quality marijuana was grown on the slopes of the Sierra Nevada de Santa Marta, much of it shipped to the North American market, while domestic growers around Manizales, Medellín, the sabana of Bogotá, and scattered throughout Cauca and Nariño supplied domestic users.[10]

In response to police arrests of buyers and sellers in 1968, the trafficking of drugs became more organized and sophisticated by 1969. In August, leaders of syndicates met over a three-day period near Caldono, just off the Pan American highway between Cali and Popayán, to draft a marketing plan. By 1971, Medellín emerged as the drug capital of the nation, with traffickers investing in laboratories where coca paste was refined into cocaine powder and then shipped out to Central America and the United States, earning 5,000 percent profit in the transaction. As always, repressive measures from police and governments only displaced production and trafficking networks from one place to another. For example, the initial U.S. "drug war" declared by Richard Nixon in 1969 led to a crackdown on smuggling between the U.S./Mexican border; in response, Colombian growers planted and smuggled more marijuana into the U.S. market, in essence, subsidized by U.S. repression against Mexican suppliers. In addition, although it was known that cocaine laboratories operated in fincas around Itagüí, La Estrella, Bello, Copacabana, and Girardota, any measures against them only displaced the labs to other areas of the country. With marijuana and cocaine use increasing among people eighteen to twenty-five in the United States throughout the 1970s, Colombian traffickers looked beyond the low-price domestic market to the much larger and more profitable U.S. market.[11]

While the drug trade expanded, articles in *Cromos* questioned whether the hippies presented a revolutionary danger. The cultural and moral revolution implicit in the new music and culture, the sexual revolution, and the use of marijuana acquired political value both for those who "dropped out" as well as for those who rejected inherited systems of order. The value placed on non-violence, however, distinguished them from past and present armed revolutionary movements. The promoter of the Ancón concert, Gonzalo Carolo, reportedly wielded enough political power to force the resignation of two of Medellín's mayors (still appointed by the national government in Bogotá), a charge that Carolo denied. He was quite sophisticated and independent in his political analysis and critical of the dark side of drug use and sexual predation while organizing various hippie artisan craft shops and then using proceeds from sales to organize concerts in poor neighborhoods and to give food to the needy. While Carolo's power came not from being a hippie but in being industrious and smart, Fanny Buitrago explored the dark side of hippie utopianism of the early 1970s, the one that led to the occult, spiritism, hustlers, and the Manson Family. That road led toward death and to the apocalypse awaited by some Christian sects. For Buitrago, the mania for youth also included ugly practices where companies fired well-paid and experienced employees over fifty, replacing them with cheaper, younger, and less-prepared eighteen- to thirty-year-olds, the cycle continuing into the future to sustain a low-paid workforce and stagnant enterprises.[12]

In part, the culture of the early 1970s tried to digest what it could of the previous decade. An Italian movie crew filmed its interpretation of Camilo Torres, using Colombian actors and military units in the production. *Inmortalidad* featured "anti-reina" María Victoria Uribe playing the role of Camilo's college girlfriend, while Natanael Díaz, an Afro-Colombian theater actor, was cast as Camilo, the priest and revolutionary. That casting decision raised questions about race and authenticity, the answers being that Camilo was a symbol who transcended race and color, while the Black Power Movement in the United States had placed black people at the forefront of the struggle against the system. Logistically, it also helped the filmmakers when they shot on Colombian bases and used military units in various scenes, so the military would not be suspicious that the film was about Camilo Torres. Although *Inmortalidad* received honorable mention distinctions at film festivals in Cannes and Venice, it could not be shown in Colombia given its subject and politics.[13]

A concert in Bogotá by James Brown in 1973 momentarily resurrected hippiedom in the capital, the hippie scene seemingly having waned by then. With seventeen thousand in attendance and a thick smell of marijuana filling the Coliseo el Campín, it seemed as though the resurrection of the new wave had been realized. With the driving rhythm of soul and the chemical and social ecstasy of a show, the concert signaled that the freedom of the sixties was still alive in the seventies; a Carlos Santana concert later that year and one by Camilo Sesto in 1974 brought other international acts to Colombia, but both were marred by logistical and legal issues.[14]

While news coverage of the James Brown concert did not mention his black pride message, *Mujer* did feature an elegant model of color, Lucía Londoño, on its magazine cover in August 1969. The antioqueña Lucía noted that racism still existed in Colombia, citing fellow Medellín residents who found her skin too dark, allowing that paisas were exceptional entrepreneurs but also exceptionally conservative. Nonetheless, Londoño opined that her color determined her recent success, signaling an opening to color in national Colombian culture. But while Colombians still avoided direct questions about race and color in their country, they did pay much attention to the status and role of women in modern society. Similar to Soledad Acosta de Samper a century earlier, Colombians looked back to history for foundations and then puzzled over the complexities of modern changes and challenges. *Cromos* published articles on key women who made Colombian independence possible, while other pieces looked back over the history of fashion and beauty in the country.

In the late sixties and early seventies, conferences of women met in Colombia to work collectively at addressing modern problems. One hundred twenty women involved in social service programs met in Cali in 1969, addressing issues connected to exploding and young populations, poverty, education, poor housing, and family planning. While development in the nation required addressing these issues, the topic of sex and the family highlighted the complexities found in a single topic. The conferees found that many Colombian families failed to understand the function of sex within the family unit: that sex was legitimate and could be satisfying; that prostitution and illicit relationships often resulted from the ignorance of the former; that a lack of sexual education maintained a double standard about sex between men and women; and that unplanned pregnancies often led to unsafe abortions, or to rejection or abandonment of young children. With 25 percent of young women—many of them illiterate—beginning sexual relations before age sixteen, and 70 percent before they were eighteen, the social and demographic cost of not providing sex education and effective birth control was clear. In cities with large black populations like Cartagena, where 40 percent of the population lived in shantytowns, or in Buenaventura, where that number doubled to 80 percent, rural levels of poverty and lack of education now defined urban centers. Although the title of the article was "The Colombian Woman and Her Responsibility for Development in the Country," future trends looked grim, indeed.[15] While it was still women's "responsibility" to deal with all these complex issues because they pertained to the family, the National Front elites, gendered male, got an implied pass. Subsequent conferences in 1970 and 1971 brought women from across the Americas to Bogotá, addressing family planning, divorce, civil marriage, and social service, one delegate concluding that "woman will only be liberated when she is sexually and economically independent."[16]

For rural campesinas or shantytown dwellers in the mushrooming cities, living outside the margins of "civilized progress" demonstrated the limits of development. Without access to schools and education, economic security and decent-paying jobs, or safe water or aqueducts to make agriculture possible, poor women lived as dependents of male partners. Rural women heard the repeated promises of politicians who claimed that their children wouldn't die in ignorance, that soon they'd have their own parcels of land and factories to offer employment, promises unrealized but repeated every two years to carry the next election. In shantytowns around the cities, those decent women who followed bourgeois values rented marginal land, stayed at home, and depended on their male partners for support. More rebellious women invaded lands and took what they needed and did not depend on a man, getting money any way they could to feed their children. Once again, rural campesina women were labeled "key" to development, but the Colombian government never supported the structural conditions where all people could enjoy a higher standard of living.[17]

The issue of sex remained an important theme at women's conferences and in the pages of *Cromos* throughout the 1970s, a topic of interest to readers who often received no sexual education from schools, church, or family. International conferees from Nicaragua and Ecuador were surprised to learn that divorce was not legal in Colombia, while other conferees criticized frivolous and expensive fashions—as had Colombians a century earlier—and questioned the meaning and importance of virginity in modern society, while disagreeing on the divisive issue of abortion. A scientific and medical article on sexuality reframed the topic around rational and psychological parameters, separating it from its traditional religious framework. While scientific sexuality made for a dry read, an interview with the 1971 Carnival queen of Barranquilla restored the spice to popular, Caribbean sexuality. Asked if old age or being single was the worst hell for women, she quipped, "Hell is arriving single at old age. Better said; being a virgin at old age." Asked if she had plans for the future, she said, "None. My generation doesn't live off the inertia of the past or the illusions of the future. Our world is the present, today, here, now." Asked what she would do if she knew that she would die tomorrow, she answered, "make love."[18]

Young women saying or doing the nontraditional marked a break with the past in a present under construction. In 1969, a young and pretty woman from Barranquilla who owned a bus company appeared on the Miami television series *Adivina en qué trabajo?* This *What's My Line?* Spanish-language spin-off featured Anita Dávila, describing how she founded her company and what she did to keep it going. Not only boss of the company, she drove when necessary and repaired buses with the mechanics. Anita also appeared on occasion as a model in fashion shows in Barranquilla. Her company drove children to their schools around Barranquilla, hiring young women to drive the ten buses. In various businesses over the previous twenty years, her next business project was a bus line for tourists, hiring drivers who spoke two or three languages.[19]

While Anita's elegance and style balanced her nontraditional work, the young smiling faces of nuns couldn't blunt fears that they might be "rebel nuns." Following the teachings of Vatican II and the elaboration of the theology of liberation from the Medellín Conference in 1968, some young nuns at the Colegio Marymount in Bogotá began to teach using the social reality around their students as a pedagogical tool. They encouraged students to learn collaboratively and critically, becoming agents of their own insight, rather than passive consumers of rigid, memorized lessons. In a Cold War setting, the nuns were labeled "Marxists," presumably in league with Communists or revolutionary guerrilla groups. The resulting controversy ended with the sacking of the new-wave nuns, their replacement with more senior and conservative sisters, and the closing of the school. The young nuns had, perhaps, pressed too quickly against traditional teachings and established authority in a patriarchal society, especially in a political environment where the legal Left was officially excluded from access to government power and where armed insurgents, therefore, sought power via the end of a gun.[20]

As a member of the Colombian Communist Party and ex-queen of the Universidad Nacional, María Arango de Marroquín reminded some Colombians of María Cano, a fellow paisa who had organized for the Left two generations before. María Arango seemed to have a rebel spirit, having been beaten by police, hounded by the authorities, and known as the "dangerous witch" (bruja peligrosa) by the counter-guerrillas. She was tall and thin, with fine features. She tried bourgeois social life but rejected it after feeling that as a woman she became an object. She encountered Marxism as a student at the Universidad Javeriana and then transferred to the Universidad Nacional. At the Nacional, she recognized the university pageants as false and antipopular, a mere social act that disconnected the sovereign from the true situation of students. She decided to subvert the process, as would María Victoria in 1968, becoming university queen in the early 1960s and then speaking publically and rallying students to action. She married fellow Communist Álvaro Marroquín and started a family, initially living in the Barrio Policarpa to organize migrants for social and political action. Friend of French revolutionary theorist Regis Debray and the revolutionary priest Camilo Torres, María Arango was interviewed by *Mujer* magazine in 1970, saying that she loved the Communist Party because it wasn't paternalistic, allowing women to develop politically. She added that "the party gave me the possibility of being a woman."[21] As

FIGURE 8.1 *María Arango, la vida burguesa, courtesy* Mujer de América *(Aug. 1970, p. 12), Editorial Andes.*

FIGURE 8.2 *María Arango, Vendiendo votos para los candidatos de su partido comunista, courtesy* Mujer de América *(Aug. 1970, p. 13), Editorial Andes.*

with the case of Anita Dávila, María Arango's appearance made her momentarily less threatening as she challenged Cold War barriers even more aggressively than had the Marymount nuns. However, neither María's looks nor her activism saved her from assassination in 1998, leaving her a victim, like thousands of other Colombians, of intolerance and impunity.[22]

The problem of being a poor woman with limited education, dependent on men for economic necessities, and socially and politically subordinate to men historically led some women toward prostitution. Although prostitution in Bogotá was an old topic, prostitution in the 1970s seemed more organized and international in its scope. Young women were often approached by a professional seducer, who pulled the women into a compromising situation and then abandoned them, leaving them little choice other than to sell their dignity to earn their survival. Traditional gender constructions that taught that men were full of desires and good women had none continued the division of love within the home and sex outside it. With an estimated 150,000 prostitutes in Colombia, the sex trade at the top used photographs and telephones to connect elite clients in expensive hotels to high-priced prostitutes, while down in the streets women exchanged sex for gifts, money, or food. Young Colombian women from fourteen to seventeen years old were in demand as sex workers in neighboring Venezuela, Panama, and Ecuador, while between 1960 and 1965, some five hundred such girls were enticed to venture to the United States to work as maids in phantom jobs that led to bordellos. With real wages stagnant at mid-1950s levels and many more young women looking for work in cities, and with office jobs paying between eighteen and twenty-five dollars a week, even secretaries and receptionists were drifting into prostitution. Culturally, Colombia's reputation for beautiful women combined with a strong patriarchal power structure and the wages of misery to feed "the oldest profession" with a new generation of marketed women.[23]

In December 1971, a national women's conference in Bogotá focused on economic issues addressing salary discrimination, the rights of working women, the rights of rural campesinas, social and legal issues like abolition of the Concordat, full citizenship rights for women, and equal educational opportunities for males and females through university. But the big news at the conference was the presence of Betty Friedan, the North American sociologist, cofounder of the National Organization of Women (NOW), and author of *The Feminine Mystique*. Friedan missed her plane in New York and arrived late to the conference, seemingly unclear on the realities facing Colombian women. *Mujer* described Friedan as intelligent, enthusiastic, expressive, but ugly and unkempt. Asked if the war of feminism was against men or against pretty women, Friedan denied that feminism was a war, more a search for liberation by way of equality, citing Gloria Steinem, who went from *Playboy* bunny to NOW, as evidence that feminism had nothing against physically attractive women. Although many of the top male newspapermen avoided the conference—some joking about the butch women present—Friedan argued that the biggest obstacle to feminism didn't come from men but from women full of self-hate, people unable to believe in themselves. Subsequent opinions about NOW in later editions of *Mujer* faulted its style of feminism as too competitive with males, making both feminism and machismo traumatic for society. While the worthy goal of equal opportunity was shared, the magazine implied that reaching that goal should be done gracefully.[24]

If North American feminism seemed to push too hard against the conservatism of Colombian society, fashion, too, demanded its due attention. The skirt length war between the mini, the midi, and the maxi placed fashion squarely at the center of a contest between generations, classes, and moralities. The slender, hip, and young Fanny Buitrago loved the mini for the freedom it represented and the beauty it revealed, noting, however, that the fashion required that one keep her body lean. With more skin revealed and with more nude or seminude photographs appearing in *Cromos*, she sensed the "light touch" of Opus Dei in labeling the mini scandalous. She loved the bright colors found in the new acrylic fabrics, colors finally giving life to dark Bogotá. The pressure back to the maxi seemed not only reactionary—a cloistering of the female form by male designers—but also cost more money to pay for the extra fabric. Fanny and others noted that fashion could be capricious and paradoxical, but it could also be political.[25]

What did more exposed female skin signify? For those who looked to nature, skin was wholesome and organic but needed care given the extra exposure to the sun. Getting the perfect tan, lightly toasting the skin, seemed to please both nature and fashion. Becoming brown not only served as a status symbol for whites—symbolizing leisure—but also opened room for models of color like Lucía Londoño. The sexy, erotic reading of skin and the exposed body pushed against religious tradition as the interaction between the exposed and the covered played with the viewer's imagination. With large blue eyes, blonde hair, and a slightly husky voice, Colombian model Ylva Tarud recognized that advertising was based on sex appeal but saw in her own image many flaws, quipping that "only conformists consider themselves beautiful." From the model immortalized by the Spanish painter Francisco Goya came the resurrection of "La Maja Iberia" pageant in Zaragoza, Spain, the Goya's image of the clothed maja—not the nude—being the model that the international aspirants sought to emulate. The Colombian representative to the 1972 contest, Rocío Durcal, had the languid, swanlike eyes required, and was given the mantilla and hairstyle needed to complete the look of the southern Spanish beauty mixed with gypsy allure. She praised La Maja Iberia pageant for its focus on the intelligence, authenticity, and sincerity of the contestants, rather than focusing simply on their physical attributes. Rocío refused to enter the Señorita Colombia pageant, as it took measurements to determine beauty and required that contestants pose in swimsuits. While Goya's nude maja painting got him dragged before the Inquisition in 1815, the dressed maja reaffirmed Hispanist orientations in Colombian beauty as it acknowledged but covered the female form.[26]

While the maja looked back to the Iberian roots of Mediterranean beauty, a series of articles in *Mujer* explored both the obligation as well as the cost of modern beauty. Science, now, could beautify women, a benefit for the daughters of Eve. Laboratories pursued chemical solutions to cover or improve problem areas on the face, while plastic surgeons could alter the shape of the nose, eyes, chin, or lips, and lift or change the size of breasts, all in the pursuit of commercial beauty. By 1971, one didn't have to leave the country for their services, as plastic surgeons practiced in both large and medium-sized cities, attracting Venezuelans and Ecuadorans to Colombia to partake of their technical expertise.

Nutritionists also used science, urging women to use reason in order to alter their diet as they aged, cutting down on calories and fat, because "staying thin was staying young." Exercise for those over forty improved health, as it maintained a body not worn, tired, depressed, or poorly oxygenated. While beauty products could help those over forty, it was best to care for yourself starting when you were young. But while the Colombian post office issued stamps of beauty queens Luz Marina Zuluaga and Liliana Gómez, the National Queen of Bambuco, the pursuit of beauty could be prohibitively expensive; hair care, cosmetics, weight-loss solutions, and plastic surgery could easily break the household budget, requiring a reduction of the food budget— one way to keep everyone in the household thin. And why could men look as natural as God had made them while women were pressed into the slavery of the latest beauty aid?[27]

On the tenth anniversary of its creation, Ana de Karpf reviewed the achievements of the previous decade of the magazine *Mujer*. Along with breaking old taboos around virginity, sexual education, marriage and divorce, and prostitution, the magazine ignored the gossip about international movie stars, instead taking on a decidedly pro-Colombian and nationalist stance on fashion and other pertinent themes for its readers. De Karpf hoped that someday the most elegant woman in Colombia would only wear fabrics and designs made in the country, rather than relying on foreign contraband purchased with scarce funds. Fashion, seen in this light, was not frivolous but both economically important and politically powerful. While skirt length wars and hot pants punctuated female fashions over the previous decades, it was in men's fashions that a true revolution transpired. Men's fashions were far less austere and conservative than in the early 1960s, with color and softness touching the edge of the feminine in unisex fashions.[28]

As a textile and design center, Medellín played an active role in defining Colombian fashion trends through the 1970s. The department's promotional magazine *Antioquia Turística* embraced the miniskirt as a bold fashion trend and as an allure to attract tourism to the department. Fashion shows in Medellín in 1970 reinforced fashion nationalism by presenting bold and colorful designs based on the long flowing shawl of the Guajira peninsula, building off the fashion rebirth of the ruana in previous decades. To address the mini/midi/maxi skirt length debate, pragmatic paisa designers incorporated hot pants worn underneath a midi-length shirtdress unbuttoned from the waist down, revealing bare legs while walking. In a similarly daring subscription drive for *Antioquia Turística*, the magazine ran photographs of apparently nude models strategically covered by—guess what?—copies of *Antio-quia Turística*. The fashion-forward stance and the nude phase of Colombian beauty during the early 1970s certainly challenged the traditional and modest fashions favored by conservatives and the Catholic Church in Antioquia. Economic recession and increasing inflation, fueled by a deepening economic recession in the United States and higher energy costs after 1973, eroded both traditional values in the city and the foundations of Colombian industry and fashion. Amidst economic problems and changing social values in 1975, the factories ended their alliance with the Catholic Church and the authoritarian control and religious education of female textile workers. By the late 1970s, inflation and industrial recession intensified, increasing unemployment among factory workers just as Medellín's drug cartels became the city's new but dangerous economic motor.[29]

The regional pageants created at the dawn of the National Front era in the late 1950s and early 1960s set the stage for the national pageant and were held in the months prior to the Señorita Colombia contest in November. In June and July, the Reinado del Bambuco in Neiva, Huila, and the Reinado del Folclore in Ibagué, Tolima, maintained their regional and national popularity, acting as escape valves in departments ripped apart during La Violencia. In September and October, the Reinado del Mar on the North Coast in Santa Marta presented national and international candidates in bathing suits, requiring that they swim well and be graceful in the water. As the Señorita Colombia pageant neared, the national newspaper *El Tiempo* cosponsored with Max Factor a straw poll for the people's favorite. Colombians submitted over 53,000 entry forms for the contest, reinforcing the image of an inclusive and democratic beauty pageant at a time when most voters abstained from National Front presidential elections.[30]

Medellín captured the national crown for the second time in 1969 when Antioquia's candidate, María Luisa Riascos, won the national pageant in Cartagena; María was also the winner of the *El Tiempo* straw poll, receiving twice as many votes as the runner-up. For the first time, the pageant was broadcast on national television in black and white with a two-hour tape delay. Bikinis were getting smaller and more common, with competitors showing more cleavage. Contestants had to answer the stock questions about their opinion of and favorite character from *One Hundred Years of Solitude* (even though García Márquez satirized the proliferation of Colombian queens in the 1960s[31]) and their attitudes about divorce, marriage, and birth control. *Cromos* suggested that the national pageant broke down regional egotism, as it brought Colombians together to celebrate the beauty of the nation's women, noting also that many contestants had lived or studied outside

Colombia, bringing with them international perspectives on national realities. María arrived in Cartagena with twenty-five suitcases and one hundred
outfits, taking the crown home to Medellín, where she was received by a
crowd of three hundred thousand people.[32]

As host of the national pageant, Cartagena enjoyed the economic benefits of the annual contest in the midst of the city's independence celebrations conducted since 1846. Competing departmental committees ran large
advertisements in the city's newspapers promoting their candidate while bolstering newspaper revenue. Competing liquor companies used departmental
candidates to pitch their rum and aguardiente to consumers. Musicians, sales-
people, hucksters, fans, and tourists poured into the city's streets, hotels, restaurants, and bars, bringing the urban party into full bloom. The competitiveness of the pageant and the outcome of the Señorita Colombia pageant
often involved ugly controversies, mostly raising questions about the justice
of the selections and integrity of the judges. The 1970 winner, Piedad Mejía
Trujillo, had a perfect face but was criticized for having too much fat around
her thighs and hips, thereby not being a good Colombian representative in
international pageants. A modern and opinionated queen, Piedad admired
Fidel, Che, and Camilo, supported the Cuban Revolution, and suggested that
revolution might be forthcoming in Colombia. She opposed the positions
of the Catholic Church on birth control and divorce and supported hippie
values and lifestyles. Fellow Caldas resident Luz Marina Zuluaga defended
the modern personality of the department's first national queen, saying that
in her day all one needed was a pretty face and good body.[33] The judges in the
1971 contest were verbally challenged by contestants who wondered if they'd
been paid off in exchange for their decision. The 1974 winner was physically
attacked at two o'clock in the morning by supporters of a rival contestant. As
the National Front ended its formal tenure, the Señorita Colombia pageant
was losing its civility and perceived integrity.[34]

Both the national pageant and the popular pageant in Cartagena juxtaposed the beautiful with the ugly, the masculine with the feminine, the rich
with the poor, the popular with the elite, black with white. On the pages
of Cartagena's *El Universal*, the newspaper commonly ran photographs of
shapely and sexy beauty queens stylishly posed in swimwear, and on the next
page photographs of the ugly, dangerous, and poor male "vagos" and "criminales" who had also poured into the city. Most of these poor men, termed
morenos or negritos, were preemptively rounded up by the police to improve security during the fiestas. Both symbolically and literally, Colombian
beauty—feminine, elite, and white—had to be separated and protected from
the Colombian beast—masculine, poor, and black. The neglected and poor

Chocó department remained outside governmental interest, and the self-designated Señorita Chocó stated plainly that racial discrimination did exist in Colombia. While Señorita Chocó of 1971 had to fight to be included in the pageant, placing a respectable fifth, she couldn't win for her department or her race because "the Colombian woman is not black." However, in the popular pageant in the city, one needed to be at least partly black to represent the city's population. Thus, the majority black Caribbean population was included in Cartagena's November festivities, albeit in a subordinate position to the national pageant. But beyond being morena, one had to be attractive, polished, poised, sweet, and a good speaker who won the crowd and worked for the improvement of the community. The Reina Popular carried the responsibility of maintaining the happiness of the people of Cartagena. The winner was selected by a panel of judges, but the crowd could sway them to the popular will with enough collective and firm lobbying.[35]

Atlántico department brought home its fourth national crown in 1971 when Barranquilla native María Luisa Lignarolo won the Señorita Colombia pageant. María Luisa was a modern queen who had just returned to Colombia from Europe, where she had studied languages and modeling. She opined that virginity was of little importance to young women and that pageants could neither solve nor justify Colombia's problems. Of Italian and Dutch ancestry, she wasn't religious, couldn't fry an egg, knew she'd make a horrible housewife, and didn't like typical Colombian music but danced cumbia and mapalé very well. While María Luisa symbolized the modern and international city that Barranquilla aspired to be—apparently so different from colonial and traditional Cartagena—her win couldn't disguise the fact that the 85 percent black majority of Barranquilla faced customary and effective segregation from power positions in the city. Economic and social power still resided with whites, with no important businesses owned by blacks, no black members at the country club, and no young women of color amongst the city's debutantes. At the city's famous Carnival celebration in 1970, the clear crowd favorite was Miss Jamaica, the only black woman invited to participate, but the judges picked a white contestant instead.[36] Modern attitudes from a symbolic queen did not equal social equality. The inherited sense of proper place and power was as firmly intact in Barranquilla as it was in Cartagena.

Valle del Cauca's place in the 1970s was winning the Señorita Colombia pageant, claiming the crown in 1972, 1974, and 1976. Valle and, by extension, Cali cemented their reputations as the land of beautiful women and pageant queens. The extravagance of the 1972 pageant prior to the oil crisis and resulting economic difficulties of 1973 was exemplified by the candidate from Santander, who arrived in Cartagena with a wardrobe worth at least 250,000 pesos; with the average daily wage being 20 pesos, the cost of her clothing equaled the wages earned over a lifetime for an average Colombian. The 1974 winner was a tall but poor girl from Tuluá, who in some photographs resembled Rita Hayworth. She arrived in Cartagena with pneumonia, won the crown, survived a 2:00 a.m. physical and verbal attack from some members of the Atlántico delegation, and then went to bed for a month to recover. The 1976 winner was "discovered" by a barber in Buga and arrived in Cartagena with a Valle del Cauca delegation of four hundred people. General Omar Torrijos, political leader of neighboring Panama, blended into the crowd celebrating the Reina Popular of Cartagena, drinking rum and dancing with the victorious queen. Valle had now won the national crown seven times, far more than any other department to date, but would have to wait until 2003 for its next triumph.[37]

As capital of Valle, Cali reveled in its 1970s successes as a national leader of Colombian beauty but also nostalgically looked backward to seemingly simpler times. In a skinny tabloid format, the *Revista Occidental* of Cali featured reinas, wedding couples, and film stars of the past, the only contemporary content being advertisements and current beauty queens. Amidst the rising inflation and unemployment of the 1970s, it looked back to the first Miss Colombia pageant in 1932, describing it as "better times" even if that year coincided with the depths of the Great Depression. In a more playful mood, *Revista Occidental* joked that readers should breathe slowly, remain calm, and don sunglasses while enjoying photographs of current bathing beauties to avoid nervous attacks when confronted with such modern and sensuous allure.[38]

Caleños boasted in a late 1970s tourist guide that the city's environment, traditions, and racial mixtures created the modern beauty that made Cali famous throughout Colombia and the larger world. Cali's tropical climate shaped the city's women like its tropical flora: tall, thin, and graceful like palms. *La piel canela* (the cinnamon skin) of the city's beauties marked their distinctive quality, a perfect proportional mixture of indigenous, white, and black ingredients, producing agile and harmonic bodies that shone even in a simple dress, accented by a particular and proud walk. This beautiful and beneficent mestizaje created an exaltation of the city's beautiful women, one where "caleñas knew that men admired them and they liked the admiration." Caleñas carried with them a confident vanity, one that was flirtatious and pleased with male compliments and attentions. According to its boosters, Cali was a tropical center of beauty, of open and harmonious sexual expression, and therefore a powerful tourist attraction.[39]

Race had also made Cali a center of salsa excellence by the late 1970s.

Although not invented in Cali (apparently salsa was molded in and around New York City by immigrants from the circum-Caribbean Basin), salsa had caught on with the black vallecaucano population and would soon conquer mestizos and the middle class. The city didn't have the best bands, but it did have the best salsa dancers, the dance requiring athletic moves and quick steps, aided by the acrobatic and harmonious bodies of caleñas. According to tourist boosters, all caleñas knew how to dance salsa—apparently because blackness made you a natural dancer—again, in a hot, tropical, and sexy setting open to educating tourists.[40]

Colombian beauty went through its nude stage in 1973 and 1974, with topless models appearing on the cover and inside the pages of *Cromos*. Most of the models were from Europe, with some American and Colombian women and a few *Playboy* models sprinkled in. Filmed in 1973 and released in 1974, a Colombian/Italian/German production made one of many Amazon sexploitation movies of this era. Featuring nude or topless young actresses for foreign release and clothed actresses for screening inside Colombia and filmed near Girardot in the Magdalena Valley, the production gained comment in *Mujer* mainly because Colombians couldn't see the uncensored version released internationally. Starring Miss Chocó 1973, the film featured Colombian beauty but of the sort meant to titillate the sexual fantasies of international viewers.[41] This and other lowbrow but very popular productions brought an erotic interpretation to issues involving changing mores about sex, gender, and power.

The year 1973 also brought an oil crisis to the world, leading to scarcity of supply and higher prices for energy around the globe. Colombia's neighbor and OPEC member Venezuela became the envy of Colombians and a destination for migrants and beauty queens. The 1973 Señorita Colombia pageant included the humorous insights of satirist Daniel Samper Pizano, who quipped that "with Watergate in the United States and the Golan Heights in the Middle East, why shouldn't the pageant in Cartagena have its crisis, too?" He noted that "being a queen is difficult, but being a queen candidate in Colombia is for machos." Forced indoors by a strong rainstorm, the candidates paraded in bikinis in the Casa del Marqués de Valdehoyos, a site where, two hundred years earlier, slaves had been bought and sold. For Samper, Colombians, more than any other people, gave beauty pageants myriad mythic characteristics. Over a four-day period the national pageant created a new mythic queen, one feeding the myths and altars of the collective Colombian unconscious.[42] Samper, like other observers, saw through the pageant's artifice but still felt its power.

Although Samper was sure that the Caribbean coast would take home another crown, having won one-third of the national titles while shutting out Bogotá, it was Santander that won its second title in 1973. Of Danish and Colombian ancestry, Ella Cecilia Escandón won the crown without handing out free liquor and spent less than half that of the Bolívar delegation (which was rumored to have purchased the 1971 crown). Historically, Santander was the center of Colombian beauty a century before; perhaps its modern role in the Colombian petroleum industry served it well in the context of the 1970s oil shocks. Santander won the crown in 1978 as well, as Catholic hierarchs criticized the extravagance of the frivolous national pageant at a time of crisis. In spirited defense of the pageant, columnist Lucas Caballero "Klim" argued, "In a period like the present, dominated by violence, demoralized by corruption, undermined by drugs, polluted by unscrupulous functionaries, feminine beauty is one of the few things that reconciles man with life." Pageant judges were looking for a prototypical "Latin beauty," but one with intelligence, culture, personal warmth, and charm. The winner, Ana Milena Parra, had those characteristics and, probably helpful as well, arrived in Cartagena aboard the private jet of Carlos Ardila Lülle, one of the richest men in Colombia and a booster of Santander and her queen.[43]

Bogotá muddled through the pageants of the early 1970s. The capital and biggest city of the land unfortunately lacked folkloric vitality and the warm climate conducive to bikini culture. It did host the first Reina Nacional de los Ciegos (National Pageant of the Blind) in 1971 and became a center for the developing model industry in the early 1970s. The search for a model of the year in 1974 included young women in bikinis, looking a little out-of-place and uncomfortable, photographed for *Cromos* inside clubs in Bogotá. The economic recession of that year and the next made the Miss Colombia pageants in Cartagena events of austerity; delegations spent less on their queens while the expensive and extravagant fantasy costumes were eliminated.[44]

While Colombian sports teams continued to lose internationally, and liquor wars for market control during Cartagena's annual celebrations raged between distilleries based in Bolívar and Antioquia, Bogotá broke through and won the 1975 and 1977 Miss Colombia crowns in Cartagena. With the formal stage of the National Front ending in 1974, perhaps Bogotá no longer carried the political burden of an elite-directed fix following La Violencia. Clearly, the delegation from Bogotá was better organized, arrived in Cartagena in number and with clout, and came to win. Moreover, *Cromos* played a more active role in prepageant publicity in both 1975 and 1977, giving favorable coverage to the candidates from Bogotá.[45]

Both winners from Bogotá emulated the look of svelte U.S. models and television actresses of the mid-1970s. They were not "typical Latin" beauties;

their eyes were green or blue, and their hair went from 1975 shag to 1977 flick à la Farrah Fawcett-Majors of U.S. television's *Charlie's Angels* fame. The 1975 victor, María Elena Reyes Abisambra, came from a middle-class, non-elite family, her mother a costeña of Lebanese ancestry. She studied odontology at the Universidad Javeriana, knowing that she would need to support herself with a career and fearful that the pageant would take away time from her studies. She was smart and direct and had to be convinced to represent Bogotá in the national pageant. Her competitor from Cartagena invested about one-half the total (120,000 pesos) of that spent two years before by the Bolívar delegation and aspired to be a political leader of the Left. The Academia de Historia de Cartagena boycotted the November 11th Independence Celebrations, saying that the beauty pageant and the drunken crowd it attracted disrupted the solemn and dignified air that the historical anniversary deserved. (Conversely, homosexuals demonstrated a more public and celebratory presence when crowning their drag queen in Cartagena in 1975.) Other newspaper articles questioned whether the national pageant should continue at all, given the insecurity, immorality, and impunity afflicting the nation. Complaints and criticisms about the pageant and its outcomes usually lasted about a week and then were forgotten until the next year. Ironically, Colombia seemed to need the national pageant expressly at times of crisis, as society was unable to build a strong nationalist belief in a still weak and ineffectual state. After the 1975 pageant, María Elena returned to Bogotá, where the normally taciturn capital residents gave her a warm reception. She hoped that her city would become more secure and tranquil, and she pledged to be the queen of peace for all Colombians. Asked what she would propose to stop the wave of kidnapping, she replied, "the death penalty."[46]

By 1977, extravagant spending at the national pageant had returned, with gold lamé adding a kitschy touch of wealth. Shirley Sáenz Starnes brought Bogotá its second crown. Described as the "prototypical international beauty, with blue eyes, chestnut hair, white skin, perfect measurements,"[47] Shirley, like a number of the other contestants, mirrored the popularity of the windswept, flip hairstyles made famous by *Charlie's Angels*. Her "typical campesina outfit" took three months to embroider and finish—a far cry from campesina dress of the past. The runner-up pledged to become the "vice-queen of flora and fauna," signaling an awakening environmental movement.[48]

Shirley finished fourth at the 1978 Miss Universe pageant, her international beauty carrying her into the select group of finalists. Colombia also placed fourth at Miss Universe in 1974 and 1977, maintaining Colombian beauty's presence on the global stage. *Cromos* took a critical stance against the 1975 Miss Universe pageant held in El Salvador, noting the political and economic forces from the United States that shaped both the pageant and its outcome. The article noted that Salvadoran students had vowed to disrupt the pageant to protest its cost to the government in demonstrations that ultimately were answered with bullets by an increasingly repressive Salvadoran regime. It also stated that the Latin American contestants were robbed of their deserved place in the pageant; they protested after the coronation by throwing their national sashes into the swimming pool at the Sheraton Hotel.[49]

The 1977 pageant broke the color barrier, selecting Miss Trinidad & Tobago as the first black Miss Universe; Miss America did the same in 1984 with the ascension of Vanessa Williams in a historic but contentious breakthrough. In Colombia, Señorita Chocó continued to be the incarnation of black Colombia before the nation, with Chocó's queens pressing the rest of the country to pay attention to a resource-rich but structurally poor department. Miss Chocó 1978 noted that the department's roads were much like those of two hundred years earlier, while illiteracy and disease levels were extremely high. The seventeen-year-old queen, Lucina Herrera Mosquera, argued that women should break barriers established by men and should liberate themselves not individually but socially, by working for and with the people to improve the collective future.

In the 1970s politics of international pageants, the participation of South Africa raised boycotts and protests—like those seen in sporting events—to confront the reality of racism and exclusion in that nation and in the larger world. However, Colombia would not select its first black Señorita Colombia until 2001, and charges of discrimination were routinely leveled against the pageant over the last third of the twentieth century. In that context, Miss Chocó 1957, Nazly Lozano, backed the creation of a new pageant, Miss Black International 1976, to be hosted in Buenaventura. Nazly became a congressional leader in the 1960s and hoped that the port of Buenaventura would attract contestants from around Africa, the Caribbean, and the Americas. Like the Chocó, however, Buenaventura had a broken or absent infrastructure, high unemployment, and high crime rates. A high wall, much like that of Berlin, separated the modern port from the decrepit urban center, a contrast of economic potential separated from, and maintaining, social misery.[50] Although the Miss Black International pageant still exists, it is not clear if it was held in Buenaventura in 1976. However, one could suggest that Buenaventura and the Chocó symbolized the socioeconomic exclusion inherited from the colonial period that barred nonwhite Colombians from access to elite-controlled wealth and power.

Nevertheless, for those select young women who won the national crown in Colombia, their future as ex-queens led to wealth and physical comfort. Most wed the year after their reign, marrying rich men, then moving into large homes with swimming pools. Their beauty and the fame they garnered in the pageant process ensured future wealth. By the late 1970s, with their astrological signs prominent, the top five finalists at the Señorita Colombia pageant went on to represent Colombia internationally at Miss Universe, Miss International, Miss Caribe, Miss Joven Internacional, and Miss World. National and international pageants, and media coverage of them, seemed to proliferate during the 1970s. Although the beauty looked increasingly commercial and stale, big money poured in to fuel contests over female beauty and male status. Silicone breast augmentations and liposuction became more available in Colombian cities as science and commerce promised the look and proportions standard in pageants. At the local level in Cartagena, the Reina Popular competition remained intense, with winners drawing attention and governmental resources to the services and streets in their home neighborhoods.[51]

If Luz Marina made Colombia famous for its beautiful women in 1958, drug production and trafficking made it infamous by the late 1970s. On the North Coast, from the northeast La Guajira peninsula to the southwest Gulf of Urabá next to Panama, marijuana and cocaine trafficking brought jobs, wealth, and violence. By the late 1970s, 70 percent of the marijuana imported into the United States came from Colombia. Just on the North Coast, thirty to fifty thousand small farmers depended on marijuana cultivation for their livelihood, while another fifty thousand gained employment from the trade. With an estimated fifty million marijuana smokers in the United States in 1979, the economic and employment picture looked bright, indeed. As the state weakened in both countries—Colombia from La Violencia and the breakdown of the judicial system, and the United States from the military loss in Southeast Asia and the Watergate Scandal—society seemed to be calling the shots. While visiting the United States, a young Ernesto Samper found marijuana smoked openly in New York City by professionals at work, in restaurants, and in parks, with the police overwhelmed by the volume of use. With drug use part of American culture and law becoming more tolerant of its use, Samper, like many Americans, suggested that marijuana be legalized. Samper echoed the opinion of ex-president López Michelsen that Colombians weren't corrupting Americans; rather, Americans were corrupting themselves. With drug trafficking organizations inside both countries becoming more sophisticated and violent, Samper asked if repression should only be the responsibility of Colombia while Americans hypocritically preached one line while snorting another.[52]

From Cali to Buenaventura, from Medellín to the Gulf of Urabá, small-scale cocaine smugglers made enough profits from their first few deals in the early 1970s to expand their trafficking operations to feed the booming demand for cocaine in the United States. With an estimated 4.1 million regular users in 1977—including 10 percent of young Americans aged eighteen to twenty-five who had tried cocaine—the United States drug culture was nearing its demand apex, and cocaine was becoming a marker of an elite luxury consumption status symbol. In Medellín, cocaine replaced the ailing textile sector as the most dynamic economic enterprise in the city, one with a notable but masked multiplier effect. In Antioquia's corridor to the Caribbean at the Gulf of Urabá, a banana boom brought wealthy investors, expanding plantations, and fifty thousand new jobs. At the port in Turbo, the fourteen million banana boxes shipped to the United States offered cover for cocaine shipments to Tampa and Miami; in Miami, Colombians went to war with Cuban-run smuggling operations for control of the cocaine wholesale business in Florida. In Apartadó, the banana/cocaine boom of the 1970s increased the population of the city from four thousand in 1965 to fifty thousand in 1975. Although banana workers made the highest wages in the coastal region, prices for food and consumer goods were also very high, and the booming city of Apartadó had no secondary school. Given the complete lack of educational training, young women couldn't study business or complete professional training to become a secretary. Prostitution became the only thriving business for women, with female migrants from the interior adding to the estimated one thousand prostitutes working in the city.[53]

The banana and cocaine booms stimulated economic growth, but both had high social costs. Politics remained stable and static thanks to the National Front, challenged by Rojas Pinilla and ANAPO and giving rise to the urban guerrilla movement, M-19. Culturally, some students adopted elements of hippie culture, as did middle-class students in the United States in the 1970s, part of the inheritance of the previous decade. Colombian opinions and discussions about sexuality, birth control, divorce, and women's rights signaled a social evolution toward modern ideas. Beauty standards alternated between the homegrown "typical Latina" to the imported international blonde, a reflection of Colombia's ongoing search for the authentic while maintaining contacts with a wider world. However, decreasing voter participation and support for the National Front also found resonance with popular displeasure with and cynicism about the Concurso Nacional de Belleza, both politics and pageants increasingly seen as corrupt elite fixes.

Chapter 9

PULCHRITUDE, THE PALACIO, AND POWER, 1979–1985

The nation's economy outperformed the Colombian political system during this last period under review, repeating the pattern witnessed thirty years earlier during La Violencia. High coffee prices bolstered by expanding production of petroleum, natural gas, nickel, coal, bananas, emeralds, marijuana, and cocaine kept the economy growing while much of Latin America entered the "lost decade" of economic contraction during the 1980s. However, while the economy grew, inflation increased to about 25 percent annually, open unemployment hovered at about 15 percent, and income distribution remained highly skewed in both urban and rural areas. Although one-third of women worked in 1985 and female employment had more than doubled since 1964, minimum wages still paid a miserable three dollars a day. Structurally, the assassination of Gaitán and the containment of Rojas Pinilla blocked the florescence of populism in Colombia, allowing the two traditional parties to pursue moderate and measured economic policies. Those policies maintained or increased wealth concentration and kept the majority of Colombians marginal to economic progress, apparently the price of political stability.[1] The social costs of this stable economic and political model included increasing levels of violence, insecurity, and insurgency.

The Liberal administration of Julio César Turbay Ayala (1971–1972) and that of maverick Conservative Belisario Betancur (1982–1986) maintained the logic and patterns inherited from the National Front; power and positions were shared between the two traditional parties, with neither administration nor party pursuing significant reforms. Both parties seemed content to play the politics of clientelism, mobilizing reliable rural voters while avoiding fresh policies or programs. Turbay bent to U.S. pressure to eradicate marijuana cultivation in Colombia, but Colombian growers were most hurt by the resulting high-quality *sinsemilla* planted around the United States from California to Maine, Alaska to Hawaii.[2] Turbay bent to military pressure to try civilians in military courts and to allow torture of prisoners believed to be insurgents, policies that only built public sympathy for the victims and for the insurgents confronting the state. Turbay, an old-school party hack and manipulative professional politician, only reinforced the perception that real political change could arrive solely via revolutionary violence. On the other hand, Betancur, the paisa commoner, pursued negotiations and dialogue with various guerrilla groups, but deals fell apart when the president could not deliver on the structural reforms sought by the insurgents. Economic expansion in the context of political stagnation led to social marginalization for more Colombians; Colombia still had infant mortality levels twice those of Costa Rica, and while 80 percent of homes now had access to electricity, some 66 percent did not have potable water. Public faith in institutions—be they the state or the church—dropped in the face of structural cynicism and callousness.[3] Emblematic of the times, Colombian filmmakers during the early 1980s focused on La Violencia, saying that today "nuestra realidad es el horror . . ."[4]

In addition to the FARC, the ELN, and the ELP, the M-19 joined the insurgent ranks in late 1973, emerging as an outgrowth of frustration to exclusionary democracy and antisocial development. Formed by former members and supporters of Rojas Pinilla's ANAPO, M-19 claimed that the 1970 presidential election was stolen from ANAPO by the National Front. M-19's first significant act was the theft of Simón Bolívar's sword, symbolizing the Liberator's imagined support for twentieth-century reforms. On New Year's Eve 1978 and New Year's Day 1979, M-19 made off with about five thousand weapons from the Canton Norte military arsenal in Bogotá, having dug an extensive tunnel under and into the armory. In 1980, they seized the Dominican Embassy in Bogotá during a diplomatic reception, holding fourteen ambassadors for a large ransom before receiving safe conduct out of the country. Influenced by the urban guerrilla tactics of the Montoneros of Argentina and the Tupamaros of Uruguay, the M-19 had a flair for the dramatic, high-profile operation. Like other South American urban guerrilla movements, the M-19, *la guerrilla chévere* (the cool guerrilla), cultivated a Robin Hood image, stealing food and goods and then distributing them in poor urban neighborhoods. Operating in the shadow of civil and military power in central Bogotá, the M-19 was a particular embarrassment to the Colombian armed forces, creating an enmity that would be fully expressed five years later at the Palacio de Justicia.[5] Although the four guerrilla groups did not often coordinate their actions and did not present a coherent project for the nation, they nonetheless won widespread sympathy from urban intellectuals, the urban poor, landless peasants, and the huge numbers of urban and rural residents living without basic services. As argued by David Bushnell, the falling confidence in the nation's political institutions gave a level of legitimacy to the armed groups as they struggled against the established order, a dynamic that one could easily track back to 1948.[6]

Regardless of the larger national problems, the local queen contests in Cartagena remained a big draw. In 1979, the seventeen-year-old "attractive trigueña" Julia Teresa Martínez, a high school student at Soledad Acosta de Samper, won the reina popular contest. Thirty thousand spectators packed the bullring for the four-hour event, the crowd craning to hear during the last three hours after the sound system quit but respectful of the judges' decisions. Julia Teresa lived in a new neighborhood outside the city center, one that still lacked bus service; the new queen dutifully requested bus service for her community. The sixty thousand pesos she won as queen would go to fixing up the family home. Unfortunately, the rector of her school expelled Julia Teresa for winning the crown. Her teachers and fellow students rallied around their sovereign and pressured successfully for the rector to readmit her. Winning the local crown helped put her community and school on the municipal map, brought necessary funds to improving the family home, with, hopefully, some left over to travel beyond Barranquilla, the only place she knew besides Cartagena. In conjunction with the reina popular pageant, a *reinado infantil* attracted sixty-one girls—twice as many as the reina popular—five to ten years old, with sponsoring companies ensuring that each participant received a gift. The queen, chosen from a cross-color slate of competitors, received a bicycle, a watch, and a doll, memorable gifts and honors for a young girl.[7]

Cartagena reveled in various pageants that served as preludes for the national pageant. Although the reina popular was still responsible for "controlling the happiness of the people of Cartagena," in 1981 the reinado popular competed simultaneously for municipal and media attention with a competing pageant, that of the "Reina de la Simpatía," sponsored by several big liquor and beer distributors. That year it seemed that the corporate pageant trumped the municipal pageant. Other pageants in the early 1980s, like the "Diosa del Mar," or that of the Carnival in Barranquilla, attracted regional and international participation, reinforcing a pattern also apparent during La Violencia: while the interior of the country plunged into political and economic violence, most of the North Coast found refuge in relative peace and pageants.[8]

The marijuana smuggling center around Santa Marta certainly bucked the trend found elsewhere on the North Coast. Gun violence followed the drug trade, leading to increased murder rates and intensified public insecurity. The dead were usually from far away; they wore dark glasses, drove Ford pick-up trucks, carried .45 caliber pistols, gambling millions at local casinos. Well-to-do local girls were often by their sides at the casinos when the shooting began. The shootings and subsequent funerals pushed tourists away from Santa Marta's resorts. Because of the violence, the biggest local party, the

Reina del Mar pageant, which attracted candidates from around the Caribbean Basin, was canceled from 1976 to 1978. In 1979, public and private leaders pushed successfully to revive the pageant; apparently, the wave of shootings had diminished. No one was shot during the 1979 pageant and street parties. The city forgot about its past trauma, forgot about the sewage spilling daily onto 14th and 15th avenues, forgot about political divisions, forgot about the companies that wanted to develop and pollute beachfront property. To restore civic pride and the pageant, to become once again the City of the Sea, Santa Martans surrendered to temporary amnesia.[9]

Political and economic trends affecting the nation also shaped national pageant politics from 1979 to the early eighties. Between 1979 and 1981, drug money inflated the costs of reinados, effectively shutting out some candidates and departments while favoring the emerging cocaine centers of Antioquia, Valle, and Amazonas. Drugs and their impact on daily life and institutions and increasing levels of violence in urban areas made cities like Cali, Medellín, and Pereira appear to be veering out of control. Reflecting these themes, beauty took on a more grown-up, sexual, cynical, and commercial quality. Television transmission in color of the national beauty pageant after 1980 increased the size of the viewing audience, while that same year, the Reinado del Coco was canceled in San Andrés because of increasing violence.[10]

Three million Colombians watched the television broadcast of the 1979 Señorita Colombia pageant from Cartagena. Big money flowed to the candidates from Antioquia, Cauca, and Santander; one party in honor of María Patricia Arbeláez, Señorita Antioquia, cost 750,000 pesos (about $18,000). Bogotá's candidate, supported by a delegation of eighty, including the governor of Cundinamarca and the mayor of Bogotá, was the great grandchild of Liberal caudillo Rafael Uribe Uribe, and the great great great grandchild of doña Trinidad Callejas, famous for her beauty in the 1830s. The judges almost stole the show; Mexican actor Jaime Moreno had appeared nude in *Playgirl* and Fabergé and Babe perfume spokesperson Margaux Hemingway commanded attention with her six-foot frame, supermodel stature, and literary lineage. Already a regular at Studio 54 in Manhattan, the twenty-four-year-old Hemingway had a drug and alcohol habit not quite as large as the striking fact that the Federal Reserve Bank in Miami held more cash than all the other Federal Reserve Banks in the United States. That those dollars came from the cocaine market was an open secret; Antioquia's win in 1979 suggested that Medellín's leadership in that bullish market did not hurt the future chances of Antioquia's queen.[11]

Since the private sector was the principal promoter of the pageant, it was logical that the geography of Colombian beauty would mirror centers of dynamic enterprise. A geography of national beauty queens revealed the historic importance of Valle, Atlántico, and Antioquia, with Cali, Barranquilla, and Medellín respectively serving as the political and commercial centers of those departments, dominating the Señorita Colombia pageant over the previous three decades. Hometown Cartagena, Santander with Bucaramanga and Barrancabermeja as economic motors, and Bogotá, the national capital and latter-day winner of the pageant, filled out the geographic and economic winners who normally controlled the outcome of the pageant. For those departments without the economic means or political connections, the path to the crown was both expensive and crowded with well-connected competitors. As always, discrimination, be it racial, social, economic, or geographic, worked against candidates outside the centers of social, economic, and political power.[12]

Even with the Señorita Colombia pageant generating 400 million pesos in economic activity, with fantasy costumes now costing 250,000 pesos each, competitors from remote provinces made a run at the crown in Cartagena in 1980. With RCN television running twelve hours of pageant programming over four days and with an estimated eleven million possible viewers, Señorita Colombia was the biggest national event of the year. Doña Teresa Pizarro de Angulo, a driving force on the Señorita Colombia organizing committee, underscored that the pageant was the biggest tourist event in Cartagena and in Colombia, one that promoted the nation to the wider world. Other organizing committee members argued that the pageant's most important role was to integrate Colombia; that the pageant, rather than civic pride, national institutions, or the rule of law, fulfilled that sovereign purpose was left unspoken. Geographic integration came to Cartagena via two competitors from the southern border of the country: Nariño sent Magda Martínez, the niece of 1959 Señorita Colombia, Stella Márquez; and the Territory of Amazonas sent its first queen. Sixteen-year-old Ivonne Maritza Gómez, whose grandparents, reportedly, were of the Miraña people, made a dramatic arrival as the indigenous princess accompanied by the long-haired, well-muscled, and deeply tanned Cápax, who, like Tarzan, always seemed to have jungle animals nearby. The extravagance of Señorita Amazonas's splash in Cartagena raised rumors that the cash behind her candidacy, supplied by her future husband, came from the drug trade. The 1980 winner would earn a Fiat 147 automobile, a one-million-peso contract with a soap company, 300,000 pesos (about six thousand dollars), four jewels valued at 100,000 pesos each, cosmetics for ten years, and the national crown.[13]

Although a computer projection broadcast by a radio station predicted that Señorita Nariño would win the pageant, Señorita Santander, Nini Johana Soto, claimed the crown. Santander won the crown three times between 1973 and 1980, perhaps buoyed by rising oil prices as well as by that department's historic reputation for beautiful women. Because of a dispute over the nomination rights, Nini could not represent Colombia in the Miss Universe pageant, and even argued before Congress to be permitted to do so. Nonetheless, she was runner-up in the Miss World pageant, the best international showing since Luz Marina's victory at Miss Universe in 1958. Meanwhile, the good people of Nariño claimed that the crown had been stolen from their southern department. The mayor of Pasto, the governor of Nariño, and the minister of labor all protested the decision, while a group of younger men took more direct action by stoning the building from which RCN broadcast the pageant.[14]

Nini started a new life once she became Señorita Colombia. She could count on the appreciation of the Colombian people at the many events that required almost constant travel. She recognized the social and economic benefits included in being the nation's sovereign. But for other pageant winners, the competitiveness of the pageants and the constant demands made on young women bordered on abuse. The promise of the crown pushed candidates to the physical breaking point, involving, at times, sabotage done to fellow competitors. Past Miss World and Miss Universe winners complained about the twenty-hour workdays that came with the crown, a regimen that left them near exhaustion. It was clear to 1980 Miss Universe Shawn Nichols Weatherly that the organizations and people who wanted her time did not see her as a person, instead only as a vehicle for profit. In reaction to the corporate and corporal beauty of modernity, some who wrote on the subject yearned for another beauty, the internal beauty extolled in literary circles a century before, one that valued the steadiness, talent, and skill of those women who couldn't enthrall with their looks.[15]

Nini Johana was first runner-up to Miss Venezuela at the 1981 Miss World pageant, part of a remarkable run of triumphs at international beauty contests by Colombia's neighbor. In the midst of booming prices for oil, Venezuela's first success came in 1979 when Maritza Sayalero won the Miss Universe crown. Prior to her coronation, she had roomed with Miss Colombia, Ana Milena Parra (both admitted to recent nose jobs). After the coronation, Martiza's mother commented to *Cromos* that "we've won a queen but lost a daughter, at least for the next few months" as eighteen-year-old Maritza became the "property of the Miss Universe contest" and ceased to pertain to her family over the next year. The Venezuelan ambassador to Australia, where the pageant was held, stated that Venezuela's triumph at Miss Universe became a type of popular sedative, as over the previous two and one-half years all that Venezuelans talked about was politics; now, at least, people could talk about beauty queens and the success of their nation's women on the global stage.[16] Venezuela repeated its success at Miss Universe in 1981 with a win by blonde Irene Sáez Conde, one of five blondes among the finalists that year. Irene paid all of her own expenses to the pageant and donated her earnings to charity. She later became mayor of a wealthy district of Caracas and a leading presidential candidate in 1998 before being displaced by former colonel and eventual president Hugo Chávez. With oil prices booming or busting, with national politics functional or in disarray, Venezuela won the Miss Universe crown an unprecedented six times between 1979 and 2009, the country presenting carefully crafted, professionally coached young women who bridged elements of the North Atlantic and Mediterranean beauty ideals.[17]

While Venezuela rode the wave of petroleum's fortunes to become a beacon of modernity and development in northern South America, Colombia fell under the shadow of an increasingly violent and profitable drug trade. Both the Drug Enforcement Agency (DEA) and *Cromos* designated cocaine as the drug of the eighties, displacing the now criticized marijuana of the sixties and seventies. Marijuana, by the early eighties, was reported in the Colombian media as an antisocial and dangerous drug, while cocaine was seen as a modern, social, nonaddictive, and sophisticated drug of white-collar workers. While *Cromos* "packaged" each drug according to its respective market trends, also emerging in the early 1980s was the planting of coca bushes in remote areas of Cauca, Huila, Caquetá, and the Llanos. Now, poor indigenous farmers in Cauca, for example, could plant coca amongst coffee or bananas and refine the coca leaf into coca paste before selling it to a trafficker who refined it further into cocaine hydrochloride powder. Whereas most of the coca grown and refined into coca paste came from Bolivia and Peru, and with U.S. "drug war" policies aimed at eradicating coca planting and trafficking there, Colombia had the laboratories to refine the coca paste into cocaine powder. Both market logic and the focus of U.S. drug policy shaped a strategic effort to vertically integrate the production of coca leaf into coca paste into cocaine powder all in Colombia.[18]

Where coca leaf took root, dollars and consumer goods followed. Peddlers trudged the dirt roads and paths that led to coca towns, bringing consumer goods and medicines formerly available only in larger towns and cities. Campesinos replaced old adobe roof tiles with new rust- and waterproof synthetic roofs, building garages near the road that housed "chivas"—folk-art buses painted with altars for the Virgen del Carmen—with new chassis and motors. Every Sunday, trucks arrived carrying new all-terrain motorcycles, big-ticket items snatched up immediately and paid for with cash at markets that used to offer oranges.[19]

Poor farming families in remote rural areas could become rich once they discovered the commercial difference between banana leaves and coca leaves. Dagoberto Corrales, an aged indigenous patriarch, had always kept a few coca bushes and had chewed coca all his life. Once the market for coca expanded commercially because of the foreign demand for cocaine, he ripped out his coffee and banana trees and planted one hundred thousand coca bushes. One ton of coca leaf earned 120,000 pesos (about $2,400), and yielded two kilos of cocaine powder, worth 40,000 dollars in Bogotá, and once cut and distributed in the retail U.S. market reportedly yielded a million dollars. Dagoberto had enough cash in his pocket to offer a police officer a bribe of 100,000 pesos ($2,000) not to burn his crop. Apparently, he also had access to mobile cocaine laboratories in the mountains of Cauca, as local youth carried kilos of cocaine from his land to larger urban markets. In urban markets like Bogotá, foreign tourists came in search of pure cocaine at twenty-five dollars a gram—when cut cocaine retailed for about eighty dollars a gram in U.S. markets—or journeyed to lovely Popayán in Cauca where cocaine sold for twelve dollars a gram.[20] In the sixties, Colombia was marketed as a tourist destination because of its natural attractions, highlighted by its beautiful women. By the early eighties, cheap drugs became the new attraction.

The ugly side of this high-risk, high-reward bonanza was a skyrocketing level of homicides. Pereira, a city of about two hundred thousand inhabitants located in the "golden triangle" between Medellín, Cali, and Bogotá, had more than 900 murders from late 1979 to late 1980 and 1,140 in 1981, an astoundingly high number of homicides (570 per 100,000 inhabitants) even for a city ten times its population. Among the murdered were several judges and police officers. The shooters, as in Santa Marta, were not from the area, belonging to various death squads, paramilitary groups, and drug trafficking organizations. They carried out their version of street justice while the formal judiciary was paralyzed by death threats and lack of police protection.[21] Although it seemed merely to be a strategic transshipment point not directly involved in the production or consumption of cocaine, Pereira became a killing field.

Proceeds from the drug industry flowed into banks, real estate, legitimate businesses, art markets, and various sports, including boxing, soccer, and auto, bicycle, and horse racing. Money bought favor from parties and politicians, judges, journalists, police and army officers, and logically, from beauty queens and models. The 1981 Señorita Colombia came from Antioquia, whose capital city, Medellín, was emerging as the cocaine capital of the world. On a balcony above Cartagena's Plaza de la Aduana, Julio Iglesias, an emerging pop icon of the 1980s, serenaded the pageant crowd below. Money bought quality entertainment, lavish parties, wardrobes, jewelry, hair stylists, makeup artists, and pageant coaches. Money, as in politics, bought access to power, in this case to beautiful women and to pageants that introduced the emerging rich of the drug industry to national society. Drug bosses bet with one another on the outcome of the pageants, and on how high "their" candidate would place. Rumors circulated that the bosses of the Medellín and Cali cartels divided the queens between them, leading to cocaine-fueled orgies after the pageant. Pageants allowed the new rich to launder some of their newfound wealth in increasingly gaudy spectacles. María Teresa Gómez, 1981 Señorita Colombia, married well, as had most national beauty queens before her. Her husband, Dairo Chica Arias, a stable hand, horse trainer, and mounted bullfighter for the Ochoa brothers—three high-level cocaine smugglers from Medellín—became a launderer of his employers' money, staging bullfights all over Colombia. At their 1983 wedding, Dairo gave his bride a white Mercedes Benz sports car. The Ochoa brothers gifted the couple a chess set with gold pieces. When Dairo asked why that gift, the Ochoa brothers responded, "So that you would see how a pawn can take a queen."[22] Regardless of her later marriage, María Teresa's victory brought big crowds into the streets of Medellín to celebrate her victory. As in previous years, thousands drove around honking car horns, shouted "Antioquia," sang the departmental and national hymns, liberally drank aguardiente, danced the *son*, and screamed themselves hoarse before retiring. The governor of Antioquia and the mayor of Medellín flew to Cartagena so they could accompany their queen back home.[23] The social and political power of being queen hadn't been altered, even if the economics had evolved.

Time and money had also changed the regional pageants established twenty years before out of the ruins of La Violencia. The Reinado del Bambuco in Neiva had grown in size by the early 1980s, even if some locals from Huila criticized it for losing its folkloric roots. Although not officially a beauty pageant, the reinado still required competitors to cover the aesthetic bases while also demonstrating skill in various bambuco dances. With Catalina providing the requisite swimsuits and liquor companies pushing their products while backing their queens, the corporate and commercial side of pageants was evident. But the crowd still mattered, and the winner had to sway the crowd, which could then influence the judges' decision. With television host Pacheco on hand to animate the crowd, the event had energy, perhaps enhanced by the five hundred thousand bottles of aguardiente consumed. Many municipalities in Huila and the majority of neighborhoods in Neiva did not participate in the reina popular contest, one resident saying, "this isn't for the people, and it's not to have fun, it's not to sing or dance. This has become one big drunk."[24] Downriver at Girardot, huge crowds from Bogotá flocked to the Reinado del Turismo Nacional and jammed the streets, often sleeping there too, as local hotels filled quickly. Bogotanos still craved the caloric and social warmth of *tierra caliente* and now had the leisure money to spend on yet another National Front-era reinado.[25]

Both the connections and tensions between popular and elite definitions of modern beauty and Colombian identity were most frequently played out in November in Cartagena. The popular festivities in the city's neighborhoods leading up to the national beauty contest set the local and popular stage for the national and elite contestation of beauty and power. At times, people saw these discrete events as part of one big party, an error corrected in 1982. That year, the Frente de Barrios Pobres (Poor Neighborhoods Front) threatened to sabotage the traditional November 11th and Concurso Nacional de Belleza celebrations unless families facing displacement from their neighborhoods received some public lands with services in compensation. The lengthening of the airstrip at the Crespo airport—to service bigger jets carrying more tourists—involved the displacement of at least three hundred families from the Barrio San José. The families protested, arguing that the airport threatened both residents and travelers, with the Frente pushing for compensation if the families were forced to move. The mayor of Cartagena and the governor of Bolívar—the governor appointed by the president, the mayor chosen by the governor, and neither popularly elected—cynically suggested that the residents move voluntarily or wait for the barrio to be bulldozed, with residents receiving no compensation. This antidemocratic demonstration of geographic, social, and political power was further punctuated that year when municipal authorities did not organize the traditional October and November parties, instead turning them over to businesses intent on profiting off the crowd. The October parties were a flop, and when the day came to crown the Reina Popular, so few people bought the now required tickets that the organizers opened the bullring for free to all comers.[26]

The 1982 Miss Universe pageant in Lima, Peru, presented a striking blend of power and marginalization. The pageant, described as one of the most organized (therefore modern) events in the world, was held in chaotic Lima in the midst of an international debt crisis, the expanding insurgency of Sendero Luminoso, and the growing might of a record-setting and destructive El Niño weather event in 1982–1983. Extraordinary security limited popular and press contact with the candidates, but nonetheless, limeños pressed to get a glimpse of the "Misses" and poured into the streets and plazas of central Lima in enthusiastic numbers not seen since the populist heyday of Victor Raúl Haya de la Torre. Feminist protestors rallied against the logic and cost of the pageant, alleging that it cost the Peruvian treasury $650,000, carrying signs protesting the objectification of women and the building of tourism at the expense of female dignity. Writer Mario Vargas Llosa and former Miss Universe Gladys Zender represented Peru on the large judges' panel, while outgoing queen Irene Sáez of Venezuela was described as cold and indifferent but still very beautiful. Thirteen candidates of color formed a "Third World" block in protest against the pageant, alleging discrimination and pushing for equal treatment with white candidates.[27]

The discrimination necessary to select the 1982 Señorita Colombia queen led to some controversy but also to the consolidation of a family dynasty. Seventeen-year-old Julie Paulín Sáenz Starnes won the crown for family and Bogotá. Often lauded for her blue eyes that changed to green, gray, or steel blue depending on the light, Julie Paulín was the sister of 1977 winner Shirley Sáenz Starnes. She was the fourth daughter of the family to participate and excel in beauty pageants and spoke English well, bolstering her chances in future international pageants. Upon her return to Bogotá, a crowd braved the light, cold rain, shouting "ganamos" (we won) as Julie Paulín paraded downtown toward the Plaza de Bolívar. Her high school mates said she was prettier after having won the crown. The controversy came from Barranquilla and the department of Atlántico, whose queen refused to accept the title of Second Princess, instead angling to enter the Reina de las Reinas competition to select the Colombian representative for Miss Universe. Allegedly, her father had tried but failed to buy economic and political favor at the Señorita Colombia pageant, a claim later denied. As part of a long-standing regional feud, Atlántico threatened not to send another queen to Cartagena, arguing that its queens had received poor treatment over the past dozen years. *Cromos* concluded that the Reinado Nacional de Belleza had entered a war footing, with intense competition among wealthy departments, and where money counted more than the personal qualities of the contestants, most of whom had grown up in luxurious circumstances.[28]

When asked about the needs of her home department, Señorita Antioquia, Marta Nohara Calle, replied that the lack of employment made security and solidarity tenuous. Manufacturing jobs in and around Medellín disappeared in the early 1980s as import tariffs on textiles declined, leaving many urban workers unemployed. Those jobs that did remain were subcontracted to unregistered firms in the informal sector that employed women at less than the minimum wage of three dollars a day. Although Marta had the body and sultry looks of a beauty queen, she complained that she was a queen without power, one who could not complete significant works but who could only collaborate at parades, dances, and banquets. When asked what they would do if they had power, most of the 1982 departmental queens answered that they would survey the country's problems and then invest in education, health, and employment programs targeted at the most vulnerable: children, the aged, and the poor. Asked what crime they would punish most severely, most listed murder, massacre, kidnapping, and crimes against children.[29]

Colombia entered a perfect storm in the early 1980s, blending economic liberalization, a weak state, and the power and destructiveness of petroleum and drug economies. Much like the situation of Mexico in the early twenty-first century, the result was an explosion of homicides, kidnapping, and terrorism. Petroleum production in Putumayo and coca paste (bazuco) production in Caquetá generated significant new profit streams and waves of killing, yet residents still lived without potable water, sewers, electricity, decent roads, and adequate schools and health clinics. Texaco produced 100,000 barrels daily from wells around Orito but invested nothing in the social development of Putumayo because the Colombian government did not require it. Children suffered from malnutrition, dysentery, anemia, malaria, parasites, and infectious diseases. Under the streets of Orito ran black gold; on the surface, people lacked elementary public services and lived on the margins of modernity's subterranean bounty. In the remote town of Cartagena del Chairá in the Caquetá, school-aged children migrated from larger towns during vacations to this tiny town on the Río Caguán to prostitute themselves for five thousand pesos (about sixty dollars). The new money arrived in 1980, when traffickers displaced from La Guajira came to the Caquetá showing former corn and yucca farmers how to plant coca and process it into coca paste. Overproduction of coca leaf subsequently lowered its price, while coca paste fetched eighty pesos a gram in Cartagena del Chairá and ten times that in Bogotá or Medellín. The paste could be further refined into cocaine powder or smoked, like crack, giving an intense but short-lived high. Although FARC guerrillas prohibited its use, local and national youth did smoke it, easily becoming addicted while damaging their minds and bodies. Regardless of the economic boom, residents of the Caquetá lacked basic services and lived poor lives, one local doctor reportedly operating by lantern light on patients lying on stretchers. The bazuco bonanza brought waves of murders; social, moral, and economic desolation; and the law of silence as residents refused to speak out in fear of retaliation. While *Cromos* incorrectly foresaw the swift decline of the coca and cocaine trade in Colombia, it did raise alarm bells about another dangerous drug, heroin. With opium poppy being grown in former

La Violencia centers of the Llanos and Tolima, a future in which heroin was produced for four hundred pesos a gram and sold in the United States at six hundred dollars a gram suggested huge new profits and tremendous social costs.[30]

At the center of the wholesale drug market, social costs intensified. Medellín, now the city with the highest urban unemployment figures in the nation, experienced an 85 percent increase in homicides in the decade since 1973. The question of who was shooting whom yielded multiple answers. Urban guerrillas of the EPL and ELN targeted police and military officers and civilian government collaborators. Urban gang members extorted local businesses, used drugs, survived unemployment, and killed to impose street justice. Death squads killed those deemed "antisocial," given elastic definitions of those deemed dangerous to public order. Paramilitaries, often composed of police and military officials, took merchants' money to protect businesses and to impose their sense of justice. Other groups like MAS (Muerte a Secuestradores), funded by the Ochoa brothers, linked drug traffickers' vengeance against guerrilla groups who kidnapped for large ransoms. In a city of 1.5 million, the local police only had ten patrols. In the first six months of 1983, eight hundred people (an obvious estimate) were murdered; 88 percent were male, most in their twenties. "High-value" victims included government officials, judges, police officials, union leaders, army officials, high school principals, and university professors.[31] Local police on the street openly shared their "five times and you're dead" rule: on the fifth arrest of any person, they'd take him out back and shoot him.[32] The deathly silence from public officials about these extrajudicial assassinations evinced the lack of a sovereign and legitimate state that could guarantee the life and property of Colombian citizens within the law.

As with coffee, cattle, petroleum, and manufacturing, the cocaine trade yielded profits that bought political influence. Connections between drug traffickers who bought protection, influence, and complicity from political leaders formed in the 1970s. In the wake of the defeat of Liberal candidate Alfonso López Michelsen for the presidency in 1982, Pablo Escobar, a violent, rising star of the cocaine business in Medellín, alleged that he gave the Liberal leader Ernesto Samper a check for 23 million pesos for the López Michelsen campaign. Samper countered that the Conservative party was behind the allegations, challenging those making the charges to produce the check, and noting that the amount of the alleged donation varied depending on the day. Samper did not explicitly deny the allegation and would not guarantee that drug money did not filter into political and electoral campaigns at the departmental and local level. He still favored the legalization of marijuana in Colombia, noting that a hundred thousand people cultivated the herb in the Sierra Nevada de Santa Marta and that its use was common in the United States. He did not favor the legalization of cocaine, disingenuously arguing that there was no social conflict connected to coca while noting at the same time the physical damage done to the body by cocaine.[33] Although Samper was out front on the issue of marijuana legalization, his position on coca and cocaine seemed out of touch with reality, and his political side step around the question of drug money in politics left him suspect. As president of Colombia from 1994 to 1998, Samper faced a bitter scandal in 1994–1995 over allegations that Cali cocaine money flowed into his presidential campaign, a scandal amplified by the ill-advised and ineffective "drug war" pushed by the United States in Colombia. Samper became a symbol of the link between drugs and politics both as a pragmatic, professional politician and as a person leading a political system greased by patronage augmented by drug money.[34]

On the 450th anniversary of the founding of Cartagena, contestants gathered for the thirtieth time to compete in the 1983 Señorita Colombia pageant. Cartagena resident and early favorite Susana Caldas Lemaitre created quite a buzz in the local and national media, as she was described as a classic beauty: white, blonde, with soft green eyes and a symmetrical figure. Despite its threatened boycott, Barranquilla sent its own blonde, Joyce Smith, a high school student in England familiar with but dismissive of punk rock. Joyce won the award for the best eyes, receiving a gold necklace as her prize. The 1983 pageant winner would receive over two million pesos in cash and contracts. Matching the blondes from the coast, Santander sent the tall and shapely Angela Patricia Janiot, who in the 1990s began a successful career as a news anchor for CNN en Español. Drug lords made their social introduction at the 1983 pageant, socializing with queens in the hotels, cultivating positive public relations with the media, laundering money, and placing bets on "their queen" with one another. *Cromos* partnered with Max Factor and the pageant to revive the drawing in which readers of *Cromos* cut out entry forms found in the magazine, filled in the predicted winner's name, and then either sent them to the magazine or placed them in special boxes wherever Max Factor cosmetics were sold. The entry forms had to be original and not photocopied to be valid, the winner to receive a new Mazda automobile. With 85 percent of urban women faithfully following developments and with circulation of magazines like *Cromos* tripling their production runs during pageant season, the drawing was good business for the companies involved. Further adding to the power and appeal of cosmetics, only three of the seventeen competitors who paraded before the judges without makeup were deemed to have naturally pretty faces.[35]

A week before the national contest, the Reina Infantil and Reina Popular pageants attracted numerous competitors and spectators. The Reina Infantil drew seventy-eight participants from in and around Cartagena, the largest field yet, with the top three gaining cash prizes and school scholarships. Cartagena's 450th anniversary also drew thirty-five "morenitas" to the Reina Popular pageant, the queen to receive three hundred thousand pesos in cash and other gifts. The winner, María Eugenia León Garcia, hoped to erase her neighborhood's marginal reputation by promoting education and literacy in Cartagena. Her neighborhood, La Esperanza (Hope), had only one school, making it difficult for young people in the district to excel in a competitive and dynamic future.³⁶ Both these pageants followed the Miss America formula—promoting female education—as they also illustrated the social marginalization making such pageants necessary.

Although the Catholic Church had not exercised much direct influence over the organizers or the participants in the Reinado Nacional de Belleza since 1961, the pageant did give Church officials the opportunity to speak out on various national issues. With the nation focused on Cartagena and the national pageant, Monsignor Iván Cadavid spoke in Cali against public and private initiatives to build more affordable housing in urban areas. He argued that such projects only stimulated more rural to urban migration, increasing already high levels of urban unemployment, hunger, familial decomposition, and prostitution. He argued that the key issue for Colombia and the world was not war and peace, but work and food. He noted that 150,000 Colombian children died each year from malnutrition and that 3 million lived in rural areas without basic municipal services: schools, health care, recreation. Only 17 percent of rural children aged 7 to 18 years received basic education, an injustice that promoted migration to cities and, ironically, bolstered the size and importance of Reina Popular pageants like those in Cartagena.³⁷

Much to the delight of the three hundred thousand spectators in Cartagena's streets, the city's and Bolívar's own Susana Caldas Lemaitre won the 1983 Señorita Colombia pageant. Licorera de Bolívar gifted her 150,000 pesos for expenses, a donation probably more important to the liquor company than to "Sussy," for the quintessential "golden girl" of pure stock (de pura cepa) oozed a sweet blonde reflection of refinement and modernity that impressed the judges and won the crowd. Some said that her win represented a gift to the people on the city's anniversary. It had been twenty-two years since Bolívar had claimed the crown; "Sussy" was embraced as the most beloved of all the national queens. With former Miss Universe and fellow blonde Irene Sáez on the judge's panel and with the Nordic blonde Xuxa becoming a pop phenomenon in Brazil, blondes seemed to hint at the presence and

FIGURE 9.1   *Susana Caldas (1983) in* Las más bellas, *p. 205, courtesy Concurso Nacional de Belleza (Cartagena, Colombia).*

promise of wealth, development, and modernity. Like Xuxa in Brazil, where intensive marketing of multiple Xuxa products created huge profits, Sussy, with her gold earrings, gold rings, gold bracelets, golden hair, and gold crown and scepter, suggested the Midas touch. Sussy was a beautiful international symbol of power and prestige, an otherworldly goddess—like Xuxa for Brazilians—a queen positioned above the toil and grit of ordinary Colombians.[38]

For an ordinary school girl to become a beauty queen required the talent and labor of coaches, publicists, and photographers. Lena Pinzón taught the European high fashion method, coaching her young students how to walk, act, and feel like queens. If her students *felt* like queens, then, presumably, they could acquire the magnetism necessary to exude sovereign status in their every movement. Publicist Michel Arnau was hired by Medellín business and civic groups to take Antioquia's queen and make her a winner in Cartagena. Antioquia picked a young, dark-haired model, one considered to have homegrown beauty (belleza colombiana criolla) but one the same age as the Medellín youth who smoked or trafficked in bazuco. As a peer, she could deliver a more effective antidrug message to youth, while also demonstrating that Medellín and Antioquia weren't such horrible places. For photographer Hernán Díaz, careful photographic construction and the wide distribution of those photographs could make a departmental queen stand out from the rest. He complained that the pageant had devolved since the late 1950s, with ordinary girls enhanced with nose jobs and breast implants but lacking the elegance of the earlier queens. For Díaz, the Señorita Colombia pageant would continue to be "the apotheosis of the ridiculous, the annual confirmation of machismo, and in my particular case a necessity."[39]

Who became queen and who became vice-queen had seemed to follow a pattern since the 1950s. Although the Catholic Church no longer exercised direct influence over the pageant, a concordat evolved wherein queens were more spiritual and heavenly, while runners-up were flesh-and-blood sex symbols of this world. While a queen was often described as "very pretty," she was termed neither a "seductress" nor "statuesque." If queens were the stuff of fairy tales, runners-up were the constructed beauties found in the novels of Dashiell Hammett or Ian Fleming. Queen and vice-queen demarcated the realms of heaven and earth, salvation and sin, dream and desire. Although international pageants favored the corporeal beauty of this world, the Señorita Colombia pageant remained faithful to its traditional roots. In one famous illustration of this pattern, Doris Gil Santamaría won the 1957 crown while termed "Miss Heaven," but it was runner-up Luz Marina and her exuberant body who brought Colombia its one and only Miss Universe crown in 1958.[40]

On the silver anniversary of Luz Marina's triumph and upon completion of the thirtieth pageant, various publications reviewed the history of the pageant. *Carrusel* tracked how the early pageants, for married and unmarried women, evolved from candidates with pretty faces from prominent families to a revealed body with symmetrical measurements of 90–60–90. Reporters asked past queens to reminisce about the year they won the title and to share beauty secrets with readers. *Cromos* published a long article, framed as an inside story revealing the inside dirt and gossip from past pageants. That article stretched over forty pages, while analysis from ten journalists who shared their thoughts and observations about the pageant covered just four. Most journalists denied any deep interest in covering the pageant, but did so as part of their jobs. A few concluded that the pageant was a peculiar manifestation of Cartagena's monarchist society, one where people marginal to power ached to be close to royalty. If nothing else, the pageant created a diversion and a shared topic of conversation for young and old, rich and poor. Many commented on the irrational appeal of the pageant in the midst of serious national and international crises. A few noted that the pageant exploited young women in an alcohol-fueled exhibit of secondary sexual characteristics. Fernando González Pacheco (Pacheco) vowed never to return to the pageant, while Daniel Samper concluded that the pageant represented a search for nonexistent perfection.[41]

Classic questions reemerged in various magazines in the mid-1980s, much as they had a century earlier. The dualism of Mary/Eve, Mother/Medusa, Madonna/Witch now marked a male need to define females in order to control his own fears and maintain his status. If woman became, as Simone de Beauvoir suggested, "a sexual companion, a reproducer, an erotic object, an Other through which he looks for himself," then females becoming selves exposed myriad male fears. Comments on fashion lacked the tension between imported progress and national dress expressed a century earlier about the corset, noting that most people followed the hegemonic power of fashion while oblivious to that power. In female fashion, the brassiere, the miniskirt, and blue jeans were extolled for having changed female fashions around the globe, in the process revealing female curves for male enjoyment. Connecting the dots between sex, fashion, advertising, and power, sociologist Elssy Bonilla de Ramos cited the works of Thorstein Veblen and Michel Foucault to reveal how predominant social relations framed advertising to legitimize those social relations of power, which then were demonstrated in the world of consumption. Sex became a vehicle to define and stimulate consumption, distorting the reality of increasing numbers of women working in the marketplace by marketing women as sexual objects to promote goods. Certainly, publicity now defined consumption and fashion, having supplanted homespun cloth and handmade clothes, as it also sold beauty as power in a consumer society. Logically, another analyst noted how beauty and sex had become a marker of "conspicuous consumption" and a vicarious expression of power in the subterranean world of narco-trafficking.[42]

In the urban centers of narco-trafficking, analysts in Medellín promised a modern future for women, whereas boosters in Cali preferred to bask in comfortable tradition. Sociologist Elsa Ruiz defended Medellín as a site of opportunity, freedom, and evolution for Colombian women. She claimed that the city helped break down archaic roles and the pernicious ethic of the cult of domesticity; women could grow beyond stereotypes and engage in a dialogue about the city's unfolding future. This optimistic picture of women's roles in Medellín ignored the threat of the one hundred death squads operating in the city, some specifically targeting feminists. In a decidedly boosterish tone, a Cali book focused on race, noting that a few white elites and some blacks had avoided racial "contamination" of mixing beyond the color line, while most of the city's population was of mixed ancestry. Blacks and mulattos were described as happy extroverts who enjoyed singing, dancing, and sports, friends of flashy and extravagant outfits. In Medellín, the city's modern promise obscured its postindustrial drug war horror; in Cali "happy fashionable blacks" seemed, as in the nostalgic past, to be no threat to existing white power structures.[43]

Although difficult to quantify, income from illegal drug sales equaled 65 percent of the income from legal exports from 1980–84. Over the period from 1980 to 1995, narco-dollars brought thirty-six billion dollars into Colombia, more than coffee or petroleum. Pablo Escobar became an alternate congressman in the Chamber of Representatives in 1982, demonstrating how economic power bought political position. His associate, Carlos Lehder, used his Bahamian island, Norman Cay, to fly in tons of cocaine to the United States market. Lehder returned to his hometown of Armenia, and promptly bought up land, urban real estate, and businesses, to go along with his cars, trucks, and aircraft. He, of course, underreported his wealth to avoid paying taxes. Logically, narco-dollars contributed even more to land concentration, Colombia already the world's leader in unequal land distribution. Crime, corruption, and homicide also boomed with the drug trade. Escobar's very clear "plata o plomo" (silver or lead) offer left little room for judges and police officers to enforce the law. Whereas murder was the seventh leading cause of death in 1973, it was number one by 1986. Homicide levels tripled between 1980 and 1993, with Medellín being both cocaine and murder capital of the world. Antioquia had murder rates three times the national average in 1991: 245 per 100,000 inhabitants.[44]

Insurgency and counterinsurgency added to the body count. In the mid-1980s the FARC opened new fronts in areas of weak state presence and grew to about four thousand armed fighters, offering peasant farmers protection and justice, while taxing big landowners. The ELN cashed in on the petroleum boom in Arauca, taxing oil and pipeline companies in exchange for not blowing up oil pipelines; it became the wealthiest of the guerrilla groups. The EPL opened a new front in northern Antioquia, while the M-19 pursued a wide range of political and armed outreach. In the midst of negotiations with the Colombian government, both the insurgents and the Colombian military pursued a mixed fighting and talking strategy. In August 1984, military crackdowns and the assassination of M-19 leader Carlos Toledo Plata led to the insurgent seizure of Yumbo, an industrial city twelve minutes north of Cali. Apparently, the purpose of this joint operation between the M-19 and a dissident front of the FARC was to protest the killing of Toledo Plata, to hold a press conference, and to demonstrate power. They picked Yumbo as a site symbolizing what was wrong with Colombia: a heavily polluted industrial city with high unemployment and the highest infant mortality in the country. Although several military units were stationed nearby, none responded to the attack until a brigade from Cartago arrived almost three hours later. Three police officers and seven insurgents were killed in the initial firefight, but then another thirty-two civilians were slain after the insurgents retreated, apparently in retribution by the army's Third Brigade.[45]

The *Cromos* reporter covering the seizure of Yumbo was impressed by the professionalism and intelligence of M-19 leaders Carlos Pizarro León-Gómez and Rosemberg Pabón. Likewise, a follow-up *Cromos* interview with Antonio José Navarro Wolf presented a serious political analyst more interested in bringing democracy than Marxism to Colombia. Citing Rousseau, Navarro Wolf argued that democracy depended on equality and participation, both sorely missing in Colombia. He criticized the Colombian government for the inefficiency and inflexibility holding up the cease-fire, and noted that some military officers and members of the political class did not want to pursue a national dialogue with insurgents to bring peace and reform to Colombia. For the M-19, the transition from armed struggle to legal political activity proved elusive throughout 1984.[46]

Another armed group made Colombian violence yet more beastly in the mid-1980s and thereafter. Paramilitary groups, often born as frontier self-defense groups, became the military muscle of big landowners, either legitimate farmers and ranchers or narco-traffickers who became hacendados. The paramilitaries attacked insurgent groups and fended off the taxes they charged in their zones of control. Moreover, they carried out a merciless campaign against anyone suspected of supporting insurgents, especially targeting the civilian population living in frontier insurgent zones. As a counterguerrilla group, the paramilitaries were far more mobile and effective than the national army. The army still organized for conventional war and was woefully slow to react to insurgent attacks as seen in Yumbo. Yet military and paramilitary members often coordinated activities, blurring the line between legitimate state actors and the shadowy activities of death squads.[47]

The militarization of the U.S. drug war by the Reagan Administration added more violent fuel to the Colombian fire. As with supply-side Reagan-omics, the U.S. approach in Colombia was to destroy drug supplies and to arrest and deport high-level drug traffickers. The United States wanted to spray the herbicide Paraquat on drugs from the air as was done in Mexico in the 1970s; when the Colombians refused, the parties agreed on glyphosate as an alternative. The goals of drug interdiction and counterinsurgency blurred once U.S. Ambassador to Colombia Lewis Tambs coined the phrase "narco-guerrilla," suggesting a link between drug traffickers and insurgents. When an ELN unit was arrested, reportedly with 150 tons of marijuana, that link seemed at least plausible. The extradition of Colombians to the United States to stand trial for drug offenses further enmeshed U.S. foreign and Colombian domestic policies. The U.S. government requested that over 150 Colombians be extradited to stand trial in the United States; drug traffickers promised to kill five American diplomats for each Colombian extradited, a stand ap-plauded by a spokesperson from the M-19. Although the Colombian foreign ministry tried to convince Washington to change its drug war tactics, the job of overseeing the extradition process fell to Minister of Justice Rodrigo Lara Bonilla. As attorney general, Lara Bonilla took an aggressive stance against drug traffickers, involved in a joint DEA and Colombian National Police seizure of a huge cocaine laboratory complex at Tranquilandia. In re-taliation, Attorney General Lara Bonilla was assassinated on April 30, 1984. Thereafter, arrest orders and property seizures from top traffickers (Lehder, Escobar, Ochoa, and Porras) were announced by the Colombian government. In the months that followed, Pablo Escobar offered to pay Colombia's foreign debt of about ten billion dollars, his father was kidnapped but then rescued by a force employed by Escobar, Ambassador Tambs was threatened and told to leave the country, the U.S. embassy was bombed, and Tambs left Colombia and was replaced late that year. Multiple layers of violence intersected in Colombia in 1984, a process stimulated both by U.S. demand for drugs and U.S. government drug wars in Colombia, a dynamic that would rage through the next decades.[48]

As the drab gray year of 1984 wore on, the October 12 Columbus Day ob-servance openly revealed patterns of racism in Colombia against indigenous and black populations. Of course, Colombia was not exceptional in those patterns shaped in the Americas during the colonial era and refined there-after; it was just coming out of the closet. Governmental and nongovernmental spokespeople noted that the indigenous throughout Colombia faced racial and social discrimination and educational obstacles that maintained their low social and economic status. Pushing the issue on indigenous rights and agency, in 1984 the Movimiento Armado Quintín Lame, a multicultural pro-indigenous self-defense force, carried out its first armed action in Cauca. For the larger black and mulatto populations of Colombia, the social situation was both more complex and somewhat more hopeful. With Colombia's ethnic composition reported as 2.2 percent indigenous, 6 percent black, 24 percent mulatto, 47.8 percent mestizo, and 20 percent white, what North Americans termed the "black" population totaled at least 30 percent of the nation. Reportedly, the 1960s were in Colombia, as in the United States, a turning point in black/white relations, with interracial relationships and marriages becoming more socially acceptable. Nevertheless, parents expressed relief when children retained "good hair" as they grew up. In cities like Quibdó in the Chocó—where blacks made up 99 percent of the population—some blacks moved up into lower- and middle-level governmental positions once the white elite left in the mid-1960s. However, leadership positions in the armed forces, national government, and the Catholic Church effectively excluded blacks. In areas of Bogotá and Cali, customary segregation barred blacks from access to some restaurants, clubs, and hotels.[49] Small changes at the local level promised a less openly racist future for some, while the overall logic of white supremacy survived as it did in most of the Americas.

Regardless of the unfolding dramas gripping the nation, the national media dedicated much of October to the departmental candidates competing for the Señorita Colombia crown and much of November to the pageant and its aftermath. Early favorites included the candidates from Sucre, Nariño, Santander, Antioquia, and Valle, but the pageant was celebrating its 50th anniversary, so much to the surprise and consternation of most spectators, the crown remained in Cartagena, won by Señorita Bolívar, Sandra Borda Caldas. Sandra was the cousin of Sussy Caldas, the previous year's winner, but that familial link was later denied by pageant officials. Sandra was also rumored to be related to Doña Tera, the matriarch of the pageant, a link also denied. Rejection of the judges' decision resounded from across the country, with Santander and Antioquia threatening to boycott the 1985 pageant. The popular poll and drawing contest run by *Cromos* also confirmed the questions raised about the outcome, as Valle, Atlántico, and Sucre topped the rankings, with Bolívar a distant seventh. In an editorial in *El Tiempo*, Enrique Santos Calderón validated some of the criticisms aimed at beauty pageants in Colombia but noted that with 90 percent of televisions tuned to the national pageant and with M-19 crowning a queen of peace in Florencia, Caquetá, pageants, like it or not, were a marker of "Colombianness" for an underdeveloped nation whose people sought an escape from unglamorous reality in a spectacular party. Another article in *El Tiempo* noted that the national pageant was the only unifying phenomenon for Colombians, one that could momentarily stem the tide of pessimism while raising a unified voice of hope. While that sentiment was pretty, reporters found Colombians all over the country who angrily voiced their discontent with the 1984 pageant outcome.[50] If the nation only had the pageant to restore luster to a tarnished dream, by 1984 both the nation and the pageant seemed to be losing the people.

Throughout 1985, the M-19 engaged in multifaceted discussions with the government of Belisario Betancur, and deadly conflicts with the Colombian armed forces and paramilitary forces. The multiple factions and popular organizations represented by the M-19 made it difficult for the group to speak with a consistent or unified voice. The guerrilla group lost key leaders in the process of negotiating peace with the Colombian government: Jaime Bateman, dead in a plane crash in 1983; Carlos Toledo Plata, assassinated three days before a ceasefire in 1984; a grenade attack in 1985 against Antonio Navarro Wolf in a Cali café, his wounds requiring a leg amputation; the killing of Iván Marino Ospina in Cali in 1985. As a result, the M-19 met in Los Robles, southeast of Cali, in February 1985 to discuss future strategy and to select new leadership. The meeting attracted national media, Catholic priests and nuns inspired by liberation theology, international representatives from Panama and Ecuador, all in spite of the Colombian armed forces' attempts to prohibit access to Los Robles. A large rally in favor of the M-19 and their goal of peace and democracy filled Bogotá's main square, the Plaza de Bolívar, in March 1985, evidence of continued popular support for M-19 goals despite the confusion of ongoing talks punctuated by fresh acts of violence.[51]

Newly selected leader Álvaro Fayad explained to *Cromos* in June 1985 that the choice for M-19 and the nation wasn't between war and peace, but between oligarchy and democracy, between hopelessness and a new society. He argued that the main goals for the nation centered on liberty, dignity, and democracy. Although the M-19 recognized the good intentions of President Betancur, it would not simply opt for a cessation of hostilities with the government until real social, economic, and political reforms were completed. Consistent with its roots growing out of Rojas Pinilla's challenge to the National Front in 1970, the M-19 envisioned a more inclusive and democratic Colombia, one where the government guaranteed the right to education, public services, industrial and agricultural development, one where taxes funded social development rather than flowing to the already wealthy. While the M-19 angled for structural reforms, the wealthy elite, the Colombian armed forces, and the paramilitaries refused to give up any wealth and power, causing the Betancur government to appear to be one of violence, not of peace. It was also clear that President Betancur did not have control over the armed forces and that members of his government maintained connections with paramilitary groups who attacked the M-19 and its supporters. By October 1985, analysts were talking of the "Salvadorization" of the M-19 as it sought a power-sharing agreement with the Colombian government.[52]

The M-19 and the Colombian armed forces locked into an attack/counterattack cycle throughout 1985. The August killing of M-19 commander Iván Marino Ospina led to the attempted kidnapping or assassination of army commander General Rafael Samudio Molina in October. Samudio Molina, a Hall of Fame member of the School of the Americas, survived the attack in Bogotá. M-19 units also assaulted an army battalion in Armenia, a strategic city between Bogotá, Cali, and Medellín. From their southern stronghold in Caquetá and Valle del Cauca, the M-19 was now flexing armed muscle in coffee country, as well as carrying out urban operations in the nation's capital. Military platoons patrolled Bogotá's main street, La Séptima, signaling both the fluidity of the situation and the relative weakness of the Betancur government. The escalation of violence would bring the M-19 and General Samudio Molina and his forces into a dramatic encounter weeks later at the Palacio de Justicia.[53]

As during the trauma of La Violencia and the cynicism of the National Front, Colombia always had beauty and pageants as masks to cover ugly social and political realities. At the twenty-fifth Reinado Nacional de Bambuco in Neiva, Huila, tough kids from Bogotá's Barrio Kennedy rumbled with some drunks from Cali in a testosterone- and alcohol-fueled status contest amongst adolescents. Heavy aguardiente consumption seemed to be the norm for tourists who descended upon the town for twelve days of drinking, feasting, and dancing. Cheap tickets for the coronation allowed the presence of a popular audience, the coronation appearing more like a party during a political campaign than a wholesome pageant. As part of the neighborhood pageant, the Reina Popular in 1985 hoped to elevate and dignify her post and pledged to work on paving the streets in her neighborhood and on improving public services. At the other end of the class spectrum, the 1985 Soberana de la Ganadería (Livestock Sovereign) likewise pledged not to be just an ornament but to promote the livestock industry. She spoke French, English, Italian, and Portuguese to complement her Spanish, lived one-third of her life outside Colombia, and had just completed a commercial art program in Montreux, Switzerland.[54] Neiva's Reina Popular and the national Soberana de la Ganadería inhabited opposite socioeconomic poles that defined Colombia: one represented the majority society underserved by the state and with limited opportunities; the other, the international elite who worked to expand their wealth and power.

The Miss Universe pageant symbolized that larger and wealthy world, one conquered by Luz Marina in 1958 and one in 1985 at the age of Christ (33) at his crucifixion. Although expectations were high—as they were for a peace agreement with M-19—Sandra Borda didn't make the semifinalist cut. Nonetheless, it was the most watched television program in the world, and Colombians took some solace when half-Colombian Deborah Carthy, Miss Puerto Rico, won the crown. Deborah's father was Colombian and Deborah subsequently returned to Bogotá to reunite with her Colombian family. Miss Uruguay, Beatriz Andrea López Silva, also visited Colombia and won the Reina Internacional de las Flores pageant in Medellín. Beatriz was fourth runner-up at Miss Universe and represented the tall (1.78 m, 5′10″), strikingly lean dimensions then in fashion.[55]

While *Cromos* readers pondered the case of model and actress Amparo Grisales and the connection between Colombian beauty and narco-trafficking, and debated where the public policy line was between eroticism and pornography, the Nevado del Ruiz, a slumbering volcano awakening to greater activity, became national news in September 1985. As in a fairy tale, the sleeping, snow-white mountain now began to roar like a menacing lion. Starting late in 1984, this tallest of Colombian volcanoes (5,389 meters, 17,680 feet) began emitting a taller and more powerful emission of hot gas and steam, with sulfur yellowing the summit's snow. On September 11, the volcano released ash that fell on surrounding communities, with loud noises from the crater and earthquakes becoming more frequent. Experts warned that Armero, on the Lagunillas River, was most at risk. Modern Armero was rebuilt in 1845 directly on top of a volcanic mudflow (lahar) after an eruption by the Nevado del Ruiz that year. A similar event occurred in 1595, burying the river valley and killing 636 people. Experts warned that something like this would recur but could not predict when. It was known that in November 1984 a landslide sixteen kilometers above Armero had dammed the Lagunillas River gorge, increasing the likelihood of future catastrophic flooding. Experts urged local people to be vigilant in monitoring the upper river gorges, but most were difficult to access and permanently cloud covered. Although noting the risks, volcanologist Armando Murcia pointed to the future tourism boom likely to focus on the volcano once danger passed. As smoking volcanoes offered a spectacular and natural beauty, experts soothed local fears by likening the Nevado del Ruiz to a baby: taking its temperature, checking its humor and internal functions, and studying what it vomited. Nonetheless, they warned residents around the mountain to have an escape plan and be ready to run at any time.[56]

One week after the Nevado del Ruiz story, *Cromos* playfully labeled the Señorita Colombia candidate from Caldas, lying west of the smoking volcano, "A Volcano Named María Cecilia" (Un volcán llamado María Cecilia). The eighteen-year-old Universidad Javeriana student from Manizales sought to promote Caldas, saying that in her pretty department people were happy and hospitable and that visitors always had a good time. She hoped that the upset caused by the Nevado del Ruiz would soon pass so life could get back to normal. She had fine features, thick wavy hair, but unlike her voluptuous compatriot, Luz Marina Zuluaga, she was painfully thin, her shoulders, arms, and hips showing little evidence of body fat. *Cromos* continued the volcano theme in subsequent editions running up to the national pageant, covering the "explosion of candidates." It highlighted candidates planning to become dentists or hearing specialists so they could, as women and queens, help others.[57]

The two-month media run-up to the national pageant cast candidates into established categories by geography and race. Señorita Chocó, Jessika Quintero, represented not only Chocó but also black Colombia. She had lived the past fifteen years in Bogotá as part of the growing black community in the capital, where her coordinating committee handled publicity, fund-raising, her wardrobe, and glamour classes. She studied English and modeling in the United States—both important tools especially in international pageants—presenting herself as a polished and sophisticated candidate. Reportedly, black candidates had little chance to move up pyramidlike pageant ranks because cosmetic companies lost so much money when black women won the Miss Universe or Miss World pageants. Other candidates with little chance of winning—from Sucre, Huila, Tolima, Cesar, Magdalena—promoted the attractions of their respective departments, their participation in the pageant illustrating the competitiveness of life. Big-city candidates from Bogotá, Medellín, Cali, and Barranquilla could count on greater media attention and the social, economic, and political clout that came with wealth and power. By 1985, private businesses, including drug traffickers, supplied funding for all the candidates, deflecting criticism of scarce public monies flowing to the pageant when basic social services went unfunded. As always, Cartagena was billed as "La Ciudad Heroica," a community momentarily separated from the violence, insecurity, hunger, and unemployment that defined the larger nation, a "Fantasy Island" worthy of the UNESCO designation as a Cultural Heritage of Humanity.[58]

Cartagena hosted the traditional Reina Popular competition prior to the national pageant, attracting thirty-nine candidates. Most were between sixteen and nineteen years old, stood 1.6 to 1.7 meters (5'3"–5'6"), weighed forty-nine to fifty-four kilos (108–119 pounds), and measured close to the standardized body proportion (90/60/90 cm) regimen. To lower the pageant costs for the aspirants, the formal gown contest was canceled. The winner fit the standard representing "typical Cartagenan beauty": cinnamon skin, black hair, brown eyes. The differences between the Reina Popular and Reinado Nacional de Belleza pageants centered on class, color, education, and social status levels. To bridge this gap, the Reina Popular participated in a limited way in the Reinado Nacional activities, using beauty as a democratic tool of integration. However, according to 1984 Señorita Bogotá, Angela Marcela Sanmiguel, the huge distance in wardrobes and cultures between the popular and elite queens led to humiliation and marginalization for the forgotten queen, the Reina Popular. She didn't receive any support or instruction on how to pose, walk, or act like a queen, and she wasn't allowed to parade with the other departmental candidates. Security forces kept the popular masses away from the departmental queens, a further illustration of nonintegration between the two estates, as the public went crazy if a queen neared, a symbol of unreachable and fleeting power.[59]

Six of the departmental queens arrived on Monday, November 4, at Cartagena's Crespo Airport onboard a rented Avianca 747. Although Avianca predicted heavy tourist traffic to the pageant, most of the plane was taken up by the queens and their delegations. The Crespo airport extension facilitated the splashy arrival of a few queens at the expense of displaced local families. Power, not the popular, was on display at the national pageant. The queens dressed in "typical Spanish costumes" to punctuate the cultural and racial origins of power in Colombia. Rum, cumbia, fantasy costumes, and floats punctuated the next two days, as the coast again became the symbolic beach offering relief for a troubled and grey interior.[60]

Those troubles recaptured center stage on Wednesday, November 6, when twenty-eight M-19 guerrillas stormed and took control of the Palacio de Justicia building in Bogotá's main square, the Plaza de Bolívar. Striking ironies punctuated the drama over the next twenty-seven hours. As the symbolic heart of the nation, the Plaza de Bolívar honored the memory of the Liberator, with the words of his rival, Francisco Paula de Santander, affixed to the stone façade of the Palacio de Justicia, which proclaimed, "Colombianos: Si las armas os han dado la independencia, las leyes os darán la libertad" (Colombians: If arms have given you independence, laws will give you liberty). The last time that the Palacio de Justicia had been destroyed was April 9,

1948, following the assassination of Gaitán; arguably, the Colombian judicial system never recovered from the resulting partisanship and chaos of La Violencia. The M-19 column that took control of the Palacio de Justicia, across the square from Congress and two blocks from the presidential palace, was named in memory of Iván Marino Ospina, assassinated three months before. General Samudio, who survived an M-19 attack the previous month, coordinated the armed forces' counterattack on the Palacio de Justicia, working to break up any public demonstrations supporting the M-19. In many ways, this very personal military contest between the M-19 and the armed forces demonstrated the failure of politics and the negotiations trumpeted by President Betancur. Arms and militarization, not laws and democracy, controlled the confrontational logic between the two groups as they had done over the previous year.[61]

The guerrillas took control of the building and the people inside after 11:30 a.m. An hour later, tanks appeared in the Plaza de Bolívar as the sundry armed forces prepared a frontal assault on the building. Hostage and Chief Justice Alfonso Reyes Echandia called President Betancur—two blocks away—to request a ceasefire from government forces, but Betancur would not take the call. Betancur publically stated that he would not negotiate with terrorists, toeing the Reagan Administration line. Fighting became fierce as the army used 90mm cannon shells to break through the heavy bronze doors of the Palacio, while M-19 guerrillas fired .50 and .30 caliber machine guns to slow access to the building. The Plaza Bolívar became a war zone, with television coverage cutting away from the drama to broadcast a soccer match and the Señorita Colombia pageant. By 2:30 p.m., about 140 people were liberated from the lower floors of the Palacio, but some of those people, especially the cafeteria workers, were later tortured and murdered by government forces, a result of army paranoia about fifth column collaborators amongst the building occupants. Chief Justice Reyes Echandia continued to place increasingly alarming calls to request a ceasefire, warning that all the non-combatants in the building would be killed. However, the government did not have a single contact person, so calls went to Congress, army personnel, police personnel, the Red Cross, and reporters. Betancur's only direct action in this drama was to send his presidential palace guard to reinforce the various and uncoordinated armed forces attacking the building. By 5:00 p.m., Reyes Echandia recognized that the government had abandoned the judges and the civilians in the Palacio de Justicia as the building burned overnight.[62]

The final armed forces offensive commenced the next day, November 7, at 1:00 p.m. Most of the surviving M-19 guerrillas and Supreme Court justices were confined to a fourth floor bathroom. Soldiers fired rockets that tore holes in the bathroom wall, allowing bullets and grenades to pass into the bathroom, killing judges and hostages inside. Women and the wounded were allowed to leave the bathroom, as the remaining M-19 guerrillas, declaring they preferred to die like machos, were killed by soldiers after their ammunition was spent. The total number killed inside the Palacio was unclear, with estimates ranging from fifty-five to one hundred. Eleven judges were killed; Chief Justice Reyes Echandia was shot through the thorax and killed by a bullet used by government forces. Judge Carlos Horacio Urán was taken alive out of the Palacio by armed forces and then shot through the head; his body was found in the Palacio the next day. General Samudio ordered any M-19 prisoners be "terminated." Other civilian survivors became "disappeared," presumably tortured and killed in or near the Canton Norte, their bodies dumped into common graves. Although the M-19 hoped for another spectacular "golpe revolucionario publicitario" (revolutionary publicity action), it confronted Colombian armed forces intent on total annihilation of any group threatening government institutions, regardless of the cost to the citizenry. The military's dirty war now penetrated the nation's symbolic heart, with President Betancur a spectator to the tragedy, the Supreme Court justices dead in the ruins of the Palacio de Justicia.[63]

News of the battle and massacre trickled in to the reinas in Cartagena, as television coverage was restricted by the government and many Cartagenans were intent on partying. Once again, the geographic temper of the country seemed to hold true: violent politics in the interior mountains; sun, beach, and diversion on the coast. Nonetheless, once the Palacio was retaken and the gravity of the situation set in, the mayor of Cartagena refused to turn over the keys of the city at 6:00 p.m., "owing to the absurd tragedy experienced by the nation."[64] News of the killing of the justices arrived an hour later. Señorita Tolima, María Patricia Troncoso, was personally touched because Justices Alfonso Reyes Echandia and Manuel Gaona Cruz had been her law professors. Discussions ensued as to whether the pageant should be canceled as an expression of solidarity for the nation's pain, with some insisting that the show must go on. A radio commentator in Cartagena argued that the pageant generated close to 500 million pesos in spending, sustaining 10,000 jobs, and that it would be a mistake to cancel an event worked on all year. The compromise the next day was to cancel the official opening of the pageant and instead to hold a mass in memory of the dead at the Palacio de Justicia. Apparently, lack of coordination resulted in thirteen of the eighteen reinas arriving late, just ten minutes before the mass ended.[65]

Security for the coronation ceremony resembled the battle forces that had taken the Palacio de Justicia: 250 marines, regular and secret police, sharpshooters. None of that security was necessary at the Señorita Colombia pageant, in stark contrast to the light security swept away by the M-19 at the Palacio de Justicia five days earlier. Señorita Guajira, María Monica Urbina Pugliese, won the peninsula's first crown (although she lived in Bogotá). A glamor class graduate, she had the face of an Italian actress. A cigarette seller on a Cartagena street reported that he was happy that Guajira won the crown in compensation for the theft of coal, salt, and natural gas taken from the peninsula by foreign companies. The 1985 pageant ended clouded by the smoke from the ruins of the Palacio de Justicia, with no public disorder and no reinas crying following the pageant judgments.[66]

Continuous earth tremors commenced on the Nevado del Ruiz the day before the coronation of the 1985 Señorita Colombia. Two days later, on November 12, a group of scientists toured its summit but found no evidence of imminent danger, and so did not order an evacuation. On November 13 at 3:06 p.m., an initial blast from the Arenas crater began to shower pumice and ash on the town of Armero, seventy kilometers downstream from the summit. A local priest, archaeologist, and the mayor urged the citizens of the city to remain calm, as the ash fall was similar to one that had fallen two months earlier. At 9:08 p.m. the volcano released molten rock for the first time, setting off pyroclastic flows that melted the summit ice cap; residents could not see the summit due to darkness and a raging storm. Between 10:00 and 11:00 p.m., residents felt a hurricane-force wind rip down the Lagunillas River gorge, followed by a ten-meter-high wall of rock, ice, mud, and debris. Moving at fifty kilometers an hour (thirty-one miles an hour), the *lahar* buried most of the city of Armero. It also flattened the town of Chinchiná, toward the Rio Cauca. About 23,000 people died that night in the worst natural disaster in Colombia's history.[67]

Colombians, intelligent, sensitive, and tough, picked over the twin disasters of the Palacio de Justicia and the Nevado del Ruiz, seeking comprehension and responsibility. As in a García Márquez novel, both were deemed chronicles of a death foretold. The government ignored reports of an impending M-19 attack on the Palacio de Justicia and decreased rather than increased security for the building prior to November 6. The M-19 seriously miscalculated its attempt to put the Betancur government on trial and to broadcast its political message through the Colombian media, ignoring the fact that the armed forces—not the Betancur government—were leading the war against it. Moreover, the Colombian government did precious little to prepare an evacuation plan for the people around the Nevado del Ruiz, though cognizant of the volcano's history and the probable trajectory of mudslides. Liberal politicians and future presidents Ernesto Samper and César Gaviria took positions on the Palacio de Justicia critical of Betancur and the Conservative Party, the political class preparing for the next round of elections. Aid for the Nevado del Ruiz disaster victims seemed not to arrive; commentators speculated that it, too, would show up as patronage in the next round of elections. As usual, the Colombian people were left to fend for themselves as both humankind and nature abandoned them to their fate.[68]

But Colombians still had beauty to cover the ugly scars left after November 1985. The evening after the dramatic disaster around the Nevado del Ruiz, Miss World was crowned in London. A blonde Icelandic woman with an unpronounceable name won the pageant, while Colombia was represented by a caleña. But the trauma of the Palacio and the volcano blunted Colombian interest in that pageant. As the Palacio sat in ruins for years in the main center of Colombian governance, some of the letters of Santander's words still dangling ever more ironically from the destroyed façade, the Miss Colombia pageant of 1986 hit new lows. Extravagant spending on a single trousseau could have paved two neighborhoods in any Colombian city, other than Armero. Increased prize money and the lure of the crown and scepter created open hostility among candidates. Plastic surgery depreciated natural beauty as more and more candidates went under the knife for various procedures.[69] If late in the twentieth century feminine beauty was still described as mysterious, intricate, and incomprehensible, were impending death squad assassinations, military and paramilitary massacres, guerrilla attacks and kidnappings, and terrorist truck bombs more obvious, simple, and comprehensible? The beast of Colombian violence and death raged after 1985, while Colombia, so naturally beautiful, continued to worship at the altar of the feminine, the fertile, the life-giving, the peaceful beauty that warmed the heart against cold, hard reality. Beauty gave Colombians their shared positive national identity especially in periods of their history when systems and institutions failed so spectacularly to become more inclusive and democratic and as alternatives went down in flames. Sadly, it appears that modern Colombian identity will need beauty to palliate the ugliness of violence and inequality well into the twenty-first century.

CONCLUSION AND EPILOGUE TO 2011

Looking backward from the tumultuous events of November 1985, one can appreciate how and why beauty has served as a marker for Colombian identity and modernity over the last two centuries. From the long colonial period, elite Colombians and foreigners maintained a preference for the white beauty ideal, one with a strong Spanish national identification. As fashions from Paris and New York came and went, Colombians frequently embraced the happy synthesis of beauty found in southern Spain, one that was multiethnic and stylized but also racially white. Women of the countryside, especially women of color, could be beautiful if healthy, virtuous, steady, and intelligent. More frequently they were imaged as ugly if sick, poor, ill-clothed, uneducated, or nonwhite. In short, Colombians embraced the white side of their diverse past and society, akin to the national racial myths espoused in Argentina, the Dominican Republic, or the United States.

The traje nacional or traje típico symbolized various complex goals: to create a national fashion expressing Colombian national identity, to blunt the changes brought by urbanization and modernization for a conservative country still actually or nostalgically rural, and to escape the partisan and social violence so prevalent throughout the nation's century. The traje nacional as adopted in the nineteenth century and reprised during the twentieth century National Front pageants served as a marker of Colombian identity but ironically illustrated ongoing violence and insecurity as it signaled the failure of modern republican politics.

The internal beauty found in character, virtue, and faith offered a deeper understanding of beauty, one that nonetheless reinforced traditional gender constructions of morally superior females serving as the cornerstones of family and religion as they bore the weight of patriarchal structures. That inner beauty perhaps was more democratic, as appearance and race and class meant less, but was also traditional in limiting women to proscribed and supportive roles. The Catholic Church sided heavily with the traditional restraint of female freedom, insisting on modest dress and behavior for women, once again standing with tradition and patriarchy against modern freedoms.

Attitudes about beauty frequently accompany social power, as seen in the Colombian elite preference for Spanishness as the anchor of national racial identity. But beauty also reflects economic and political power, as illustrated throughout this book. The female artisans of Santander were by reputation the nation's most beautiful women in the mid- to late nineteenth century because their economic earnings increased their attractiveness as it earned them respect as Spanish. Medellín and Antioquia by extension built on gold and coffee exports to develop an industrial economy, all symbols of wealth promoted by a sense of racial superiority over the rest of the country. Cali and Barranquilla rode the waves of their economic prosperity, adorned by the reputations of their beautiful women of many hues. Politically, the proximity of powerful men and politicians alongside beautiful women benefited both gendered players as it gained each more attention and status and promoted their respective social and political positions. When Rafael Reyes and Rojas Pinilla needed to build political consensus for their respective governments, they reinforced their political and social power through public rituals of beauty and order. When drug lords in the 1980s desired social acceptance as new elites, they conspicuously spent large sums of money at beauty pageants.

Those pageants held in Colombia, and in other cultural settings throughout the Americas, re-created the hierarchy of order of diverse societies inherited from the colonial period, but performed in modern societies disguised in democratic wrapping. Drawing from both European and African monarchical traditions, pageant judges selected a queen to reign but not to govern, thereby including the subaltern in an elite-controlled and nondemocratic ritual, one endlessly repeated to reflect the present as it honored the past. Momentarily, the powerless became powerful, and then the old order was restored. The beauty celebrated at those pageants was so vital because Colombians have so few other positive national symbols and because the terror of the beast reinforced gender roles—women should be beautiful, men should be powerful—as violence, insecurity, and governmental exclusiveness closed options for future reform and liberation. In Colombia, the beast and beauty reside in different wings of the same menacing castle.

Modern pageants grew out of the mass mobilizations and horrific tragedies of World War I. Uniformed women serving their nations during wartime set the stage for the new postwar uniforms of ball gowns, swimsuits, and high heels. Stimulated by invitations from international pageants, Colombia hosted national beauty contests in 1932 and 1934, but thereafter, the pageant languished until 1947. Between those years, the most important Liberal reforms of the twentieth century introduced modern economic, social, and political change to Colombia, with athletic, uniformed beauty symbolic of the drive toward public progress. Interestingly, wars in Europe set the stage for national and international pageants, but Colombians didn't need them when effective national reforms in the 1930s and 1940s made symbolic sovereigns unnecessary. World War II revived the gendered definitions of male violence and female beauty, again the postwar era resuscitating national and international beauty pageants. Once Liberal reforms ebbed as political violence flowed after 1946, pageants regained importance in Colombia.

Colombia needed beauty in the decade following Gaitán's murder in 1948, as violence raged, the economy grew, and administrations went from Laureano Gómez to Rojas Pinilla and then to the National Front. Beauty softened and civilized the competitive masculine worlds of mass sports, militarization, and vicious violence. The chaos of La Violencia led to an affirmation of Colombia as a Spanish nation, while French and Italian films reasserted a Mediterranean beauty type favorable to Colombia in international pageants. General Rojas Pinilla manipulated the power of beauty and pageantry, as had Rafael Reyes a half-century earlier, to build support and legitimacy for his administration. It was clear in 1958, as it was over the next decade, that Colombia was a country rich in resources and beautiful in its cultural and physical geography. But even as Luz Marina was crowned Miss Universe, it was also clear that beauty could not control the beast of violence.

The National Front system signaled a return to civilian government but also the continuation of an exclusionary democratic system. The partisan quality of La Violencia faded, but predatory economic violence was joined by revolutionary guerrilla bands in the mid-1960s. The marketing of Colombian beauty as the pacific and positive face of the nation intensified during the National Front with the proliferation of regional pageants and festivals often centered in regions deeply scarred during La Violencia—events structured as nonpartisan, participatory, and inclusive. In essence, the elite-directed National Front promoted the celebration of the best of feminine beauty and the best of traditional culture as a pitch for popular support for what was actually an exercise in embracing Colombia's elitist and nonmodern core.

Sex, drugs, and rock 'n' roll spread into larger cities by the late 1960s and 1970s, promoting an ethos of liberation and the emergence of a small counterculture. Women discussed and wrote articles about sexuality, birth control, marriage, and abortion, opening public awareness and education on formerly taboo topics. Attitudes among some beauty queens echoed the liberationist spirit, but they represented a tiny minority in a large and diverse nation. Although some of those social and cultural attitudes mirrored those of much of the rest of the modern world, the political stagnation and economic inequality of Colombia kept most women poor and dependent on males. With wages for women stuck at mid-1950s levels well into the 1980s, prostitution remained a means of survival for many women, as sex in marketing became a vehicle to define and stimulate consumption, distorting the reality of increasing numbers of women working in the marketplace.

The beast of violence remained a specter over Colombian reality through much of the history between 1845 and 1985, shifting dynamics and logics between partisan, economic, and ideological struggles in cyclical fashion over time. At root in all this violence was the inability of Colombian government and its officers to fashion a sovereign national state, one seen as legitimate and representative of the Colombian people. Unable to uphold the law or to guarantee the lives and property of its citizens, unable to build an inclusive identity for the nation, the dysfunction and rot at the top of the Colombian power structure left room at the local level for armed groups to become autonomous agents who imposed their own agendas. By the 1970s and 1980s, death squads, insurgent groups, paramilitary organizations, cocaine and emerald cartels, and the armed forces of Colombia all employed violence to attack perceived threats and to expand their power while failing to gain broad national support for their actions.

Violence raged in Colombia in the decade after 1985, fed by the drug trade, attacks by surviving insurgent groups, massacres by paramilitary groups employed by drug cartels and in league with military officers, and assassinations carried out by death squads intent on social or ideological "cleansings." Medellín remained "murder capital" and "cocaine capital" of the world, with the city routinely enduring between three thousand and sixty-five hundred homicides per year during the late 1980s and early 1990s; by the early 1990s when homicides peaked, the city's authorities only made one arrest for every one thousand murders. Intimidation of witnesses, judges, police officers, and a clearly ineffectual judicial system fed a culture of silence that allowed killers immunity from arrest and prosecution. Murder rates spiked in Cali as the competing "Cali cartel" of bankers, merchants, and landowners warred with their social inferiors in the "Medellín cartel" for control of production, shipment, and marketing of cocaine. Murder rates also jumped in Bogotá from 1985 to 1993. Although political and terrorist violence took a dramatic toll in big cities, more cotidian domestic, interpersonal, social, and economic violence harvested most victims, with the highest risk factors found after paydays or on weekends and holidays, in poor or decomposing neighborhoods where alcohol and firearms were close at hand, those killed usually young and male. By the late 1990s, nearly 70 percent of all homicides and murders in the country were committed in Bogotá, Medellín, and Cali; the rural violence of the past had morphed into the urban violence of the late twentieth century.[1]

Drug trafficking and violence responded both to national and international dynamics. More liberal economic policies led to factory shutdowns and increasing unemployment, as seen most clearly in Medellín. Lower prices for coffee, sugar, and cotton on world markets hurt Colombian farmers, pushing some into the high-risk but also much more profitable drug production business. U.S. antidrug programs in Bolivia and Peru designed to decrease coca leaf and coca paste production ended up stimulating the expansion of both in Colombia, allowing Colombians to count on a more reliable leaf supply to be refined into cocaine powder. Low-grade cocaine paste, or *basuco*, was dumped on the domestic market, stimulating its use and resulting in turf wars fought by rival urban gangs to control distribution and sale. Ironically, it was the United States that funded both sides of the drug war in Colombia; counter-drug programs had the "balloon effect" of concentrating coca leaf and cocaine production in Colombia while an estimated thirteen million addicted and casual U.S. consumers spent an estimated 67 billion dollars on illegal drugs in 1999. The United States was number one in illegal drug use in the world, and functioned as the demand motor for Colombian drug production and trafficking. While only an estimated $3.5 billion of the $67 billion returned to Colombia, the total spent by U.S. consumers totaled about one-quarter of the entire Colombian gross domestic product in 1999. It was U.S. demand for drugs, U.S. currency as the medium of exchange, and U.S. weapons that flowed both to the Colombian government for counterinsurgency and counterdrug programs and to drug trafficking organizations via an unregulated trade in semiautomatic weapons that propelled the beast of drug violence in both countries.

The U.S. "drug war" in Colombia intensified after 1989 as the not-so-Cold War neared its end and the United States moved into its next global campaign, the "War on Drugs." Although President Richard Nixon had demonstrated that treating users and the demand side was a much more efficient and cost-effective approach to drug abuse in the United States, each subsequent president attacked the supply side, a hopeless and unwinnable campaign given high U.S. consumer demand for drugs. The Reagan Administration's slogan of "Just Say No" made explicit denial of drug use a moral and professional imperative in the United States. Although designed as a defensive retort for school-aged children to imagined drug pushers outside the school yard fence, for adults it meant silence; adults couldn't have an adult and analytical discussion on why the United States was number one in drug use. That Americans lived in a highly competitive, individualistic, consumer-centered society, that they craved immediate gratification, conspicuous consumption, and unrestricted greed, and that they valued freedom in the abstract while distrusting intrusive government in their private lives, remained unexamined. Instead, for Reagan, the trouble was *out there*, and "America" was under assault from dastardly foreign evildoers. Reagan's "City on a Hill" allusions rekindled the idealist pretenses in American foreign policy that America was God-blessed and had a special mission in the world and that Americans were moral, sober, and righteous souls. If evil or conflict threatened the American body politic, it had to come from outside "America"; the sins of drug use and drug abuse couldn't theologically or politically be inside the USA.

The aggressive actions of Reagan's successor, George H. W. Bush, in the "drug war" banished the "wimp factor" from domestic politics with the U.S. invasion of Panama and steeply increased military assistance to Colombia in 1989. "Operation Just Cause"—or "Operation Just Because" as critics quipped—focused on arresting the de facto head of government and commander of the Panamanian Defense Forces and School of the Americas graduate, Manuel Noriega, on drug charges pending in U.S. courts. That Noriega had been on the CIA payroll since 1967, had worked with Bush Sr. when he headed the CIA in 1976 to 1977, and that he received a raise in his CIA salary in the 1980s for his Cold War service in Central America remained unspoken until later. Noriega was involved in laundering money from drug profits, as were bankers in Colombia and the United States, and he did regulate the flow of cocaine from Colombia through Panama en route to big markets in the United States. Once Noriega was arrested and brought to trial via an illegal U.S. invasion of another sovereign nation, with 2,500 to 4,000 Panamanians killed by the blunt instrument of war, cocaine shipments across Panama increased as the governor on cocaine trafficking sat in a Florida jail as his eager successors competed to meet the U.S. market demand.

While Noriega was less an asset as the Cold War cooled and more of a liability as Drug War rhetoric and programs took the strategic U.S. foreign policy stage, emergency U.S. military assistance to Colombia of $65 million was used to make war in Colombia in 1989. U.S. insistence that the Colombian drug cartel leaders be extradited to the United States to stand trial for murder and drug trafficking—convictions promising the death penalty given the venue—prompted billionaire cartel leaders to wage both a focused and a terrorist war against the Colombian government and society. Hundreds of journalists, labor leaders, judges, and police officers were killed; presidential candidates from the Liberal Party and two new leftist parties were assassinated while on the campaign trail; hundreds of Colombian civilians died and thousands were wounded from car and truck bombs, precursors of the homegrown terrorist bombing in Oklahoma City in 1995. However, psychologically, terrorist bombs in Bogotá and Medellín, or onboard an Avianca jet en route to Cali, taught millions of Colombians that their already shaky urban environment could be blown apart suddenly and without warning. By late 1989, Bogotá became a nocturnal ghost town after waves of assassinations and terrorist bombings sealed the city's residents indoors against a cold and dark night.

The C-130's, small attack planes, and helicopter gunships sent from the United States as emergency military assistance gave the Colombian armed forces greater mobility and firepower in attacking the Medellín cartel. U.S. and Colombian military and intelligence operations focused on killing or capturing the top echelon of the Medellín cartel: the arrest and extradition of Carlos Lehder to the United States in 1987; the killing of Gonzalo Rodríguez Gacha in 1989; the arrest of Juan David and Jorge Luis Ochoa in 1991. That left the kingpin, Pablo Escobar, identified in 1989 by *Forbes* magazine as the seventh-richest person in the world, with personal wealth estimated at $25 billion dollars. Escobar was the most violent and feared billionaire businessman in the world and a target for myriad enemies. Highly secretive and covert U.S. Army Special Operations from Delta Force and Centra Spike/ Gray Fox, along with CIA and DEA officers, shared communications and actions with the Colombian National Police and with a death squad known as Los Pepes, founded by the Castaño Brothers to kill all known associates of Pablo Escobar. Cali cartel leaders and former Medellín cartel associates financed and supported the activities of Los Pepes, often intermingled with U.S. Special Forces and CIA and DEA agents, to find and kill Escobar, an operation completed in 1993. Thereafter, the Cali cartel emerged as the major cocaine trafficking operation in Colombia and the world, until six of its seven top leaders were arrested in 1995. Of course, decapitating the top management of lucrative and far-reaching business operations only opened more market and profit opportunities for new leaders to build more adroit, more compartmentalized structures to ship more product to international markets. These "cartelitos" expanded coca leaf plantations inside Colombia, bought semiprocessed coca base from various sources, refined the base into cocaine powder, and smuggled record amounts of cocaine into the huge United States market by the late 1990s. The infamous Colombian cartels had been destroyed and Colombian and American government leaders congratulated themselves for this "victory" in the war on drugs, as the U.S. government nurtured the beast of violence in Colombia while denying the apparent reality that the United States was the root cause for drug violence in both countries.

The one billion dollars of counter-narcotics aid that Colombia received in the decade after 1989 from the United States government fueled wars against both narcotics and insurgents; Americans supplied weaponry, training, and logistical and communications support, while Colombians did the bulk of the fighting and dying. Rhetorically, American Cold War justification for attacking Marxist/Leninists guerrillas shifted to attacking the narcoguerrillas in the 1990s with the "new" militarized war on drugs. But insurgent numbers and areas of operation expanded rapidly after 1986, especially for the FARC and the ELN. The FARC grew from 3,600 insurgents in 1986 to 7,000 in 1995 and more than doubled again by the year 2000 to an estimated 15,000. The ELN had 800 insurgents in 1986—almost four times that total in 1995—growing to about 5,000 by the year 2000. Insurgents expanded operations into new and richer zones of the country, both rural and urban; by the late 1980s, FARC units controlled the eastern heights above Bogotá. By 1996, insurgents operated in almost 60 percent of Colombian municipalities. Ironically, the FARC profited from the U.S. war against the cocaine cartels by building networks of rural support among coca leaf farmers and then taxing the leaf, base, and cocaine trade. The ELN cashed in on oil exploration and pipelines in Arauca, extorting huge sums of money from petroleum companies for not destroying the exposed pipelines. Both groups could offer competitive salaries and outfit and arm recruits given increasing revenues, especially in hard economic times like those of the 1990s. Extortion and kidnapping spiked in the late 1980s and late 1990s, netting both the FARC and ELN hundreds of millions of dollars. Colombians and foreigners, rich and poor, felt the sting of extortion and the dread of kidnapping, which could occur in urban centers, on main roads between major cities, or en route to and from work or school. The FARC and ELN profited mightily but paid a high political cost as their former ideological and revolutionary war gave way to socioeconomic opportunism.[2]

Other insurgents left the armed struggle and began legal, political activities. Sectors of the FARC joined with the existing Colombian Communist Party and other leftists to form the Unión Patriótica (UP) in 1985. But 1986 UP presidential candidate Jaime Pardo and 1990 UP presidential candidate Bernardo Jaramillo both were murdered prior to their respective elections. The M-19 laid down its weapons in 1990 to take part in elections as well, and received more support than the UP, but the M-19 presidential candidate and former guerrilla chief, Carlos Pizarro, was also slain in 1990; Antonio Navarro Wolf replaced Pizarro as the M-19 presidential candidate and won almost 13 percent of the votes cast.[3] Bernardo Gutiérrez took most of the EPL with him into legitimate political work after 1991, but EPL members were hunted by the armed wing of the FARC because Manuel "Tirofijo" Marulanda never forgave Gutiérrez for leaving the FARC before heading the EPL. But the former FARC members of the UP also met ferocious repression from paramilitaries and death squads who slaughtered between three thousand and five thousand UP members in the decade after 1985. For "Tirofijo" and other FARC and ELN commanders, insurgents laying down their weapons equaled a death sentence in a civil society where the Colombian government could not or would not protect the legal political work of leftists. And, of course, business was brisk for both the FARC and ELN and they were winning major engagements against the Colombian armed forces, so insurgent violence continued.

The most fearsome beasts of violence in the late twentieth and early twenty-first centuries were the paramilitaries. Evolving from partisan or bandit groups during La Violencia, becoming civil defense militias in the employ of ranchers, merchants, oil companies, or narcotics traffickers in the early 1980s, by the late 1980s they were the clear ideological enemies of insurgent groups and of anyone who espoused sympathies for reform or revolution. From 1986 to 1989, narco-landowner-paramilitary leaders in the Magdalena Medio pursued an extermination campaign against new political parties, human rights groups, union leaders and members, peasant organizations, public officials, and journalists. Suspicion of leftist sympathies often led to horrific tortures and widespread massacres inflicted on the civilian population by paramilitary forces in Chocó, Urabá, Córdoba, Sucre, César, Putumayo, and Caquetá—all former insurgent strongholds.[4] The Castaño Brothers, former Medellín cartel members whose father was kidnapped and murdered by the FARC in 1981, became after 1997 the public face of the AUC (Autodefensas Unidas de Colombia), an organization that also profited from the dismantling of the Medellín and Cali cartels. They taxed coca leaf and trafficked most of the cocaine, becoming wealthy landowners with political power, paying higher salaries than the FARC. The AUC grew to 5,000 armed men by the year 2000. As an anti-insurgent shock force it usually targeted unarmed civilians and often worked in league with the Colombian armed forces and government, even while the Colombian attorney general estimated that the paramilitaries had slaughtered 140,000 Colombians over a thirty-year period and forcibly displaced millions of rural Colombians in a widespread and vicious terrorist campaign.[5] Interestingly, both the FARC and AUC web pages—before they were blocked from public view—stated that their rival organizations existed because the Colombian government lacked sovereignty.

Both the FARC and AUC benefited from the new constitution drafted in 1991, in the midst of political and institutional crises. Decentralization of political power and governmental revenue opened the way for the direct elections of mayors and governors and a shift of government revenue to local and departmental organizations, but in those areas of FARC and AUC operations, both groups formed political networks to control or influence politics and tapped into governmental funds to support their respective operations.

Constitutional guarantees of greater political, religious, human, and social rights promised greater freedoms for all Colombians—including indigenous and black communities, women, and non-Catholics—but also intensified political contestation in wide areas of the nation where the Colombian state was not sovereign. The ban against extradition reduced the intense drug violence fanned by U.S. policy, giving narcotraffickers and AUC and FARC leaders momentary relief from harsh U.S. justice (Colombia outlawed the death penalty), but the extradition prohibition was repealed under U.S. pressure in 1996. The judicial system was reorganized but remained underfunded and politicized, so an independent and strong judiciary could not enforce many provisions and articles in the promising Constitution of 1991.[6]

Beauty surrounded by increasing insecurity, violence, and crime once again represented the search for peace in a troubled nation. But beauty queens who symbolized peace and who became crowd favorites could not deliver on that promise when males controlled politics, economics, and instruments of violence and terror. Colombians tried to forget about the violence and terrorism defining their country in the months before, during, and after the national beauty pageant in Cartagena, as they had done a generation before during La Violencia, but the pageant and its queens could only address rather than fix the country's deep problems. Many of the pageant contestants in the decade after 1985 had prepared themselves to be queens since childhood. They read only what was necessary to compete in the pageant, underwent plastic surgery, escaped concrete reality by professing their belief in astrology, reincarnation, metaphysics and the dark arts, and wore extravagant costumes paid for by powerful men in the wings. Money from rich drug traffickers from Medellín, Cali, Bogotá, and the North Coast flowed to departmental and national queens, with mafiosos opening modeling schools to launder money and to attract single, attractive young women to private dalliances at their residences. In popular opinion, none of this was sinister but rather normal—rich and ambitious men using beautiful young women as objects of sexual fascination and social status.

Colombians grappled with the question of whether their country was ready to elect its first black queen in 1987 and 1994—as usual the candidate from the Chocó—but answered negatively as "Una negra no podía ser Señorita Colombia" (A black woman cannot be Miss Colombia).[7] Questions persisted on the meaning of race, identity, and beauty, whether drug money bought judges' decisions, and how beauty reflected or concealed larger Colombian reality. Colombia fared well on the international stage at Miss Universe pageants, placing third in 1986 and 1990 and second in 1992, 1993, and 1994, reinforcing Colombia's global fame for strikingly beautiful women; however,

FIGURE 10.1   *Paula Andrea Betancourt y Carolina Gómez (1993),* in Las más bellas, *p. 265, courtesy Concurso Nacional de Belleza (Cartagena, Colombia).*

the counterimage of a nation infamous for drugs and violence—and reported DEA influence over the judges in 1994—kept the Miss Universe crown away from Colombia.[8]

Paramilitary massacres, cycles of insurgency, counterinsurgency, periodic peace negotiations, and drug politics hounded the presidencies of Ernesto Samper (1994–1998) and Andrés Pastrana (1998–2002). Samper's thin victory in the 1994 presidential election led his Conservative challenger Pastrana to allege that Samper had accepted $6 million in campaign donations from the Cali cartel. That allegation and a long investigation into the web of drug money in Colombian politics dominated most of Samper's presidency. In retaliation, the Clinton Administration decertified Colombia in 1996 and 1997 for insufficient progress in the war on drugs. Although the leadership of the Medellín and Cali cartels had been dismantled by 1995 and thousands of Colombians had died in the U.S.-propelled drug war, that effort and those sacrifices seemed meaningless. Pastrana followed Samper into the presidency, staking his government on reaching a peace agreement with the FARC, a failed if gallant effort. By 2000, former U.S. Army general and current White House drug czar Barry McCaffrey sounded the alarm that increasing quantities of heroin and cocaine sent from Colombia to the United States amounted to a national security threat against the United States and its people. The U.S. Congress passed the Plan Colombia aid project, a $1.3 billion package for the next two years, about 80 percent of it for police and military equipment and operations. Lame duck President Clinton—who had barely survived an embarrassing personal and political scandal of his own—waived conditions that the Colombian armed forces meet minimum human rights standards, even though Colombia consistently had the worst human rights record in all of South America. According to political scientist Brian Loveman, "Human rights violations and politically inspired murders in Colombia exceeded levels in the worst military dictatorships in South America. Colombia's many 'dirty wars' took more victims than state terrorism, insurgency, and counterinsurgency in Brazil, Chile, Argentina, and Uruguay combined from the 1960s to 1990."[9] The U.S. government persisted in exporting its war and its drug problem to Colombia, regardless of the attendant human rights atrocities.

Colombian beauty made a big international splash in global mass media near the turn of the twenty-first century. The hip-shaking, belly-dancing songwriter and performer Shakira went from brunette to blonde upon receiving an award at the 1999 Señorita Colombia pageant. She then mastered English and Portuguese to open markets for her music in Brazil and the United States, adding some French, Italian, and Arabic for the European, North African, and Middle Eastern markets. Born in Barranquilla and of Lebanese and Southern European ancestry, Shakira became the most recognized and popular Latin American performing artist, her musical hybridity blending rock, pop, Latin, and Arabic influences. She was proudly Colombian and always spoke of her country with pride and love when interviewed around the world. Her talent, creativity, drive, and social development projects for poor Colombian youth were matched by a costeña's style, sensuality, and sex appeal. She became the most successful Colombian artist ever, and second only to Gloria Estefan as the biggest-selling female Latin performer, while "Hips Don't Lie" was the best-selling song and web video in the 2000s.[10]

An innovative ugly-duckling television soap opera, "Yo soy Betty, la Fea" became a sensation in Colombia from 1999 to 2001 and was subsequently spun off into twenty other productions worldwide, making it the most popular telenovela ever. Awkward but smart, industrious but naïve, Betty represented huge numbers of diligent, sincere, and good Colombians ignored because of their class and looks. With braces, a unibrow, big red glasses masking intense dark eyes, an unflattering wardrobe, and greasy hair, Betty startled many of her glamorous, conniving, but lazy employees at a Bogotá fashion house, but her good character and brilliance in economics and finance helped her save the company from bankruptcy, and eventually she got her man, the president of the company. Her transition from ugly duckling to swan occurred after she left Bogotá and took work in Cartagena with a fashion designer for the Señorita Colombia pageant; she got a new wardrobe and haircut, waxings, makeup, and new glasses and lost the braces, making her more conventionally attractive upon her return to Bogotá.[11] But it was Betty's inner beauty—her virtue, character, and loyalty—that shone through regardless of situation or appearance. On the side, the jokes and insights about the gulf between the elite and the popular in Colombia were just delicious.

Colombia witnessed another striking evolution of beauty's definition in 2001 when the Señorita Colombia pageant elected its first black queen, Vanessa Alexandra Mendoza Bustos, representing Chocó. It had been forty-four years since Nazly of Chocó had broken the color line at the national pageant, one hundred and fifty years since slavery had been abolished in the country, and decades since the pageant and Colombia had been called racist. Like other pageant contestants through the decades such as Luz Marina Zuluaga, runner-up in 1957 and Miss Universe 1958, Vanessa Mendoza did not come from an elite background; she was said to be from a large, poor, but hardworking family, from a town in Urabá that most Colombians had never heard of and couldn't find on a map, becoming a Cinderella success story who symbolized a new beginning for the nation. For once, the clear audience favorite also received the highest point totals from the pageant's judges; the two Cartagenas, usually dichotomized between white and black, elite and popular, national pageant and popular pageant, found in Vanessa an inclusive queen. The photograph of Vanessa and accompanying text on the *Cromos* cover of November 12, 2001, transmitted strong but complex messages. The upper torso and head shot showed the queen with scepter and crown, hair swept up and back, diamond earrings and ring, perfect makeup and facial

FIGURE 10.2 *Nuestra Reina, Vanessa Mendoza,* Cromos *cover, Nov. 12, 2001, courtesy* Revista Cromos.

features, with her right hand covering her mouth as she prepared to blow a kiss to the audience. Her complexion was lightened by a brown background, soft lighting, airbrushing, and lens filter, her name in tan block letters, with a larger and proud white font proclaiming her, Nuestra reina, Our queen. While Vanessa, reportedly, had not dreamed of becoming queen like many of the other competitors, and although many Colombians believed that the country didn't deserve a black queen, as "Our queen," the *Cromos* cover signaled, at least, the acceptance of a "whitened black" candidate as an exemplar of Colombian beauty. With a stunning face, fit body, muted voice, and legs that seemed to go to her neck, to some Colombians, Vanessa was so pretty that she seemed white.[12]

Vanessa was white and black, like most Colombians, Brazilians, and Americans of African ancestry. Vanessa was white through her mother, whose parents were identified as "bogotanos de pura cepa," bogotanos of pure stock, connecting Vanessa to the capital's white social elite.[13] She was racially whitened through her ancestry, by the focus on her flawless face, by the *Cromos* cover, and by winning the national crown in a country still ambivalent but beginning to open up to its diverse multicultural reality. She was black by representing the Chocó, by being described as poor—but didn't appear to be—and by dedicating her triumph to "her Chocanoan countrymen, her family, and her race."[14] She was traditional and black through her hometown of Unguía, located on a finger of northern Chocó reaching northwest into Panama, part of the other rural and black coastal Colombian lowlands. Her natural beauty was accentuated by her statement that she had not had plastic surgery, the only contestant that year to make such a claim. She knew that if she stayed in Unguía she had no future, so she looked to the other Colombia, the one on the other side of the Atrato River, the Unguía swamp, and the Urabá Gulf, to reach Turbo, Apartadó, and then modern Medellín. She had heard of modern paisa technology, of computers that communicated with the entire world; she studied tourism and hotel management, and then found lucrative work as a fashion model. Her beauty and style attracted support from fashion designers and businessmen in Medellín who financed her preparation and trip to Cartagena for the national pageant.[15] In Cartagena she was dubbed "the black Barbie" for her resemblance to the Mattel doll, a popular moniker that made her a modern commodity acceptable for white consumption.[16]

Vanessa's path to queen of Colombia was opened both by her actions and beauty and by the Constitution of 1991. Article 7 stipulated that "the State recognizes and protects ethnic and cultural identity of the Colombian nation," thus expanding the state's ideological and legal recognition of black and indigenous communities as part of white and mestizo Colombia. Article 55 and Law 70 of 1993 established the process by which some black Colombians could be recognized as belonging to black communities with rights to ancestral lands that formerly had been property of the state. For the first time in its history, the Colombian government recognized Afro-Colombians, 26 percent of the country's population, as an ethnic minority.[17] With rural black communities totaling 93 percent of the population in the tropical forests of the Pacific lowlands, the future of a more inclusive and multicultural Colombia seemed promising in the Chocó.[18]

Expedited land grants to Afro-Colombian communities in northern Chocó—Vanessa's home region—began in 1996 and distributed 10 million hectares (24.7 million acres) to black communities over the next five years. But simultaneous with these land grants and the promised embrace of multiculturalism and sustainable development, direct attacks from the Colombian army and paramilitary units commenced on the black communities in and around Riosucio, upriver from Vanessa's hometown of Unguía. In December 1996 and April 1997, military planes bombed and strafed communities in and around Riosucio indiscriminately, with paramilitary units on the ground terrorizing the defenseless population with torture, dismemberment, and massacre. Tens of thousands of black Colombians started the exodus from the Chocó, seeking refuge in big cities like Bogotá. The humanitarian disaster of internally displaced persons reached between 3.6 million to 5.2 million Colombians in the decades after 1985, with one-third of those estimated to be black, 72 percent women and children. Only Sudan rivaled Colombia's ignoble distinction for the most internally displaced persons (internal refugees) in the world, with many more displaced persons than countries like Iraq or Afghanistan.[19]

The competing logic gutting the promise of multiculturalism and sustainable development was paramilitary neoliberalism. The 1992 Plan Pacífico, part of a larger development plan for the "Pacific Rim," envisioned massive road, dam, even interoceanic canal projects in the tropical forest lowlands of the Colombian Pacific to exploit the varied and rich natural resources of the Chocó, long a center of Colombian gold mining. Neoliberals dreamed of huge profits from timber, fisheries, cattle ranching, and industrial agriculture. As an outgrowth of Reaganomics—private enterprise good, government bad—the market fundamentalism of the Washington Consensus championed the private sector's role in determining economic and political priorities in the world, limiting governmental interference with market expansion. The problem by 1996 for those focused on primitive accumulation of natural resources was that Afro-Colombians and indigenous peoples lived on the land and had, or would soon receive, collective titles to their ancestral lands; redistribution of land, resources, and status to marginal black or indigenous communities to bolster their social viability was antithetical to the political and economic logic of neoliberalism. The solution in 1996 and thereafter for the Colombian state, national and transnational business interests, and the paramilitary was to use the terror of violence as a vehicle to depopulate targeted lands and to displace those black and brown Colombians in the way of white progress. Without residents, titles of land to black and indigenous communities could be voided, opening the way for African palm or coca plantations, or mining, timber extraction, deforestation, and big cattle ranches. Neoliberalism needed paramilitary terrorism as an instrument to impose its economic and political program while gutting the competing and contradictory goal of social inclusion and communal welfare inscribed in the Constitution of 1991. This pattern was not new in Colombian history; it *was* Colombian history. Using violence as a mechanism of displacing residents and extracting wealth for elites began with the Spanish conquest, continued through the long colonial period with some legal restrictions, and then intensified with liberal economic policies on the coffee, cattle, and coca frontiers in the modern era, leading to the re-embrace of neoliberalism and terrorism at the turn of the twenty-first century.[20]

The competing claims of multiculturalism and neoliberalism collided when Vanessa Mendoza was named Miss Colombia, as thousands and then millions of Colombians were forced from their homes in the name of profit and power. On one side, Vanessa's win signaled a symbolic recognition of diversity and multiculturalism in Colombia; one could be a stunning black beauty, albeit whitened for popular and commercial consumption, and represent the nation proudly on the international stage. But on the other side lurked the terror of the beast, once again employed against the poor, the ethnic, the dark, in a merciless campaign supported by national and international businesses and state and para-state killers to ensure modern white supremacy and elite enrichment. Vanessa's victory reconciled the double-edged sword that brought Colombian history and its many contradictions into one totemic instrument: one side was clean, bright, and smooth like a sexy plastic doll; the other was sharp, rusty, jagged, and bloody like the executioner's axe. Ironically, the Chocó became more recognizably Colombian after Vanessa's singular victory—as had Nariño after Stella Márquez won Miss Colombia in 1959—while it also became more Colombian as terror and violence ripped through the department. As always, the beauty queen integrated and thereby annulled the complex contradictions of reality.[21] And then, in Colombia, there was always next week's pageant.

Part of the shifting geography of terror into Chocó and into southern Caquetá and Putumayo followed the inherited logic of post-1945 Cold War anticommunism against insurgent groups woven together with post-1980 drug war violence. The FARC and the paramilitary AUC competed with one another for the expanding coca fields in the south while also contesting control for the cocaine smuggling routes in the north. Taxing the drug trade, kidnapping, extortion, and terrorist attacks against the civilian population made both groups wealthy and much feared. However, AUC coordination with the Colombian armed forces shielded it from public condemnation as long as the common enemy was the guerrillas, even as the AUC was responsible for most massacres and human rights atrocities. By the millennium, U.S. government representatives serving in Colombia were obsessed with breaking the FARC while often silent about AUC massacres and drug trafficking, seemingly oblivious to readily apparent historical patterns in Colombia. The FARC's roots stretched back to the peasant republics of the 1930s and land battles in the Sumapaz; La Violencia gave the leadership valuable combat experience; U.S. counterinsurgency programs made them an organized insurgency in the mid-1960s; U.S. demand for drugs and U.S. drug wars against cartels made both the FARC and the AUC more powerful and dangerous threats to a still exclusionary and nonsovereign Colombian state. Once again, U.S. policy chased the tail of the Colombian tiger rather than confronting the head of the beast; destroying the leadership of the Medellín or Cali cartels, the FARC, the ELN, or the AUC wouldn't solve Colombia's security issues but merely lead to its evolution as long as the Colombian government was not sovereign, inclusive, and popularly legitimate.[22]

The terrorist attacks in the United States on September 11, 2001, rebranded U.S. global hegemonic policies as the War on Terror, an absurd policy given that war *is* terror. Nonetheless, the "new" strategic objective integrated earlier Cold War and drug war programs and approaches in Colombia and in the rest of the world. U.S. designation of the FARC, the ELN, and the AUC as foreign terrorist organizations made Colombia Ground Zero in U.S. hemispheric security programs in Latin America as Colombia had three of the four such designated groups in the region, the fourth being the Sendero Luminoso (Shining Path) in Peru.[23] With the Plan Colombia program, Colombia became the third-largest recipient of U.S. military aid in the world, after the special cases of Israel and Egypt.

Colombians elected the independent paisa Álvaro Uribe in the first round of presidential elections in 2002, signaling their distaste for the two previous presidents, Liberal Ernesto Samper and Conservative Andrés Pastrana. Samper's drug politics scandals and Pastrana's failed peace negotiations with the FARC weakened the presidency, a power that Uribe vowed to restore with aggressive actions against the FARC backed by firm U.S. military commitments. While mayor of Medellín in 1982–1983, Uribe had personal dealings with Pablo Escobar and the Ochoa Brothers of the Medellín cartel, and as governor of Antioquia from 1995 to 1997, he mobilized and employed paramilitary groups to attack the FARC in Medellín and in Urabá. The tough-talking, hardworking, bookish but telegenic Uribe fit Colombian stereotypes of paisa efficiency, intelligence, and superiority, and Uribe had a blood feud with the FARC since members of that insurgent group had killed his father in 1983, giving him a personal bond with Colombians who also feared the FARC.

Uribe's goal of bringing security to all Colombians required a major expansion of the size and capabilities of the armed forces; Uribe's basic strategy built governmental sovereignty through military superiority over competing armed groups, not by building on the rule of law. U.S. assistance programs and taxes on the rich provided the funds to expand the size of the armed forces fourfold by 2010. By 2004, the government claimed to have police or military presence—if not a monopoly on force—in all Colombian municipalities. Coordinated military and paramilitary operations pushed the FARC and ELN out of urban centers of operation while also targeting insurgent strongholds in the countryside. Murder and kidnapping rates fell in major urban centers—notably in Bogotá, Medellín, Cali, and Barranquilla—which were also key cities polled by the government to measure impressive public support for President Uribe. Violence and insecurity did not end; they just shifted away from urban areas where most Colombians, especially middle- and upper-class citizens, embraced Uribe as a can-do savior. Resource-rich rural communities eyed by national and international businesses and strategic border zones with Panama, Ecuador, and Venezuela experienced intense violence as state, paramilitary, and guerrilla groups battled for position in or for control of the drug economy. The rhetoric about democracy and human rights would wait until the peace was won by war.[24]

Over the course of his two presidential terms (2002–2010), Uribe managed to maintain high popular support as he took the war to the FARC, demobilized some but not all of the paramilitary AUC units, reduced urban crime, and stimulated economic growth. Both the FARC and ELN lost about one-half of their estimated combatants during the first decade of the new millennium, many to desertions and acceptance of government terms to disarm as morale swung away from the insurgents and to the more offensive armed forces. The FARC lost many top commanders from 2004 to 2011 to arrest, airstrikes, death in combat, or, in the case of Manuel "Tirofijo" Marulanda, to heart attack; the FARC's aura of invincibility was tarnished with these high-profile successes by the Colombian government. As a top ally of the Bush Administration in South America, Uribe and Colombia could count on massive U.S. military training and intelligence-sharing operations to attack the FARC, making use of the AUC as counterinsurgency shock forces less necessary. Over a two-year period after 2003, about thirty-one thousand AUC members surrendered and demobilized in exchange for light or no prison sentences and protection from extradition to the United States on drug trafficking charges. Critics charged that many of those weren't paramilitary members at all, but former insurgents or opportunistic and unemployed Colombians taking advantage of short-term government subsidies. Moreover, those AUC members who committed gross human rights violations—massacres, forced displacements of civilians, and disappearances—received amnesties and were not held accountable to the law or to Colombian society. However, like the FARC, the AUC top leadership was thinned either in combat or by murder within the organization, with fourteen top leaders extradited to the United States in 2008 by an Uribe government concerned that paramilitary cooperation with Colombian investigators might reveal criminal connections to the Uribe coalition.[25]

The dark side of the Uribe administration included contempt for law and for political opposition, paramilitary influence and presence in regional and national politics, ongoing human rights abuses often involving government officials or the Colombian armed forces, and illegal wiretapping of political opponents and judges. Much like Nixon or Fujimori, President Uribe didn't know when to take his foot off the power accelerator. From 2006 to 2008, a series of "parapolitics" scandals revealed and investigated the extent of paramilitary power in the Uribe camp. Between 2007 and 2009, DAS (Department of Administrative Security) officials revealed paramilitary penetration of DAS, death threats made by DAS to Colombians investigating paramilitary links to Uribe, and illegal wiretaps of judges, politicians, and journalists done by Uribe's secret police. Moreover, with most official killing no longer being outsourced to the paramilitaries, now Colombian troops faced charges of kidnapping and then killing innocent civilians, dressing them as guerrillas, so that their officers got pay raises, extra vacations, and promotions as evidence of success against insurgency. These "false positives" revealed a body bag culture—like that of U.S. commanders in Vietnam—involving thirteen hundred operations and about two thousand victims.[26] Moreover, if you were a labor member or organizer, journalist, priest, or nun, your life was also in peril in Colombia before and after Uribe's reign. In 2010, 60 percent of all trade unionists killed in the world were Colombian; about three thousand trade unionists were murdered in Colombia since 1986, on average one every three days. Colombia had the lowest percentage of organized workers in all the Americas for good reason: business, paramilitary, and state terrorism.[27] Nowhere in the Americas were journalists under more threat than in Colombia after 1992; twenty-eight journalists were murdered in Colombia during the Uribe years (only Iraq, the Philippines, Algeria, and Russia had more murdered journalists than Colombia). Finally, in strikingly Catholic Colombia, between 1984 and September 2011, two bishops, seventy-nine priests, eight monks and nuns, and three seminarians were murdered;[28] the international silence about these killings of Colombian religious workers was in marked contrast to the outcry over Spanish or American clergy killed in El Salvador during the 1980s. However, in El Salvador in 1980 or Colombia in 2005, it didn't really matter who you were to be marked for assassination if the U.S. government fed the beast of violence. In Uribe's Colombia, if you tried to organize and work in dignity, report and read responsible journalism, or organize for a better future as you prayed for protection, you could die.

Beauty, of course, soothed the reality of the beast of violence even if the U.S. press reported that Colombia had turned the corner toward peace and justice. The Bush administration needed a foreign policy success story overseas, and Colombia fit the bill. ABC created a spin-off of the Colombian telenovela sensation, re-creating *Ugly Betty* as a comedy-drama series, with Betty now working in a New York fashion house, living in a Latin household, and dealing with immigration issues. Running from 2006 to 2010, ABC used the series to make money and to bolster its "Latin" programming as it retold the story of inner beauty. A much more voluptuous outer beauty was found in the curves and wit of Sofía Vergara, whom ABC showcased starting in 2009 in its hit sitcom *Modern Family*. Sofía plays Gloria, from a homicide-ridden Colombian city, married to an older American husband; she is drop-dead gorgeous but also direct, smart, and strong, like many Colombian women. From Barranquilla, like Shakira, Sofía had to dye her hair darker to appear "typically Latina," whereas Shakira went blonde to cross over to a North American audience, while both proved that they were talented, engaged, creative, and socially responsible, much more than the sum of their impressive parts.

Beauty and the beast remained entwined in Colombia as Uribe's administration neared its end. Uribe's support and associations with paramilitarism proved embarrassing and a political liability for Colombia's international image. Some paramilitary units stayed in the drug trafficking and displacement/land theft businesses, with homicide rates spiking upward in Medellín in 2008 after the extradition to the United States of paramilitary drug boss Diego Fernando Murillo (a.k.a. Don Berna). Don Berna counted among his former associates Pablo Escobar and the Castaño Brothers and had cleared Medellín of competing gangs and drug syndicates, becoming the boss of both security and drug trafficking in the city. His monopoly on violence brought homicide rates down after 2003, with homicide rates lower in Medellín than in New Orleans, Baltimore, and Washington, DC, by 2007. However, with Don Berna extradited to the United States—and luckily for Uribe, not talking to U.S. investigators—a new drug/turf war erupted in Medellín after 2008. Although the city now boasted impressive new museums and corporate

headquarters, swank new clubs and restaurants, and a brighter, more positive image, a return to the bad old days threatened Medellín's makeover.[29]
However, with the nation-state gendered female as modern Colombian beauties represented the country around the world, males continued to specialize
in the beastly world of violence, drugs, and paramilitary terror, connecting
Colombia to its troubled identity. Internationally, the United States subsidized both sides of the drug business with weaponry, intelligence, cash, and
a seemingly insatiable appetite for drugs; by 2006, marijuana was the biggest
cash crop in the United States.[30]

The election of Uribe's defense minister, Juan Manuel Santos, to the presidency in 2010 opened the future to a post-Uribe era. Although Uribe continued to have high approval ratings and often worked to undercut his successor, Santos signaled a rapprochement with the judiciary, a relationship
damaged by Uribe, as he formally moved away from parapolitics and pursued
compensation for displaced victims so they could recover lands seized ille-
gally by the paramilitary. Santos, a member of Bogotá's traditional political
elite, was distancing himself and his government from the tough-talking paisa
cowboy, Uribe.[31]

The U.S. Congress rewarded Santos and Colombia with a Free Trade
Agreement in 2011, one pushed hard for by Caterpillar, G.E., and Walmart
inside Washington. Canadian mining and oil companies had already cashed in
on access to the Colombian trade zone with their own Free Trade Agreement
in 2009. With gold prices at record highs, Medellín and Antioquia's tradition of wealth production found new corporate partners in Canada and the
United States. Small Colombian farmers worried that they could not compete with subsidized American agriculture, some suggesting that they could
turn to coca as an alternative crop.[32] Big American banks eyed the Colombian market, hopeful that more trade would boost the balance sheet as it
also offered logical access to the billions of liquid assets generated by the
international drug trade; perhaps the U.S. mortgage market would soon be
floated by an infusion of cocaine capital generated between Colombia and
the United States. As usual, this trade agreement will benefit elites the most,
will give middle-class consumers a window of access to cheaper and better-
quality goods, while the poor will pay the bill with loss of jobs, resources, and
futures. With the majority of Colombians poor, most in the country will lose.
Violence will erupt, again, in the Pacific lowlands, in Arauca, Cauca, and the
Putumayo/Caquetá, as domestic and international companies and drug traffickers jockey for resource and transportation access. In racial terms, white
elites will win, brown and black Colombians will lose, a continuation of the
colonial hangover.

Paramilitary neoliberalism will lead to more violence, terror, displacement, and exclusion, gutting the Constitution of 1991's promises of greater multicultural and inclusive democracy in Colombia. Beauty will continue to mask the terror of the beast, and Colombia, soon, might again win the Miss Universe crown; the country is "re-open for business," and billionaire investors, like Miss Universe pageant owner Donald Trump, are banking on high growth rates fueled by abundant natural resources, graced by some of the most beautiful women in the world. Colombia, indeed, has plenty of beautiful women who can dazzle the international imagination as much as Luz Marina did in 1958 when her symbolic reign bridged the terror of La Violencia with the exclusive elitism of the National Front. Tragically, Colombia still needs beauty as the positive weight to balance the negative reality of an elitist, exclusive, and nonsovereign state, one that cannot deliver peace, security, or inclusion for its citizens.

NOTES

INTRODUCTION

1. What is now Colombia was known as Gran Colombia from 1819 to 1830, Nueva Granada from 1830 to 1863, and Colombia thereafter. I will use the name *Colombia* to refer to the country regardless of the official title at the time.

2. South American nations like Brazil, Argentina, Chile, Uruguay, and Paraguay have all placed well in such championships and have built part of their twentieth-century national and international reputations around them.

3. Colombia won the Miss Universe pageant in 1958 out of the ashes of La Violencia and at the beginning of the National Front; Venezuela won in 1979, 1981, 1986, and 1996 as bipartisan liberal democracy unraveled, and recently in 2006 and 2009 during the Chávez administrations; Brazil won in 1963 as civilians pushed aggressive reforms and in 1968 during a full-blown military dictatorship.

4. A series of experiments in the 1980s found that infants as young as three months old preferred faces deemed by adults to be attractive to others rated unattractive. See Linda A. Jackson, *Physical Appearance and Gender: Sociobiological and Sociocultural Perspectives* (Albany: State University of New York Press, 1992), pp. 75–77.

5. Miss Puerto Rico has won Miss Universe five times (1970, 1985, 1993, 2001, 2006) in an elite group, only trailing Venezuela (six titles) and the United States (seven crowns). As both culturally Latina and nationally American—the Commonwealth of Puerto Rico is U.S. territory—the selection of Miss Puerto Rico in 1993 could be seen as a synthetic candidate who represented both Latin America and the United States at a moment of greater economic hegemony, sparking nationalist concerns for protective sovereignty. Research on beauty and identity in Puerto Rico would be fascinating.

6. A regional, national, and international analysis of the impact of the rubber boom in northwest Amazonia: *Red Rubber, Bleeding Trees: Violence, Slavery, and Empire in Northwest Amazonia, 1850–1933* (Albuquerque: University of New Mexico Press, 1998).

7. It strikes me that a study of the notion of beauty among the blind would be fascinating. I found John Berger's *Ways of Seeing* (London: Penguin Books, 1972) a useful primer on how to analyze visual texts.

8. See Eccehomo Cetina, *Jaque a la reina: mafia y corrupción en Cartagena* (Bogotá: Planeta, 1994); and Pedro Claver Tellez, *El lado oscuro de las reinas: sus amores, sus pasiones, sus intimidades.* (Bogotá: Intermedio Editores, 1994).

9. *Las mujeres en la historia de Colombia, vol. 1, Mujeres, historia y política; vol. 2, Mujeres y sociedad; vol. 3, Mujeres y cultura* (Bogotá: Editorial Norma, 1995); see especially volumes 4, 5, and 6 of the *Nueva historia de Colombia* (Bogotá: Planeta Colombiana Editorial, 1989).

10. See Suzy Bermúdez Q., *Hijas, esposas y amantes: género, clase, etnia y edad en la historia de América Latina* (Bogotá: Ediciones Uniandes, 1992); Catalina Reyes Cárdenas, *La vida cotidiana en Medellín, 1890–1930* (Bogotá: Colcultura, 1996); and Patricia Londoño Vega and Santiago Londoño Vélez, "Vida diaria en las ciudades colombianas," in *Nueva historia de Colombia*, vol. 4 (Bogotá: Planeta Colombiana Editorial, 1989), pp. 313–399.

11. Lois W. Banner, *American Beauty* (Chicago: University of Chicago Press, 1983), pp. 3–5.

12. Amelia Simpson, *Xuxa: The Mega-Marketing of Gender, Race, and Modernity* (Philadelphia: Temple University Press, 1993).

13. Ellen Zetzel Lambert, *The Face of Love: Feminism and the Beauty Question* (Boston: Beacon Press, 1995); Naomi Wolf, *The Beauty Myth: How Images of Beauty Are Used against Women* (New York: Doubleday, 1991).

14. Colleen Ballerina Cohen, Richard Wilk, and Beverly Stoeltje, eds., *Beauty Queens on the Global Stage: Gender, Contests, and Power* (New York: Routledge, 1996).

15. Jackson, *Physical Appearance and Gender.*

CHAPTER 1

1. For geographic introductions to Colombia, see Frank Safford, *The Ideal of the Practical: Colombia's Struggle to Form a Technical Elite* (Austin: University of Texas Press, 1976), pp. 21–24; and Krzysztof Dydyński, *Colombia, a Lonely Planet Travel Survival Kit*, 2nd ed. (Hawthorne, Victoria: Lonely Planet Publications, 1995), pp. 28–30.

2. For a short but insightful overview of twentieth-century Colombian history, see Brian Loveman and Thomas M. Davies, Jr., "Colombia," in Che Guevara, *Guerrilla Warfare: With Revised and Updated Introduction and Case Studies by Brian Loveman and Thomas M. Davies Jr.*, 3rd ed. (Wilmington, DE: Scholarly Resources, 1997), pp. 233–267.

3. Raymond Leslie Williams and Kevin G. Guerrieri, *Culture and Customs in Colombia* (Westport, CT: Greenwood Press, 1999), pp. xvi, 26, 29.

4. Safford, *Ideal of the Practical*, pp. 21–25.

5. Gabriel García Márquez, *One Hundred Years of Solitude*, translated from the Spanish by Gregory Rabassa (New York: Avon Books, 1971).

6. See Dydyński, *Colombia*, and Guillermo Abadía Morales, *ABC del folklore colombiano*, 6th ed. (Bogotá: Panamericana, 1998).

7. For the colonial history of the Chocó, see William Frederick Sharp, *Slavery on the Spanish Frontier: The Colombian Chocó, 1680–1810* (Norman: University of Oklahoma Press, 1976); and for a general overview of the geography and folklore of the Pacific coast, see Abadía Morales, *ABC del folklore*, pp. 81–93.

8. My apologies to those readers who desire more attention to beauty in Boyacá, Cesar, the Llanos, Córdoba, and Sucre; my archival research focused on big cities and extrapolated out, leaving smaller cities and their surrounding departments somewhat unattended.

9. UABG (M) *Gloria* no. 9 (julio-ago. 1947), p. 6.

10. Selden Rodman, *The Colombia Traveler* (New York: Hawthorne Books, 1971), p. 151.

11. An example: "Who won the Pasto beauty contest this year?" "No one." Rodman, *Colombia Traveler*, pp. 154–155.

12. Safford, *The Ideal of the Practical*, p. 31; Williams and Guerrieri, *Culture and Customs in Colombia*, p. 3.

13. Williams and Guerrieri, *Customs and Culture in Colombia*, pp. 2–5.

14. Malcolm Deas, Efraín Sánchez, and Aída Martínez, *Tipos y costumbres de la Nueva Granada: la colección de pinturas formada por Joseph Brown en Colombia entre 1825 y 1841 y el diario de su excursión de Bogotá a Girón en 1834* (Bogotá: Fondo Cultural Cafetero, 1989), pp. 174.

15. Deas, *Tipos y costumbres*, p. 183.

16. On the llanos, see Jane Rausch, *The Llanos Frontier in Colombian History* (Albuquerque: University of New Mexico Press, 1993); and for Amazonia, see Stanfield, *Red Rubber, Bleeding Trees*.

17. David Bushnell, *The Making of Modern Colombia: A Nation in Spite of Itself* (Berkeley: University of California Press, 1993), pp. 208, 286–87; Safford, *Ideal of the Practical*, p. 24; Patricia Londoño and Santiago Londoño, "Vida diaria en las ciudades colombianas." In *Nueva historia de Colombia*. Vol. IV (Bogotá: Planeta, 1989), pp. 327–37; Dydyński, *Colombia*, p. 37.

18. Safford, *Ideal of the Practical*, pp. 3–5, 10, 29.

19. Luis LaTorre Mendoza, *Historia e historias de Medellín: siglos XVII, XVIII, XIX* (Medellín: Ediciones Tomás Carrasquilla, 1972), pp. 412–414.

20. Londoño and Londoño, "Vida diaria" p. 340; Magdala Velázquez Toro, "Condición jurídica y social de la mujer," in *Nueva historia de Colombia*, vol. 4 (Bogotá: Planeta, 1989), p. 22.

21. On the hermosa Catalina, see pp. 11–13; p. 41 for "La India Anica"; p. 74 for Guillermina; and p. 118 for Eva, all in Camilo S. Delgado, *Historias, leyendas y tradiciones de Cartagena*, vol. 1 (Cartagena: Tip. "Mogollon," 1911).

22. This marvelous source could serve as the base for an interesting paper. Joaquín Posada Gutiérrez, "Fiestas de la Candelaria en la Popa," in *Museo de Cuadros de Costumbres* (Bogotá: Impreso por Foción Mantilla, 1866), pp. 81–90. Apparently, it can also be found in Posada's *Memorias histórico-políticas*.

23. Posada Gutiérrez, "Fiestas de la Candelaria," p. 82.

24. Ibid., pp. 83–86; for descriptions of various popular Colombian dances, see Williams and Guerrieri, *Culture and Customs in Colombia*, pp. 32–33.

25. Posada, "Fiestas de la Candelaria," pp. 87–88.

26. Ibid., p. 89.

27. Londoño and Londoño, "Vida diaria," p. 359; "Danzas de Colombia: El bulle-rengue," *Colombia Ilustrada* (enero–junio 1970): 25-32; "Danzas de Colombia: El currulao," *Colombia Ilustrada* (enero–abril 1972): 19-28.

28. Josefina Amezquita de Almeida, *La mujer: sus obligaciones y sus derechos* (Bogotá: Ediciones AA, 1977), pp. 8-11; Williams and Guerrieri, *Culture and Customs*, p. 37; Velásquez Toro, "Condición jurídica," pp. 9-15; Londoño and Londoño, "Vida diaria," pp. 387-391.

29. Jackson, *Physical Appearance and Gender*, pp. 1-9; Geoffrey Cowley, "The Biology of Beauty" *Newsweek* (June 3, 1996): 61-66.

30. Jackson, *Physical Appearance and Gender*, pp. 8-19; Banner, *American Beauty*, p. 226.

31. Banner, *American Beauty*, pp. 11-13.

32. *Ibid.*, p. 41.

33. For a fascinating analysis of race, gender, beauty, modernity, and marketing in Brazil, see Simpson, *Xuxa*.

34. Rachel Kemper, *Costume* (New York: Newsweek Books, 1977), pp. 10-12, quote on p. 15; Aída Martínez Carreño, *La prisión del vestido: aspectos sociales del traje en América* (Bogotá: Planeta Colombiana Editorial, 1995), pp. 10, 17, 25.

35. Kemper, *Costume*, pp. 11, 78; Martínez Carreño, *La prisión del vestido*, pp. 33-35.

36. Kemper, *Costume*, p. 11; Martínez Carreño, *La prisión del vestido*, pp. 44-45, 51-52; Aída Martínez Carreño, *Un siglo de moda en Colombia, 1830-1930* (Bogotá: Fondo Cultural Cafetero, 1981) p. 1.

37. Kemper, *Costume*, pp. 122-126; Nancy Bradfield, *Costume in Detail: Women's Dress, 1730-1930* (Boston: Plays Inc., 1968), p. 86.

38. Deas and Martínez, *Tipos y costumbres*, pp. 136-137.

39. Martínez Carreño, *Un siglo de moda*, pp. 1-5; ibid., *La prisión del vestido*, pp. 141-142.

40. Martínez Carreño, *Un siglo de moda*, p. 24; Martínez Carreño, *La prisión del vestido*, pp. 52-54, 143-144; Deas and Martínez, *Tipos y costumbres*, pp. 105, 107, 113, 133.

41. Antonio Montaña, *Cultura del vestuario en Colombia* (Bogotá: Fondo Cultural Cafetero, 1993), p. 31; *En busca de un país: la comisión corográfica; selección de dibujos de Carmelo Fernández, Enrique Price, y Manuel María Paz, con texto introductorio de Gonzalo Hernández de Alba* (Bogotá: Carlos Valencia Editores, 1984), n.p. (illustra-tion—"Llapanga i mestizo del Cauca).

42. On Cartagena, see Martínez Carreño, *La prisión del vestido*, pp. 177-178; on Piedecuesta and the portraits of rural women, see Deas and Martínez, *Tipos y cos-tumbres*, pp. 101, 103, and 183; on nudity and the *aguadoras* of Bogotá, see Martínez Carreño, *La prisión del vestido*, pp. 26-27, 143-144.

43. Loveman and Davies, "Colombia," p. 236.

44. For other sources in English on violence patterns in nineteenth-century Colombia, see Safford, *Ideal of the Practical*, p. 44; and David Bushnell, "Politics and Violence in Nineteenth-Century Colombia," in *Violence in Colombia: The Contempo-*

rary Crisis in Historical Perspective, ed. Charles Bergquist, Ricardo Peñaranda, and Gonzalo Sánchez (Wilmington, DE: Scholarly Resources, 1992), pp. 11–30.

CHAPTER 2

1. For a political overview of this period, see Rodman, *Colombia Traveler*, pp. 42–45; for social insight, see Suzy Bermúdez, "Debates en torno a la mujer y la familia en Colombia, 1850–1886." *Texto y Contexto* (Bogotá) 10 (Enero–Abril 1987): 111–144.

2. See Bushnell, "Politics and Violence in Nineteenth-Century Colombia," pp. 11–30; and Javier Ocampo López, *Historia básica de Colombia* (Bogotá: Plaza & Janes, 1994), pp. 241–243.

3. Safford, *Ideal of the Practical*, pp. 18, 185–86; Marco Palacios, *Entre la legitimidad y la violencia: Colombia, 1875–1994* (Bogotá: Grupo Editorial Norma, 1995), pp. 26–54.

4. Ocampo López, *Historia básica*, pp. 237–258; Bushnell, "Politics and Violence," pp. 13–15; Palacios, *Entre la legitimidad*, pp. 15, 42–43; Stanfield, *Red Rubber, Bleeding Trees*, pp. 70–74.

5. Safford, *Ideal of the Practical*, p. 187; Palacios, *Entre la legitimidad*, p. 39.

6. Safford, *Ideal of the Practical*, p. 38; Ocampo López, *Historia básica*, pp. 247–249; Palacios, *Entre la legitimidad*, pp. 16, 31.

7. Brian Loveman, *No Higher Law: American Foreign Policy and the Western Hemisphere since 1776* (Chapel Hill: University of North Carolina Press, 2010), pp. 88–90, 107, 200–202.

8. Ibid., pp. 105–107, 110, 175.

9. Williams and Guerrieri, *Culture and Customs of Colombia*, pp. 6–7; Palacios, *Entre la legitimidad*, p. 36; Safford, *Ideal of the Practical*, pp. 45, 121.

10. Palacios, *Entre la legitimidad*, p. 17.

11. *Ibid.*, p. 18.

12. Bermúdez, "Debates en torno", p. 126.

13. Ibid., pp. 112–114; Suzy Bermúdez, "La mujer y la familia en América Latina: Dos elementos claves para entender el mantenimiento de las jerarquias sociales, raciales, y sexuales, 1850–1930," *Revista de Antropología* (Bogotá) 2, nos. 1–2 (1986): 104–108.

14. Martínez Carreño, *La prisión del vestido*, pp. 118–19; ibid., *Un siglo de moda*, pp. 8–12, 24–5; Palacios, *Entre la legitimidad*, pp. 25, 37–38.

15. *El Pobre*, Nov. 30, 1851; *El Zipa*, Oct. 11, 1877, Jan. 9, 1879.

16. Miguel María Lisboa, *Relación de un viaje a Venezuela, Nueva Granada, Ecuador* (Caracas: Ediciones de la Presidencia de la República, 1954), pp. 261–262, 273–274; *Viajeros colombianos por Colombia*, Prólogo de Gabriel Giraldo Jaramillo (Bogotá: Fondo Cultural Cafetero, 1977), pp. 5, 66, 239, 241.

17. Isaac Farwell Holton, *New Granada: Twenty Months in the Andes* (New York: Harper and Brothers, 1857), pp. 244–245.

18. *Ibid.*, p. 440.

19. *Ibid.*, pp. 171, 380–382; on an internal "difficult beauty" as expressed in nineteenth-century British literature and in lived experience, see Lambert, *The Face of Love*.

20. Banner, *American Beauty*, p. 5.

21. Rosa Carnegie-Williams, *Un año en los andes o aventuras de una lady en Bogotá*, trans. Luis Enrique Jiménez Llaña Vezga (Bogotá: Tercer Mundo, 1990), p. 69 (indias), 92–93 (negra); Miguel Cané, *Notas de un viaje sobre Venezuela y Colombia* (Bogotá: Imprenta de la Luz, 1907), p. 136.

22. Carnegie-Williams, *Un año en los andes*, pp. 54, 66, 90.

23. *Ibid.*, pp. 91, 96, 105–106.

24. Cané, *Notas de viaje*, pp. 161–163.

25. Martínez Carreño, *Un siglo de moda*, pp. 8–12.

26. *Viajeros colombianos por Colombia*, pp. 246–253.

27. Safford, *Ideal of the Practical*, pp. 32, 214; Palacios, *Entre la legitimidad*, p. 17.

28. *Viajeros colombianos por Colombia*, pp. 175, 190.

29. *Ibid.*, p. 191.

30. Friedrich von Schenck, *Viajes por antioquia en el año de 1880* (Bogotá: Banco de la República, 1953), pp. 18–21.

31. *Ibid.*, pp. 18–25.

32. Palacios, *Entre la legitimidad*, p. 19.

33. *Ibid.*, p. 54.

34. Schenck, *Viajes por Colombia*, pp. 12, 23.

35. Geoffrey Cowley, "The Biology of Beauty," *Newsweek* (June 3, 1996): 61–66.

36. Schenck, *Viajes por Colombia*, p. 47.

37. Juan Bautista López O., *Costumbres, tercera época*, vol. 2 (Manizales: Biblioteca Popular de Autores Caldenses, 1981), pp. 29–34.

38. Lisboa, *Relación de un viaje*, p. 320.

39. *Viajeros colombianos por Colombia*, p. 143. ("Las señoras son en general muy bellas, espirituales, expansivas y alegres, y reúnen a la elegancia o la gentileza de las formas una gracia en el decir, en la mirada y la sonrisa, verdaderamente encantadora"; ". . . una fealdad dolorosa: flacas, largas, sombrías, pálidas como espectros, lúgubres como las sombras errantes en medio de las tumbas . . .")

40. Sensuous poems found in *La Floresta: periódico literario dedicado al bello sexo del estado* (Cartagena) 1, no. 12 (Oct. 31, 1879); heaven/hell dichotomy in *El Amigo de las Damas* (Cartagena) no. 3 (Apr. 16, 1874).

41. *El Amigo de las Damas* no. 17 (Feb. 21, 1875).

42. *La Floresta* 1, no. 6 (Nov. 30, 1879).

43. Ibid. 1, no. 2 (July 31, 1879).

44. Ibid. 1, no. 5 (Oct. 31, 1879).

45. Ibid. 1, no. 6 (Nov. 30, 1879).

46. Holton, *New Granada*, pp. 59, 63.

47. Schenck, *Viajes por Colombia*, pp. 53, 56–57; "Diario de sucesos de Cali," in

Boletín histórico del Valle (Cali; July 1934): 249–275; Palacios, *Entre la legitimidad,* pp. 44–45.

48. Palacios, *Entre la legitimidad,* pp. 20–21; Schenck, *Viajes por Colombia,* pp. 58–59; *Viajeros colombianos por Colombia,* pp. 79, 119.

49. *Viajeros colombianos por Colombia,* p. 258.

50. *Ibid.,* pp. 31, 258, 263; Stanfield, *Red Rubber, Bleeding Trees,* pp. 57–58; Fredrick Pike, *The United States and Latin America: Myths and Stereotypes of Civilization and Nature* (Austin: University of Texas Press, 1992).

51. Miles Lambert, *Fashion in Photographs 1860–1880* (London: B. T. Batsford, 1991), pp. 10, 34, 81, 127–128; Kemper, *Costume,* pp. 132–33; Bradfield, *Costume in Detail,* pp. 162, 228.

52. Banner, *American Beauty,* p. 14.

53. *Biblioteca de Señoritas,* Jan. 9, 1858, p. 10.

54. *Ibid.,* Feb. 12, 1859, pp. 44–46.

55. *Ibid.,* Sept. 16, 1858, pp. 2–3.

56. *Ibid.,* Jan. 8, 1859, p. 2 ("Tenemos que cultivar nuestro corazón, nuestro espíritu, nuestra persona bajo todas sus condiciones para hacerla tan bella, tan agradable, tan seductora como sea posible)."

57. *Ibid.,* Jan. 3, 1858, p. 8.

58. *Ibid.,* Jan. 16, 1858, pp. 18–19; May 22, 1858, p. 165; June 12, 1858, p. 189.

59. *Ibid.,* Aug. 14, 1858, pp. 6–7.

60. *Ibid.,* May 29, 1858, p. 173; June 4, 1859, pp. 16–17.

61. *El Iris,* Feb. 11, 1866, p. 1; Feb. 13, 1867; Nov. 16, 1867, p. 256.

62. *Ibid.,* Mar. 10, 1867.

63. *Ibid.,* Mar. 3, 1867, pp. 113–19; June 24, 1866, pp. 262–263.

64. *Ibid.,* Aug. 17, 1867, pp. 43–44 ("convertirse un poco en actrises"); Banner, *American Beauty,* pp. 106–127.

65. *El Iris,* Aug. 17, 1867, p. 45; Nov. 9, 1867, p. 240.

66. Frank Safford and Marco Palacios, *Colombia: Fragmented Land and Divided Society* (New York: Oxford University Press, 2001), pp. 225–226.

67. *La Aurora: periódico dedicado al bello sexo,* nos. 1–24 (1868–1869).

68. *Ibid.,* no. 2 (Oct. 31, 1868), p. 10 ("ningun país ha sido dotado como el nuestro, por la Providencia, con seres mas anjélicas, mas nobles, mas santos, que lo que lo son nuestras hermosas antioqueñas").

69. *Ibid.,* no. 1 (Oct. 24, 1868), p. 2 ("Nuestro periódico será limpio, puro, noble, como el alma de las virtuosas antioqueñas a quienes se dedica").

70. *Ibid.,* no. 5 (Dec. 12, 1868), pp. 34–37.

71. *El Hogar,* May 16, 1868, pp. 127–128; Sept. 12, 1868, pp. 257–259; Sept. 26, 1868, pp. 273–274; Oct. 31, 1868, pp. 313–314; May 1, 1869, pp. 129–130.

72. *Ibid.,* Jan. 23, 1869, pp. 25–26.

73. *Ibid.,* Jan. 1, 1870, pp. 385–386; Cohen, Wilk, and Stoeltje, *Beauty Queens on the Global Stage.*

74. *El Hogar*, Apr. 10, 1869, p. 109 ("deben tener el cinto de Vénus i no el asta de Marte"); Mar. 21, 1870, pp. 479–480.

75. *Ibid.*, Mar. 13, 1869, p. 85.

76. *El Verjel Colombiano: periódico literario, dedicado al bello sexo*, Oct. 23, 1875, pp. 82–88 ("a una divinidad en figura humana," p. 84); story continues Oct. 30, 1875, pp. 89–96; Nov. 6, 1875, pp. 97–103; and Nov. 13, 1875, pp. 105–108.

77. *Ibid.*, Nov. 20, 1875, pp. 117–118.

78. Ibid., Dec. 11, 1875, p. 144.

79. *Ibid.*, Mar. 25, 1876, pp. 191–192.

80. *Ibid.*, Feb. 24, 1876, pp. 155–159.

81. *Ibid.*, Apr. 1, 1876, pp. 195–197.

82. Perhaps *O Sexo Feminino* of Rio de Janeiro, first published in 1873, also should be a contender for this honor. See Francesca Miller, *Latin American Women and the Search for Social Justice* (Hanover, NH: University Press of New England, 1991), pp. 44, 69.

83. *La Mujer: lecturas para la familia: Revista quincenal redactada exclusivamente por señoras y señoritas, bajo la dirección de la señora Soledad Acosta de Samper*, no. 1 (Sept. 1, 1878), p. 1 ("para auxiliar á sus compañeros de peregrinación en el escabroso camino de la vida, y ayudarles á cargar la grande y pesada cruz del sufrimiento"). For more background on Acosta de Samper, see Bermúdez, "Debates en torno," pp. 121–133; and Velásquez Toro, "Condición jurídica" en *Nueva Historia de Colombia*, vol. 4, pp. 40–41.

84. *La Mujer*, no. 10 (Feb. 5, 1879), p. 240.

85. Ibid., no. 2 (Sept. 18, 1878), p. 47; for background on Langtry, see Banner, *American Beauty*, pp. 136–139.

86. Ibid., no. 15 (May 5, 1879), p. 76; no. 21 (Aug. 5 1879), p. 220; no. 23 (Sept. 5, 1879), pp. 267–268; no. 43 (Aug. 15, 1880), p. 171.

87. Ibid., no. 22 (Aug. 20, 1879), p. 239 ("no puede haber modestia sin orgullo, ni orgullo sin aparente modestia. En cambio la vanidad, que á veces confundimos con el orgullo, no tiene en sí ni un atomo de modestia ó de orgullo. La vanidad, cuando llega á adueñarse de un corazón, no permite que la rivalice otro sentimiento y reina despóticamente").

88. Ibid., no. 7 (Dec. 15, 1878), pp. 152–253; no. 39 (June 15, 1880), pp. 74–75; no. 45 (Sept. 15, 1880), pp. 208–209; no. 46 (Oct. 1, 1880), pp. 227–28.

89. *La Familia: Lecturas para el hogar, bajo la dirección de la señora Soledad Acosta de Samper*, no. 4 (Aug. 1884), pp. 227–228; no. 8 (Dec. 1884), p. 474; no. 9 (Jan. 1885), p. 542.

CHAPTER 3

1. David Bushnell, *The Making of Modern Colombia: A Nation in Spite of Itself* (Berkeley: University of California Press, 1993), p. 140; Safford and Palacios, *Colombia*, p. 239; Palacios, *Entre la legitimidad y la violencia*, p. 47.

2. Bushnell, *Making of Modern Colombia*, pp. 140–143; Safford and Palacios, *Colombia*, pp. 245–246; Palacios, *Entre la legitimidad y la violencia*, pp. 47–50.

3. Bushnell, *Making of Modern Colombia*, pp. 144; Safford and Palacios, *Colombia*, p. 246–247; Palacios, *Entre la legitimidad y la violencia*, p. 50.

4. *Colombia 1886: Programa centenario de la constitución* (Bogotá: Biblioteca Luis Ángel Arango, 1986) pp. 10–11, 20; Palacios, *Entre la legitimidad*, p. 55.

5. Carlos Uribe Celis, *La mentalidad del colombiano; Cultura y sociedad en el siglo XX* (Bogotá: Ediciones Alborada, 1992), pp. 10, 51.

6. Bushnell, *Making of Modern Colombia*, p. 147.

7. *Colombia 1886*, p. 38.

8. *Ibid.*, pp. 76–79.

9. On press censorship see, Williams and Guerrieri, *Culture and Customs in Colombia*, p. 60; *La Mujer* serie I, no. 1 (Oct. 30, 1895).

10. *La Mujer* serie I, no. 2 (Nov. 6, 1895), pp. 9–10.

11. Ibid., p. 11; serie II, no. 13 (Dec. 18, 1895), p. 98–99.

12. *La Mujer* serie III, no. 26 (Jan. 15, 1896), pp. 341–343.

13. *La Mujer* serie II, no. 18 (Jan. 18, 1896), p. 140.

14. *La Mujer* serie III, no. 32 (Mar. 7, 1896), pp. 249–251, 269–270.

15. *La Mujer* serie IV, no. 55 (July 9, 1896), pp. 457–459.

16. *La Mujer* serie I, no. 3 (Nov. 9, 1895), pp. 17–19; no. 4 (Nov. 13, 1895), pp. 25–28; no. 8 (Nov. 27, 1895), pp. 59–60.

17. *La Mujer* serie I, no. 1 (Oct. 30, 1895), p. 4; serie III, no. 40 (Apr. 11, 1896), pp. 318–19; serie III, no. 26 (Feb. 15, 1896), pp. 341–343.

18. *La Mujer* serie V, no. 88 (Jan. 6, 1897), pp. 706–708.

19. *La Mujer* serie V, no. 85 (Dec. 16, 1896), pp. 673–676.

20. *La Mujer* serie III, no. 37 (Mar. 28, 1896), pp. 291–293.

21. *La Mujer* serie V, no. 96 (Feb. 23, 1897), pp. 801–803.

22. *La Mujer* serie V, no. 114 (July 9, 1897), pp. 1020–1021.

23. *La Mujer: Organo del bello sexo* serie V, no. 105 (Apr. 27, 1897), pp. 910–912.

24. *La Mujer: Organo del bello sexo* serie V, no. 105 (Apr. 27, 1897), pp. 909–910 ("en el hogar seductoras; y junto al lecho del dolor, sublimes!").

25. Soledad Acosta de Samper, *La mujer en la sociedad moderna* (Paris: Garnier Hermanos, 1895).

26. Acosta de Samper, *La mujer*, pp. 414–418.

27. Banner, *American Beauty*, pp. 8, 154–158, 203.

28. Banner, *American Beauty*, p. 148.

29. *Revista Ilustrada* (Bogotá, 1898) quoted in Martínez C. *Un siglo de moda*, p. 12; ". . . si hay en el mundo seres que deban especial gratitud a ese gran adelanto de la civilización son sin duda las bellas damas de la culta Bogotá a quienes costumbres y tradiciones ya vetustas condenaban a una vida claustral madre de anemias y neurosis . . ."

30. *Revista Ilustrada*, no. 3 (Aug. 4, 1898), p. 48; *El Sport* (July–Aug. 1899).

31. *El Sport* no. 7 (Aug. 20, 1899), p. 49.

32. Safford and Palacios, *Colombia*, pp. 249–51; Bushnell, *Making of Modern Colombia*, pp. 149–154.

33. *Lecturas para el Hogar; revista literaria, histórica e instructiva. Redactada exclusivamente por Soledad Acosta de Samper*, vol. 1, nos. 1–12 (Mar. 1905–Mar. 1906).

34. *El Hogar Católico*, serie 6a no. 51 (July 16, 1912), pp. 489–493.

35. *El Hogar Católico*, serie 6a no. 51 (July 16, 1912), pp. 523–524.

36. Bushnell, *Making of Modern Colombia*, pp. 155–165.

37. *Bogotá Ilustrado*, no. 5 (Mar. 30, 1907), pp. 72–74; no. 7 (June 18, 1907), pp. 106–109: *La Ilustración*, no. 2 (Sept. 1908), p. 21.

38. Londoño and Londoño, "Vida diaria," 358–359.

39. *La Ilustración*, no. 5 (Jan. 1909), p. 61; no. 6 (Mar. 1909).

40. *Sociedad de Mejoras Públicas* (Agosto 17, 1912), pp. portada-6, in FAES (M).

41. Felix Serret, *Viaje a Colombia, 1911–1912*, trans. and prologue by Luis Carlos Mantilla R., O.F.M. (Bogotá: Biblioteca V Centenario Colcultura, 1994), p. 70; Cámera de Comercio de Cali, Centro de Estudios Históricos y Sociales, "Santiago de Cali," *Tertulias del Cali Viejo* (Cali: XYZ Impresores, 1995), pp. 48–54, Banco de la República, Centro de Documentación Regional (BRCDR).

42. Williams and Guerrieri, *Culture and Customs in Colombia*, p. 64; Sala Valle del Cauca, *Despertar Vallecaucano*, no. 104 (Oct. 1990), p. 11, Biblioteca Departamental (Cali; BD).

43. *Cromos*, Oct. 25, 1965, pp. 18–20.

44. Serret, *Viaje a Colombia*, p. 272; *El Porvenir*, Nov. 10, 1910, Archivo Histórico, Archivo General del Distrito, Cartagena de Indias (AH); *Bogotá Ilustrado*, no. 3 (Jan. 1907), p. 38.

45. *El Porvenir*, Oct. 13, 1912, AH; Banner, *American Beauty*, pp. 257–261; Martínez Carreño, *Un siglo de moda*, p. 19.

46. *El Porvenir*, Nov. 15, 1910, AH.

CHAPTER 4

1. Bushnell, *Making of Modern Colombia*, pp. 161–169; Safford and Palacios, *Colombia*, pp. 271–276; Rodman, *Colombian Traveler*, p. 47.

2. Banner, *American Beauty*, pp. 166, 218.

3. Martínez Carreño, *Un siglo de moda*, p. 19.

4. *Cromos*, Jan. 1916–May 1917 (passim).

5. *Cromos*, May 12, 1917–Dec. 7, 1918.

6. *Tolima, revista ilustrada* 1 no. 2 (Sept. 8, 1918), front cover.

7. Bernardo Merizalde del Carmen, A. R., *Estudio de la costa colombiana del Pacífico*. (Bogotá: Imprenta del Estado Mayor General, 1921), pp. 80, 152.

8. Londoño and Londoño, "Vida diaria," p. 325; *Diario de la Costa*, Nov. 1918, Nov. 14, 1919.

9. *El Porvenir*, Nov. 11, 1919; Nov. 15, 1920; Nov. 16, 1921; Oct. 12, 1922; Nov. 16, 1922; Oct. 12, 1923; Nov. 9, 1923.

10. *Películas*, May 1919, June 1920, Dec. 1922; *El Porvenir*, Oct. 14, 1919; Londoño and Londoño, "Vida diaria," p. 366.

11. Londoño and Londoño, "Vida diaria," pp. 328–335, 354, 382; *Cromos*, 1919–1921 (passim).

12. *Cromos*, 1919–1921, covers.

13. *Cromos*, 1921–1924 covers; Feb. 18, 1922; Apr. 28, 1923; *Suplemento de la Revista Cromos*, Aug. 18, 1923.

14. *Suplemento de la Revista Cromos*, Mar. 30, 1923; May 26, 1923; June 2, 1923.

15. *Cartas sobre el feminismo* (Cartagena, 1925), Biblioteca Nacional (Bogotá; BN).

16. Bushnell, *Making of Modern Colombia*, p. 169.

17. Ibid., *Making of Modern Colombia*, p. 165; Londoño and Londoño, "Vida diaria", p. 330.

18. Londoño and Londoño, "Vida diaria," pp. 331, 342.

19. Ibid., "Vida diaria,", pp. 331, 343–344; Safford and Palacios, *Colombia*, p. 276.

20. Vásquez Toro, "Condición juridical," NHC IV, 32–33; Luz Gabriela Arango, *Mujer, religion e industria: Fabricato, 1923–1982* (Medellín: Universidad Externado de Antioquia, 1991), p. 303.

21. Velásquez Toro, "Condición juridical," NHC IV, pp. 22–23; Bushnell, *Making of Modern Colombia*, p. 175.

22. Velásquez Toro, "Condición juridical," NHC IV, pp. 19–20.

23. *Antioquia Histórica*, Oct. 1926, pp. 307–309, Universidad de Antioquia, Biblioteca General (Medellín; UABG); *Progreso*, Nov. 3, 1926 and Dec. 15, 1928, Fundación Antioqueña para los Estudios Sociales (Medellín; FAES).

24. Jorge Iván Marín Taborda, "María Cano," in *Las mujeres en la historia de Colombia, vol. 1*, pp. 157–160.

25. Ibid., pp. 162–171; Velásquez Toro, "Condición juridical," NHC IV, pp. 42–43; Bushnell, *Making of Modern Colombia*, p. 179.

26. "Entre nosotros se tiene por norma que la mujer no tiene criterio propio, y que siempre obra por acto reflejo del cura, del padre, del amigo. Creo haber educado mi criterio lo suficiente para orientarme." Cited in Marín Taborda, "María Cano," p. 171.

27. "No existían ciertas libertades y derechos que ahora se reconocen en la mujer. Pero entonces, como ahora, lo esencial era y sigue siendo movilizar a la gente; despertarla del marasmo; alinearla y poner in sus manos las banderas de sus tareas concretas. ¡Y que las mujeres ocupen su lugar!" Cited in Marín Taborda, "María Cano," p. 171.

28. Sala Valle del Cauca, *Despertar Vallecaucano* (Sept. 1989): 24–25, BD.

29. Uribe Celis, *La mentalidad del colombiano*, p. 49.

30. "Para que la humanidad sea mejor y mas bella . . . ," *Diario de la Costa*, Oct. 11, 1924, p. 5, AH.

31. "El día de la raza," *Diario de la Costa*, Oct. 12, 1929, AH.

32. "El reinado de Zoila I," *Diario de la Costa*, Oct. 8, 1925, p. 1; "El mundo estudiantil: mensaje real de doña Emilia I," ibid., Oct. 9, 1925; "La reina de los estudiantes del Tolima y los leprosos de Agua de Dios", ibid., Nov. 9, 1925, p. 3, all in AH.

33. *Diario de la Costa*, Nov. 14, 1927, p. 7, AH.

34. Concurso Nacional de Belleza, *Las más bellas: historia del Concurso Nacional de Belleza; Colombia, 60 años*. Cartagena de Indias: Junta Organizadora del Concurso Nacional de Belleza, 1994, pp. 15–16; "En 1922 también hubo reinado de belleza," *El Universal*, Nov. 9, 1984, p. 6.

35. Banner, *American Beauty*, pp. 249, 264, 269; Sarah Banet-Weiser, *The Most Beautiful Girl in the World* (Berkeley: University of California, 1999), pp. 36–37.

36. Banner, *American Beauty*, pp. 207–208.

37. *Las más bellas*, p. 17.

38. *Cromos*, Nov. 12, 1927.

39. Bushnell, *Making of Modern Colombia*, p. 180.

CHAPTER 5

1. Bushnell, *Making of Modern Colombia*, p. 180.

2. *Ibid.*, pp. 181–182; Safford and Palacios, *Colombia*, p. 288.

3. Bushnell, *Making of Modern Colombia*, p. 185; Safford and Palacios, *Colombia*, p. 289.

4. Bushnell, *Making of Modern Colombia*, pp. 183–184; Londoño and Londoño, "Vida diaria," p. 336.

5. For war coverage, see *Cromos*, Sept. 24, 1932; for Miss Universe and Miss Colombia, see *Cromos*, Apr. 16, 1932.

6. *Cromos*, Apr.–Dec. 1932 (passim); *Las más bellas*, pp. 18–21.

7. Londoño and Londoño, "Vida diaria," pp. 336–337, 349–350.

8. Bushnell, *Making of Modern Colombia*, pp. 185–90; Safford and Palacios, *Colombia*, pp. 290–296.

9. *Cromos*, 1934–1938 (passim); *Las más bellas*, pp. 22–25.

10. *Cromos*, Mar. 16, Sept. 7, 14, 21, Dec. 9, 1935.

11. Ibid., Dec. 15, 1935.

12. *Progreso*, no. 64, p. 1023, FAES.

13. Londoño and Londoño, "Vida diaria," p. 355.

14. Robert H. Davis, *Historical Dictionary of Colombia*, 2nd ed. (Metuchen, NJ: Scarecrow Press, 1993), pp. 430–433.

15. Londoño and Londoño, "Vida diaria," pp. 390–391.

16. Ibid., pp. 361; Davis, *Historical Dictionary*, pp. 422–423; Williams and Guerieri, *Culture and Customs*, pp. 49–55.

17. "Simboliza las glorias del pasado y los anhelos nobles de progreso y engrandecimiento material y moral de mi patria chica," *Diario de la Costa* 3, Nov. 16, 1937.

18. *El Fígaro*, Nov. 9, 1939; *Diario de la Costa*, Nov. 16, 1941; Nov. 6, 1943.

19. *El Fígaro*, Oct. 10, 1941, AH; Cámara de Comercio y Centro de Estudios Históricos y Sociales, Santiago de Cali, *Tertulias del "Cali Viejo," segundo libro*, (Cali: Impresora Feriva, 1998), BRCDR.

20. *Progreso*, Sept. 1939, pp. 80–81; Nov. 1939, pp. 144–145; Oct. 1941, pp. 869–875; all in FAES.

21. Ibid., Apr. 1940, FAES.

22. Velásquez Toro, "Condición juridical," pp. 27–30; Gabriela Peláez Echeverri, *La condición social de la mujer en Colombia* (Bogotá: Editorial Cromos, 1944), pp. 14–15, 64.

23. Safford and Palacios, *Colombia*, pp. 288–90; *Cromos*, 1937–1939 (passim).

24. *Cromos*, Nov. 12, 1938; Dec. 10, 1938.

25. Ibid., Oct. 21, 1938; Sept. 14, 1939.

26. Ibid., 1941–1944 (passim); Londoño and Londoño, "Vida diaria," pp. 338–346.

27. *Cromos*, May 10, 1941; May 16, 1942; Sept. 19, 1942.

28. Ibid., July 31, 1943.

29. Ibid., Oct. 13, 1945; Apr. 28, 1945.

30. *Diario de la Costa*, Nov. 1, 5, 1941; Oct. 31, 1943, Nov. 3–6, 1943.

31. Ibid., Nov. 1944.

32. Lucila Rubio de Laverde, *Ideales feministas* (Bogotá: Ediciones Nuevo Mundo, 1950), pp. i–v, 37, 115–125, 153–60.

33. Bushnell, *Making of Modern Colombia*, pp. 196–200.

34. *Cromos*, Sept. 27–29, Nov. 1947; *El Relator* 1–12 (Nov. 1947); *El Tiempo* 2–18 (Nov. 1947); *Las más bellas*, pp. 26–31.

35. Safford and Palacios, *Colombia*, pp. 318–319; Bushnell, *Making of Modern Colombia*, pp. 197–200; Velásquez Toro, "Condición juridical," p. 54.

36. Safford and Palacios, *Colombia*, p. 319; Bushnell, *Making of Modern Colombia*, pp. 201–204; *Cromos*, Jan.–Apr. 1948 (passim).

37. *El Relator*, Apr. 12–15, 1948; Bushnell, *Making of Modern Colombia*, p. 202.

CHAPTER 6

1. Herbert Braun, *The Assassination of Gaitán: Public Life and Urban Violence in Colombia* (Madison: University of Wisconsin Press, 1985), p. 171.

2. Bushnell, *Making of Modern Colombia*, pp. 203–204; Safford and Palacios, *Colombia*, pp. 346–347, 367–369.

3. Bushnell, *Making of Modern Colombia*, pp. 206–209; Safford and Palacios, *Colombia*, pp. 319–321.

4. Bushnell, *Making of Modern Colombia*, p. 205; Safford and Palacios, *Colombia*, pp. 347–351; Herbert Braun, "La dialéctica de la vida pública," in Rafael Pardo, comp., *El siglo pasado: Colombia, economía, política y sociedad* (Bogotá: Tercer Mundo, 2001): 215, 251.

5. Safford and Palacios, *Colombia*, pp. 319–321.

6. Londoño and Londoño, "Vida diaria," p. 355; *Cromos*, Mar. 12, 1949.

7. Londoño and Londoño, "Vida diaria," p. 370.

8. *Cromos*, 1949–1951 (passim).

9. Ibid., Jan. 8, 1949; Jan. 22, 1949; Oct. 18, 1949; Oct. 29, 1949.

10. Ibid., Jan. 8, 1949; Jan. 22, 1949; Feb. 12, 1949.

11. Ibid., Sept. 17, 1949; Sept. 23, 1950; July 7, 1951; *Gloria*, no. 31, July and Aug. 1951, pp. 21–23, 31–32.

12. *Las más bellas*, pp. 32–37, 295; *Cromos*, Sept. 17, 1949; Oct. 10, 1949; Nov. 5, 1949; Nov. 12, 1949; Nov. 19, 1949; Nov. 26, 1949; Jan. 21, 1950; Jan. 28, 1950; Feb. 18, 1950.

13. *Cromos*, May 28, 1949; Jan. 28, 1950; Feb. 18, 1950.

14. Ibid., Apr. 8, 1950; Dec. 15, 1951.

15. "1951: biografía de un año más," ibid., Dec. 29, 1951.

16. *Cromos*, Oct. 13, 1951.

17. *Las más bellas*, pp. 38–41, 295–296; *Cromos*, Nov. 11. 1951; Dec. 1, 1951; Dec. 15, 1951.

18. *El Relator*, Feb. 8–13, 1950; Nov. 7–13, 1951; Safford and Palacios, *Colombia*, p. 319.

19. *Progreso*, Dec. 1949, p. 27; *Gloria*, July and Aug. 1951, pp. 21–31.

20. Velásquez Toro, "Condición juridical," pp. 20–21; Archivo de Memoria Visual de Antioquia, Club Union, (CU 1), Archivo Histórico de Antioquia (Medellín; AHA); *El Tiempo* Nov. 4, 1951, p. 15.

21. Archivo de Memoria Visual de Antioquia, Fondo Carlos Rodriquez, AHA; Club Union, fotos 1274–1297 (CU 3).

22. *El Universal*, Nov. 6, 1955, p. 1; *El Fígaro*, Nov. 10, 1958.

23. Bushnell, *Making of Modern Colombia*, pp. 211–213; Michael Stanfield, "U.S. Military Aid and Violence in Colombia: Patterns and Perspectives," unpublished manuscript, March 2001.

24. Safford and Palacios, *Colombia*, pp. 321–22.

25. *Las más bellas*, pp. 42–47; *Relator*, Nov. 13, 1953; *Cromos*, Aug. 15–Dec. 19, 1953; Rojas also appeared at the opening of the 1954 "Vuelta a Colombia" bicycle race. See Londoño and Londoño, "Vida diaria," pp. 370–371.

26. *Las más bellas*, pp. 42–47, 296.

27. Safford and Palacios, *Colombia*, p. 324; Bushnell, *Making of Modern Colombia*, p. 216; *Cromos*, Aug. 15, 1953; *El Tiempo*, Nov. 6, 1953, pp. 4, 12.

28. Safford and Palacios, *Colombia*, p. 322–24; Bushnell, *Making of Modern Colombia*, p. 219–20.

29. Safford and Palacios, *Colombia*, p. 351–54; Bushnell, *Making of Modern Colombia*, p. 222.

30. *Cromos*, 1954 passim; Aug. 1, 1955. Miss USA and Miss Universe are now owned by Donald Trump and his partners, which explains a lot. See Banet-Weiser, *Most Beautiful Girl*, pp. 44–47.

31. *Cromos*, May 23–Dec. 12, 1955; *El Relator*, Nov. 2, 8, 13, 15, 1955; *Las más bellas*, pp. 48–53.

32. Williams and Guerrieri, *Culture and Customs*, p. 45; Rodman, *Colombia Traveler*, pp. 61–62; Bushnell, *Making of Modern Colombia*, p. 222.

33. *Cromos*, July 7, 15, 29, 1957.

34. Ibid., July 7, 15, 29, Aug. 19, 26, 1957.

35. Ibid., Sept. 16, Oct. 7, 14, 1957.

36. Ibid., Nov. 4, 1957.

37. Ibid. ("Nazly es una afortunada síntesis de la belleza americana y un símbolo de las virtudes afirmativas del pueblo chocoano . . .").

38. *Cromos*, Nov. 18, 1957.

39. Ibid., Nov. 11, 1957; *El Tiempo*, Nov. 4, 5, 12, 1957; *El Relator*, Nov. 4, 1957.

40. *Las más bellas*, pp. 54–59, 296; *Cromos*, Nov. 18, 1957.

41. *Cromos*, Nov. 25, Dec. 2, 1957.

42. Ibid., Dec. 2, 1957; Safford and Palacios, *Colombia*, p. 324; Bushnell, *Making of Modern Colombia*, p. 223; Velásquez Toro, "Condición jurídica," pp. 58–59.

43. *Cromos*, 1957–1958 (passim); *El Relator*, Nov. 4, 1957, p. 20.

44. *Cromos*, May 19, June 23, 30, Aug. 4, 1958; *El Relator*, June 20, 25, 1958.

45. *Cromos*, June 16, July 14, Aug. 4, 25, 1958 ("el nombre de Colombia será identificado con una figura dulce y poética de mujer . . ."); "Alberto Vargas," *Wikipedia*, accessed Oct. 10, 2010, http://en.wikipedia.org/wiki/Alberto.

46. *Cromos*, Aug. 4, 11, 25, 1958 ("Pienso en Colombia y en Caldas, y en las mujeres colombianas que están luchando por una patria mejor").

47. *Cromos*, Aug. 25, 1958; *El Tiempo*, Aug. 26, 1958, p. 1; *Las más bellas*, pp. 60–65.

48. *Cromos*, Sept. 1, 8, 29, 1958; *El Tiempo*, July 27, 1958; *El Relator*, July 28, 29, 1958.

49. *El Relator*, July 17, 1958, p. 11.

CHAPTER 7

1. Bushnell, *Making of Modern Colombia*, pp. 225–225; Safford and Palacios, *Colombia*, pp. 324–325, 353; Rodman, *Colombia Traveler*, pp. 63–64.

2. Safford and Palacios, *Colombia*, pp. 299–309; Safford, *Ideal of the Practical*, pp. 240–242.

3. Banet-Weiser, *Most Beautiful Girl*, pp. 2–9, 186–187.

4. *Colombia Turística*, Aug. 1958; Banet-Weiser, *Most Beautiful Girl*, pp. 190–194.

5. *Colombia Turística*, Aug, Sept./Oct. 1958 ("Porque ella ya no es ella sino su raza").

6. *Colombia Turística*, Oct./Nov. 1959, June 17, 1960, July 1961, Dec. 5, 1963.

7. *Colombia Ilustrada*, Jan.-Apr. 1972, pp. 19–29; Jaime Sierra García, *Diccionario folclórico antioqueño* (Medellín: Universidad de Antioquia, 1983), pp. 71–75, 121–128.

8. Peter Wade, *Music, Race, and Nation: Música Tropical in Colombia* (Chicago: University of Chicago Press, 2000), pp. 44–52, 141–146, 187, 206–208.

9. *Cromos*, Oct. 19, 26, Nov. 9, 1959.

10. Ibid., Nov. 16, 23, 1959; *Las más bellas*, pp. 66–71, 296.

11. *Las más bellas*, pp. 66–71, 296; *El Tiempo*, Nov. 1, 1959, Nov. 11, 1969; *El Universal*, Nov. 10, 11, 17, 1959; *El Relator*, Nov. 13, 1959; *Cromos*, July 23, 1962.

12. *El Universal*, Nov. 15, 19, 1959; *El Tiempo*, Nov. 9, 1959.

13. *El Universal*, Oct. 1, 1959, Nov. 1, 6, 15, 1960, Oct. 30, 1963.

14. *El Relator*, Nov. 2–12, 1959.

15. *El Relator*, Nov. 4, Dec. 22, 27, 1959.

16. *Cali, ciudad de América* (Cali: Carbajal y Cia, 1967), pp. 66–67; "VI Pan American Games, Cali, Colombia," http://www.la84foundation.org/8saa/PanAm/cali .htm.

17. *El Tiempo*, Sept. 6, 1961; *Noticias Culturales*, 1961–1975, passim.

18. *Cromos*, 1961–1964, passim.

19. Ibid., July 10, 1961, July 2, 9, 1962; *Mujer*, Jan. 1962.

20. *El Tiempo*, Nov. 15, 1961; *Las más bellas*, pp. 72–77, 297.

21. *Mujer*, Jan. 1962; *Cromos*, July 9, 1962.

22. *Cromos*, Oct. 9, 1961; "Advertising: She Does," *Time*, Aug. 11, 1967, http:// www.time.com/time/magazine/article/0,9171,899732,00.html.

23. *Cromos*, July 16, 1962, Aug. 20, 1962; *Mujer*, Aug.–Sept. 1962, p. 26.

24. *Mujer*, Aug.–Sept. 1962; *Cromos*, July 23, Oct. 22, Nov. 12, 1962.

25. *Mujer*, Feb. 1962, pp. 21–25; Davis, *Historical Dictionary*, p. 347; *El valle del cauca*, p. 21.

26. *Cromos*, Nov. 19, 1962; *Mujer*, Aug.–Sept. 1962, pp. 14–15; *Las más bellas*, pp. 78–83.

27. *El Universal*, Nov. 10, 1962, p. 6; Simpson, *Xuxa*, pp. 2–6, 38; *Cromos*, Sept. 21, 1964, p. 52; Carl N. Degler, *Neither Black nor White: Slavery and Race Relations in Brazil and the United States* (Madison: University of Wisconsin Press, 1986).

28. *Cromos*, Nov. 19, 1962.

29. *Mujer*, Jan.–Feb. 1964, pp. 8–13.

30. *Cromos*, July 20, 1964.

31. Ibid., Dec. 16, 1963, Nov. 9, 1964; *Mujer*, Aug. 1965, pp. 17–18.

32. *Cromos*, July 29, Aug. 5, Nov. 2, 1963, July 6, 1964.

33. "Leonor destila feminidad por todos los poros," *Mujer*, Jan.–Feb. 1964, p. 17.

34. *Cromos*, Nov. 18, 25, 1963; *El Universal*, Nov. 10, 14, 1963, p. 1.

35. "Las gentes necesitan sus pequeños dioses a quienes adorer," *El Tiempo*, Dec. 13, 1963, p. 10; Nov. 16, 1964, p. 14; Dec. 12, 1964, p. 9; *Cromos*, July 29, 1963.

36. Bushnell, *Making of Modern Colombia*, pp. 225–230, 291; Rodman, *Colombia Traveler*, p. 68.

37. Bushnell, *Making of Modern Colombia*, pp. 244–245; Safford and Palacios, *Colombia*, pp. 354–359.

38. Davis, *Historical Dictionary*, p. 492; Safford and Palacios, *Colombia*, pp. 300, 358–359; Bushnell, *Making of Modern Colombia*, pp. 244–245; *Cromos*, Aug. 9, 1965.

39. *Cromos*, Oct. 18, 1965; Uribe Celis, *La mentalidad del colombiano*, pp. 94–95.

40. Bushnell, *Making of Modern Colombia*, pp. 239, 243; Safford and Palacios, *Colombia*, pp. 300–301, 326–327.

41. "La vida es una cosa, que nos imponen sin nuestro consentimiento." *Mujer*, Sept. 1964, pp. 10–12.

42. ". . . la política debe ser actividad exclusiva de los hombres. Nosotras debemos perfilarnos hacia el hogar." *Las más bellas*, pp. 92, 90–95.

43. *Antioquia Turística*, no. 1, Apr. 30, 1965.

44. *El Tiempo*, Nov. 16, 19, 1965; *Mujer*, Apr. 1965, pp. 16–17; May 1965, pp. 8–9; Aug. 1965, pp. 17–18.

45. *Cromos*, Oct. 19, 1964; Nick Bromwell, *Tomorrow Never Knows: Rock and Psychedelics in the 1960s* (Chicago: University of Chicago Press, 2002).

46. *Mujer*, Apr. 1966, pp. 16–17; Nov. 1966, pp. 13–16.

47. Ibid., Nov. 1967, pp. 32, 47; *Cromos*, Aug. 7, 1967.

48. *Cromos*, July 10, 1967, Dec. 4, 1967; *El Tiempo*, Nov. 5, 1966, p. 8.

49. *El Tiempo*, Nov. 5, 1966, p. 8; Nov. 7, 1966, p. 12; *Mujer* May 1967, pp. 28–29: *Cromos*, Oct. 3, 1966; Kemper, *Costume*, pp. 147–148.

50. *Las más bellas*, pp. 96–113.

51. *Cromos*, Oct. 30, 1967, July 31, 1967.

52. *Mujer*, Aug. 1966, pp. 20–22; May 1968, pp. 10–12.

53. *Cromos*, July 11, 25, 1966; *Mujer*, Aug. 1967, pp. 14–15.

54. *Cromos*, July 1, 1968; Aug. 19, 1968.

55. Ibid., Nov. 27, 1967, Oct. 31, 1966; Ricardo Rondón, "Leonor González Mina. El alma de la Negra Grande de Colombia," Sept. 30, 2004, http://www.caribenet.info /oltre_rondon_negragrande_colombia.asp?l=

56. *Cromos*, Nov. 18, 1968.

57. Ibid., Sept. 30, 1968; "Marta Traba," Sept. 28, 2010, http://es.wikipedia.org /wiki/Marta_Traba.

58. *Cromos*, Dec. 9, 1968.

59. Ibid., Dec. 16, 1968.

60. Ibid. ("una comedia para vender cosméticos, whiskey y desaburrir del tedio a la alta sociedad").

61. Ibid. ("Cartagena durante el reinado es una ciudad sucia donde la gente tiene la piel negra"; ". . . coqueta, casi morbosa satisfacción de su metamorfosis sexual. La ambigüedad de ser confundidos con el eterno femenino, ejercía en ellos una secreta excitación, cierta nostalgia y devoción al culto de lo prohibido").

62. "Voice of the Women's Liberation Movement," CWLU Herstory Website, October 1968, http://www.uic.edu/orgs/cwluherstory/CWLUArchive/voices/voices 4-1.html.

63. *Cromos*, Oct. 28, 1968 ("Algo bello es algo que es. Yo diría que la belleza es lo cotidiano, y lo bello es lo real. . . . la mujer bella es la que vive su vida, que no se preocupa sólo por la belleza física y por estar bien vestida. La mujer bella de hoy es la inconforme con los estatutos, con las normas dictadas y toda esa cosa . . ."); Elisabeth Fog, "María Victoria Uribe Alarcón," Aug. 31, 2007, http://www.universia.net.co /galeria-de-cientificos/ciencias-sociales-derecho-y-ciencias-politicas/maria-victoria -uribe-alarcon/tambien-hay-tiempo-para-el.html; Banet-Weisner, *Most Beautiful Girl*, p. 210.

64. *Las más bellas*, pp. 114–119; *El Tiempo*, Nov. 11, 1968, p. 15 ("Considero que debe ser vital . . . Pues activa, obviamente").

CHAPTER 8

1. Bushnell, *Making of Modern Colombia*, pp. 233–236, 241.

2. Bushnell, *Making of Modern Colombia*, pp. 238, 276–277.

3. *Cromos*, Dec. 13, 1971; *Mujer*, Oct. 1973, pp. 26–31.

4. Bushnell, *Making of Modern Colombia*, pp. 229–230; Rodman, *Colombia Traveler*, p. 73; Safford and Palacios, *Colombia*, pp. 330–331.

5. *Mujer*, July 1969, pp. 6–11.

6. Ibid., Mar. 1970, pp. 16–17.

7. Ibid., Sept. 1969, pp. 24–26.

8. *Cromos*, July 12, 1971, pp. 8–9, 29–31, 65; Dec. 20, 1971, pp. 58–63.

9. *Mujer*, Aug. 1972, 25–28.

10. *Cromos*, Dec. 20, 1971, pp. 58–63; Sept. 10, 1973, pp. 47–49.

11. Ibid., Dec. 20, 1971, pp. 58–63; Sept. 10, 1973, pp. 47–49; Schneider Institute for Health Policy, Brandeis University, "Substance Abuse: The Nation's Number One Health Problem," Feb. 2001, http://www.rwjf.org/files/publications/other/SubstanceAbuseChartbook.pdf (pp. 13–16).

12. *Cromos*, Aug. 24, 1970, p. 63; Oct. 19, 1970, p. 63; Oct. 25, 1971, pp. 28–29; Aug. 28, 1972.

13. Ibid., July 10, 1972, pp. 32–35.

14. Ibid., Sept. 10, 1973; Oct. 22, 1973; Dec. 4, 1974.

15. *Mujer*, Aug.1969, pp. 14–15; "La mujer colombiana y su responsabilidad en el desarrollo del país," *Cromos*, Nov. 3, 1969, pp. 26–29.

16. *Cromos*, July 20, 1970; "la mujer solo se libera cuando se independiza sexual y economicamente," *Mujer de América*, Oct. 1971, pp. 62–63.

17. *Mujer*, Mar. 1970, pp. 28–29; May 1970, pp. 50–53; Mar. 1972, pp. 17–21.

18. *Cromos*, Nov. 15, 1971, pp. 62–65; Nov. 29, 1971, pp. 66–69; Nov. 8, 1971.

19. *Mujer*, Jan./Feb. 1970, pp. 8–19.

20. Ibid., June 1979, pp. 10–11, 66–67.

21. Ibid., Aug. 1970, pp. 12–17.

22. *El Tiempo*, Apr. 18, 26, 1998.

23. *Mujer*, June 1970, pp. 30–36; July 1970, pp. 10–13; *Cromos*, Nov. 29, 1971, pp. 70–73.

24. *Mujer de América*, Jan./Feb. 1972, pp. 30–36; Aug. 1973, pp. 8–9.

25. *Cromos*, Nov. 24, 1969, p. 16; Dec. 1, 1969, p. 34; Nov. 9, 1970, p. 67.

26. *Mujer*, June 1969, pp. 22–24, 46–47; May 1972, pp. 18–20; Sept. 1973, pp. 77–80.

27. Ibid., Apr. 1971), p. 75; May 1971, p. 32; June 1972, pp. 66–67; July 1973, pp. 56–57; Jan. 1974, p. 56.

28. *Mujer de América*, June 1971, p. 49; Dec. 1971, pp. 14, 80–82.

29. *Antioquia Turística*, Mar./Apr. 1969, pp. 28–29, 32; Jan./Feb. 1970, pp. 45, 55; *Cromos*, July 27, 1970, pp. 78–9; Aug. 30, 1971, pp. 48–9; Arango, *Mujer, religión e industria*, pp. 118–120.

30. *Cromos*, July 14, 1969, pp. 62–63; Oct. 13, 1969; Sept. 7, 1970, pp. 46–49; Oct. 27, 1969, pp. 93–95; *El Tiempo*, Nov. 5, 1969, p. 9; Nov. 9, 1969, p. 9; Nov. 12, 1969, p. 24.

31. "Stripped of their earthly splendor for the first time, they marched by, preceded by the universal queen: the soybean queen, the green-squash queen, the banana queen, the meal yucca queen, the guava queen, the coconut queen, the kidney-bean queen, the 255-mile-long-string-of iguana-eggs queen, and all the others who are omitted so as not to make this account interminable." "Big Mama's Funeral," in Gabriel García Márquez, *Collected Stories* (New York: Harper and Row, 1984), p. 199.

32. *Cromos*, Nov. 10, 1969, pp. 8–11; Nov. 24, 1969, pp. 102–107; Dec. 8, 1969, p. 12; *Las más bellas*, pp. 120–125.

33. *El Tiempo*, Nov. 12, 1970, p. 13; Nov. 13, 1970, p. 12; Nov. 14, 1970, p. 5.

34. *El Universal*, Nov. 9, 13, 1969; Nov. 7, 1970, p. 3; Nov. 1, 1972, p. 1; *Las más bellas*, pp. 130, 132, 154.

35. *El Universal*, Nov. 1, 6, 1970; Nov. 7, 1969; Oct. 27, 1972; *El Espectador: Edición de la Costa*, Nov. 4, 6, 1978; *El Tiempo*, Nov. 7, 1971, p. 16A; Nov. 11, 1971, p. 1, *Las más bellas*, pp. 132–134 ("la mujer colombiana no es negra").

36. *Las más bellas*, pp. 132–137; Rodman, *Colombia Traveler*, p. 143.

37. *Las más bellas*, pp. 138–143, 150–155, 162–167; "Concurso Nacional de Belleza de Colombia," Nov. 16, 2010, http://es.wikipedia.org/wiki/Concurso_Nacional_de_Belleza_de_Colombia.

38. *Revista Occidental*, Jan./Feb. 1977, p. 13; Oct. 1980, p. 27.

39. "La caleña sabe que la admiran y le gusta que la admiran." *Guía práctica y turística de Cali* (Cali: Prensa Moderna, 1978), pp. 5–6.

40. Ibid., p. 6.

41. *Mujer*, Oct. 1973, p. 14; June 1974, pp. 83–86.

42. *El Tiempo*, Nov. 12, 1973, p. 16A; *Las más bellas*, pp. 144–149 ("Ser reina es una tarea difícil, pero ser candidata a reina de Colombia es 'para machos'"; "¿Si hay un Watergate en Estados Unidos y unas colinas de Golán en el Oriente Medio, por qué el reinado de Cartagena no ha de tener sus crisis?")

43. *Las más bellas*, pp. 144–149; 174–179 ("En una época como la presente, dominada por la violencia, desmoralizada por la corrupción, minada por la droga, polucionada por los funcionarios inescrupulosos, la belleza feminina es una de las pocas cosas que reconcilian al hombre con la vida . . .").

44. *El Tiempo*, Nov. 13, 1971, p. 11A; *Cromos*, July 11, 1974, pp. 12–15; July 18, 1974; Aug. 7, 1974, pp. 51–57; Nov. 13, 1974, pp. 54–58; *El Tiempo*, Nov. 7, 1974, p. 1B; Nov. 9, 1974, p. 1B.

45. *Cromos*, Aug. 28, 1974; *El Tiempo*, Nov. 11, 1975, p. 1B; *Las más bellas*, pp. 156, 168; *El Universal*, Nov. 7, 1975.

46. *Cromos*, Oct. 1, 1975, pp. 92–93; Oct. 15, 1975, pp. 100–101; Nov. 12, 1975, pp. 4–10; Nov. 19, 1975; *El Tiempo*, Nov. 12, 1975, p. 1; Nov. 14, 1975, p. 7B; Cetino, *Jaque a la reina*, p. 192; *Las más bellas*, p. 160; *El Tiempo, Lecturas Dominicales*, Nov. 9, 1975, p. 3.

47. *Las más bellas*, p. 168 ("el prototipo de la belleza internacional, con ojos azules, pelo castaño, piel blanca y medias perfectas").

48. *El Tiempo*, Nov. 13, 1977, pp. 16A; *Las más bellas*, pp. 168–173.

49. *El Tiempo*, Nov. 14, 1977, p. 16A; *Las más bellas*, pp. 288–289; *Cromos*, July 23, 1975, pp. 6–13.

50. *El Tiempo*, Nov. 9, 1978, p. 5D; Nov. 8, 1978, p. 1B; *Cromos*, Nov. 5, 1975, pp. 82–83.

51. *Cromos*, 1975–1978, passim; July 28, 1976, pp. 58–61; Nov. 1, 1978, pp. 36–45; *El Universal*, Nov. 10, 1976; Nov. 17, 1976, pp. 1, 6.

52. *Cromos*, Oct. 15, 1979, pp. 20–23; U.S. Library of Congress, "Colombia: Drugs and Society," 1988, http://countrystudies.us/colombia/59.htm.

53. Paul Gootenberg, *Andean Cocaine: The Making of a Global Drug* (Chapel Hill: University of North Carolina Press, 2008), pp. 301–12; U.S. Library of Congress, "Colombia: Drugs and Society," 1988, http://countrystudies.us/colombia/59.htm; *Cromos*, Sept. 3, 1975, pp. 96–97; "Aquí el único porvenir es la prostitución," Sept. 24, 1975.

CHAPTER 9

1. Bushnell, *Making of Modern Colombia*, pp. 268–277.

2. U.S. government estimates track a tenfold increase in the production of domestic marijuana, from 2.2 million pounds in 1981 to 22 million pounds in 2006, worth $35.8 billion, making it the top cash crop in the United States. See Jon Gettman, "Marijuana Production in the United States (2006)," *The Bulletin of Cannabis Reform*. http://www.drugscience.org/Archive/bcr2/intro.html.

3. Bushnell, *Making of Modern Colombia*, pp. 249–253, 257–261, 276–278.

4. *Despertar Vallecaucano* 105 (Dec. 1980): 42 ("our reality is horror").

5. Safford and Palacios, *Colombia*, pp. 359–360; Bushnell, *Making of Modern Colombia*, pp. 246, 253–254; Davis, *Historical Dictionary*, pp. 341–342.

6. Bushnell, *Making of Modern Colombia*, p. 256.

7. *El Espectador: Edición de la costa*, Nov. 2, 5, 8, 1979.

8. Ibid., Nov. 2, 4, 5, 1980; Nov. 9, 10, 1981.

9. *Cromos*, Aug. 6, 1979, pp. 83–89.

10. *El Tiempo*, 1979–1981 (passim); *Cromos*, 1979–1983 (passim).

11. *Cromos*, Nov. 12, 1979, pp. 150–153, 190–197; *Las más bellas*, pp. 180–185; Lowell Bergman, "U.S. Companies Tangled in Web of Drug Dollars," *New York Times*, Oct. 10, 2000, http://www.columbia.edu/cu/fehdp/corp1.html.

12. "En Colombia hay discriminación racial," *Carrusel*, Oct. 12, 1979; "Distribución geográfica de la belleza colombiana," *El Tiempo*, Nov. 6, 1980, p. 2-E.

13. *Cromos*, July 29, 1980, pp. 66–68; Nov. 7, 11, 18, 1980; *Carrusel*, Oct. 3, 1980, p. 7; Nov. 13, 1981; Cetina, *Jaque a la reina*, p. 24.

14. *Cromos*, Nov. 18, 1980, pp. 100–117; *El Espectador: Edición de la costa*, Nov. 13, 1980, p. 3B; *Las más bellas*, pp. 186–191.

15. *Revista del Jueves*, Nov. 5, 12, 1981; Jaime Jaramillo Panesso, *Con olor a medallo* (Medellín: Galaxia Impresores, 1989), pp. 101–103.

16. *Cromos*, July 30, 1979, pp. 53–4, 59–60, 102 ("Hemos ganado una reina, pero hemos perdido una hija . . ."; "propriedad del concurso de Miss Universe y dejó de pertenecer a su familia").

17. Ibid., July 28, 1981, pp. 94–97; "Miss Universe," Nov. 28, 2010, http://en.wikipedia.org/wiki/Miss_Universe.

18. *Cromos*, Aug. 4, 1980, pp. 89–90; Aug. 25, 1981, pp. 45–52, 54–62.

19. Ibid., Aug. 25, 1981, pp. 45–52, 54–62.

20. *Cromos*, Aug. 25, 1981, pp. 45–52, 54–62.

21. Ibid., Sept. 8, 1981, pp. 30–34.

22. "Para que usted vea cómo un peón se puede comer a una reina." Cetina, *Jaque a la reina*, pp. 79–80; *Las más bellas*, pp. 192–97; *Cromos*, Nov. 17, 1981, pp. 8–12, 35–43.

23. *El Espectador: Edición de la costa*, Nov. 16, 1981.

24. "Éstas ya no son pa'l pueblo, ni pa' divertirse, ni pa' cantar, ni pa' bailar. Se convirtieron en pura 'tomata.'" *Cromos*, July 7, 1981, p. 57.

25. Ibid., July 8, 1980, pp. 70–77; July 7, 1981, pp. 54–60; Oct. 20, 1981, pp. 144–145.

26. *El Espectador: Edición de la costa*, Nov. 5, 1982, p. 9A; Nov. 10, 1982, p. 1.

27. *Cromos*, July 27, 1982, pp. 44–47.

28. Ibíd., Sept. 28, 1982, pp. 79–81; Nov. 23, 1982, pp. 40–43; *El Tiempo*, Nov. 15, 16, 18, 1982; *Las más bellas*, pp. 198–203; *El Espectador*, Nov. 16, 1982, p. 1B.

29. *Cromos*, Oct. 26, 1982, pp. 134–135; Nov. 12, 1982, pp. 10–15; Bushnell, *Making of Modern Colombia*, pp. 270–271.

30. *Cromos*, Oct. 26, 1982, pp. 54–60; "Aquí nace el bazuco," Aug. 23, 1983; Sept. 6, 1983, pp. 41–44.

31. *Cromos*, Sept. 6, 1983, pp. 16–19.

32. Medellín police street interview with author, January 1985, Medellín, Colombia.

33. *Cromos*, Aug. 2, 1983, pp. 20–23.

34. Safford and Palacios, *Colombia*, pp. 339–340, 369.

35. *Cromos*, Sept. 27, 1983, pp. 80–82; Oct. 4, 1983, pp. 49–51; Oct. 11, 1983, pp. 78–81; Oct. 18, 1983, pp. 84–89; *El Tiempo*, Nov. 11, 1983, p. 1C; Nov. 13, 1983, p. ultima A; *El Universal*, 14, 15 nov. 1983; *Las más bellas*, pp. 204–209; Cetina, *Jaque a la reina*, p. 83.

36. *El Universal*, Nov. 3, 1983, p. 4; Nov. 5, 1983, p. 5; Nov. 6, 1983; *El Espectador: Edición de la costa*, Nov. 8, 1983, p. 1.

37. *El Tiempo*, Nov. 11, 1983, p. 2D; *Cromos*, Nov. 22, 1983, p. 87.

38. *El Espectador: Edición de la costa*, Nov. 3, 1983, p. 3; Nov. 14, 1983, p. 14A; *El Universal*, Nov. 13, 1983, p. 1; Nov. 14, 1983, p. 2; *Las más bellas*, pp. 204–209; Simpson, *Xuxa*, passim.

39. *Cromos*, Nov. 15, 1983, pp. 71–74 ("la apoteosis del ridículo, la confirmación annual del machismo y en mi caso particular una necesidad").

40. Ibid., Nov. 22, 1983, pp. 86–89.

41. *Carrusel,* Nov. 4, 1983, pp. 4–6, 22–23; Nov. 11, 1983; *Cromos,* Nov. 8, 1983, pp. 69–119; Nov. 15, 1983, pp. 79–82.

42. *La Cabala* no. 1 (1982): 13; *Actualidad* no. 130 (1988): 36–37; Elssy Bonilla de Ramos, "Publicidad y sexualidad: ¿El poder en lo irrelevante?" *Texto y Contexto* (May-Aug. 1984): 185–200; Rodrigo Parra Sandoval, "A propósito de: 'Belleza y poder. La publicidad: ¿El poder de lo irrelevante? De Elssy Bonilla de Ramos.'" *Texto y Contexto* (Mayo-Aug. 1984): 255–257.

43. Elsa Ruiz, "La mujer en la ciudad," in *Ciudad: Revista de Asuntos Urbanos* 1 no. 1 (June 1983): 116–117; Fundación Grupo 80, *El Valle del Cauca* (Cali: Albon S.A., n.d. [1980?]: pp. 6–7.

44. Safford and Palacios, *Colombia,* pp. 308–309, 315, 361–369; Bushnell, *Making of Modern Colombia,* pp. 252, 262–63; *Cromos,* Sept. 25, 1984, pp. 16–19.

45. Bushnell, *Making of Modern Colombia,* pp. 246–247, 255; *Cromos,* Aug. 21, 1984, pp. 4–13.

46. *Cromos,* Oct. 16, 1984, pp. 34–37.

47. Safford and Palacios, *Colombia,* pp. 364–367; Bushnell, *Making of Modern Colombia,* p. 265.

48. Gootenberg, *Andean Cocaine,* p. 313; Bushnell, *Making of Modern Colombia,* p. 263; *Cromos,* Dec. 18, 1984, pp. 128–155.

49. *Cromos,* Oct. 9, 1984, pp. 30–47; Bushnell, *Making of Modern Colombia,* p. 247.

50. *Cromos,* Nov. 13, 1984, pp. 14–24, Nov. 27, 1984, pp. 86–91; *Carrusel,* Oct. 5, 1984, pp. 10–13; *El Tiempo,* Nov. 11, 1984, p. 4A, Nov. 13, 1984, p. 1C, Nov. 13, 1984, p. 1, Nov. 14, 1984, p. última A; *Las más bellas,* pp. 210–215; Cetina, *Jaque a la reina,* pp. 142–144.

51. *Cromos,* Feb. 25, 1985, pp. 26–29; May 6, 1985, pp. 26–31; July 2, 1985, pp. 12–17; Oct. 15, 1985, pp. 36–41.

52. Ibid., July 2, 1985, pp. 12–17; Oct. 15, 1985, pp. 36–41.

53. Ibid., Sept. 2, 1985, pp. 30–34; Oct. 28, 1985, pp. 24–31; "Rafael Samudio Molina," Nov. 6, 2010, http://es.wikipedia.org/wiki/Rafael_Samudio_Molina.

54. *Cromos,* July 8, 1985, pp. 56–61; Aug. 20, 1985, pp. 74–75.

55. Ibid., July 22, 1985, pp. 84–88, 96–98, 100–103; Aug. 20, 1985, pp. 56–58; Sept. 16, 1985, pp. 16–23.

56. Ibid., May 27, 1985, pp. 46–49; Oct. 7, 1985, pp. 98–101; Sept. 30, 1985, pp. 64–66; Oct. 21, 1985, pp. 46–49; Dr. Vic Camp, Department of Geological Sciences, San Diego State University, "How Volcanoes Work: Nevado del Ruiz (1985)" http://www.geology.sdsu.edu/how_volcanoes_work/Nevado.html.

57. *Cromos,* Sept. 30, 1985, pp. 68–71; Oct. 15, 1985, pp. 60–66.

58. Ibid., Sept. 16, 1985, pp. 60–63; Oct. 7, 1985, pp. 66–73; Oct. 21, 1985, pp. 54–65; Oct. 28, 1985, pp. 94–107; *Carrusel,* Nov. 1, 1985.

59. *El Espectador: Edición de la costa,* Nov. 1, 1985, p. 1; Nov. 3, 1985, p. 10a; *El Tiempo,* Nov. 11, 1985, p. 1b.

60. *Cromos,* Nov. 14, 1985, pp. 120–139.

61. Ibid., Nov. 14, 1985, pp. 139–140; *El Tiempo,* Nov. 7, 1985, p. 1; Ana Carrigan,

The Palace of Justice: A Colombian Tragedy (New York: Four Walls Eight Windows, 1993), pp. 215–216, 227–228.

62. *El Tiempo*, Nov. 7, 1985, pp. 1, 6a; Carrigan, *Palace of Justice*, pp. 59–60, 114, 118–120, 123–124, 131, 137, 148.

63. Carrigan, *Palace of Justice*, pp. 231, 245–247, 251, 257, 270, 272–273; *El Tiempo*, Nov. 8, 1985, pp. 1, 8a; Nov. 9, 1985, pp. 1, 2a; Nov. 10, 1985, pp. 1, 8a; "Un video inédito confirma que un magistrado salió vivo del Palacio de Justicia: Luego apareció asesinado," *Semana.com*, Jan. 4, 2011, http://www.semana.com/wf_InfoArticulo.aspx ?idArt=105903.

64. *Cromos*, Nov. 14, 1985, p. 144 ("debido a la absurda tragedia vivida por la nación).

65. Ibid., Nov. 14, 1985, pp. 145–150; *El Tiempo*, Nov. 9, 1985, p. 1B.

66. *Cromos*, Nov. 14, 1985, pp. 14–21; *El Tiempo*, Nov. 13, 1985, pp. 1B, 2B; *Las más bellas*, pp. 216–221.

67. Dr. Vic Camp, Department of Geological Sciences, SDSU, "How Volcanoes Work: Nevado del Ruiz (1985)," http://www.geology.sdsu.edu/how_volcanoes_work /Nevado.html; *Cromos*, Nov. 19, 1985, pp. 8–21, 102–107.

68. *El Tiempo*, Nov. 15, 1985, pp. 1, 1C, 7C, 8A, 8C; Nov. 16, 1985, p. última-F.

69. *Cromos*, Nov. 25, 1985, pp. 62–64; *Consigna*, Nov. 17, 1986, pp. 42–43.

CONCLUSION

1. Safford and Palacios, *Colombia*, pp. 360–361; María Victoria Llorente, Rodolfo Escobedo, Camilo Echandía, and Mauricio Rubio, "Violencia homicida y estructuras criminales en Bogotá," *Sociologias* (Porto Alegre, Brazil), no. 8 (July–Dec. 2002): 172–205.

2. Safford and Palacios, *Colombia*, pp. 362–364.

3. Bushnell, *Making of Modern Colombia*, pp. 258–259, 265–266.

4. Safford and Palacios, *Colombia*, pp. 364–366; Bushnell, *Making of Modern Colombia*, p. 265.

5. "Revealed: The Secrets of the Murderous Castaño Brothers," *The Telegraph*, accessed Dec. 2011, http://www.telegraph.co.uk/news/worldnews/southamerica/colom bia/3391789/Revealed-The-secrets-of-Colombias-murderous-Castano-brothers .html.

6. Bushnell, *Making of Modern Colombia*, pp. 251, 267, 279.

7. *Las más bellas*, p. 228.

8. Ibid., pp. 222–276, 291–293; Claver Téllez, *El lado oscuro*, p. 102; Cetina, *Jaque a la reina*, pp. 83–109.

9. Loveman and Davies, *Guerrilla Warfare*, p. 259.

10. "Shakira," *Wikipedia*, accessed Dec. 2011, http://en.wikipedia.org/wiki /Shakira.

11. "Yo soy Betty, la fea," Wikipedia, accessed December 2011, http://en.wikipedia .org/wiki/Yo_soy_Betty_la_fea.

12. *Cromos*, Nov. 12, 2001, pp. 52–80.

13. *Carrusel*, Nov. 23, 2001, p. 16.

14. *Aló*, Nov. 13–29, 2001, p. 28 ("El triunfo es para mis coterráneos, mi familia y mi raza").

15. *Carrusel*, Nov. 23, 2001, pp. 16–17.

16. Gregory J. Lobo, "La bella y la bestia: Colombia entre el consenso y la coerción, o sobre el multiculturalismo y la violencia racial neoliberal," *Revista Iberoamericana* 74, no. 223 (Apr.-June 2008): 515–519.

17. Colombia has the third largest population of African descent on the mainland of the Americas, after Brazil and the United States.

18. Ulrich Oslender, "Another History of Violence: The Production of 'Geographies of Terror' in Colombia's Pacific Coast Region," *Latin American Perspectives* 35, no. 5 (Sept. 2008): 85.

19. Oslender, "Another History of Violence," pp. 85–91; Lobo, "La bella y la bestia," pp. 522.

20. Oslender, "Another History of Violence," pp. 92–97; Lobo, "La bella y la bestia," pp. 520–523.

21. Oslender, "Another History of Violence," pp. 96–97; Lobo, "La bella y la bestia," pp. 525–526.

22. Michael Stanfield, "Ayuda militar estadounidense y violencia en Colombia," conference paper at La Construcción de la Paz y la Cooperación Internacional en Colombia—Universidad Javeriana (Bogotá, July 2001).

23. U.S. Department of State, Foreign Terrorist Organizations, http://www.state.gov/s/ct/rls/other/des/123085.htm.

24. Forrest Hylton, "The Cold War That Didn't End: Paramilitary Modernization in Medellín, Colombia," in *A Century of Revolution: Insurgent and Counterinsurgent Violence during Latin America's Long Cold War*, ed. Greg Grandin and Gilbert M. Joseph, pp. 338–367 (Durham: Duke University Press, 2010).

25. "Colombia Timeline," *BBC News*, http://news.bbc.co.uk/2/hi/americas/1212827.stm; "Profile: Alvaro Uribe Velez," *BBC News*, http://news.bbc.co.uk/2/hi/americas/3214685.stm.

26. "Profile: Alvaro Uribe Velez," *BBC News*, http://news.bbc.co.uk/2/hi/americas/3214685.stm; "Alvaro Uribe casts long shadow over Colombia election," *BBC News*, http://www.bbc.co.uk/news/10131095.

27. "40 Union Members Slain Last Year in Colombia," *Latin American Herald Tribune*, http://www.laht.com/article.asp?ArticleId=351727&CategoryId=12393; "Human Rights in Colombia," *Wikipedia*, http://en.wikipedia.org/wiki/Human_rights_in_Colombia.

28. "Priest Hacked to Death in Colombia," *Thaindian News*, http://www.thaindian.com/newsportal/uncategorized/priest-hacked-to-death-in-colombia_100563434.html; "Journalists Killed in Colombia," CPJ, Committee to Protect Journalists, http://www.cpj.org/killed/americas/colombia/.

29. Sara Miller Llana, "Medellín, once epicenter of Colombia's drug war, fights

to keep the peace." *Christian Science Monitor*, Oct. 25, 2010, http://www.csmonitor
.com/World/Americas/2010/1025/Medellin-once-epicenter-of-Colombia-s-drug
-war-fights-to-keep-the-peace; Nadja Drost, "In Medellín, a Disturbing Come-
back of Crime," *Time*, Feb. 25, 2010, http://www.time.com/time/world/article/0,8
599,1967232,00.html.

30. Ronaldo Munck, "Deconstructing Violence: Power, Force, and Social Transformation," *Latin American Perspectives* 35, no. 5 (Sept. 2008): 3–19; Jon Gettman,
"Marijuana Production in the United States (2006)," Drug Science.Org, http://www
.drugscience.org/Archive/bcr2/cashcrops.html.

31. Daniel Wilkinson, "Death and Drugs in Colombia," *New York Review of
Books*, May 24, 2011, http://www.nybooks.com/articles/archives/2011/jun/23/death
-and-drugs-colombia/?pagination=false.

32. Mark Drajem, "The Benefits of a U.S.-Colombia Free-Trade Deal," *Bloomberg
Businessweek*, April 14, 2011, http://www.businessweek.com/magazine/content/11_17
/b4225032089913.htm.

SELECTED BIBLIOGRAPHY

ARCHIVES AND LIBRARIES

Bogotá

Banco de la República, Biblioteca "Luis Ángel Arango" (BRB)
Banco de la República, Hemeroteca "Luis López de Mesa" (BRH)
Biblioteca Nacional (BN)

Cali

Archivo Histórico de Cali (AHC)
Banco de la República, Centro de Documentación Regional (BRCDR)
Biblioteca Departamental (BD)
Universidad del Valle, Departamento de Bibliotecas (UVB)

Cartagena

Archivo Histórico, Archivo General del Distrito, Cartagena de Indias (AH)
Concurso Nacional de Belleza (CNB)

Medellín

Archivo Histórico de Antioquia (AHA)
Archivo de Memoria Visual de Antioquia (AMVA)
Fundación Antioqueña para los Estudios Sociales (FAES)
Universidad de Antioquia, Biblioteca General (UABG)

NEWSPAPERS AND MAGAZINES

El Amigo de las Damas (Cartagena, 1874–1875)
Antioquia Histórica (Medellín, 1924–1974 passim)
Antioquia Turística (Medellín, 1965–1973)
La Aurora: periódico dedicado al bello sexo (Medellín, 1868–1869)
Biblioteca de Señoritas (Bogotá, 1858–1859)

Bogotá Ilustrado (Bogotá, 1906–1908)
Carrusel: Suplemento de El Tiempo (Bogotá, 1977–1985)
Colombia Ilustrada (Medellín, 1969–1973)
Colombia Turística (Medellín, 1958, 1960–1972)
Consigna (Bogotá, 1976–1978)
Cromos (Bogotá, 1916–1985)
Diario de la Costa (Cartagena, 1916–1946)
El Día (Bogotá, 1849–1854)
El Espectador: Edición de la Costa (Cartagena, 1978–1979)
La Familia (Bogotá, 1884–1885)
El Fígaro (Cartagena, 1939–1960)
La Floresta (Cartagena, 1879–1881)
Gloria: Publicación Mensual de Fabricato (Medellín, 1946–1953)
El Hogar (Bogotá, 1868–1870)
El Hogar Católico (Bogotá, 1907–1914)
La Ilustración (Bogotá, 1908–1909)
El Iris (Bogotá, 1866–1868)
Lecturas para el Hogar (Bogotá, 1905–1906)
Modas y Propaganda (Bogotá, 1922)
La Mujer (Bogotá, 1878–1881)
La Mujer (Bogotá, 1895–1897)
Mujer de América (Bogotá, 1961–1974)
Noticias Culturales (Bogotá, 1961–1975)
El Pasatiempo (Bogotá, 1878)
Películas (Bogotá, 1919–1920, 1922)
El Pobre (Bogotá, 1851)
El Porvenir (Cartagena, 1908–1927)
Progreso (Medellín, 1939–1949)
El Relator (Cali, 1917–1952)
Revista del Jueves–El Espectador (Bogotá, 1977–1985)
Revista Femenina (Medellín, 1938–1942)
Revista Ilustrada (Bogotá, 1898–1899)
Revista Ilustrada para Las Familias (Chattanooga, Tennessee, 1922–1923)
Revista Occidental (Cali, 1968–1986)
El Sport (Bogotá, 1899)
Suplemento de la Revista Cromos (Bogotá, 1922–1923)
El Tiempo (Bogotá, 1911–1917, 1922, 1926, 1937–1985)
Tolima, revista ilustrada 1, no. 2 (Sept. 8, 1918)
El Universal (Cartagena, 1955–1987)
Variedades (Bogotá, 1921–1922)
El Verjel Colombiano: periódico literario dedicado al bello sexo (Bogotá, 1875–1876)
El Zipa (Bogotá, 1877, 1879)

BOOKS AND ARTICLES

Abadía Morales, Guillermo. *ABC del folklore colombiano*. 6th ed. Bogotá: Panamericana, 1998.

Acosta de Samper, Soledad, *La mujer en la sociedad moderna*. Paris: Garnier Hermanos,
1895.

Amezquita de Almeida, Josefina. *La mujer: sus obligaciones y sus derechos*. Bogotá: Ediciones AA, 1977.

Arango, Luz Gabriela. *Mujer, religión e industria: Fabricato, 1923–1982*. Medellín: Universidad Externado de Colombia, 1991.

Banet-Weiser, Sarah. *The Most Beautiful Girl in the World*. Berkeley: University of California Press, 1999.

Banner, Lois. *American Beauty*. Chicago: University of Chicago Press, 1983.

Berger, John. *Ways of Seeing*. London: Penguin Books, 1972.

Bergquist, Charles W. *Coffee and Conflict in Colombia. 1886–1910*. Durham, NC: Duke
University Press, 1978.

Bermúdez, Suzy. "Debates en torno a la mujer y la familia en Colombia, 1850–1886."
Texto y Contexto (Bogotá) no. 10 (Enero–Abril 1987): 111–144.

———. "La mujer y la familia en América Latina: Dos elementos claves para entender el mantenimiento de las jerarquias sociales, raciales, y sexuales, 1850–1930."
Revista de Antropología (Bogotá) 2, nos. 1–2 (1986): 104–108.

Bermúdez Q., Suzy. *Hijas, esposas y amantes: género, etnia y edad en la historia de América
Latina*. Bogotá: Ediciones Uniandes, 1992.

Bonilla de Ramos, Elssy. "Publicidad y sexualidad: ¿El poder en lo irrelevante?" *Texto
y Contexto* (May–Aug. 1984): 185–200.

Bradfield, Nancy. *Costume in Detail: Women's Dress 1730–1930*. Boston: Plays Inc., 1968.

Braun, Herbert. *The Assassination of Gaitán: Public Life and Urban Violence in Colombia*.
Madison: University of Wisconsin Press, 1985.

———. "La dialéctica de la vida pública." In *El Siglo Pasado, Colombia: economía,
política y sociedad*, compiled by Rafael Pardo, pp. 213–254. Bogotá: Tercer Mundo
Editores, 2001.

Bromwell, Nick. *Tomorrow Never Knows: Rock and Psychedelics in the 1960s*. Chicago:
University of Chicago Press, 2002.

Bushnell, David. *The Making of Modern Colombia: A Nation in Spite of Itself*. Berkeley:
University of California Press, 1993.

———. "Politics and Violence in Nineteenth-Century Colombia." In *Violence in
Colombia: The Contemporary Crisis in Historical Perspective*, edited by Charles Berg-
quist, Ricardo Peñaranda, and Gonzalo Sánchez, pp. 11–30. Wilmington, DE:
Scholarly Resources, 1992.

Cali, ciudad de América. Cali: Carbajal y Cia., 1967.

Cané, Miguel. *Notas_de viaje sobre Venezuela y Colombia*. Bogotá: Imprenta de la Luz,
1907.

Carnegie-Williams, Rosa. *Un año en los andes o aventuras de una lady en Bogotá*. Translated by Luis Enrique Jiménez Llaña Vezga. Bogotá: Tercer Mundo, 1990.

Carrigan, Ana. *The Palace of Justice: A Colombian Tragedy*. New York: Four Walls Eight Windows, 1993.

Cartas sobre el feminismo. Cartagena, 1925. BN.

Cetina, Eccehomo. *Jaque a la reina: mafia y corrupción en Cartagena*. Bogotá: Planeta, 1994.

Claver Tellez, Pedro. *El lado oscuro de las reinas: Sus amores, sus pasiones, sus intimidades*. Bogotá: Intermedio Editores, 1994.

Cohen, Colleen Ballerino, Richard Wilk, and Beverly Stoeltje, eds. *Beauty Queens on the Global Stage: Gender, Contests, and Power*. New York: Routledge, 1996.

Colombia 1886: programa centenario de la constitución. Bogotá: Biblioteca Luis Ángel Arango, 1986.

Concurso Nacional de Belleza. *Las más bellas: historia del Concurso Nacional de Belleza; Colombia, 60 años*. Cartagena de Indias: Junta Organizadora del Concurso Nacional de Belleza, 1994.

Cowley, Geoffrey. "The Biology of Beauty." *Newsweek*, June 3, 1996: 61–66.

Davis, Robert H. *Historical Dictionary of Colombia*. 2nd ed. Metuchen, NJ: Scarecrow Press, 1993.

Deas, Malcolm, Efraín Sánchez, and Aída Martínez. *Tipos y costumbres de la Nueva Granada: La colección de pinturas formada por Joseph Brown en Colombia entre 1825 y 1841 y el diario de su excurción de Bogotá a Girón en 1834*. Bogotá: Fondo Cultural Cafetero, 1989.

Degler, Carl N. *Neither Black nor White: Slavery and Race Relations in Brazil and the United States*. Madison: University of Wisconsin Press, 1986.

Delgado, Camilo S. *Historias, leyendas y tradiciones de Cartagena*. Vol. 1. Cartagena: Tip. Mogollon, 1911.

Delpar, Helen. *Red Against Blue: The Liberal Party in Colombian Politics. 1863–1899*. Tuscaloosa: University of Alabama Press, 1981.

"Diario de sucesos de Cali." *Boletín histórico del Valle* (Cali) July 1934: 249–275.

Dix, Robert H. *The Politics of Colombia*. New Haven, Conn,: Yale University Press, 1986.

Dydyński, Krzysztof. *Colombia, a Lonely Planet Travel Survival Kit*. 2nd ed. Hawthorne, Victoria: Lonely Planet Publications, 1995.

En busca de un país: la comisión corográfica; selección de dibujos de Carmelo Fernández, Enrique Price, y Manuel María Paz, con texto introductorio de Gonzalo Hernández de Alba. Bogotá: Carlos Valencia Editores, 1984.

Freedman, Rita. *Beauty Bound: Why We Pursue the Myth in the Mirror*. Lexington, MA, 1986.

Fundación Grupo 80. *El Valle del Cauca*. Cali: Albon S.A., [1980].

García Márquez, Gabriel. *Collected Stories*. New York: Harper and Row, 1984.

García Márquez, Gabriel. *One Hundred Years of Solitude*. Translated from the Spanish by Gregory Rabasssa. New York: Avon Books, 1971.

González Marín, María del Carmen. "La retórica de la belleza." *Arbor: Ciencia, Pensamiento y Cultura* (Madrid) 47, no. 579 (Mar. 1994): 127–136.

Gootenberg, Paul. *Andean Cocaine: The Making of a Global Drug*. Chapel Hill: University of North Carolina Press, 2008.

Groot, José Manuel. *Cuadros rústicos de costumbres nacionales*. S,L, 1858.

Guía práctica y turística de Cali. Cali: Prensa Moderna, 1978.

Guy, Donna. *Sex and Danger in Buenos Aires: Prostitution, Family, and Nation in Argentina*. Lincoln: University of Nebraska Press, 1991.

Henderson, James. *When Colombia Bled: A History of the Violencia in Tolima*. University, Ala.: University of Alabama Press, 1985.

Holton, Isaac E. *New Granada: Twenty Months in the Andes*. New York: Harper and Brothers, 1857.

Hylton, Forrest. "The Cold War That Didn't End: Paramilitary Modernization in Medellín, Colombia." In *A Century of Revolution: Insurgent and Counterinsurgent Violence During Latin America's Long Cold War*, edited by Greg Grandin and Gilbert M. Joseph, 338–367. Durham: Duke University Press, 2010.

Jackson, Linda A. *Physical Appearance and Gender: Sociobiological and Sociocultural Perspectives*. Albany: State University Press of New York, 1992.

Kemper, Rachel H. *Costume*. New York: Newsweek Books, 1977.

Lambert, Ellen Zetzel. *The Face of Love: Feminism and the Beauty Question*. Boston: Beacon Press, 1995.

Lambert, Miles. *Fashion in Photographs 1860–1880*. London: B. T. Batsford, 1991.

Las mujeres en la historia de Colombia. Vol. 1, Mujeres, historia y política; Vol. 2, Mujeres y sociedad; Vol. 3, Mujeres y cultura. Bogotá: Editorial Norma. 1995.

LaTorre Mendoza, Luis. *Historia e historias de Medellín: siglos XVII, XVIII, XIX*. Medellín: Ediciones Tomás Carrasquilla, 1972.

Legrand, Catherine. *Frontier Expansion and Peasant Protest in Colombia, 1850–1936*. Albuquerque: University of New Mexico Press, 1986.

Lisboa, Miguel María. *Relación de un viaje a Venezuela, Nueva Granada, Ecuador*. Caracas: Ediciones de la Presidencia de la República, 1954.

Llorente, María Victoria, Rodolfo Escobedo, Camilo Echandía, and Maurico Rubio. "Violencia homicida y estructuras criminals en Bogotá." *Sociologias* (Porto Alegre) no. 8 (July/Dec. 2002): 172–205.

Lobo, Gregory J. "La bella y la bestia: Colombia entre el consenso y la coerción, o sobre el multiculturalismo y la violencia racial neoliberal." *Revista Iberoamericana* 74, no. 223 (Apr.-June 2008): 515–528.

Londoño Vega, Patricia, and Santiago Londoño Vélez. "Vida diaria en las ciudades colombianas." In *Nueva historia de Colombia*, vol. 4, pp. 313–399. Bogotá: Planeta Colombiana Editorial, 1989.

López O., Juan Bautista. *Costumbres, tercera época*. Vol. 2. Manizales: Biblioteca de Autores Caldenses, 1981.

Loveman, Brian. *No Higher Law: American Foreign Policy and the Western Hemisphere since 1776*. Chapel Hill: University of North Carolina Press, 2010.

Loveman, Brian, and Thomas M. Davies Jr. "Colombia." In Che Guevara, *Guerrilla Warfare: With Revised and Updated Introduction and Case Studies by Brian Loveman and Thomas M. Davies Jr.*, 3rd ed., pp. 233–267. Wilmington, DE: Scholarly Resources, 1997.

———, eds. Che Guevara, *Guerrilla Warfare: With Revised and Updated Introduction and Case Studies by Brian Loveman and Thomas M. Davies Jr.*, 3rd ed. Wilmington, DE: Scholarly Resources, 1997.

Marín Taborda, Jorge Iván. "María Cano." In *Las mujeres en la historia de Colombia*, vol. 1, 157–160. Bogotá: Editorial Norma, 1995.

McGreevey, William Paul. *An Economic History of Colombia, 1845–1930.* Cambridge, England: Cambridge University Press, 1971.

Martínez Carreño, Aída. *La prisión del vestido: aspectos sociales del traje en América.* Bogotá: Planeta Colombiana, 1995.

Martínez Carreño, Aída. *Un siglo de moda en Colombia, 1830–1930.* Bogotá: Fondo Cultural Cafetero, 1981.

Martz, John. *Colombia: A Contemporary Political Survey.* Chapel Hill, N.C: University of North Carolina Press, 1962.

Melo Lancheros, Livia Stella. *Valores femeninas de Colombia.* Bogotá: Carvajal Hermanos, 1966.

Merizalde del Carmen, Bernardo, A. R. *Estudio de la costa colombiana del Pacífico.* Bogotá: Imprenta del Estado Mayor General, 1921.

Miller, Francesca. *Latin American Women and the Search for Social Justice.* Hanover, N.H.: University of New England Press, 1991.

Montaña, Antonio. *Cultura del vestuario en Colombia.* Bogotá: Fondo Cultural Cafetero, 1993.

Munck, Ronaldo. "Deconstructing Violence: Power, Force, and Social Transformation." *Latin American Perspectives* 35, no. 5 (Sept. 2008): 3–19.

Museo de Cuadros de Costumbres. Bogotá: Impreso por Foción Mantilla, 1866.

Nash, June, and Helen Icken Safa. *Women and Change in Latin America.* South Hadley, MA, 1985.

Nueva Historia de Colombia. Tomos 4, 5, y 6. Bogotá: Planeta Colombiana Editorial, 1989.

Ocampo López, Javier. *Las fiestas y el folclor en Colombia.* Bogotá: El Ancora Editores, 1985.

———. *Historia básica de Colombia.* Bogotá: Plaza & Janes, 1994.

Oquist, Paul. *Violence, Conflict, and Politics in Colombia.* New York: Academic Press, 1980.

Ortiz Riano, Cleofe. "Salud y belleza." *Amigos Volando* (Cali) no. 85 (Marzo 1991): 58–66.

Oslender, Ulrich. "Another History of Violence: The Production of 'Geographies of Terror' in Colombia's Pacific Coast Region." *Latin American Perspectives* 35, no. 5 (Sept. 2008): 77–102.

Palacios, Marco. *Coffee in Colombia, 1850–1970: An Economic, Social and Political History.* Cambridge, Eng.: Cambridge University Press, 1980.

———. *Entre la legitimidad y la violencia: Colombia, 1875–1994.* Bogotá: Editorial Norma, 1995.

Palma, Milagros. *La mujer es puro cuento: simbólica mítico-religiosa de la feminidad aborigen y mestiza.* Bogotá: Tercer Mundo, 1992.

Pardo, Rafael, comp. *El siglo pasado: Colombia, economía, política y sociedad.* Bogotá: Tercer Mundo Editores, 2001.

Park, James. *Rafael Núñez and the Politics of Colombian Regionalism, 1863–1886.* Baton Rouge, La.: Louisiana State University Press, 1985.

Parra Sandoval, Rodrigo. "A proposito de: 'Belleza y poder. La publicidad: ¿El poder de lo irrelevante? De Elssy Bonilla de Ramos.'" *Texto y Contexto* (May–Aug. 1984): 255–257.

Payne, James L. *Patterns of Conflict in Colombia.* New Haven, Conn: Yale University Press, 1968.

Peláez Echeverri, Gabriela. *La condición de la mujer en Colombia.* Bogotá: Editorial Cromos, 1944.

Pescatello, Ann M., ed. *Female and Male in Latin America: Essays.* Pittsburgh: University of Pittsburgh Press, 1973.

Pike, Fredrick. *The United States and Latin America: Myths and Stereotypes of Civilization and Nature.* Austin: University of Texas Press, 1992.

Posada Gutiérrez, Joaquín. "Fiestas de la Candelaria en la Popa." In *Museo de Cuadros de Costumbres,* 81–90. Bogotá: Impreso por Foción Mantilla, 1866.

Ramsey, Russell W. "The Colombian Battalion in Korea and Suez." *Journal of Inter-American Studies,* 9, no 4 (Oct. 1967): 541–560.

Rausch, Jane. *The Llanos Frontier in Colombian History.* Albuquerque: University of New Mexico Press. 1993.

Reyes Cárdenas, Catalina. *La vida cotidiana en Medellín, 1890–1930.* Bogotá: Colcultura, 1996.

Ricci, Margoth, "Después de las fiestas, las cuentas." *Consigna* (Bogotá) 4, no. 150 (Nov. 30, 1979): 52–54.

Rippy, J. Fred. *The Capitalists and Colombia.* New York: Vanguard Press, 1931.

Rodman, Selden. *The Colombia Traveler.* New York: Hawthorne Books, 1971.

Rolly, Katrina and Caroline Aish. *Fashion in Photographs, 1900–1920.* London: B.T. Batsford, 1992.

Rubio de Laverde, Lucila. *Ideales feministas.* Bogotá: Editorial Nuevo Mundo, 1950.

Ruiz, Elsa. "La mujer en la ciudad." *Ciudad: Revista de Asuntos Urbanos* 1, no. 1 (June 1983): 116–117.

Safford, Frank. *The Ideal of the Practical: Colombia's Struggle to Form a Technical Elite.* Austin: University of Texas Press, 1976.

Safford, Frank, and Marco Palacios. *Colombia: Fragmented Land, Divided Society.* New York: Oxford University Press, 2001.

Sánchez, Gonzalo, and Ricardo Peñaranda, comps. *Pasado y presente de la Violencia en Colombia*. Bogotá: CEREC, 1986.

Sánchez, Gonzalo. "La Violencia in Colombia: New Research, New Questions." *Hispanic American Historical Review* 65, no. 4 (Nov. 1985): 789–807.

Schenck, Friedrich von. *Viajes por Antioquia en el año de 1880*. Bogotá: Banco de la República, 1953.

Serret, Félix. *Viaje a Colombia, 1911–1912*. Trans. and prologue by Luis Carlos Mantilla R., O.F.M. Bogotá: Biblioteca V Centenario Colcultura, 1994.

Sharp, William Frederick. *Slavery on the Spanish Frontier: The Colombian Chocó, 1680–1810*. Norman: University of Oklahoma, 1976.

Sierra García, Jaime. *Diccionario folclórico antioqueño*. Medellín: Universidad de Antioquia, 1983.

Simpson, Amelia. *Xuxa: The Mega-Marketing of Gender, Race, and Modernity*. Philadelphia: Temple University Press, 1993.

Stanfield, Michael Edward. *Red Rubber, Bleeding Trees: Violence, Slavery, and Empire in Northwest Amazonia, 1850–1933*. Albuquerque: University of New Mexico Press, 1998.

Stern, Steve J. *The Secret History of Gender: Women, Men and Power in Late Colonial Mexico*. Chapel Hill: University of North Carolina Press, 1995.

Stoner, K. Lynn. "Directions in Latin American Women's History, 1977–1984." *Latin American Research Review* 22, no. 2: 101–134.

Tertulias del "Cali Viejo", Segundo Libro. Cali: Impresora Feriva, 1998.

Universidad Nacional de Colombia. *Mujer, amor y violencia*. Bogotá: Tercer Mundo, 1991.

Uribe Celis, Carlos. *Los años veinte en Colombia: Ideología y cultura*. Bogotá: Ediciones Alborada, 1991.

Uribe Celis, Carlos. *La mentalidad del Colombiano: Cultura y sociedad en el siglo XX*. Bogotá: Ediciones Alborada, 1992.

Velásquez Toro, Magdala. "Condición jurídica y social de la mujer." In *Nueva Historia de Colombia*, vol. 4, 9–60. Bogotá: Planeta Colombiana Editorial, 1989.

Viajeros colombianos por Colombia. Prólogo de Gabriel Giraldo Jaramillo. Bogotá: Fondo Cultural Cafetero, 1977.

Wade, Peter. *Music, Race, and Nation: Música Tropical in Colombia*. Chicago: University of Chicago Press, 2000.

Williams, Raymond Leslie, and Kevin G. Guerrieri. *Culture and Customs of Colombia*. Westport, CT: Greenwood Press, 1999.

Wolf, Naomi. *The Beauty Myth: How Images of Beauty Are Used against Women*. New York: Doubleday, 1991.

UNPUBLISHED MANUSCRIPTS

Stanfield, Michael. "Ayuda militar estadounidense y violencia en Colombia." Conference paper at La Construcción de la Paz y la Cooperación Internacional en Colombia. Universidad Javeriana, Bogotá, Colombia, July 2001.

Stanfield, Michael Edward. "U.S. Military Aid and Violence in Colombia: Patterns and Perspectives." Invited lecture at the University of California, Berkeley, March 2001.

CPSIA information can be obtained at www.ICGtesting.com
Printed in the USA
LVOW01s0740140115

422407LV00004B/6/P